Rural Worlds Lost

RURAL WORLDS

LOST THE AMERICAN SOUTH 1920–1960

JACK TEMPLE KIRBY

Louisiana State University Press
Baton Rouge and London

Designer: Laura Roubique
Typeface: Times Roman
Typesetter: G & S Typesetting, Inc.
Printer: Thomson-Shore, Inc.
Binder: John H. Dekker & Sons, Inc.

LIBRARY OF CONGRESS CATALOGING-IN-PUBLICATION DATA

Kirby, Jack Temple.
  Rural worlds lost: the American South, 1920–1960.

  Includes index.
  1. Southern States—Rural conditions—History—
20th century.   2. Rural-urban migration—Southern
States—History—20th century.   I. Title.
HN79.A13K57   1986   306'.0975   86-10253
ISBN 0-8071-1300-X
ISBN 0-8071-1360-3 (pbk.)

To
Theodosia Palmer Kirby
and to the memory of
Theodosia Yarbrough Palmer

Contents

Illustrations

Photographs

Figures

Maps

Tables

Preface

THE NEW SOUTH ENTERED THE AMERICAN
language at least as early as 1866, when Georgia's Benjamin H. Hill
proclaimed the miraculous transformation of the former Confederacy to
a New York audience. By *new* Hill meant a South unburdened of slavery, secessionist feeling, and a host of habits and practices out of step
with industrializing, urbanizing America. Hill's successor as New South
spokesman, the Atlanta publisher Henry W. Grady, went much further.
During the 1880s Grady and like-minded colleagues declared that
southerners had become creatures of the bourgeois world—entrepreneurs, mechanics, hustlers—progressives who had put the primitive
worlds of the village, farm, and plantation behind them. So positive and
eloquent were Grady and his generation of publicists that after most of
them were dead, serious scholars of the early twentieth century accepted their proclamations as truth.[1]

Subsequently, the hyperbole and fraud of this rhetorical New South

1. Paul M. Gaston, "The 'New South,'" in Arthur S. Link and Rembert W. Patrick
(eds.), *Writing Southern History: Essays in Historiography in Honor of Fletcher M.
Green* (Baton Rouge, 1965), 316–36; Gaston, *The New South Creed: A Study in Southern
Mythmaking* (New York, 1970), 87–88. Gaston cites usage of the term *New South* as early
as 1862 (*New South Creed,* 18).

were exposed. Industries and cities did indeed grow from Grady's time onward, but well into this century the region remained overwhelmingly rural and poor. The expression *New South* nevertheless survived. Both scholars and (probably) the better informed among the public understand that since 1865 the region has undergone a number of fundamental changes and that the phrase is hardly adequate to describe or even symbolize them all.[2] Still, the New South endures, like so many other confusing historical tags. *Romantic* and *progressive* are others, but neither has been called into service to describe a chronology so lengthy as the New South's.

One of the objectives of this book is an accurate periodization of this New South, for it needs subdivision. *New* has always implied cities and factories, for example. Grady and his fellows were merely prescient (to put the matter generously): industrial production workers did not outnumber farmers until the late 1940s, and a majority of the southern population did not become urban until the 1950s. So the New South as proclaimed in the late nineteenth century did not actually appear until after World War II. The postwar era, then, might logically be termed the New South. Or, stuck as we seem to be with the same usage for seven and a half prewar decades as well, our times would become the New New South. (I concede that logical adjustments of past errors sometimes cross the border to silliness.) Conversely, the long period of persisting rural poverty, of sharecropping and mule power, and of semiprimitive backwoods and mountain cultures—between the Civil War and, say, 1940—would be the Old New South. The collapse of this rural southern world, its economic systems and ways of life, is the subject of this book.

The four decades between 1920 and 1960 encompass the great transformation. Change was most intense during the two middle decades— the 1930s and 1940s—when the Great Depression, New Deal farm programs, and the demographic chaos occasioned by World War II all conspired to end or alter the main elements of the old systems. The broader chronological scope, 1920–1960, presents the old and new in stark contrast. Despite an ongoing black exodus (which began about 1915), the rural south in 1920 was much as it had been in the 1870s; in fact, it was in certain respects worse off. The plantation monoculture subregions were larger; much more southern land was worn or ruined; the "Mexican" cotton boll weevil, unknown until the 1890s, was completing its

---

2. See C. Vann Woodward, *Origins of the New South, 1877–1913* (Baton Rouge, 1951), ix–x; George B. Tindall, *The Emergence of the New South, 1913–1945* (Baton Rouge, 1967), ix–x.

northeastwardly course to the limits of the cotton kingdom; and southern farm staples were about to encounter a price crisis perhaps worse
than those of the end of the previous century. By 1960 about nine million southerners had migrated from the region, more millions had
settled in southern towns and cities, sharecroppers and mules had become rare, and southern farms and rural communities, both now vastly
reduced in numbers and souls, more closely resembled those of the
North and West than the prewar South. The southern countryside was
thus enclosed and depopulated as dramatically as was rural England toward the end of the eighteenth century.

My method in relating this watershed of southern history is indicated
by the three divisions of the book: structural change in agriculture, the
effects of structural change upon people at work and in communities,
and rural-to-urban migration. Three other principles also govern this
work. First, I have emphasized the diversity of the South in terms not
only of race but of topography and crop types, which fundamentally
relate to farming systems and to what is broadly called culture. Second,
I have attempted to write about southern life and institutions in the context of other American regional modes. Comparison aids description,
even if it does not necessarily establish truth. And third, while I have
made use of records and papers of planters, farm editors, and other "articulate" spokesmen of the region, as well as federal and state government documents, I have tried to focus more upon the experiences of the
masses of southerners whose interests and values were seldom well
served or reflected by the "articulate."

Finally, a word about biases or, as I would prefer, values and informed opinions. My subjects are the mechanization of farming and the
demise of what are called traditional rural communities—rural modernization. Since modernization arose in most of Europe and in every other
American region before it swept the South, the process has assumed the
aura of inevitability and is generally accounted as another aspect of
progress, something good, which is not to be doubted.[3] Questions of
inevitability are, of course, metaphysical, not historical, and I would
prefer not to touch them with a ten-foot hoe. Yet because inevitability
implies a certain organic or God-given naturalness and rightness in historical developments, the construction demands response, for what we
call modern agriculture is the work not of invisible divine forces but of
a determined corps of men and women and their government. In the

---

3. See, for example, Thomas D. Clark, *Three Paths to the Modern South: Education,
Agriculture, and Conservation* (Athens, Ga., 1965).

United States their work and opinions had become so irresistible by World War I that alternatives to a depopulated countryside and machine-driven farming were hardly to be heard. Nature (in the form of droughts, blights, and pests) seemed to conspire with the agricultural modernizers. By 1933 southern farmers in particular had but one question before them: would they accept expensive but labor-saving agricultural science, governmental regulation, and subsidies, or would they perish? It was no question at all. By that late date mechanization and depopulation did indeed seem inevitable.

So in writing this book I have tried to be critically sensitive to these ambiguous and quixotic matters of inevitability and progress. In sum I think that the best-intended plans of good people and governments sometimes go awry. The modernization of farming and the end of the Old New South brought both benefits and great sorrow. This is little less than the folks who lived through the changes said themselves, and it may be sufficient. I could hardly have written this book from a nostalgic or romantic perspective either, having seen so much of the testimony of ordinary citizens of the Old New South. As the following pages will demonstrate, there was much that was unhealthy and unhappy about the old rural life, as well as much that was personable and humane. The passing of that South, for better or worse, is done. This is merely an attempt to measure dimensions and plumb some of the human meaning of this seismic event.

Acknowledgments

NO SHARECROPPER AM I, BUT LIKE EVERY other scholar who is not independently wealthy, my dependency upon patrons is profound. Most important and numerous of my benefactors are the taxpayers of Ohio. They support Miami University, which in turn has generously supported my work. Many Ohio taxpayers are southerners who left the old country under trying circumstances that I have tried to describe in this book, and I hope they will find my efforts a particularly fitting return on their investment. (Native Yankees among my patrons also share the work ethic and may come to a similar conclusion for different reasons.) At Miami my old friend and longtime department chairman, Richard M. Jellison, orchestrated two free semesters for travel, research, and writing, as well as teacher-friendly schedules for all the semesters in between. Colleagues on the Miami Faculty Research Committee also channeled subsidies my way for three summers of work at southern research institutions. Beyond Ohio, my institutional patrons include the American Council of Learned Societies and the American Philosophical Society (Johnson Grant No. 1592); they also funded summer travel.

Over the past seven years I have traveled more than twenty thousand miles around the South (most of it by car), collecting material for this book. The sojourns ranged from Washington, D.C., to Gainesville, Florida; from Frankfort, Kentucky, to College Station, Texas; and to a great many places in between. The locals treated me with professional courtesy at every library, archive, and museum, but I am especially grateful to a few research professionals whose help was transcendent: Elizabeth Alexander of the P. K. Yonge Library at the University of Florida; Russell Baker of the Arkansas History Commission, Little Rock; Helen Boyd of the Arkansas County Agricultural Museum in Stuttgart, Arkansas; John Ezell of the Western History Collection, University of Oklahoma; Milo B. Howard and Mimi Jones of the Alabama Department of Archives and History, Montgomery; Allen W. Jones of the Auburn University Archives; Bobby Roberts of the manuscripts library at the University of Arkansas, Little Rock; and the late Jimmy Shoalmire of Mississippi State University's Mitchell Library.

Much of the framework of this book rests upon a foundation of tedious labor in federal agricultural censuses, and several former graduate students at Miami—Ann Rebecca Boggs, Sharon Edwards, Ann Heiss, and Roderick Nimtz—were prodigious diggers on my behalf. Their association, like that of typists Dale Thomas and Pamela Messer, was as pleasurable as productive.

When my own drafting was done, I imposed upon able colleagues around the country for critical readings of various chapters. I am eager to repeat my thanks to Numan V. Bartley, John N. Dickinson, Robert Freymeyer, Michael J. Hogan, Winston Kinsey, Raymond H. Pulley, John Shelton Reed, and Joel Williamson. H. L. Mitchell, who is a marvel and a breathing artifact of the period of my study, lent me photographs from his collection, read and corrected the chapter on race relations, and graciously respected my differences in interpretation of his beloved Southern Tenant Farmers' Union. Pete Daniel read the entire manuscript twice and made it better. He knows more about the old flue-cured tobacco culture—and a great many other things southern and rural—than anyone I know less than seventy years of age. Three of the chapters have appeared previously in different forms: Chapter 2 in *Agricultural History,* LVII (July, 1983), 257–76; Chapter 7 in the same journal, LVIII (July, 1984), 411–22; and Chapter 9 in the *Journal of Southern History,* XLIX (November, 1983), 585–600. I am grateful to the editors of both journals, as well as to their anonymous consultants.

This book is dedicated to my mother and her mother. My grandmother was a Florence County, South Carolina, farm girl who in 1903 married a young man who was leaving a Georgetown County farm. My grandfather's long working life was spent in more than a dozen country crossroads and small towns along the South Atlantic coast from Georgia through Virginia, extracting lumber and pulpwood from the native pine forests. He became a creature of business and the automobile, but I think that my grandmother was never reconciled to life in town and car. When I knew her (from the 1940s until her death in 1969), she seemed still a denizen of her early, lost world—the farm, the extended family, and a rustic landscape whose silence was broken only by human and animal voices. She advised my father and me on planting our large garden from her well-worn almanac. Her namesake, my mother, who was born and raised in those saw- and pulpmill towns, seems more than any of her seven siblings to have inherited the first Theodosia's outlook. I cannot say precisely how these two women influenced the writing of this book, but the *feeling* atop my social science must in part derive from having known them.

Rural Worlds Lost

Everywhere . . . folks were apathetic about . . . book
farming.
—A FORMER MISSISSIPPI AGRICULTURAL EXTENSION
AGENT ON HIS EXPERIENCES, *ca.* 1911–1920

I was a mule farmin man to the last; never did make a
crop with a tractor.
—A RETIRED ALABAMA FARMER, ON THE 1940s
AND 1950s

I had the pleasure of watching a small farmer near
Fresno furrowing out for irrigation with a horse-drawn
walking plow, and I could not help but meditate on the
unique position of the West. . . . I do not believe there
was another horse-drawn piece of equipment on a
cotton farm in the whole San Joaquin Valley in 1949.
—A CALIFORNIA COTTON OIL EXECUTIVE, 1949

Prologue

Homesteads, Bonanzas, and Hydraulic Societies

MOST OF THE RURAL WESTERN WORLD HAS
undergone what is called modernization over the past two centuries.
Countrysides have been almost depopulated; machines have displaced
men, women, children, and work animals; and the corporate system has
come to dominate in the production of food and fiber. The South was the
last region of the United States to experience the process, which continues today at various speeds over much of the earth. The process is also
known as development or progress, and hardly anyone who might begin
this book does not know its course. So there will be few surprises in the
ending of this story. Much of the plot, indeed, will be told in this prologue. The surprises, rather, may lie in causes, timing, and human consequences. Consideration of these matters properly begins with the
American national context, within which a lagging South stood exposed, then was drawn inexorably toward "progress."

There have been several American paths to economic development in
the countryside. One is the mode of the plantation and monoculture,
characteristic of most of the South and most unhappy in its consequences for people and for the land. This mode and its destructive
course will be described in the next chapter. Another is the eastern and
corn belt experience, which affirmed the highest hopes of small private

capitalism and balanced agricultural-industrial economies. Then there were various corporate farming enterprises across the plains and far West and the remarkable hydraulic agricultural societies of the far West, especially in California, which combined corporate (or corporate-style) scale, state governmental assistance, and massive federal guidance and financial support. By the early 1930s, as their anachronistic plantation system began to collapse, southerners and those who would help them had these other experiences before them as lessons and as models of hope, and perhaps of choice.

Through the eighteenth and nineteenth centuries, across the Northeast, then the old corn belt (Ohio through Iowa), Americans spread family farms in what is regarded as the classic fashion. Young men and women struck out on their own, purchased modest acreage, cleared land for corn and vegetables, fenced their crops, herded a few milk cows and swine, and built cabins. Each year they cleared more land and improved their homes until the forests were largely cut and the countryside took on its modern appearance. Capital for this process was private and modest, on the individual level. Young farmers in the nineteenth century might receive a gift or small inheritance from their parents of five hundred or a thousand dollars, which was sufficient to begin. More commonly boys and young men would take jobs in cities or hire out to established farmers for a few years, saving nearly all their pay, then start out on their own. Country merchants usually supplied credit and carried small mortgages for nearby beginning farmers. By about 1860 banks became more common as mortgage holders and short-term creditors. Meanwhile farming attracted population to market towns, which responded to farmers' demands for services not only financial but mechanical and technical. Blacksmiths became manufacturers of plows, mowers, hay rakes, corn planters, grain harvesters, and threshers. Agricultural development supported and paralleled urban industrial development. Gradually many of the cities grew past the function of serving farmers to become complex economic entities whose dynamic began to consume the farm land that gave them birth.[1]

Yet not every farmer in this eastern–middle western model was an

1. Clarence H. Danhof, *Change in Agriculture: The Northern United States, 1820–1870* (Cambridge, Mass., 1969), vii, 76–81, 181–250; Ann Rebecca Boggs, "From Rural-Agricultural to Urban-Industrial: An Overview of the Evolution of Butler County in Southwestern Ohio, 1880–1960" (M.A. thesis, Miami University, 1982); Douglas F. Dowd, "A Comparative Analysis of Economic Development in the American West and South," *Journal of Economic History,* XVI (December, 1956), 558–74.

owner. Tenancy was nearly as common as in the notorious postbellum South. During the last quarter of the nineteenth century 24 to 35 percent of all the farms in relatively prosperous Iowa were operated by tenants. Tenancy rates in the corn belt remained high in the twentieth century, too: Ohio 28.4 percent in 1910 and 26.3 percent in 1930; Indiana 30 percent in 1910 and 1930; Illinois 41.4 percent in 1910, 43.1 percent in 1930; and Iowa 37.8 percent in 1910 and 47.3 percent in 1930. Middle western farm tenancy can hardly be compared to the southern pathology of virtually permanent dependency, however. In the corn belt renters typically paid cash or cash equivalent shares of crops or livestock for use of land, and they owned sophisticated equipment beyond the reach of all but a tiny minority of southern tenants. Northern tenancy, in fact, was usually not a permanent condition but was rather a temporary status on the ladder to ownership.[2]

Another measure of the corn belt's relative agricultural health—and of the South's illness—is the relationship of tenants to landlords. In the South renters were rarely related by blood or marriage to landlords; in the Middle West such relationships were common. In Ohio, typical of the corn belt in 1930, 35.3 percent of all farm tenants were related to their landlords. In the north-central and northwestern sections of the state, rates ranged between 40 and 50 percent. (Livestock-sharing was the common form of contract.) Ohio's overall average was lowered somewhat by the northeastern counties, where nearby industrial cities attracted young relatives away from farms, and the southern counties, where migrants, often from the nearby Appalachian South, crowded in to rent from strangers.[3]

The infrequency with which southerners rented to relatives is only partly explainable by the fact that so many tenants were black and most landlords white. The phenomenon is a mark of the region's special agricultural history, crowded with too many people, too little money, and of its reliance upon markets and credit sources over which southerners held little mastery. The poor renter-relative ratios virtually define the limits of the South within such border states as Missouri, Oklahoma, and Texas. In the seven cotton- and corn-growing counties of southeastern-

2. Donald L. Winters, *Farmers Without Farms: Agricultural Tenancy in Nineteenth Century Iowa* (Westport, Conn., 1978), 14, 65–91; *Thirteenth Census of the United States, 1910: Agriculture,* VI, 413, 463, 507, VII, 307; *Fifteenth Census of the United States, 1930: Agriculture,* II, 31.

3. I. W. Moomaw, "Farm Tenancy Areas in Ohio," Ohio State University and Ohio Agricultural Experiment Station *Bulletin,* No. 144 (August, 1941), 14–15, and Table 12 (Mimeograph in Land Tenure Section project files, Record Group 83, National Archives).

most Missouri, for example, only 8 percent of tenants were related to their landlords. In eastern Oklahoma fewer than 10 percent of landlord-tenant relationships included families; and in the eastern and south-eastern counties of Texas—with but five exceptions—the percentages were comparably low. The least "southern" counties in Texas, predictably, lay in the upper Panhandle and north-central and west-central sections of the state. Along Oklahoma's northwestern and western borders, 25 to 30 percent of tenants rented from relatives. And in Missouri's northern and western counties the rate reached as high as 32.7 percent. All these areas of states often called southern were in socioeconomic terms middle western or western.[4]

Beyond the humid eastern Middle West farming required more land and capital and special technical adjustments. As in the corn belt, many families successfully homesteaded the subhumid and arid Plains with hard work, savings, and the support of banks, railroad companies, and merchants. Many others failed.[5] The most important successes in the Plains, however, were made not by families working in the great tradition but by wealthy entrepreneurs and corporate managers representing distant investor-clients. These were the "bonanza" farmers, ranchers, and promoters who appeared throughout the West from the 1870s into the 1920s. Texas provides excellent examples of the phenomenon at work just beyond the borders of the plantation South.

At the beginning of the 1870s investors from Cincinnati and the East organized the Coleman-Fulton Pasturage Company in San Patricio County, near Corpus Christi. Bosses and cowboys rounded up the long-horn cattle that roamed the open range and shipped them, on the hoof, to New Orleans and Havana. By the mid-1880s fences closed the range and ended the era of the longhorn, so Coleman-Fulton fenced its own thousands of acres, imported shorthorns, and began shipping dressed beef to Chicago over recently completed rail lines. Meanwhile the com-

4. U.S. Department of Agriculture and Missouri Agricultural Experiment Station, "Farm Tenancy Areas in Missouri (A Preliminary Report)" (October, 1941), 21, 23, and Table 1, Oklahoma Agricultural Experiment Station, "Types of Tenancy in Oklahoma (A Preliminary Report)," by Owen Scott (January, 1941), 4–5, [Texas Agricultural Experiment Station (?)], "Texas Tenancy—Types of Tenancy Maps" (n.d.), esp. Figure 8 (Typescript copies of all in Land Tenure Section files).

5. Gilbert C. Fite, *The Farmers' Frontier, 1865–1900* (New York, 1966); James H. Shideler (ed.), *Agriculture in the Development of the Far West* (Washington, D.C., 1975); Thomas R. Wessel (ed.), *Agriculture in the Great Plains, 1876–1936* (Washington, D.C., 1971).

pany's director, David Sinton, then his son-in-law, Charles Phelps Taft (half brother to William Howard Taft, future president of the United States), oversaw Coleman-Fulton's evolution as a row-crop agricultural empire. Between 1904 and 1912 (while the enterprise became known as the Taft Ranch), huge teams drawing special root-pulling plows cleared the scrub from the old rangeland, and managers laid out farms and company towns. Some farms were sold to individuals, but most were rented to Anglo-American tenants (and later blacks as well) or worked by Mexican hired hands. Tenants and laborers raised feed grains for the company's cattle and, increasingly, cotton, in yields of about half a bale per acre. By the 1910s and 1920s the Taft Ranch was renowned for its enormous size and diversity of operations, for its paternalism toward employees, and as a luxurious hunting preserve for stockholders and their famous guests.[6]

The Francklyn Land and Cattle Company was a British corporation that arrived in the Texas Panhandle, along with railroads and barbed wire, as the open range there was ending. Like the Taft Ranch, Francklyn imported shorthorn cattle during the 1880s, established feeder lots, and began farming operations to achieve self-sufficiency. Huge steam-powered plows turned the High Plains sod for crops of kafir corn, wheat, hay, and finally, cotton, which became the bonanza crop of the early twentieth century. In 1919 petroleum and natural gas were discovered in the Panhandle. The resultant population growth strengthened towns and cities in the region and the Francklyn company as well.[7] Industrial growth posed no threat to capital-intensive agriculture, which—so unlike the system of eastern Texas and beyond to the Atlantic—relied upon the machine, not abundant manpower.

A contemporary corporate bonanza site was the Red River Valley of the North, a flat, lush, three-hundred-mile-long corridor from Lake Winnipeg in Canada to the tri-state junction of Minnesota and the Dakotas. Early in the 1870s, when rail lines connected this region to the East, promoter-entrepreneurs leaped to the advantage. Absentee-owned, Texas-sized farms were organized and operated by resident managers equipped (by the 1880s) with the latest and largest steam-powered machinery for the production of wheat. Promoters, managers, and eastern stockholders conceived the farms as efficient factories from the start,

6. A. Ray Stephens, *The Taft Ranch: A Texas Principality* (Austin, 1964).
7. Lester Fields Sheffy, *The Francklyn Land & Cattle Company: A Panhandle Enterprise, 1882–1957* (Austin, 1963).

and like the owners of the Coleman-Fulton and Francklyn companies in Texas, their models appear to have worked well.[8]

The ultimate corporate bonanza farmer was Thomas D. Campbell. A futurist and fearless entrepreneur, Campbell spent a decade under the tutelage of J. S. Torrance, the California financier, contractor, and corporate farmer. Campbell learned to believe in bigness and to love Wall Street as the facilitator of gargantuan projects. In 1915 the "food crisis" created by war in Europe gave Campbell his grand idea, to plow the endless plains of eastern Montana. J. P. Morgan and associates lent him two million dollars to capitalize the Montana Farming Corporation, and Campbell bought thirty-four of the largest gasoline-powered tractors available, along with land-grading machinery, harvesters, threshers, and an enormous amount of wire for fencing and lumber for workers' camps. Before 1919 his men and machines placed hundreds of thousands of acres under cultivation of wheat. When postwar prices fell and rains stopped, Campbell bought out Morgan and other investors at a bargain and organized the Campbell Farming Corporation. Campbell's giant enterprise did well during the succeeding decade, and Campbell himself—"the Plower of the Plains"—became world famous as an exemplar of modern agriculture. His maxims were borrow big, buy every piece of labor-saving machinery available, hire labor, and plant big.[9]

That Thomas Campbell emerged from California to plow the plains of Montana is of more than passing significance. For California (well before 1920) had already established the model *ne plus ultra* of heavy capitalization, superb organization, and remarkable mechanical innovation. J. S. Torrance, Campbell's mentor, was but one of the agricultural giants of the Golden State, and by no means the first. Spanish and Mexican landlords held titles to sprawling estates before annexation by the United States in 1848. Then American adventurers and the Southern Pacific Railroad monopolized most of the new state's arable acreage. From the 1860s into the 1880s they and their lessees commanded enormous cattle ranches and wheat farms. Unlike southern planters, Californians never maintained a resident peasantry but employed hordes of migrant laborers at harvest. During the 1860s and 1870s they were "blanket men" or "bindle stiffs," single Anglo-American men who migrated on foot. When many farmers switched from wheat to fruit (especially in

8. Fite, *Farmers' Frontier*, 75–93. On steam power in agriculture, see Reynold M. Wik, *Steam Power on the American Farm* (Philadelphia, 1953), esp. 82–154.

9. Hiram Drache, "Thomas D. Campbell—the Plower of the Plains," in Wessel (ed.), *Agriculture in the Great Plains*, 78–91.

the south) during the 1880s, Chinese laborers arrived on the scene. The arrival during the 1890s and 1900s of sugar beets necessitated yet more workers, this time Japanese (in the north) and Mexicans (in the south). East Indians appeared in numbers about 1909 as the Japanese began to disappear from the migrant force. Mexican laborers finally came to predominate all over the state by 1920. Meanwhile California bankers, railroads, food processors, and growers achieved the vertical integration of most of the vegetable, fruit, and beet businesses. Financiers and railroad men organized markets; processors contracted with large numbers of growers great and small; the growers organized their hordes of successive ethnic laborers. Thus were established, in the words of Los Angeles attorney and journalist Carey McWilliams, the first American "factories in the field." [10]

The Earl Fruit Company of Bakersfield in Kern County exemplified the California model. A one-unit, centrally managed enterprise, Earl Fruit during the early 1930s operated twenty-seven farms it owned outright and eleven others it leased. In addition, the company purchased fruit on contract from many small "independent" growers in the southern San Joaquin Valley. The company owned eleven packing houses in several California cities and a 95 percent interest in the Klamath Lumber and Box Company, which supplied packing boxes at cost. Earl Fruit, in turn, was a subsidiary of the DiGiorgio Fruit Corporation, which owned warehouses and distributorships in Cincinnati, Chicago, Pittsburgh, Baltimore, and New York, along with a more than one-third interest in Italian Swiss Colony vineyards and wineries and part of another winery as well. Thus, with the exception of the railway cars that transported the fruit from California to the East, Earl-DiGiorgio owned and controlled its product from tree to consumer. Fruit was a labor-intensive crop, and Earl Fruit (during the late 1930s) employed nearly three thousand agricultural workers each year and maintained 350 dwellings for them. [11] Such labor requirements were comparable to those of Mississippi's giant Delta and Pine Land Company, then the nation's largest cotton plantation, but of course, Earl Fruit kept large numbers of workers on their properties for only a fraction of the year.

10. Carey McWilliams, *Factories in the Field: The Story of Migratory Farm Labor in California* (Boston, 1939), 10–27, 48–199 (esp. 50–60). See also Richard J. Orsi, "*The Octopus* Reconsidered: The Southern Pacific and Agricultural Modernization in California, 1865–1915," *California Historical Quarterly,* LIV (Fall, 1975), 197–220.

11. Carey McWilliams, *Ill Fares the Land: Migrants and Migratory Labor in the United States* (Boston, 1942), 17–20.

Where agricultural enterprise was susceptible to labor-reduction or elimination, Californians led the nation. The wheat country of the San Joaquin Valley, where the state's first armies of migrants roamed, was ideal. From mid-May to early November rain seldom falls. The sun ripens wheat, and there is no need to cut and shock the crop for drying as in the Middle West and East. Growers realized early the possibility of combining harvesting and threshing into one operation, and the first grain combines were introduced in the Central Valley during the 1870s and 1880s, half a century before they were generally accepted and used in the Middle West. Huge contraptions drawn by great teams of horses, they rolled over expansive, flat, dry fields, not only speeding the harvest but vastly reducing labor needs. The boggy deltas of the San Joaquin and Sacramento river systems presented yet another problem and mechanical opportunity. Farmers complained at the turn of the century that the wheels of self-propelled steam tractors became hopelessly mired, and even horses equipped with twelve-inch wooden foot-enlargers could not work during the wet times. So Benjamin Holt, a New England–born engineer-manufacturer of Stockton, adapted a crawler-type track to his steam tractor in 1904. Two years later Holt applied the "caterpillar" device to a new, lighter gasoline-powered tractor with excellent results. The caterpillar tractor became enormously successful in logging and construction as well as in farming.[12]

Meanwhile, hydraulic farming societies were taking shape in the San Joaquin and Imperial valleys. Private initiative came first. In 1871 the San Joaquin and Kings River Canal Irrigation Company was incorporated to bring water to a forty-mile area, typical of the lower Central Valley, where annual rainfall usually measured less than ten inches. The canal system, completed in 1873, had a sort of democratic effect upon landholding: many huge wheat estates were broken up and sold in smaller parcels to individuals and cooperatives. During the 1910s, however, holdings were consolidated once more, banker-backed marketing cooperatives were established, and the region underwent rapid mechanization. Huge agricultural factories such as Earl Fruit were in place. Growers outside the area served by the canal company pumped underground and lake water to their fields. During the first decade of the century, they used the new gasoline-powered donkey pumps, then in the teens, electrical power. High costs and the danger of ruining land by the

---

12. Reynold M. Wik, "Some Interpretations of the Mechanization of Agriculture in the Far West," in Shideler (ed.), *Agriculture in the Far West*, 73–83; John Turner, *White Gold Comes to California* (Bakersfield, 1981), 29–32.

FIGURE 1
Tractors in Seven
California Central
Valley Counties,
1925–1959
(in thousands)

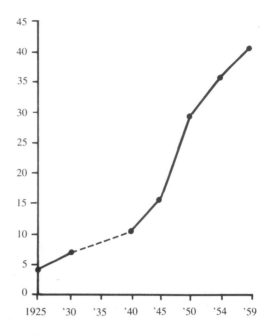

SOURCE: Censuses of agriculture, 1925–1959,
county tables. Data for 1935 not available.

spread of salt (alkalinity) from the subsoil led organized growers and
their backers to campaign for state and federal aid in bringing distant
surface water to the valley. They finally succeeded during the 1930s and
1940s, when the multimillion-dollar Central Valley Project was constructed at state and national taxpayers' expense. From the Imperial
Valley and environs to the extreme south near the borders with Arizona
and Mexico, the federal contribution to the Colorado River Irrigation
Canal, together with promotion by corporate developers, created
factory-style agriculture in the first decade of the century. The United
States Department of Agriculture established an experiment station
near Yuma, Arizona, which helped corporate farmers develop the Pima
variety of long-staple cotton in 1910. In the following decade, as the
boll weevil ravaged southeastern crops, a cotton craze raged in the Imperial Valley. As early as 1911 desert growers demonstrated avid interest
in a picking machine.[13] Thus, the California model of farming—charac-

13. Donald Worster, "Hydraulic Society in California: An Ecological Interpretation,"
Agricultural History, LVI (July, 1982), 503–15. On donkey pumps, electrical pumping,
and scarce rainfall, see Turner, *White Gold,* 33–34; Donald J. Pisani, *From the Family*

terized by economies of scale, industrial organization, and generous governmental assistance—came to embrace the principal staple of the plantation South.

Cotton was not unknown in California in the nineteenth century. A minor boom occurred around Los Angeles, in the Sacramento Valley, and elsewhere after the Civil War. Growers hired Chinese laborers to chop and harvest. But this boom ended by 1885 as southeastern cultivation underwent the great expansion that will be described in the next chapter.[14] The emergence of irrigation in the San Joaquin and Imperial valleys and adjacent Arizona deserts early in the twentieth century, however—while southeastern cotton reeled under the weevil's onslaught—created a virtually ideal environment for cotton's reappearance. The irrigated lands had obvious advantages. They were flat, dry, and capable of supporting the large cultivating machinery Californians preferred; there were no weevils, no bollworms (as yet), and fewer other pests; preharvest grasses were light, necessitating little weeding labor; harvesttime weather was almost always dry; and ranchers, as planters are called in the West, had easy access to Mexican hired workers who left when chores were done rather than remain year round like the sharecroppers of the Southeast.[15]

Imperial and Yuma ranchers turned to other pursuits around 1919–1920, when cotton prices fell and an uncharacteristic plague of insects descended upon their fields. But at that moment the future giant of the San Joaquin Valley was being born, and the United States Department of Agriculture was midwife. The "father of California cotton" was a USDA official, W. B. "Bill" Camp, a South Carolinian assigned to the new cotton field station at Shafter, Kern County, in 1917. The federal initiative was occasioned by the war. Camp's mission was to develop a source of long-staple cotton for the fabric used as the structural covers of military aircraft. (Most southeastern cotton was short-staple.) The large ranchers around Bakersfield eagerly cooperated. Indeed, officers

Farm to Agribusiness: The Irrigation Crusade in California and the West, 1850–1931 (Berkeley, 1984), 78–128, 335–439. Ronald L. Nye, in "Federal vs. State Agricultural Research Policy: The Case of California's Tulare Experiment Station, 1888–1909," *Agricultural History,* LVII (October, 1983), 436–49, discusses a very early instance of federal and state service to desert ranchers in the San Joaquin Valley.

14. Turner, *White Gold,* 23.

15. Moses S. Musoke and Alan L. Olmstead, "The Rise of the Cotton Industry in California: A Comparative Perspective," *Journal of Economic History,* XLII (June, 1982), 385–412.

of the enormous Kern County Land Company lent Camp test acreage, then deeded land for the Shafter station to the county, which in turn leased the property to the USDA. Camp, in the meantime, demonstrated the feasibility of growing Egyptian Pima with successful 1917 and 1918 crops, and equally noteworthy, he convinced westerners that folks other than black southerners could pick cotton.[16]

Then a most curious series of events transpired. The wartime long-staple cotton "emergency" passed, and Pima prices dropped out of sight. Yet Camp and the USDA persisted in the development of cotton culture in the West. There seems to have been no significant protest against this peacetime governmental promotion of competition with the forlorn, weevil-eaten Southeast. Camp found a new, better variety of cotton—Acala #8, a descendant of a strain collected near Acala, Mexico, by USDA agents in 1906—and he brought to California under federal auspices James S. Townsend, a fellow Carolinian and master gin mechanic. Townsend would show western ginners how to adapt their saws to the fine lint from Camp's new cotton, largely at taxpayers' expense. Meanwhile Acala acreage, from Riverside County in the south (near Imperial) through the San Joaquin and up into the Sacramento Valley, grew from 50,000 to 129,000 between 1922 and 1924. As one might expect, Californians pioneered mechanically while they planted big. The first aerial applications of chemicals occurred near Woodland in the Sacramento Valley in 1920, when a pilot guided a World War I training plane with his knees while dumping lead acetate on cotton fields with a coal shovel.[17]

This commitment to Acala by ranchers, ginning companies, and USDA agents led to effective agitation for a state "one variety" law in 1924. Camp appears to have initiated the movement. The California assembly complied early in the following year, designating nine districts (corresponding to counties) in which only one variety of cotton seed might be planted. Since the Shafter station was the originator of Acala #8 (and its many successors), the state government in effect secured the place of the federal government in the emerging infrastructure of the

16. William J. Briggs and Henry Cauthen, *The Cotton Man: Notes on the Life and Times of Wofford B. ("Bill") Camp* (Columbia, S.C., 1983), 30, 37.

17. Turner, *White Gold*, 36, 41–44. Arthur F. Raper, in *Tenants of the Almighty* (New York, 1943), 188, reported the migration of several Greene County, Georgia, planters to Kings County, California, following World War I; yet Turner is probably correct that the great majority of California cotton growers were not southeasterners.

Map 1
California Cotton Country

SOURCE: Adapted from John Turner, *White Gold Comes to California* (Bakersfield, 1981).

California cotton industry. In California there would be no constant private experimentation with planting seed and none of the resultant seed adulteration and degradation that had occurred in the lower Mississippi Valley. California growers also benefited from the state's experience with marketing cooperatives and vertical integration. (Some cotton ranchers had switched from fruit; and the Shafter station, it will be recalled, was located in the midst of the Earl Fruit Company's Kern County domain.) Ginners rather than banks financed early crops, but the huge successes during the 1920s finally attracted bankers' confidence, too. In 1928 W. B. Camp left Shafter and federal service for a position with the Bank of Italy (headquartered in San Francisco and later called the Bank of America), where he was concerned with agricultural credit and the management of vast bank-owned acreage. In 1933 Camp returned to public service to help administer the New Deal's Agricultural Adjustment Administration (AAA) cotton program. Finally, he and his two sons became private cotton and potato farmers in Kern County.[18]

Having brought cotton culture to San Joaquin in the 1920s, the federal government helped entrench the commodity during the Depression of the 1930s. Poor fruit prices at the onset of the decade provoked growers to rip out thousands of acres of trees and vineyards and plant their land in cotton—just in time to receive federal commodity support payments under the auspices of the AAA in 1933. AAA subsidies aided most farmers, but the largest growers received disproportionately lavish support. Carey McWilliams estimated that in 1938, only 2 percent of California growers collected 43.6 percent of all AAA payments in the state. Meanwhile the New Deal and the state undertook the Central Valley Project to irrigate the eastern and central sections of the San Joaquin Valley, and in 1937 congressional legislation guaranteed free cotton classification services and market news to all organized farm groups.[19]

With taxpayer-subsidized water on the way to all but ranchers on the western side of the valley, labor remained the most nagging problem in cotton culture. Wage rates for picking were consistently higher in California than anywhere else in the nation. In 1935, for example, western pickers received about a dollar per hundredweight of seed cotton, but southeastern workers received an average of only about sixty cents. The ranchers' problem was compounded by their own remarkable successes in increasing both acreage and per-acre yield. Between 1924 and 1936 California cotton acreage grew almost three and a half times, while yields improved from 415 to 595 pounds per acre. Labor requirements increased by a factor of twelve, according to agronomists on the scene. Throughout this period growers battled with workers, especially the Mexicans, who sought to bargain collectively. Few ranchers intended to yield to worker unions, so they looked to mechanization as their solution. The ranchers and their USDA advisors calculated that as soon as the wage rate passed $1.25 per hundredweight, picking machines, of which there were several working models already, would become cost

18. Turner, *White Gold,* 57–61, 66, 69, 72; Briggs and Cauthen, *Cotton Man,* 53, 97, 110–34, 243–66, and *passim.*
19. Turner, *White Gold,* 73–74, 76; McWilliams, *Ill Fares the Land,* 20.

FIGURE 2
Cotton Acreage
Harvested in Seven
California Central
Valley Counties,
1920–1959
(in thousands of acres)

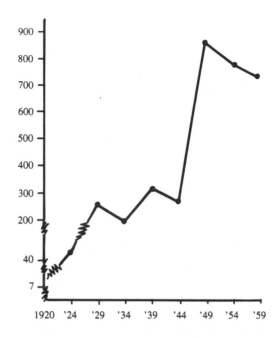

SOURCE: Censuses of agriculture, 1920–1959, county tables.

effective. By 1942 wages did reach this level, but the heavy equipment requirements of World War II prevented manufacturers and growers from acting on their formula. Once the war was over, however, the mechanization of the cotton harvest quickly came about.[20]

In 1947 cotton became California's most profitable crop, and International Harvester, Allis-Chalmers, Pearson, and John Deere were selling hundreds of spindle-type one-row picking machines. (The stripper-type machine used in western Texas and Oklahoma and in New Mexico since the early 1930s was not appropriate to Acala because it left too much trash in the lint.) By 1949 the machines had won wide acceptance. There were 850 in operation, which harvested 14 percent of the

20. Musoke and Olmstead, "Rise of the Cotton Industry in California," 398; Turner, *White Gold,* 84–87; Cletus E. Daniel, *Bitter Harvest: A History of California Farmworkers, 1870–1941* (Ithaca, 1981). The San Luis Canal finally brought surface water to the western side of the valley in 1968. Before then ranchers such as Frank C. Diener of Five Points, Fresno County, adapted oil-drilling-type derricks to pump water from deep in the earth. Turner, *White Gold,* 74, 139–40, 166; Frank C. Diener and his family, author's interviews, July 5–10, 1982, aboard the *Mississippi Queen* between Cairo and New Orleans.

state's crop. A Coalinga area rancher crowed over his success and itched for a bright future. In 1949, he reported, "our four machines harvested 1773 bales in seventy days." His crew "lost only two days because of weather. The four machines were kept operating with a seven-man crew—each man had one day a week off." The previous year, 1948, his production "cost was forty-two dollars a bale, but in 1949 it was down to twenty-seven dollars a bale, including grade loss, yield loss and machine repair and depreciation." The rancher's data on comparisons of hand-harvested and machine-harvested costs were equally impressive: "In 1948 our machine picked cotton was seven dollars a bale cheaper than the hand picked, and in 1949 it was twenty-two dollars cheaper. And we have not hit perfection yet. Someday we will be as completely mechanized as scientists can make it. And when this is done—hand thinning, weeding and picking will be a thing of the past." [21]

"Someday" was not far off. The rancher's hopes were soon fulfilled by the fine tuning of a new agricultural chemistry which had emerged from World War II. Of particular importance to cotton growers were defoliants, which, sprayed on cotton in early fall, caused plants to drop their leaves before mechanical pickers began their work. Lint would be cleaner, grade loss minimal. As for weeding, preemergent herbicides developed by the USDA and state colleges of agriculture in cooperation with the private chemical industry were already becoming available during the late 1940s. The San Joaquin Valley remained free of bollworms and weevils, but for the variety of other pests that attacked cotton, ranchers had DDT, Toxaphene, benzene hexachloride, and a number of other lethal chemical agents. During the 1950s effective helicopter and fixed-wing aerial spraying craft and equipment were in wide use, the Fresno Cotton Exchange was founded, and machine picking exceeded 50 percent of the crop. Yields improved so dramatically that growers reduced acreage to lower irrigation costs. The Southeast, meanwhile, lagged in adopting nearly every feature of this brave new world of cotton. California properly claimed ascendancy by the 1960s. [22]

California ranchers had combined the big-thinking futurism of nineteenth-century bonanza farmers with what I shall call the federal road to rural development. Always well capitalized and free of the South's resident peasantry and stagnating traditions, they grasped the guiding hand of the USDA, then squeezed life-giving water from taxpayers in Califor-

---

21. Turner, *White Gold*, 89, 103, 92–93.

22. Gilbert C. Fite, "Mechanization of Cotton Production Since World War II," *Agricultural History*, LIV (January, 1980), 190–207; Turner, *White Gold*, 87, 93, 107.

nia and the nation. By the end of the 1950s, when their superiority to southeastern cotton culture was clear, they had built a marvel of grower organization, water conservancy controls, cooperation with the USDA (perhaps control of it), and effective lobbying power. Thus the Californians defined and symbolized what is modern in agriculture. Their size and efficiency and their premonition of now-common production systems, such as vertical integration and contract farming, set the West apart and ahead of the rest of the nation.

The western mode of agricultural development was not entirely a creature of the West or of Plains bonanza farming, however. If California, in particular, came to define the modern in farming, modernity was in fact a long time aborning, and its origins are to be located in the East and the old corn belt. There, modernity is little more (or less) than the realization of values and assumptions long associated with the middle classes of the East—love of the balance sheet, the new, the technical, and the large, and belief in education as a facilitator of all those changes called progress. The townsmen of colonial Massachusetts had conceived of the public school and, beyond that, the government as facilitators of divine will. Their secular heirs, the agrarian urbanites and professors of the nineteenth-century homestead country, resolved that government should bring middle-class values and goals to primitive farmers through schooling. Most farmers resisted, it seems, at least in the short run. Many of them were close to what is thought of as a premodern class; they were traditionalists disdainful of books and change. Southern farmers and, ironically, small farmers in the far West were least touched by middle-class goals and most resistant. In the long run, however, the commercial potential of the rich American landscape, along with labor shortages and responsive technical innovations, conspired against them. Ultimately, they gave in and joined the middle class or were swept away by "progress." [23]

The modernist movement might be dated from 1857, when Justin S. Morrill first introduced in Congress a bill to provide federal aid to agricultural education. Morrill and his backers would dedicate national lands within states and territories to the establishment and support of land-grant colleges where scientific farming would be professed. While the South remained in the troubled Union, Morrill failed, but when Lin-

23. This argument is in effect an extension (backwards chronologically) of a thesis in David B. Danbon, *The Resisted Revolution: Urban America and the Industrialization of Agriculture, 1900–1930* (Ames, Iowa, 1979). See also Jack Temple Kirby, *Darkness at the Dawning: Race and Reform in the Progressive South* (Philadelphia, 1972), 131–76.

GASOLINE TRACTOR DEMONSTRATION, OKLAHOMA, 1920s

Herring Collection, Western History Collections, University of Oklahoma Library

coln's new government assumed office in 1861, a long ascendancy of eastern and middle western interests began. The Lincoln administration created the Department of Agriculture to serve its largest constituency, and in 1862 Morrill's land-grant bill became law. Iowa was the first state to accept its provisions. In 1887 Congress passed the so-called Hatch Experiment Station Act. Sponsored by a Missouri legislator, this law funded practical research at the agricultural colleges. Three years later a second Morrill Act required states of the late Confederacy to share federal grants with black citizens, and seventeen black agricultural colleges came into existence. By 1900 there were sixty-nine land-grant schools devoted primarily to educating farmers.[24]

Most farmers ignored the college movement. Enrollments were tiny, and rural folks disparaged city-born professors with backgrounds in classical studies. So the educators turned to a device now known as outreach. They established the "institute," a meeting in the countryside where experts—agronomists, animal specialists, orchardists, and so on—brought experiment station and other research directly to farmers.

24. Roy V. Scott, *The Reluctant Farmer: The Rise of Agricultural Extension to 1914* (Urbana, 1970), 26–27, 33; Alfred Charles True, *A History of Agricultural Education in the United States, 1785–1925* (Washington, D.C., 1929), 91–191, 208–10.

The origins of the institute movement may be dated to antebellum times, but its great growth occurred late in the nineteenth century and during the first decade and a half of the twentieth. The principal historian of agricultural education has argued persuasively that the growth of institutes may be attributed in considerable part to farmers' discontent during the years of declining commodity prices and struggles against rail carriers, banks, and other big businesses. Farmers organized for the first time, creating the Patrons of Husbandry (the Grange), the northern and southern Farmers' Alliances, and finally the People's party. The organizations emphasized (among other things) cooperation, improvement of the physical conditions of farm life, and education. And among the results of all the organizational activity was greater respect among farmers for learned lecturers.[25]

So the institutes grew, and after 1900 especially, their success is a milestone of the progress of middle-class aspirations among farmers. That farmers accepted instruction from lecturers supplied by railroad corporations, manufacturers, and banks (as well as those sent directly from the colleges) seems particularly noteworthy. Grangers and former Populists apparently made peace with their old enemies. Railroad and banking executives were eager to generate commercial farming business in their areas, and farm implement manufacturers, especially International Harvester, had obvious self-interest in production growth and labor savings. Railroads subsidized "institute trains" early in the century, and in 1910 International Harvester created its own successful institute department. The National Fertilizer Association, a trade group, sponsored programs beginning in 1911, and large banks—particularly middle western ones—organized institutes for the first time the same year. Between 1901 and 1914, according to the USDA, the number of farmers' institutes (of all types) grew 230 percent, from 2,772 to 8,861; and attendance catapulted from 819,995 to 3,050,151. Regional differences in support of institutes are glaring, however. The Middle West was utterly dominant in numbers of meetings and attendance throughout the period. In terms of attendance, nine northeastern states were most supportive, after the Middle West. The sparsely populated far West was weakest. In terms of the number of institutes per million rural population, the Northeast was dominant at the beginning of the century; then the Middle West emerged as regional institute leader during 1909–1910. Tellingly, by 1913–1914, the West had far surpassed all other re-

25. Scott, *Reluctant Farmer,* 64–103.

BUTLER COUNTY, OHIO, ANTIQUE MACHINERY CLUB SHOW, 1984. Above is a corn planter, *ca.* 1910, drawn by Belgian horses; below is a 1920s Farmall.

Photos by the author

gions. There were 426 institutes per million rural population held in eleven western states during that winter. The Middle West had but 198. By this time the institute movement in sixteen southern and border states had grown to 140 per million rural population—the same count as in nine northeastern states. The South had begun the century with only 18.[26] On balance, then, despite obvious headway made by agricultural education before World War I, the South lagged considerably behind the rest of the nation. The progress of modernity had begun in the North and flowered most gloriously in the West, bypassing most of those who lived below the Mason-Dixon Line and the Ohio River.

What success middle-class rural reformers enjoyed in the South was owing not so much to a fundamental conversion as to a peculiarly southern crisis. About 1893 a voracious strain of cotton boll weevil crossed the Rio Grande near Brownsville, Texas, and began to make its way northeastward. By the end of the decade the economies of entire counties in eastern Texas were devastated. Farmers, storekeepers, bankers, and railroad officers demanded federal assistance. The USDA, controlled by middle westerners who exemplified the spirit of modern research and federal solutions to practical business problems, responded promptly. The department's Bureaus of Plant Industry and Entomology went to work and established experimental demonstration farms to test methods of weevil control. In 1902 Seaman A. Knapp—a former Iowa farm editor and professor of agriculture and the principal developer (as a corporate officer) of rice culture in southwestern Louisiana—became the USDA special agent for the South. The following year he devised a novel educational enterprise on a private farm outside Terrell, Texas, which became the model for the future federal-state Agricultural Extension Service. The farmer agreed to follow Knapp's advice to the letter in cultivating a part of his land, and neighbors were invited to observe the procedures and results. Local businessmen provided a guaranty fund against failure because of book farming. The farmer succeeded—although heavy doses of costly fertilizer were probably the most significant factor in turning a profit. Soon Knapp began hiring agent-helpers to assist in other demonstrations. The program spread eastward, then northward, with the progress of the weevil. Congress increased appropriations, and in 1906 the Rockefeller-funded General Education Board began to augment public and local support for the work. By 1913 county agents were spread throughout the South, in Virginia, West Vir-

26. *Ibid.*, 104–106, 170–89, 190, 205.

Hays for the Salvation of Alabama, 1930s
ACES Photo Collection, Auburn University Archives

ginia, and Maryland as well as in the weevil-infested districts. Meanwhile Knapp, his son and successor, Bradford Knapp, and the agents fostered scientific farming among the young with boys' corn and hog clubs and girls' tomato and garden clubs. They also promoted "modern" homemaking among farm wives with a home demonstration program. Some agents (men and women) came to specialize in educational work among children and women. Finally, in 1914 Congress institutionalized and nationalized something close to Knapp's original system with the Smith-Lever Act. This law formally created the USDA Extension Service and linked it with the state land-grant colleges, which would direct the county agents' activities and report to Washington.[27]

27. Joseph Cannon Bailey, *Seaman A. Knapp, Schoolmaster of American Agriculture* (New York, 1945), 109–243; Scott, *Reluctant Farmer*, 210–313.

The legislators-of-record behind this realization of middle-class dreams were southerners—Senator Hoke Smith of Georgia and Congressman Asbury Frank Lever of South Carolina. Both had rural origins, but both had become professionals (attorneys) and city men, aligned in mind and politics with the progressives of the Middle West and the small but growing numbers of middle-class urban reformers at home in the South. Indeed, the Smith-Lever Act might have been named for middle western Republican congressmen instead of the southerners had not Democrats won control of Congress late in 1910 and had not Woodrow Wilson become president early in 1913. Legislators from Michigan and Nebraska and agricultural educators from New York to Iowa and beyond had been agitating for similar federal programs for years. The southern birth of the county agent system proved something of a hollow irony, for despite the numbers of agents in the region and despite growing attendance at southern farmers' institutes, federal programs reached a pitifully small proportion of a massive southern rural population. Middle-class goals, no matter how ardently preached or generously funded, make little headway among a people without capital, and southerners would remain for another generation in the grip of a farming system unlike anything in the North or West.[28]

Yet in the years between Seaman Knapp and Franklin Roosevelt, that minority of southerners who embraced middle-class values and benefited from federal largess would grow, in influence if not so much in numbers. Their experiences, augmented by the spectacular successes of the Plains and the West, accumulated overwhelming evidence that the Yankee version of modernity was the only road to southern salvation. The complexity of southern problems and the region's tortured path to this sort of salvation are related in the chapters following.

28. See Scott, *Reluctant Farmer,* 288–313; Kirby, *Darkness at the Dawning,* 131–76 and *passim.* Scott does not share my doleful assessment of the impact of agricultural education.

Part One
Transformations

To get money, then [the South] turned with absorbing
passion to the extension of the only practice which . . .
had yielded it: the cultivation of cotton. In the years
from 1875 to 1890 it would double its annual production of the staple; and in the next decade it would triple
it. But so far from affording the expected relief,
cotton, always fickle and dangerous, was developing
now into a Fata Morgana, the pursuit of which was actually bearing the South deeper and deeper into
trouble. . . . In the coming days, and probably soon,
[the South] is likely to have to prove its capacity for
adjustment far beyond what has been true in the past.
—W. J. CASH

Chapter 1

Modern Times and Rural Souths

IN THE BEST HISTORICAL SENSE THE SOUTH
first became modern when Indians retreated before the advance of the
earliest tobacco fields of Jamestown. European pioneers, having invented the plantation in Ireland, Brazil, and the Caribbean, brought this
frontier-settlement institution to North America early in the seventeenth
century. Later came the African slaves whose labor achieved for plantations both great size and efficiency. Physical brutality and specialized
dependency were logical components of this first economic world order.
Plantations were labor-intensive, and the indigenous red population was
inadequate and relatively unskilled. African slavery worked. Planters
and their managers, in turn, became dependent upon faraway metropo-
lises for both capital and markets for their export products. They were
agents, in effect, of the sources of power in this emerging world system.
Plantation societies had little need for cities, local manufacturing, or
technology. They were underdeveloped, in present-day parlance, by
their very modern design.[1]

American independence brought changes in economic relationships.

1. Immanuel Wallerstein, *The Modern World-System: Capitalist Agriculture and the
Origins of the European World-Economy in the Sixteenth Century* (New York, 1976), esp.
theoretical essay, 228–39.

Northwestern European capital and markets continued to be important to American planters, but during the early nineteenth century, as the northeastern United States underwent industrialization, American credit institutions, manufacturers, and consumers gradually assumed the position of metropolitan power over the southeastern plantation society. Meanwhile, six decades of the expansion of cotton culture made this plantation society the largest in the world, extending from Maryland into Texas. The South, dependent on its new metropolis in the North, remained an object for metropolitan investment and an extractive, cheap-labor supplier of raw materials. The American region bore striking similarities to other nineteenth-century plantation regions, especially northeastern Brazil, another internal colony within a New World modern state.[2]

The ravages of Civil War and the emancipation without compensation of southern slaves presented profound problems and wrought some structural changes, but the South remained a plantation society. Cultivation of cotton, tobacco, and other export staples actually expanded, as did the dependency of the region upon outside capital and markets. Commensurately, southern subregions previously independent of the world system, shrank. The former slaves, and ultimately hundreds of thousands of whites who had formerly lived outside the plantation districts, were drawn into an American version of labor and credit dependency known in virtually all the regions of the world after the end of slavery. Towns and cities and certain manufactures grew throughout the late nineteenth and early twentieth centuries, but most were of a special sort. Urban centers acted as regional branches of northern and European sources of credit, supply, and transportation; factories specialized in preliminary processing of minerals (as with the Birmingham, Alabama, steel complex) or of forest products or made textiles in the piedmonts near newer cotton fields. Before World War I there was little outside the region to attract southern migrants. Farm tenancy, especially the lowest, most dependent kind, sharecropping, expanded at dismaying rates through the 1920s, then worsened during the early 1930s. So the

2. On plantation societies (esp. New World ones), see Edgar T. Thompson, "The Plantation" (Ph.D. dissertation, University of Chicago, 1935), Chap. 1; Andre Gunder Frank, "The Development of Underdevelopment," in Robert I. Rhodes (ed.), *Imperialism and Underdevelopment: A Reader* (New York, 1970), 3–17; Frank, *Capitalism and Underdevelopment in Latin America: Historical Studies of Chile and Brazil* (New York, 1972), esp. 219–53; George L. Beckford, *Persistent Poverty: Underdevelopment in the Plantation Economies of the Third World* (New York, 1972), esp. Intro. and Chap. 1.

South in the second quarter of the twentieth century was more modern, in the traditional sense of the word, than ever, and more impoverished.[3]

The culture of export staples, especially on plantations, is the persistent and defining factor for the South in the modern world. Expansion of plantation production areas within the region, then, always amounted to an expansion of "modernity" and the end of isolated, "premodern" rural life in southern subregions where the plantations and staple culture spread. Following the Civil War (particularly during the 1870s and 1880s) the area of the cotton kingdom grew dramatically. Several factors prepared the way. Railroad development in the hilly upper piedmonts opened for the first time lands that by planters' and merchants' standards were undeveloped. Thousands of war veterans and newcomers, eager for agricultural and commercial opportunities, rushed into the hills once they were connected to the world marketplace. Merchants established general stores offering not only a wide array of outside goods but credit from metropolitan bankers. Through credit, successful merchants gained monopolies over new cotton growers' business. Hill country natives, especially the small owners and tenants, found themselves trapped in the cycle of capital and market demands of the world system. Merchants colluded with planters in supplying tenants and croppers. Merchants became planter-landlords themselves, and planters (as they had long done in black-belt and delta areas) often set up their own stores or commissaries. The two upper classes—landowners and merchants—in effect merged in many districts, consolidating at once the power of their own class and the grip of the world market economy over the latest cotton frontier.[4]

The coming of plantation agriculture gradually destroyed the tradi-

3. On southern economic colonialism during the late nineteenth century, see Morton Rothstein, "The New South and the International Economy," *Agricultural History*, LVII (October, 1983), 385–402; C. Vann Woodward, *Origins of the New South, 1877–1913* (Baton Rouge, 1951), Chap. 11; Jonathan M. Wiener, *Social Origins of the New South: Alabama, 1860–1885* (Baton Rouge, 1978); Dwight B. Billings, Jr., *Planters and the Making of a "New South": Class, Politics, and Development in North Carolina, 1865–1900* (Chapel Hill, 1979), 3–41.

4. On the post–Civil War expansion of cotton and the development of crop liens and sharecropping, see Roger L. Ransom and Richard Sutch, *One Kind of Freedom: The Economic Consequences of Emancipation* (Cambridge, Eng., 1977), 126–48; Ronald L. F. Davis, *Good and Faithful Labor: From Slavery to Sharecropping in the Natchez District, 1860–1890* (Westport, Conn., 1982), esp. 89–120; Crandall A. Shifflett, *Patronage and Poverty in the Tobacco South: Louisa County, Virginia, 1860–1900* (Knoxville, 1982); Michael Schwartz, *Radical Protest and Social Structure: The Southern Farmers' Alliance and Cotton Tenancy, 1880–1890* (New York, 1976), 62–63.

INDIANS PICKING COTTON ON THE OKLAHOMA COTTON FRONTIER, 1899

Frank Phillips Collection, Western History Collections, University of Oklahoma Library

tional structure of life in the hill country. War had already damaged or consumed homes, barns, crop fences, and life-sustaining livestock. Then came the railroaders, planters, and crop-lien merchants. Open lands were alienated, squatters and landless herdsmen were converted into tenants, and the local barter and labor-exchange economy was wrecked. When the planters and townspeople came to Georgia's upper piedmont during the 1870s they demanded laws to protect crops and other property from foraging cattle and swine—in other words, an end to the open range that had sustained small owners and the landless for many generations. The state assembly enacted legislation authorizing county option elections on the issue, and there ensued a struggle lasting through the 1880s between the new people and the old, the big and the small, those who self-consciously cried for modern protection and those who insisted that poor people with little land could not remain independent unless their herds roamed freely on open land. Gradually the modernizers won the battle. Many among the old yeomanry, herdsmen, and squatters became vigorous Populists, but they were brought under sway.[5]

The process of extending cotton dependency and ending the open range was similar in neighboring Alabama. There, the state legislature

5. Steven Hahn, "Common Right and Commonwealth: The Stock-Law Struggle and the Roots of Southern Populism," in J. Morgan Kousser and James M. McPherson (eds.), *Region, Race, and Reconstruction: Essays in Honor of C. Vann Woodward* (New York, 1983), 51–88. See also Hahn, *The Roots of Southern Populism: Yeoman Farmers and the Transformation of the Georgia Upcountry, 1850–1890* (New York, 1983), esp. 137–69.

moved before the end of the 1860s to restrict livestock in certain black belt and Tennessee River counties. By the 1880s the open range over much of the state was closed, and railroads imported fat pork from Cincinnati to feed a people who before the Civil War had fed themselves and produced meat surpluses for export. Mississippi, Louisiana, Tennessee, parts of North Carolina, and other places where modern developers spread, followed the pattern.[6]

On the fringes of the plantation districts and beyond, remnants of the open range (and the premodern economies the open range usually indicates) persisted well into the twentieth century. A central North Carolina stock dealer reported that before World War I "old field" varieties of livestock predominated—this in the midst of the piedmont textiles and tobacco belt. Remote Appalachian highlanders and some west-central Kentucky farmers ranged cattle and hogs into the 1920s. And on North Carolina's Outer Banks a petty merchant kept a wild, unfenced herd of cattle from which he slaughtered meat for home use and local sale well into the 1920s. Only then did state officials fine the merchant for failure to dip his cattle in insecticide and force him to shoot the animals before spring fattening.[7]

Yet the twentieth century did not bring stagnation to the modernizing

6. On "primitive" agriculture generally, see Ester Boserup, *The Conditions of Agricultural Growth: The Economics of Agrarian Change Under Population Pressure* (Chicago, 1965); B. A. Datoo, "Toward a Reformulation of Boserup's Theory of Agricultural Change," *Economic Geography,* LIV (April, 1978), 135–44. On the South, in addition to Steven Hahn's works cited above, see John S. Otto, "Southern 'Plain Folk' Agriculture: A Reconsideration," *Plantation Society in the Americas,* II (April, 1983), 29–36. On the closing of the southern range during the late nineteenth and early twentieth centuries, see (in addition to Hahn) Forrest McDonald and Grady McWhiney, "The South from Self-sufficiency to Peonage: An Interpretation," *American Historical Review,* LXXXV (December, 1980), 1095–1118; J. Crawford King, Jr., "The Closing of the Southern Range: An Exploratory Study," *Journal of Southern History,* XLVIII (February, 1982), 53–70; Wayne Durill, " 'Taking the Peoples Libertyes Away by Law Power': The Destruction of a Subsistence Economy in Union County, North Carolina, 1872–1885" (Paper read September 22, 1983, History of Rural Life in America Conference, Florida A & M University). Fencing laws notwithstanding, stock broke out and wandered or were never adequately penned throughout the South long after the range was closed. See Theodore Rosengarten, *All God's Dangers: The Life of Nate Shaw* (New York, 1975), 407.

7. On the persistence of open-range husbandry outside plantation districts, see, for example, Leonard Rapport, "Jim Eubanks: Horse and Cow Trader," February 3, 1939, W. O. Saunders, "Isaac ('Big Ike') O'Neal," life history, n.d. (1938 or 1939) (Both typescripts in Federal Writers' Project [FWP] life histories file, Southern Historical Collection, University of North Carolina [SHC]). Leslie Ann Stanley, oral history of William Elmo Stanley, March 7, 1973 (Microfilmed typescript, in Marshall University Oral History of Appalachia Collection [MUOHA]) reports the open ranging of hogs in Carlisle County, western Kentucky, at least as late as World War I.

dynamic on cotton plantations. Cotton fields spread westward to the "black waxy" lands below Dallas, Texas, and over much of Oklahoma. Lumber companies cleared yet more hill country and swampy lowlands, opening the way for further expansion. At the time of the Civil War hardly 10 percent of the vast alluvial lowlands of the Yazoo-Mississippi Delta were under cultivation. It was not until the late 1880s that legal conundrums were untangled, releasing the land to timber companies. So only in the early twentieth century was this future cotton empire cleared, ditched, leveed, and ready for the mule and plow. One of the last and greatest of the plantation bonanza regions was northeastern Arkansas and the bootheel of Missouri just to the north. Until World War I these rich lowlands were a heavily forested country with sparse population and local economies probably much like that of the Georgia upper piedmont forty years before. Then came lumber companies, which nearly denuded the landscape and cut drainage ditches, exposing vast expanses for agricultural development. Purchasers were in the main wealthy families (such as that of R. E. Lee Wilson) and corporations (such as Singer Sewing Machine Company). Their plantation managers subdivided huge tracts among thousands of black and white sharecroppers during the 1920s and brought this last delta frontier under the plow.[8] By 1930, of approximately twelve hundred counties in all or parts of sixteen southern states (the former Confederacy minus west Texas, plus Kentucky, eastern and southern West Virginia, eastern Oklahoma, and southeastern Missouri), more than half were committed to cotton. West Virginia was the only state usually considered southern without at least one cotton county. This vast region included many dynamic sections, such as the deltas and new western lands, but within the cotton South were also many poor, retrograde cotton counties and many newer hill area counties that never should have turned to clean-row agriculture. Greene County, Georgia, which was explored so well by the sociologist

8. On the persistence into the 1920s of cotton and its decrepit financial system, see Harold D. Woodman, *King Cotton and His Retainers: Financing and Marketing the Cotton Crop of the South, 1800–1925* (Lexington, Ky., 1968), 350–352. On early twentieth-century cotton frontiers, see Robert L. Brandfon, *Cotton Kingdom of the New South: A History of the Yazoo-Mississippi Delta from Reconstruction to the Twentieth Century* (Cambridge, Mass., 1967), 39–64; USDA Bureau of Agricultural Economics, "Mississippi Backwater Areas Study—Yazoo Segment," by R. Heberle and Udell Jolley (Typescript, November 10, 1940, in Land Tenure Section project files, Record Group 83, National Archives); early incorporation and operations papers of the Delta and Pine Land Company in the company's records, Mississippi State University Library; Donald Holley, *Uncle Sam's Farmers: The New Deal Communities in the Lower Mississippi Valley* (Urbana, 1975), 35–36 (on northeastern Arkansas).

COTTON CHOPPING WITH GANG LABOR, ALABAMA, 1930s
ACES Photo Collection, Auburn University Archives

Arthur Raper during the late 1920s and 1930s, is a classic retrograde type. Part of Georgia's original black belt, by the 1920s its lands were badly worn and eroded and infested with the dreaded boll weevil. Planters cut and sold their second-growth pine, leaving nothing of value on the land. They then began to withdraw, abandoning their property to the poor or, more commonly, to banks and insurance companies. The poor trapped rabbits in the brush of ruined old fields. Thus in Greene and other parts of the old black belt, where slaves first planted cotton, the plantation had broken down.[9] This South was no longer modern in any sense.

9. Classification of southern counties by crop type for 1930 is derived from Charles S. Johnson *et al.* (comps.), *Statistical Atlas of Southern Counties: Listing and Analysis of Socio-economic Indices of 1104 Southern Counties* (Chapel Hill, 1941), county tables by states. This volume does not include 1930 census or other data on West Virginia, Missouri, Oklahoma, and central Texas; I have classified relevant counties in these states from the county tables of the 1930 census of agriculture. On Greene County, Georgia, see Arthur F. Raper, *Preface to Peasantry: A Tale of Two Black Belt Counties* (Chapel Hill, 1936), 148 (on rabbit trapping) and *passim;* and Raper, *Tenants of the Almighty* (New York, 1943), 111–18.

Union Parish in northern Louisiana was also old cotton country, but of another type—marginal soil, white majority, few plantations. Following a disastrous drought in 1896 farmers in the parish turned to lumbering for cash. By 1920 the timber was cut out, and the people returned to more extensive cotton farming on their red clay and sandy soils. The boll weevil conspired with poor dirt to reduce production steadily and further impoverish Union farmers.[10]

Calhoun County in south-central Arkansas was similarly marginal. By the 1920s cotton was growing in the county's only decent alluvial soil, along the Ouchita River. Four-fifths of the county's land, away from the river, lay in timber or was cut over and badly eroded. Here, the open range still prevailed for small hill-farm proprietors. A New Deal worker observed in 1934 that in the "chief village," Hampton, "hogs and other livestock roam the streets at large." Citizens drew water with buckets from open wells, and there was no public library within the county.[11]

Walker County, Alabama, in the north near Birmingham, was a new cotton county in despair. Long classified as industrial, Walker became agricultural only toward the end of the 1920s when coal mines played out. Birmingham's industrial depression early in the 1930s spread further dislocation throughout the subregion. So miners and factory workers took up plows on their poor, steep hills and planted the crop that had always brought cash, however little. No plantation folk, Walker County people were mostly whites with small properties. But like the people of the black belt and the delta, they also had lien merchants—and too few livestock and vegetable gardens to sustain themselves.[12] Walker was a victim of cruel industrial circumstances and the plantation traditions of the subregions nearby.

Many retrograde cotton counties of the South (such as Greene, Georgia) still had black majorities in 1930, despite the boll weevil and migration. So did the dynamic delta cotton districts (such as northeastern Arkansas). But the newer cotton lands in Texas and Oklahoma were white dominated, as were practically all marginal hill cotton counties such as Walker, Alabama. Despite these poor correlations between land

10. Federal Emergency Relief Administration, Rural Problem Areas Survey Report No. 65, Western Cotton Growing Area: Union Parish, Louisiana (Typescript, January 14, 1935, in RG 83, NA), 1, 4.

11. *Ibid.*, Report No. 48, Western Cotton Growing Area: Calhoun County, Arkansas (Typescript, December 17, 1934), 1, 4–5.

12. "Annual Narrative Report of C. R. Edge, County Agent, Walker County, Alabama, November 30, 1940" (Typescript in Alabama Extension Service Records, Auburn University Archives).

MAP 2

The Cotton South, 1930

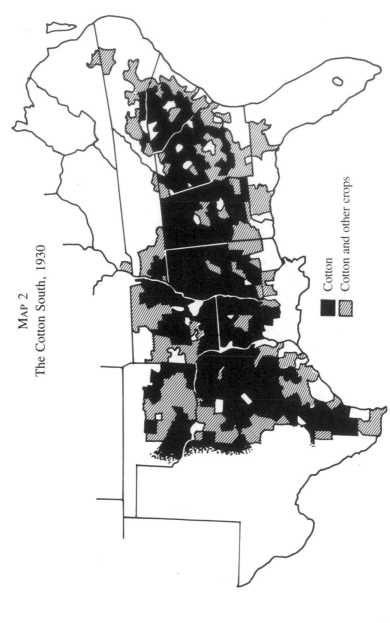

Cotton

Cotton and other crops

SOURCES: Adapted from Charles Johnson *et al.* (comps.), *Statistical Atlas; Fifteenth Census, 1930: Agriculture*, county tables.

quality and the racial composition of the farming populations, race remains a useful division of the great cotton South. For with the exception
of the new western lands, nearly all plantation counties had black majorities, and sharecropping was by far the dominant form of tenancy.
Cotton lands where whites were the majority—the West is exceptional
once more—were generally poor and hilly, and share tenants usually
outnumbered sharecroppers there. Statistics from the censuses of agriculture on representative samples of black- and white-majority cotton
counties reveal a pattern of other differences. Farms in the black plantation counties were consistently smaller—an average of sixty-four acres
in 1920, down to only fifty-six in 1930—than farms in the white areas,
which averaged about eighty-one acres in 1920 and a little more than
seventy-two acres in 1930. Black ownership of land was most common
in the same counties where black sharecropping was heaviest, too. In
fact the black-majority counties actually had more black farm owners
than white in the censuses of 1920, 1925, and 1930. Parcels were small,
however; very few blacks had large farms. Black farm owners in the
white counties totaled only about one-tenth the number of white proprietors throughout the 1920s. In neither area were farms significantly
mechanized, but the black-sharecropper plantation group had about
twice as many tractors (403 in 1925 and 805 in 1930) as the hilly white
farm counties (210 in 1925 and 370 in 1930).[13] Black-belt and delta
planters had better access to credit, of course, and some were responding in part to the black exodus of the 1920s with purchases of labor-
replacing machinery. Later the planters would grasp other capital advantages and forge far ahead of the hill farmers.

Cotton was not the only labor-intensive row crop conducive to plantations. Huge areas of Virginia, the Carolinas, Kentucky, and Tennessee, and sections of Alabama, southern Georgia, and northern Florida
were given over to cultivation of corn, tobacco, potatoes, and peanuts.
Tobacco—especially the flue-cured varieties of the South Atlantic—
was the most labor-intensive of all commercial crops. So in the coastal
plains heavily black populations of sharecroppers labored over tobacco
crops much as in the cotton fields to the west. The Kentucky-Tennessee

13. Figures calculated from county tables of the censuses of agriculture for 1920,
1925, and 1930. Black-majority counties sampled are Macon and Sumter, Alabama; Crittenden and St. Francis, Arkansas; Sumter, Georgia; Tensas Parish, Louisiana; Washington and Noxubee, Mississippi; Harrison, Texas; and Edgefield, South Carolina. White-
majority counties sampled are Clay and Fayette, Alabama; Perry, Arkansas; Forsyth and
Madison, Georgia; Sabine Parish, Louisiana; Covington and Tishomingo, Mississippi;
Trinity, Texas; and Chester, Tennessee.

MAP 3
The Row Crop South, 1930

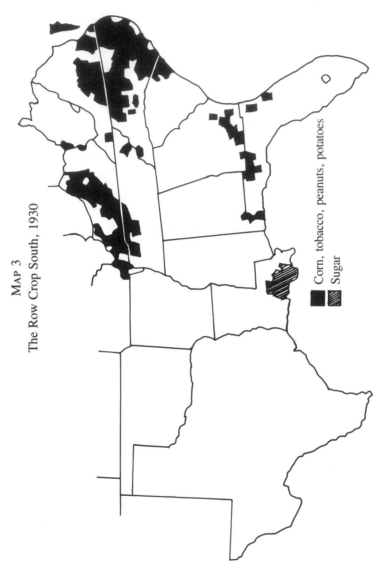

■ Corn, tobacco, peanuts, potatoes
▨ Sugar

SOURCES: Adapted from Charles Johnson *et al.* (comps.), *Statistical Atlas; Fifteenth Census: Agriculture,* county tables.

burley and corn country had fewer blacks and fewer plantations, but nonownership of farms by those who worked them—especially share tenancy (a step up from sharecropping)—was common. Tobacco was a dynamic crop, too, particularly in the lower Southeast. North Carolina growers pressed the boundaries of the staple ever southward, searching not only for better lands but for earlier-maturing crops so they might beat the competition to market and claim higher prices. By the end of the 1920s the eastern flue-cured belts extended down to southern Georgia and northern Florida. As the Carolina tobacco frontiersmen pressed southward, they brought their special knowledge to former cotton tenants and sharecroppers who had been displaced by the boll weevil and early mechanization. The owner-tenant relationship otherwise remained about the same, as the plantation form merely switched crops.[14]

In the sandy loam soils of the Virginia Eastern Shore and the Carolina coast, farmers, planters, and their tenants raised potatoes, another unmechanized crop, for urban markets near and far. Inland a few miles, in the tidewater of Virginia and North Carolina and in southern Georgia and parts of northwestern Florida and nearby southern Alabama, yet more farmers grew peanuts, another alternative to weevil-threatened cotton. By the end of the 1920s larger operators had adopted early, stationary peanut-threshing machinery, but the threshers required many hands with rakes and forks to feed them at harvest; so the machines did not substantially dislocate the southern mode of labor-intensive agriculture. The great age of peanut culture lay ahead, with advances in harvest machinery.[15]

14. Pete Daniel charts the southward advance of flue-cured tobacco culture in *Breaking the Land: The Transformation of Cotton, Tobacco, and Rice Cultures Since 1880* (Urbana, 1985), 23–38. See also Harry Crews, *A Childhood: The Biography of a Place* (New York, 1978), 27 (on southeastern Georgia); Florida Agricultural Extension Service, *The Story of Suwannee County* (N.p., [1963]), 23; E. C. Jones, "Tobacco" (Typescript, 1940, in Federal Writers' Program of Florida files, University of Florida Library). The southern extension of tobacco is also evident in the crop tables for Georgia and Florida in Charles Johnson *et al.* (comps.), *Statistical Atlas.*

15. See Charles Johnson *et al.* (comps.), *Statistical Atlas,* county tables. On peanuts, see USDA, Farm Economics Division, Economic Research Service, Agricultural Economics Report No. 7, *Peanut-Cotton Farms: Organization, Costs, and Returns, Southern Plains, 1944–1960,* by W. Herbert Brown (Washington, D.C., 1962), 13–14; Dru Flowers, oral history of Carl and Ted Forrester, January 18, 1975 (Typescript in Samford University Oral History Collection, Birmingham); advertising brochures for early peanut machinery (*e.g.,* one for a mechanical sheller, dated January 4, 1917) in Florence (Charles) Hall Pinkston Papers, Alabama Department of Archives and History, Montgomery. On potatoes, see USDA, Bureau of Agricultural Economics, "Eastern Shore Confidential Report," [by Dr. C. J. Galpin (?)] (Typescript, 1929, in RG 83, NA).

Sugar was another row crop of the plantation South. Sugar culture in southeastern Louisiana was an old enterprise, dating from colonial times. It rivaled flue-cured tobacco in labor intensiveness, but after emancipation sugar planters experimented only briefly with fragmenting their estates into tenant or sharecrop plots. Planters were dissatisfied with tenants' inattention to drainage ditch maintenance and a dozen other tasks that occupied sugar growers nearly year round. Unlike cotton and tobacco planters, who might also have preferred consolidating operations and more closely supervising labor, however, sugar men had access to New Orleans banks and acceptable interest rates. So they turned to wage labor during the 1870s, paying each full hand about a hundred dollars per year. Sugar planters reduced labor costs as much as possible for the time by planting rows far enough apart to permit cultivation with teams instead of hoes, and they were among the first in the lower South to purchase gasoline tractors during the 1910s. A series of disasters struck the sugar country during the 1910s and 1920s, however. Cane diseases decimated production; prices collapsed in 1921; anthrax killed twenty thousand head of livestock in 1924. Then the 1927 Mississippi River flood nearly ruined the industry altogether. So during the 1920s many planters turned to tenancy once more, in effect asking labor to share low prices and high risks. Many of the wage hand–tenant class departed, however, and by 1930 the sugar parishes in many respects resembled the impoverished cotton country.[16]

Rice was a very special small grain—not a row crop—that provided an alternative to labor-intensive agriculture few southerners could emulate. Low-country South Carolinians grew enormous quantities of rice in colonial times, but their industry declined to insignificance. Rice culture revived in the South around the turn of the century in southwestern Louisiana, the Arkansas Grand Prairie, and a few southeastern Texas counties. Like sugar, rice was well capitalized from its introduction, but rice culture was mechanized long before sugar or any other southern row crop and thus was the least labor intensive. A model for the new agriculture that was to evolve after 1930, rice was, fittingly, the creature of middle western pioneers to the South. During the 1880s Seaman A. Knapp, a former agricultural science professor and college president in Iowa, joined a British land development company to drain Louisiana

16. J. Carlyle Sitterson, *Sugar Country: The Sugar Cane Industry in the South, 1753–1950* (Lexington, Ky., 1953), 231–51, 308–323, 341–60, 390–391; Ralph Shlomowitz, " 'Bound or Free'? Black Labor in Cotton and Sugarcane Farming, 1865–1880," *Journal of Southern History,* L (November, 1984), 569–96.

swamps, control water, and introduce East Asian rice. The William Deering Company, manufacturers of steam-powered grain harvesters, accommodated with a machine adapted to rice. In 1894 David Abbot, another middle westerner, established effective upland irrigation. The Yankees and British formed canal companies, which charged fees to flood growing crops, and rice mills in Crowley and Lafayette, and they assisted Great Plains migrants in adapting their huge plows and threshers to rice culture. Thus was created in Cajun country a southern hydraulic culture much like the far western ones then evolving. Owner operation was common in rice, as it was in wheat in the Plains. Tenants were usually white, and they (as in the Middle West) usually owned their own equipment and paid only one-fifth their crops in rent, another one-fifth to canal companies for water. Sharecropping was rare.[17]

At the beginning of the twentieth century other Yankee immigrants in Lonoke and Arkansas counties, Arkansas, observed Louisiana operations and adapted their own middle western expertise to the peculiar geology of the Grand Prairie, which lies immediately west of the delta, stretching north to south. Until about 1900 the Grand Prairie was cattle and hay country, still much given over to tall grasses, natural food for beef. Beneath the sod lay a hard clay base, which would hold water above; beneath that lay an enormous aquifer. J. W. Fuller, an Ohio-born Nebraskan and a Union army veteran, first recognized the area's potential for rice and became an early promoter. The Arkansas process, which Fuller and others developed, was to clear the prairie grasses, line fields with levees that would hold shallow water part of the year, then pump water (using steam power) from the aquifer or nearby bayous. Before harvest, water was permitted to flow off into ditches, creeks, and other streams, out to the Arkansas and Mississippi. As in Louisiana, planters used steam plows for breaking ground, teams of horses (not small-footed mules) for levee building, and steam (later gasoline) threshers at harvest. Planters associated closely with well-drilling companies and with the new rice millers of Stuttgart, seat of Arkansas County. Between 1905 and 1909 rice culture boomed and spread from below Stuttgart up to Jonesboro in Craighead County. Native cotton

17. Joseph Cannon Bailey, *Seaman A. Knapp, Schoolmaster of American Agriculture* (New York, 1945), 109–32; Henry C. Dethloff, "Rice Revolution in the Southwest, 1880–1910," *Arkansas Historical Quarterly,* XXIX (Spring, 1970), 66–75; Pete Daniel, *Breaking the Land,* 39–62; Ralph John Ramsey, "Criteria for Classifying Louisiana Tenants" (M.A. thesis, Louisiana State University, 1940), 64–65. See also David O. Whitten, "American Rice Cultivation, 1680–1980: A Tercentenary Critique," *Southern Studies,* XXI (Spring, 1982), 98–112.

MAP 4
The Rice South, 1930

SOURCE: Charles Johnson *et al.* (comps.), *Statistical Atlas.*

NOTE: Only those counties and parishes where more than half of all acreage harvested was in rice are represented. The actual area of rice culture was somewhat larger.

planters switched to rice, and middle westerners (especially from Illinois and Iowa) migrated to take part in the bonanza. Planters who maintained some cotton acreage retained black sharecroppers, but as in Louisiana and Texas, the most common forms of tenancy were cash and share; most renting producers were white and well equipped, too. By 1927 the typical rice operation measured 329 acres, while the Arkansas-

wide average farm was but 70.[18] Enormous strides in the mechanization
of rice lay ahead, but in 1930, while nearly every row crop in the South
tottered toward disaster, rice was relatively stable.

Another agricultural South that maintained relative stability was that
which specialized in grain, dairy production, and livestock. Grain-
dairy-livestock counties were scattered over the four corners of the
broad region, from Virginia to Florida to Texas and Oklahoma, but most
lay in three upper South states: Virginia, Kentucky, and Tennessee. This
was the heart of the white South and, along with the rice country, an
agricultural subregion where ownership, not tenancy of any sort, was
the rule. Sharecropping was rare; black sharecropping was statistically
insignificant, peaking early (in 1925) and steadily subsiding to near in-
visibility thereafter. Farm sizes were smaller than in the rice areas but
much larger than cotton and tobacco units. Grain-dairy-livestock farms
averaged 140 acres in 1920 and declined only about 2 acres during the
following decade. During the 1930s farm sizes in this subregion declined another dozen acres but remained large (125 acres) by southern
standards.[19]

The secret of the modest success in the grain-dairy-livestock South
during the worst of times in a poverty-ridden plantation region was, of
course, its freedom from the labor needs of row crops. Most of each
year family labor was sufficient to care for livestock, fencing, and crops
of small grains for feed. Capital requirements for such farming were
small, too. Possession of gasoline tractors and combines would further
reduce labor needs during the 1940s and afterwards, when farm sizes
leaped and population declined. But during the first third of the century,
grain-dairy-livestock farmers achieved a rather happy balance of land,
people, horses and mules, and a few tractors. Their world more closely
resembled that of northern farmers than that of fellow southerners in the
plantation and other labor-intensive row crop subregions.[20]

Yet another agricultural South resembled parts of California, New

18. J. M. Spicer, *Beginnings of the Rice Industry in Arkansas* (N.p., 1964); R. H.
Desmarais, oral histories of J. M. Spicer, January 23, 1978, George A. Meekins, Febru-
ary 23, 1978, Mr. and Mrs. Otis Goodwin, March 23, 1978, Wilbert Gunnell, January 29,
1978 (Audio tapes, all in Arkansas County Agricultural Museum, Stuttgart); "Rice"
(Typescript, in FWP files, Arkansas History Commission, Little Rock); G. R. Jones,
"Farmer Recounts 1920 Move in Immigrant Car," Annette Greenland, "Immigrants from
Iowa Adopted Prairie as Home," both in Stuttgart (Ark.) *Daily Leader,* Centennial Edi-
tion, May 16, 1980, Sec. E, 1–2, 10.

19. See selected county tables in censuses of agriculture for 1920 and 1925; 1930 data
from Charles Johnson *et al.* (comps), *Statistical Atlas.*

20. County tables of censuses of agriculture, 1920, 1925; 1930 data from Charles

MAP 5
The Grain-Dairy-Livestock South, 1930

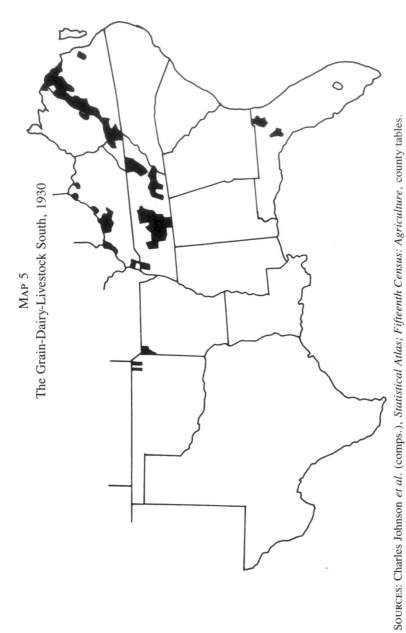

SOURCES: Charles Johnson et al. (comps.), Statistical Atlas: Fifteenth Census: Agriculture, county tables.

NOTE: The map excludes the south-central Texas cattle country and the northern Oklahoma wheat-growing area.

Jersey, New York, and other American fruit and truck garden districts that served urban populations. Most southern counties that concentrated upon citrus and commercial truck lay in central and southern Florida, but a dozen others that grew vegetables, apples, and small fruits were scattered from southeastern Louisiana and nearby Mississippi to northwestern Arkansas, the low country between Savannah and Charleston, eastern Tennessee (near Chattanooga), and central and northern Virginia. Outside Florida the fruit-vegetable specialty counties and parishes lay close to urban markets (except for Washington County, Arkansas), but all (including Florida) were also connected by rail or water routes to northeastern and middle western markets.[21]

Of course vegetables and fruits were grown throughout the South for home and local markets. In the heart of Alabama, Reuben F. Kolb, formerly a Populist politician, bred Kolb's Gem, a prized strain of market watermelon, early in the century.[22] Southwestern Arkansas and eastern Texas became better known for watermelons by the 1920s. Hope, Arkansas, promoters proclaimed that small city the watermelon capital of the world in 1926, when annual festivals and prize awards began. In September, 1935, Oscar D. Middlebrooks, a nearby Hempstead County farmer, brought to Hope a championship 195-pound melon. Yet the surrounding countryside still concentrated upon cotton (with low yields) and had little access to the migrant labor streams that made fruit and vegetable specialty areas productive and relatively prosperous.[23]

Washington County in northwestern Arkansas was a vastly different world from farmer Middlebrooks' Hempstead. Washington County farmers—nearly all of them white owner-operators—raised livestock and feed grains and a variety of fruits, including apples, peaches, grapes, and strawberries. Black pickers were available in Fayetteville, the county seat, but farmers also used migrants from the West and South who passed through at appointed times for harvest. There was practically no resident sharecrop labor.[24]

Johnson *et al.* (comps.), *Statistical Atlas.* See also selected county tables in the agricultural censuses for 1935, 1940, 1945, 1950. On the similarity of farming and rural life in southeastern Ohio and the river valleys of West Virginia (both grain-livestock) see "JL," oral history of Ardella Bruner, n.d. (*ca.* 1975) (Microfilmed typescript in MUOHA).

21. See tables in Charles Johnson *et al.* (comps.), *Statistical Atlas.*

22. William W. Rogers, "Reuben F. Kolb: Agricultural Leader of the New South," *Agricultural History,* XXXII (April, 1958), 109–19.

23. Typescript note, dated 1935, in FWP Hempstead County history files, Arkansas History Commission.

24. Charles Johnson *et al.* (comps.), *Statistical Atlas;* Fayetteville and Springdale,

MAP 6

The Fruit and Vegetable South, 1930

SOURCES: Charles Johnson *et al.* (comps.), *Statistical Atlas; Fifteenth Census: Agriculture*, county tables.

Tangipahoa Parish, Louisiana, came to specialize in strawberries around the turn of the century after local timber was cut out and the sawmill business died. Agents of the Illinois-Central Railroad, which passed through the parish, then promoted strawberry production and attracted hundreds of newcomers—Germans, Italians, and Hungarians— to grow them on tiny plots of three or four cultivated acres. Each spring crops were auctioned and shipped. The Illinois-Central took about 30 percent to Chicago during the 1920s and 1930s. Much of the crop went to nearby New Orleans and to other southern cities. Blacks from Louisiana and Mississippi sawmill settlements appear to have picked much of the Tangipahoa berry crop, but some migrants (mostly white) from near and very far away, passed through each spring, too.[25]

Florida's potential as a winter garden and citrus supplier to northeastern urban centers was perceived at least as early as the 1880s. By the 1920s the "frost proof" sections of the state had attracted not only vacationers, developers, and retirees, but vigorous settlers eager for agricultural opportunities. They spread down both coasts and across the central Florida orange belt below Orlando on farms of about a hundred acres. During the 1920s and 1930s, white owners outnumbered black about five-to-one. Owners outnumbered tenants of all classes by about seven-to-one. Sharecroppers were rare, as were tractors. The federal department of agriculture did not begin to count hired workers until 1935, but observers noted the presence and necessity of large numbers of this class of labor from early in the century. By 1940 in a selection of Florida fruit and vegetable counties hired laborers numbered ten thousand— about double the number of farm owners—and this count was probably well below the actual number. Most of Florida's hired farm workers belonged to the so-called Atlantic stream of migrants who began each year in Dade and Broward counties and worked their way northward as crops matured, to the truck gardens of coastal South Carolina, to apple picking in northern Virginia and potato-digging on the Eastern Shore of Virginia and Maryland, to New Jersey's truck crops, and so on.[26]

Arkansas, Chambers of Commerce bulletins (*ca.* 1936) in FWP, Washington County history files, Arkansas History Commission.

25. USDA, Bureau of Agricultural Economics, "A Disadvantaged Rural Area in Louisiana," by J. P. Montgomery (Typescript, 1941, in Land Tenure Section project files, RG 83, NA); Carey McWilliams, *Ill Fares the Land: Migrants and Migratory Labor in the United States* (Boston, 1942), 164.

26. Charles Johnson *et al.* (comps.), *Statistical Atlas* (for 1930 data); Florida county tables in the censuses of agriculture for 1920, 1924, 1935, 1940; McWilliams, *Ill Fares*

Yet for all of southern Florida's unsouthern agricultural prosperity and freedom from plantation-style resident labor, the state lagged behind its great competitor, California, in the critical arena of market organization. During the 1920s producers in some Florida districts cooperated privately and bargained with shippers, but the state government dawdled in providing inspection, grading, and market services. Only after 1933 did Florida's department of agriculture move—emulating California in every step—to aid growers in systematizing production and reaching faraway markets efficiently.[27]

A last agricultural South cannot be described as modern in any way, either in the very old sense of being part of the plantation society and the original world economic order or in the new sense of being well capitalized, at least partly mechanized, and connected to metropolitan markets. This was the self-sufficient South. In 1930 there were about 155 counties in the broader region where at least half of farmers' modest production was used at home. Most lay in the Appalachian highlands; another block of self-sufficient counties covered part of the Ozarks of northwestern Arkansas and the poor, hilly land of nearby northeastern Oklahoma. But other southern counties with little role in the modern scheme of economic things were scattered about the coastal plains of Texas, Mississippi, Florida, Georgia, and Virginia, in the hilly country of western Tennessee and Kentucky, and in Virginia's upper piedmont.[28]

Self-sufficient farmers raised virtually all their own food. They planted vegetables and wheat for bread; they kept milk cows, hogs, chickens, and sometimes geese and goats. Their swine and beef cattle

---

the Land, 140–48. On the eastern migratory stream, see also Donald Hughes Grubbs, "A History of the Atlantic Coast Stream of Agricultural Migrants" (M.A. thesis, University of Florida, 1959), 4–18; Florida Legislative Council and Legislative Reference Bureau, *Migrant Farm Labor in Florida* (Tallahassee, 1963), 5 and *passim.*

27. Martin M. LaGodna, "The Florida State Department of Agriculture During the Administration of Nathan Mayo, 1923–1960" (Ph.D. dissertation, University of Florida, 1970), esp. 1–3, 78–120. See also Box 29 of the Nathan Mayo Papers, University of Florida Library.

28. Charles Johnson *et al.* (comps.), *Statistical Atlas,* 7, counted 139 "self-sufficing" counties, a figure based upon 1930 census data and personal observations of field workers; the figure does not include West Virginia and Oklahoma. The agricultural censuses have no self-sufficing or subsistence classification; so when classifying counties not included in Johnson's atlas, I chose to term a county self-sufficient when the census classified it as general farming and the market values of crops sold were very low. Some of the counties I have thus classified in these two states might not have been sufficiently productive to be classified as agricultural counties at all.

usually roamed the heavily forested open range much of the year, as from earliest pioneer times, feasting on wild nuts as well as highland grasses. A Clay County West Virginian recalled that as late as the 1920s, "everybody had the woods full a hogs. Just turned them out and let them nibble on the mas[t]." In the fall men with "big dogs" would "go out and catch these hogs" for fattening and slaughter. "And we didn't want for anything to eat them days," he concluded.[29]

The rural folks themselves also used the forests, gathering wood for fuel and nuts and berries to supplement their diet. Small stores served as local exchange points for surpluses. Home crafts (such as quilt and furniture making) flourished. Cash, as in any relatively primitive economy, was needed for few things—for modest taxes; for commodities such as sugar and coffee that could not be produced at home; and for tobacco among those who could not or did not grow their own. Male members of families earned such cash from occasional "public work" as farm laborers, railroad or mine workers, seasonal county road workers, and of course, from making and selling illegal (untaxed) whiskey.[30]

Whether they hoed corn on steep Kentucky ridges or ripped up wire grass in northern Florida, self-sufficient southern farmers worked the poorest land in the region. Their cash incomes were as low as those of sharecroppers—often lower. New Dealers would call them impoverished, as they indeed seemed by the standards of the urban Northeast.[31] Yet most of these white (and a few black) folks owned their poor land and enjoyed isolation and independence unknown in the plantation South. This was particularly the case with the more remote Appalachian and Ozark rural people. For most highlanders, however, by the 1920s arcadia had already been ruined by half a century of experience with the worst side of the industrial process.

29. PC, oral history of William T. Arnold, n.d. (*ca.* 1975) (Microfilmed typescript in MUOHA).

30. Excellent surveys of rural life and work in remote Appalachia are Ronald D Eller, "Land and Family: An Historical View of Preindustrial Appalachia," *Appalachian Journal*, VI (Winter, 1979), 83–110; Eller, *Miners, Millhands, and Mountaineers: Industrialization of the Appalachian South, 1880–1930* (Knoxville, 1982), early chaps.; Michael J. McDonald and John Muldowny, *TVA and the Dispossessed: The Resettlement of the Population in the Norris Dam Area* (Knoxville, 1982), esp. 106–11. See also USDA, Bureau of Agricultural Economics and Forest Service, *Economic and Social Problems and Conditions of the Southern Appalachians*, by L. C. Gray and C. F. Clayton (Washington, D.C., 1935); USDA, Economic Research Service, Agricultural Economics Report No. 69, *An Economic Survey of the Appalachian Region* (Washington, D.C., 1965); FERA, Rural Problem Areas Survey Report No. 35, The Appalachian-Ozark Area: Searcy County, Arkansas (Typescript, January 2, 1935, in RG 83, NA).

31. See USDA, *Economic and Social Problems, passim.*

MAP 7

The Self-sufficient South, 1930

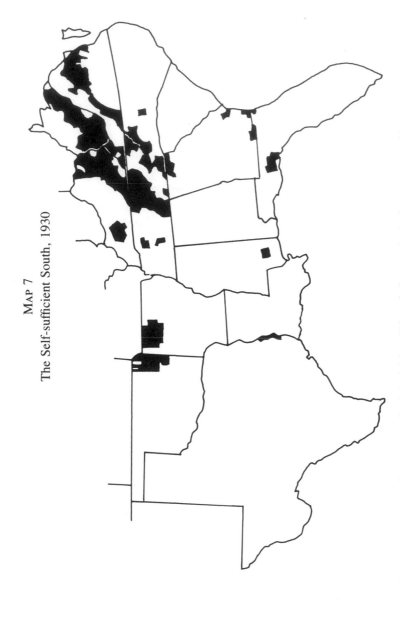

SOURCES: Charles Johnson *et al.* (comps.), *Statistical Atlas*; *Fifteenth Census: Agriculture*, county tables.

Beginning in the 1870s railroad trunk lines penetrated some of the most rugged parts of the southern Appalachians. Timbering and coal mining followed, luring many thousands from farms and alienating hundreds of thousands of acres of land from private ownership. Estimated hog production declined by about 60 percent by World War I, while lumber and mining camp workers learned to eat from stores instead of "living at home." In the more developed areas of southern West Virginia, eastern Kentucky, and southwestern Virginia the revolution was most profound. Then the timber boom ended about 1920. The coal industry overproduced during World War I and the early 1920s and nearly collapsed. Prices fell, and in much of the highland region production virtually ceased by the mid-1920s. Thousands of native miners and lumbermen went back to already overpopulated family farms. But now moisture-holding trees on ridges above their properties had been cut, the life-sustaining open-range system of animal husbandry was gone, and habits of life in a cash economy had become fixed. So families expanded fields up the ridges to accommodate returnees and turned increasingly to market tobacco as a replacement for public work.[32]

In 1930 southern subsistence farms averaged a little more than ninety acres, of which only a fraction was arable. White owner-operators predominated. Tenants of all classes were fewer than a third of the number of owners. Blacks and sharecroppers of either color were statistically insignificant. So were tractors in this cash- and credit-poor country. In a sample of ten subsistence-farming counties representing the Appalachians, the Ozarks, and sandy coastal plains, there were only 140 tractors (for all ten) in 1925; 238 in 1930; and 311 as late as 1940.[33]

Some highland sections of the subsistence South remained without railroads or even roads as late as 1930. Remote Appalachia, in fact, was the only part of the United States where the automobile was not common.[34] The absence of modern transportation usually implies the absence of a market economy and other aspects of modern wealth and dependency. So those remote sections of this particular rural South remained "primitive" very late. Other sections of the subsistence South,

32. Eller, *Miners, Millhands,* 128–60, 210–40, and *passim.*

33. County tables of the censuses of agriculture for 1925, 1930, and 1940 for Newton, Arkansas; Liberty, Georgia; King and Queen and Scott, Virginia; Johnson and Knox, Kentucky; Campbell and Sevier, Tennessee; and Logan and Randolph, West Virginia.

34. On the absence of roads, see USDA dot map, "Autos on Farms, 1930," in RG 83, NA; typescript diary of Mary Breckenridge, a pioneer public health nurse in remote eastern Kentucky during the 1920s, in SHC.

however—the coastal and hill counties bypassed by the plantation and the developed parts of the highlands—came by 1930 to resemble in some ways the worst of the plantation South. Rather like the hilly, white-majority cotton counties, they had been drawn partway into the modern world economy, suffering virtually all its ills and enjoying few of its benefits.

The plight of these rural Souths—most particularly the huge plantation one—seemed all the worse in contrast with the rest of the United States. Farmers throughout the Union had experienced the frustration of declining importance and esteem at least since the 1880s, when the pejorative *hayseed* entered the urban vocabulary of scorn.[35] Most nonsouthern rural folks had come to belong, however, to that national conspiracy of modern, or middle-class, progressive values. They were capitalists, mechanics, and futurists, ever at the business of saving labor with machines and experimenting with anything promising. Pushed farther to the rear by the emergence of the corporation, they nonetheless still belonged to the early twentieth-century liberal, corporatist polity. Yankees boosted "scientific" agriculture at fine, state-supported colleges such as Cornell and Wisconsin; they hailed Theodore Roosevelt's Country Life Commission in 1908; they realized benefits from the creation of the county agricultural extension system in 1914 and upon that founded powerful locals of the Farm Bureau Federation during World War I.[36] In the South, save for the minority of upper South progressive agriculturists and some lower South planters, the modern world of the college of agriculture and the county agent was alien. For most southern rural folks, the early twentieth century was a time of danger, of loss, of falling backward while the rest of the industrialized world sped by.

The tragedy was compounded by statistics of doom and forlorn literary symbols. The epochal federal census of 1890, for instance, had revealed the "closing" of the western frontier and the age of the pioneer-farmer. Then the 1920 enumeration showed that the American population had become statistically urban—that is, a majority lived in cities of twenty-five hundred or more souls. Not a single southern state's population met this modest definition of urban in 1920, however.[37] Meanwhile,

35. Earl W. Hayter, *The Troubled Farmer: Rural Adjustment to Industrialism* (DeKalb, Ill., 1968), 145–210.
36. Grant McConnell, *The Decline of Agrarian Democracy* (Berkeley, 1953), Chaps. 1 and 2.
37. See state population tables in Donald B. Dodd and Wynelle S. Dodd (comps.), *Historical Statistics of the South, 1790–1970* (University, Ala., 1973). Because the popu-

the year of this census also brought forth the second scalding volume of H. L. Mencken's *Prejudices,* which included the Bad Boy of Baltimore's outrageous diatribe against the South, "Sahara of the Bozart." Mencken blasted the entire region, "from the Potomac mud flats to the Gulf," for being poor, rural, antiintellectual, racist, preacher-ridden, prohibitionist, and peculiarly subject to demagoguery—in a word, antimodern. Only four years later appeared Frank Tannenbaum's *Darker Phases of the South,* in which the Columbia University social scientist surveyed several of the more doleful shortcomings of the region—its prisons, race relations, and awful agricultural system. Before the decade of the 1920s was finished came the first novels of Thomas Wolfe and William Faulkner, and Erskine Caldwell was at work on *Tobacco Road.* National attention focused on the region in all its bizarre contradictions of the progressive American norm. Southern institutions, most obviously the aged scheme of labor-intensive farming, teetered on the brink of catastrophe. They could not survive the 1930s.

---

lations of Maryland and Delaware (states included in the South as the Bureau of the Census defined it) were classified as urban in 1920, they are excluded from this study of the rural South.

I let 'em all go. In '34 I had I reckon four renters and I
didn't make anything. I bought tractors on the money
the government give me and got shet o' my
renters. . . . I did everything the government said—
except keep my renters.
—AN OKLAHOMA FARMER, *ca*. 1938

If cotton is decreased much more, day labor will be a
necessity. Since I'm trying to develop a stock farm,
sharecropping doesn't fit into my set-up at all.
—A NORTH CAROLINA PLANTER, 1939

The advance of machinery in the cotton country is dis-
tinctly irregular. It spreads, like a Hitler army, over
delta regions, river-bottom lands, and other spots where
the topography and other conditions are favorable. It
tends to avoid the roughest lands and the poorest lands.
—HERMAN CLARENCE NIXON, 1941

Chapter 2
The South on the Federal Road

PLANTATIONS DO NOT REFLECT THE ENTIRE
southern rural experience, ante- or postbellum, but they have ever been
the locus of economic power and the vanguard of change. Twentieth-
century planters, probably more so than their predecessors, were landlords, bosses, and creditors to many times their numbers. They organized and dominated much of the flatland and hill South. When planters
decided to alter their mode of production fundamentally—as they did
most dramatically during the 1930s and 1940s—much of the region was
convulsed. Millions of people were dispersed to cities. Sharecropping,
a system three-quarters of a century old in 1940, shrank rapidly to insignificance. And mules, symbols and factotums of traditional farm life,
became rare. The southern landscape was depopulated and enclosed;
agriculture at last became capital intensive.[1]

1. Twentieth-century American plantations have no specific historian, although economist Jay R. Mandle, in *The Roots of Black Poverty: The Southern Plantation Economy
After the Civil War* (Durham, N.C., 1978), assayed the dynamics of modernization in the
lower South, employing statewide census data. See also Rupert B. Vance, *Human Factors
of Cotton Culture: A Study in the Social Geography of the American South* (Chapel Hill,
1929); Charles S. Johnson, *Shadow of the Plantation* (Chicago, 1934); USDA, *Agriculture Yearbook, 1923* (Washington, D.C., 1924), 507–600; Jonathan Wiener, "Class

Planters led the way reluctantly. Members of a wary, conservative class, most seem merely to have reacted to exogenous forces. Throughout the 1920s and into the Great Depression, planters resisted the powerful forces of mechanization, cotton boll weevil infestation, and labor mobility, clinging to their archaic system and methods. Once the New Deal joined those forces, however, providing the vital component of capital, planters finally seized initiative and began the transformation of the region. World war, accelerated labor mobility, the mechanical cotton harvester, and new agricultural chemicals hastened completion of the revolutionary process that pushed southern farming toward conformity with that of the rest of the nation.[2]

The archaic plantations about to be transformed were overwhelmingly of the fragmented type. Following emancipation, landless freedmen and some whites agreed to live and work on pieces of formerly centralized estates and large farms and to share, typically "on halves," in risks and profits. (During the first third of the twentieth century, whites came almost to equal black sharecroppers in numbers.) The centralized occupance pattern of antebellum plantations dissolved as the first tenants moved from slave quarters to cabins surrounded by the fields for which they were responsible. Planters, now also landlords, supplied work stock, tools, seed, and fertilizer—and a great deal of supervision, although certainly management of fragmented plantations was not as efficient or centralized as that of slave-labor antebellum estates. Other planters, especially those in hilly, white-majority areas, divided cultivation of their land among share and cash tenants, usually white, who supplied their own work stock and tools and realized greater shares both of risks and profits. On such fragmented plantations as these planters were usually mere landlords, providing little supervision of labor. The fragmented era of plantations' history lasted longer in parts of the South than had the entire antebellum period—from the late 1860s to the 1940s and after. The painful passing of this era and the creation

Structure and Economic Development in the American South, 1865–1955," *American Historical Review,* LXXXIV (October, 1979), 970–92; Gilbert C. Fite, *Cotton Fields No More: Southern Agriculture, 1865–1980* (Lexington, Ky., 1984); Pete Daniel, *Breaking the Land: The Transformation of Cotton, Tobacco, and Rice Cultures Since 1880* (Urbana, 1985).

2. On mechanization and agricultural chemicals, see Gilbert C. Fite, "Mechanization of Cotton Production Since World War II," *Agricultural History,* LIV (January, 1980), 190–207.

of capital-intensive so-called neoplantations are the subjects of this chapter.[3]

Fragmented plantations were predicated upon and endured in a world of scarce capital and abundant labor. For most planters capital remained scarce until the 1930s, when New Deal subsidy checks and low-interest loans became available, but two interconnected threats to the supply of labor appeared as early as the 1910s. By 1915 the cotton boll weevil had crossed the Mississippi River, and by 1922, it had reached the northeastern limits of cotton culture in North Carolina and south-central Virginia. High World War I–era prices for cotton compensated for some losses, but as sociologist Arthur Raper observed in the Georgia black belt, many farmers in the worst-hit areas, where the land was already overcropped, were ruined. Landless farmers—most of them black sharecroppers—fled to cities, never again to be available as rural laborers. The boll weevil and a host of other southern miseries provided a classic push to black migration. And for the first time since emancipation, World War I–generated industrial jobs outside the region presented generous alternatives to farm work—the classic pull. Between 1910 and 1920 fully 10.4 percent (or 200,400) of the black population of Alabama and Mississippi left the region.[4]

3. The plantation typology employed here is that of University of Georgia geographer Merle C. Prunty, Jr., who first heralded the neoplantation in "Renaissance of the Southern Plantation," *Geographical Review,* XLV (October, 1955), 459–91. Prunty's student, William Theodore Mealor, Jr., elaborated the typology and described a local transformation from fragmented to neoplantations in "The Plantation Occupance Complex in Dougherty, Lee, and Sumter Counties, Georgia" (M.A. thesis, University of Georgia, 1964). On the evolution and maturity of sharecropping, see Roger L. Ransom and Richard Sutch, *One Kind of Freedom: The Economic Consequences of Emancipation* (Cambridge, Eng., 1977); Vance, *Human Factors of Cotton Culture.* Sugar plantations, which are not specifically considered here, were always rather well capitalized and experimented with the fragmented format only briefly. See J. Carlyle Sitterson, *Sugar Country: The Sugar Cane Industry in the South, 1753–1950* (Lexington, Ky., 1953), 390–91 and *passim.* Prunty defined the neoplantation as a fully mechanized unit of at least 260 acres with at least four resident hired workers. A plantation during the era of fragmentation is here defined as federal researchers understood the term during the 1930s: "a tract with five or more resident families, including the landlord." See Work Projects Administration, Division of Research, *The Plantation South, 1934–1937,* by William C. Holly, Ellen Winston, and T. J. Woofter, Jr. (Washington, D.C., 1940), xi.

4. Arthur F. Raper, *Preface to Peasantry: A Tale of Two Black Belt Counties* (Chapel Hill, 1936), 183–224; Daniel M. Johnson and Rex R. Campbell, *Black Migration in America: A Social Demographic History* (Durham, N.C., 1981), 72–76; Robert Higgs, "The Boll Weevil, the Cotton Economy, and Black Migration, 1910–1930," *Agricultural History,* L (April, 1976), 335–50. Figure calculated from U.S. Bureau of the Census, *Historical Statistics of the United States, from Colonial Times to 1957* (Washington,

Yet the boll weevil and migration did not substantially dislocate the fragmented plantation. Planters retired the worst weevil-infested fields, opened new land, rotated crops, and learned to poison pests with arsenic.[5] Tractors replaced men, women, children, and mules only in western Texas and Oklahoma, where sharecroppers and other laborers had always been relatively scarce anyway, and in parts of the black belt especially affected by migration.[6] The cotton producers of semiarid Texas and Oklahoma had the additional advantage of mechanical cotton harvesters suited to their environment—tractor- or mule-drawn strippers manufactured by the John Deere Company, which, like metal picket fences riding points forward, ripped bolls from plants. Available since the 1920s, strippers sold for only $185 each in 1931. They collected so much plant trash with the bolls that farmers often put cotton through threshers before ginning; grades and prices were considerably reduced. So even these producers at the western fringe of the South purchased few strippers during the 1920s and 1930s, as long as sufficient (and relatively cheap) labor remained available to them. In the humid southeast, where cotton foliage was more abundant, strippers were utterly impractical.[7] Probably more important, black migration notwithstanding, most landless rural southerners remained in the region. Those few planters who possessed adequate capital therefore had little incentive to acquire even tractors. So the old landscape, dotted with tenant houses, continued relatively unchanged.

A planter of Scott (Lonoke County), Arkansas, recalled that his father had purchased his first steel-wheeled tractor about 1920; yet "there

---

D.C., 1961); Donald B. Dodd and Wynelle S. Dodd (comps.), *Historical Statistics of the South, 1790–1970* (University, Ala., 1973).

5. Billy J. Burkett, oral history of J. O. Dockery, n.d. (*ca.* 1978) (Audio tape in Arkansas County Agricultural Museum, Stuttgart). Dockery began spraying arsenic powder on cotton and other crops from the air over Louisiana and Mississippi in 1924.

6. The state and county tables of the censuses of agriculture for 1925 and 1930 reveal little growth in the number of tractors except among plains farmers at the western edges of the South. Southern Tenant Farmers' Union members in western Texas reported continued land aggrandizement and mechanization from the 1920s through the 1930s. See, for example, Fred Matthews to H. L. Mitchell, September 27, 1936, microfilm roll 3, Southern Tenant Farmers' Union (STFU) Papers, Southern Historical Collection, University of North Carolina (SHC). Allen Buster was displaced from his sharecrop farm near Selma, Alabama, by his landlord's tractors during the 1920s. See Debra Ann Burks, oral history of Allen Buster, November 29, 1974 (Typescript in Samford University Oral History Program, Birmingham).

7. Gilbert C. Fite, "Recent Progress in the Mechanization of Cotton Production in the United States," *Agricultural History,* XXIV (January, 1950), 19–28.

were a lot of Negroes [and mules] on the plantation in 1941." The same was true for the giant Delta and Pine Land Company (D&PL) and its thousands of sharecropped acres in Washington and Bolivar counties, Mississippi. In 1925 D&PL owned but 3 tractors, along with 306 mules and 10 horses. Over the following sixteen years the company expanded production and purchased trucks and more tractors, but at the end of 1941, D&PL owned 978 mules, too, and provided housing for more than three thousand people.[8]

The increased mobility of farm labor and tenants of all classes did oblige planter-landlords to make one significant concession: provision of cash "furnish"—that is, cash advances for subsistence before the end of the crop year—in lieu of credit lines at plantation commissaries and country stores. Ned Cobb, a black tenant of lower Tallapoosa County, Alabama, reported that his landlord "gived me cash money" as furnish as early as 1913.[9] Most landlords did not begin the practice until after World War I, however, as Robert H. Alexander, a central Arkansas planter, recalled. He, his father, and neighboring "planters decided that since the Negroes were more mobile by that time, that they would allow them so much money a month." [10] Arthur Raper observed the phenomenon in black-belt Georgia, too. There, planters acknowledged the danger to their labor supply presented not only by Yankee industrial recruiters but by the growing ownership of automobiles among sharecroppers and renters. Cars carried the landless over improved roads to new chain stores in towns, where tenants discovered wider variety and lower prices than were offered by the landlords' establishments. So, largely to hold their laborers, planters of Greene and Macon counties adopted cash furnishing almost wholesale by the mid-1920s, virtually abandoning their traditional credit system and the controls (not to mention profits) that went with them.[11]

Cash furnishing persisted in the coastal plains of northeastern North Carolina, but it was short-lived nearly everywhere else in the plantation South. In the Georgia counties Arthur Raper studied, planters found

8. Rebecca Yarbrough, oral history of Mr. and Mrs. Robert H. Alexander, October 5, 1973 (Typescript in University of Arkansas Library, Little Rock); accountant's "Report on Examination, February 28, 1925" (Typescript), 6–7, and "Livestock—1941–42" (Manuscript, March 31, 1942), both in Delta and Pine Land Company Records, Mississippi State University Library.

9. Theodore Rosengarten, *All God's Dangers: The Life of Nate Shaw* (New York, 1975), 149.

10. Yarbrough, oral history of Mr. and Mrs. Alexander.

11. Raper, *Preface to Peasantry,* 117–78.

that petty cash could not compete with more substantial city wages; then low cotton prices during the late 1920s and early 1930s made cash scarce for them, too. So planters reinstituted a modified commissary system, distributing homegrown food to tenants against their crops, along with drastically reduced cash allowances or no cash at all. In the newer cotton lands of northeastern Arkansas, cash furnishing may never have been instituted. Certainly by the mid-1930s the landlords and managers of enormous estates were operating commissaries comparable to the most notorious Appalachian coal company stores. Arkansas tenants hardly ever saw legal tender; they were issued scrip, metal tokens made of "bronzene," or coupon books ("doodlum" or "due you" books) valid only at the planter-landlords' emporiums.[12] So planters' experiments in competition with off-farm work made little appreciable impact upon the system of management, work, and credit on fragmented plantations. The institution staggered on into the Great Depression.

The Depression-deepened crisis of southern agriculture and especially the New Deal–pumped infusions of federal money into the region finally began the end of traditional plantations. It seems impossible to generalize briefly and fairly about New Deal agricultural and rural welfare programs. They brought both succor and suffering. Perhaps a fair summary, subject to many exceptions, would be that in predominantly white, nonplantation areas of the South, the programs were inadequate as relief but positive and beneficial in the short run. In predominantly black plantation areas, on the other hand, the programs rescued and enriched planter-landlords and inflicted frustration and suffering on the already poor and landless.

The Federal Emergency Relief Administration (FERA, 1933–1934) and the Works Progress Administration (WPA, 1935–1939) provided limited and temporary aid to multitudes of poor southerners, particularly whites, in every subregion. It was estimated that during the fall of 1933, one-fifth of all Appalachian and Ozark highland families were on relief. At the same time, in the eastern cotton areas, where landlessness

---

12. Bernice Kelly Harris, "The Landlord Has His Troubles," March 5, 1939 (Typescript in FWP life histories files, SHC); Raper, *Preface to Peasantry,* 178; Howard Kester, *Revolt Among the Sharecroppers* (New York, 1936), 42–43. The STFU Papers for 1934–37 contain many references to the plantation credit systems in northeastern Arkansas that Kester described. J. E. Little, landlord to about 300 sharecroppers in southern Faulkner County, central Arkansas, apparently never made cash advances. In 1926, heyday of cash furnishing, he issued coupon books. See samples of dated coupons, daybooks, and ledgers in J. E. Little Plantation Records, Arkansas History Commission, Little Rock.

was more common and there was less subsistence capability than in the mountains, almost two-thirds of whites and somewhat less than half of all black families received emergency federal help. The FERA also lent mules and money and provided expert advice in such "problem areas" as Franklin County, North Carolina, turning tenants and small owners away from tobacco and cotton toward food production and subsistence. Such programs were short-lived, however.[13]

Highland and backwater white southerners often wax nostalgic about the New Deal. Loretta Lynn, raised during the 1930s in Appalachian Johnson County, Kentucky, wrote that "you'll see pictures of FDR on the wall" of any mountain home "because Roosevelt started the WPA . . . which gave men jobs." Her own father "would work a few days on the roads" and return "with a few dollars, as proud as could be." A mountain preacher declared with wonderful certitude that New Deal welfare and jobs relieved cash-poor southern West Virginians who had been obliged to make illegal whiskey against their religious principles.[14]

The Resettlement Administration, the Farm Security Administration (FSA), and its successor, the Farmers' Home Administration (FHA), aimed at long-term antipoverty goals: the rehabilitation of "worthy" tenants in homestead communities and the granting of low-interest, long-term loans and free supervision in agronomy to particularly promising nonlandholders. Out in Titus County, Texas, Mr. and Mrs. Dewey Blackstone, a young white couple, purchased a 61½-acre farm in 1938 with FHA assistance. The following year the Rural Electrification Administration turned on the electricity, and the Civilian Conservation Corps, yet another New Deal agency, fenced most of the property and sodded a pasture at no cost to the Blackstones except for the fencing materials. A federally subsidized tractor owned by the county then terraced most of their crop land for thirteen dollars. In 1941 the FHA decided to back Carl Forrester, an industrious tenant farmer of Houston County in southeastern Alabama. Forrester bought his own farm with an FHA low-interest loan. In 1944 he traded his mules and old plow rigs

13. Theodore Saloutos, *The American Farmer and the New Deal* (Ames, Iowa, 1982), 153–54; Pete Daniel, *Breaking the Land*, 63–152.

14. Loretta Lynn with George Vecsey, *Loretta Lynn: Coal Miner's Daughter* (New York, 1976), 31–32; Guy R. Sutphin, oral history of Rev. Raymond Atkins, n.d. (*ca.* 1975) (Microfilmed typescript, in Marshall University Oral History of Appalachia Collection). An exception to highlanders' attitudes toward the New Deal is the Norris Basin people displaced by the Tennessee Valley Authority. See Michael J. McDonald and John Muldowny, *TVA and the Dispossessed: The Resettlement of the Population in the Norris Dam Area* (Knoxville, 1982).

for a used one-row Farmall tractor, established a large peanut acreage before federal allotments were set, acquired new peanut-harvesting machinery, and moved rapidly toward the status of modern planter. By 1975 Forrester and his three sons were cultivating eleven hundred acres.[15]

Yet Congress was stingy with such small-farm programs. Many of the homestead communities were capital starved or incompetently managed or both, but their inhabitants were blamed for their failures. Between 1937 and 1947 the FSA and FHA made farm purchase loans to only 47,104 tenants (nationally), leaving in 1945 about 1.8 million nonowners who were never assisted. The FSA made loans (averaging $4,500) to a grand total of 46 tenants in the entire commonwealth of Virginia. At this miserly rate of support, the elimination of tenancy and the achievement of the Jeffersonian dream of an America of stable freeholders would have required about four hundred years.[16]

Causes of the New Deal parsimony toward the rural poor and small farmers are complex and, of course, political. Long-term solutions to poverty and change in the distribution of wealth did not figure much in New Deal policy, which aimed at recovery, not reform. Then, too, the nation's largest agricultural lobby, the Farm Bureau Federation, actively and effectively fought structural change. Between 1937 and the mid–1940s, the Farm Bureau and congressional allies crippled, then killed the FSA as well as the USDA Bureau of Agricultural Economics, a research agency whose studies were thought to comprise reform agenda. During these years the Farm Bureau was led by Edward Asbury O'Neal, a large planter-landlord from the rich Tennessee River valley region of northern Alabama.[17]

15. Texas Agricultural Extension Service, "Annual Report, 1940" (Typescript in Texas A & M University Archives, College Station), 302; Dru Flowers, oral history of Carl and Ted Forrester, January 18, 1975 (Typescript in Samford University Oral History Program).

16. Sidney Baldwin, *Poverty and Politics: The Rise and Decline of the Farm Security Administration* (Chapel Hill, 1968); Donald Holley, *Uncle Sam's Farmers: The New Deal Communities in the Lower Mississippi Valley* (Urbana, 1975): Saloutos, *American Farmer and the New Deal*, 190, 264; Ronald L. Heinemann, *Depression and New Deal in Virginia: The Enduring Dominion* (Charlottesville, 1983), 124. On FSA payments, see also Federal Works Agency, Work Projects Administration, *Summary of Relief and Federal Work Program Statistics, 1933–1940* (Washington, D.C., 1941), 78–267.

17. Arthur M. Ford, *Political Economics of Rural Poverty in the South* (Cambridge, Mass., 1973), 35–57; Grant McConnell, *The Decline of Agrarian Democracy* (Berkeley, 1953), 107–11. On the middle western and modernist biases of the USDA, see Richard S. Kirkendall, *Social Scientists and Farm Politics in the Age of Roosevelt* (Columbia, Mo., 1966). Edward A. O'Neal's Papers at the Alabama Department of Archives and History,

Planters such as O'Neal were fearful of New Deal welfare, workfare, resettlement, and small-farm support, however modest. Another large northern Alabama farmer-employer declared, "Why, they [the WPA] are going to take all our hands away from us and put them to work on the big road. They are going to give them two dollars a day, and it would break me to pay that much." [18] The self-proclaimed champion of Georgia farmers, Eugene Talmadge, wrote testily to Franklin Roosevelt, "I wouldn't plow nobody's mule for fifty cents a day when I could get $1.30 for pretending to work on a DITCH." [19] The FSA, too, seemed a threat. A Perry County, Alabama, landlord-merchant complained bitterly that an FSA agent and the county home demonstration agent had entered his plantation and offered to underwrite the independence of one of his tenants. Not only had the federal agent attempted to lure away his labor, but he had violated traditions of business and paternalism. "It has always been the custom," wrote the planter, "to first contact the landlord." [20] Such fears and incidents notwithstanding, New Deal agencies were administered in counties by local folk, almost invariably representatives of the largest property holders and employers. They generally saw to it that relief did not interfere with labor requirements and that workfare wages did not exceed local norms. Previous scholars have established this pattern, and the papers of the Memphis-based Southern Tenant Farmers' Union are filled with complaints by eastern Arkansans, especially blacks, of discrimination, even abuse, by WPA and FSA officials. [21]

Montgomery, contain materials on his presidencies of the Alabama Farm Bureau (1923–31) and the national Farm Bureau (1931–47) and his plantation operations. On Farm Bureau hostility to the FSA, see esp. "Farm Security Administration Activities in Alabama" (Undated typescript in Walter Leon Randolph Papers, Alabama Department of Archives and History, Montgomery). Randolph was a collaborator and close associate of O'Neal.

18. Luther Clark, "Looking Around with a Hay Farmer," life history of E. Leonidas Cockrell, n.d. (1938 or 1939) (Typescript in Alabama Writers' Project files, Alabama Department of Archives and History).

19. Quoted in William Anderson, *Wild Man from Sugar Creek: The Political Career of Eugene Talmadge* (Baton Rouge, 1975), 136.

20. J. C. Webb to W. G. Carr, February, 1942, Randolph Papers.

21. See David Eugene Conrad, *The Forgotten Farmers: The Story of Sharecroppers in the New Deal* (Urbana, 1965), 19–63; Paul E. Mertz, *New Deal Policy and Southern Rural Poverty* (Baton Rouge, 1978), 192–209; Donald H. Grubbs, *Cry from the Cotton: The Southern Tenant Farmers' Union and the New Deal* (Chapel Hill, 1971), 158–59; Saloutos, *American Farmer and the New Deal*, 154; J. R. Butler to Matthew S. Murray, September 7, 1937, microfilm roll 5, R. J. Julian to Butler, February 10, 1939, roll 10, Frank Sanders to Butler, March 28, 1939, roll 11, "People Refused Applications for WPA Work" (Typescript, January, 1938, roll 7), all in STFU Papers.

The keystone of the New Deal's program for the plantation districts of the South was not the WPA or the FSA but the cotton and tobacco crop-reduction and subsidy programs administered by the Agricultural Adjustment Administration (AAA). A few middle-level bureaucrats and a great many landless southerners hoped that the Depression might occasion thorough reform, the redistribution of land and the realization of the early Reconstruction dream of "forty acres and a mule" for every family.[22] But the AAA was in fact never more than a relief agency designed to raise the incomes of land-owning farmers. Administrators of the cotton and tobacco programs were able men who identified with growers and who worked with legislation that took slight notice of tenancy.

Two southerners played leading roles in New Deal programs most affecting the region—Cully A. Cobb, who headed the Cotton Section of the AAA, and Oscar Johnston, who directed the USDA cotton pool and served as first vice-president of the Commodity Credit Corporation while continuing to preside over the Delta and Pine Land Company in Mississippi. Both were exemplars of the sort of modern agriculture long championed by the USDA Extension Service, the state colleges of agriculture, and the Farm Bureau. Tennessee-born, Cobb graduated from the Mississippi Agricultural and Mechanical College in 1908, served as principal of an early agricultural high school, established boy's corn clubs in Mississippi under the auspices of the Extension Service, and then went on (in 1919) to edit the *Southern Ruralist* in Atlanta. Throughout his career in agricultural journalism he identified with the substantial farmers and planters who were his subscribers, the Extension Service, and the Farm Bureau. Johnston was Mississippi-born, an attorney by training, and a corporate manager par excellence. D&PL's owners, a British consortium, trusted Johnston—with good reason—to protect their interests. The corporation conducted its own research in agronomy, and Johnston absorbed the science as well as the business of cotton culture. While managing the cotton pool, he also participated significantly in the conception and governance of the AAA cotton program. Once Congress created the AAA in the spring of 1933, Cobb and Johnston traveled thousands of miles across the cotton South, persuad-

22. Conrad, *Forgotten Farmers;* Grubbs, *Cry from the Cotton;* Mertz, *New Deal Policy.* Much of the STFU leadership was socialist (collectivist), but sharecropper correspondence in the union's papers indicates the rank and file were not. See also H. L. Mitchell, *Mean Things Happening in This Land: The Life and Times of H. L. Mitchell* (Montclair, N.J., 1979), 38–170.

ing growers to sign contracts with the government, reduce acreage, and in return receive both higher prices and federal payments for lost production.[23]

Under this first AAA contract, cotton landlords were vaguely committed to divide government payments with their tenants, but noncompliance was seldom punished by local AAA boards, which were themselves dominated by planters. Meanwhile reports of massive tenant evictions poured into the AAA and the public press throughout the winter of 1933–1934. William R. Amberson, a professor at the University of Tennessee College of Medicine in Memphis, wrote to Cully Cobb early in March that "evictions have been ordered, apparently in direct defiance of the [AAA] contract." In one instance, he reported, "the plantation owner who is responsible for this policy is one of the local committee who oversees the acreage reduction program." An "adjustment committee" established by Cobb virtually whitewashed the scandal, however. Of 1,457 complaints against landlords investigated, the committee recommended cancellation of only 21 contracts.[24]

A group of young "liberals" within the AAA—notably Jerome Frank and Alger Hiss of the legal section and Gardner Jackson of the Consumer Council—were outraged. Accordingly, they decided to add explicit protection of tenants to the 1934–1935 AAA cotton contract. This celebrated document was apparently written by many hands. Oscar Johnston made important contributions, and Alger Hiss took a part in drafting the controversial Section 7, which dealt with tenants, even though he agreed with Johnston that the tenant-retention provision of the new contract was unenforceable. From the perspective of half a century later, it seems obvious that their situation, like that of the renters with whom they sympathized, was impossible; they were trying to protect the poor and reform society from a base within a bureaucracy dedicated to saving (perhaps enriching) the rural upper and middle classes. The furor within the AAA persisted until early in 1935, when the secretary of agriculture, yielding to Cobb and his allies, fired and silenced the liberal band.[25]

23. Roy V. Scott and J. G. Shoalmire, *The Public Career of Cully A. Cobb: A Study in Agricultural Leadership* (Jackson, Miss., 1973); Lawrence J. Nelson, "Oscar Johnston, the New Deal, and the Cotton Subsidy Payments Controversy, 1936–1937," *Journal of Southern History*, XL (August, 1974), 399–416; Nelson, "The Art of the Possible: Another Look at the 'Purge' of the AAA Liberals in 1935," *Agricultural History*, LVII (October, 1983), 416–35; Mertz, *New Deal Policy*, 25–26; Conrad, *Forgotten Farmers*, 19–82.

24. Saloutos, *American Farmer and the New Deal*, 100–103.

25. *Ibid.*; Nelson, "Art of the Possible."

A few landlords shared the federal bounty and raised tenants', share-croppers', and even hired workers' incomes as well as their own. R. B. Snowden of Horseshoe Plantation in Crittenden County, Arkansas, across from Memphis, reduced cotton acreage in favor of truck crops and dairy operations while apparently maintaining most if not all his tenant families. Snowden grossed nearly $80,000 annually during the mid-1930s. His tenants worked 212 days per year (compared with 110 elsewhere in the cotton country) and earned $517 per family, or $369 per worker—far above average. Thad Snow, a large landlord of south-eastern Missouri, not only shared with his croppers but advocated their cause in Washington.[26]

These two delta planters were hardly typical, however. By 1938 a major function of the Southern Tenant Farmers' Union in eastern Arkansas and the Missouri Bootheel was that of ombudsman to the AAA on behalf of aggrieved tenants whose landlords did not divide "conservation" payments.[27] Planters and local AAA boards could be brutal to complainers, too. In Haywood County, Tennessee, in 1936, a black share renter confronted his landlady, a white woman, over the possession of a subsidy payment. "If it's your check, I want you to have it," he declared. "If it's mine, I want it." The landlady was firm. "It's my check," the renter quoted her. "It's my land, it's my check. You don't have no land and you don't have no check coming." Since the renter was obliged to get water from the landlady's yard, he feared a dangerous racial incident if he insisted upon his rights; so he buckled, "decided to give the check up, make that crop, and leave the next year."[28] Early in 1935 Anthony O. Took of Jefferson County (near Pine Bluff), Arkansas, demanded his share of the 1934 crop payment from his landlord, who refused and ordered Took to move. Took found another place, but his new boss changed his mind, Took later testified, "when my former landlord told him I was a 'wise, inquisitive nigger.'" Took then wrote to AAA headquarters in Washington but got no satisfaction. Instead, he believed, word of his complaint was leaked back to the Pine Bluff AAA board, and "no planter would take me on as a cropper or renter. I can't

26. "Successful Farmer Grows 17 Cash Crops and Forgets Cotton" (Unidentified press clipping, *ca.* 1936, in Federal Writers' Project, Crittenden County history files, Arkansas History Commission). Snowden did not forget cotton, which still grew on about 40 percent of his cropland. See also Carey McWilliams, *Ill Fares the Land: Migrants and Migratory Labor in the United States* (Boston, 1942), 290–91.

27. AAA complaint files, 1938–40, roll 13, STFU Papers.

28. Richard Couto, "'A Place to Call Our Own,'" *Southern Exposure,* IX (Fall, 1981), 16–17.

get any credit. Everywhere I go I'm referred to as a 'smart nigger.'" [29]

Whites who did not benefit from the AAA were no less outraged. An Alabama woman demanded of Congressman William B. Bankhead in 1936, "Will you please answer if the tenant farmers are to[o] small to get help from the New Deal . . .? The big farmers . . . is the only ones that have been profited in the last 3 years." Bankhead, who was sympathetic to such arguments, could not answer. He may have been aware that over in western Mississippi the Delta and Pine Land Company had received $103,349.74 in production control payments for the previous year. [30]

Upon such capital was largely based the rise of neoplantations. The most comprehensive evidence of the AAA's impact on plantation income originates from the WPA Division of Research, which in 1934 and again in 1937 studied 246 matched plantations in seven states (the Carolinas, Georgia, Alabama, Mississippi, Arkansas, and Louisiana). Average AAA payments amounted to $1,123 in 1934, $1,237 in 1937—or 39 percent and 23 percent of net cash income, respectively. (Payments to tenants on the same plantations amounted to an average of 4 percent and 9 percent of their incomes.) In 1937 the Department of Agriculture revealed under Senate pressure that forty-six plantation owners had received AAA payments in excess of $10,000 each; the Delta and Pine Land Company received for the three crop years 1933–1935 a grand total of somewhat more than $318,000. Meanwhile the first New Deal Congress had also created the Production Credit Association (PCA), which would extend low-interest loans to farmers. By the end of 1934 fully one-fourth of the nation's 597 local PCAs were located in the seven plantation states listed above. Local boards in the lower South were busy, too, extending 48,301 loans totalling $17,137,000 before the beginning of 1935. Plantation state PCA loans were smaller on the average than those extended in states where agriculture was already mechanized, but southerners nonetheless borrowed almost one-fifth of the nation's PCA credit during the first year and a half of the program's life. [31]

29. Anthony O. Took testimony, 1937 (Typescript in "Social Correlative of Farm Tenure," Jefferson County Series, University of Arkansas Department of Agricultural Economics and Rural Sociology records, University of Arkansas Library, Fayetteville).

30. Mrs. T. B. Gaines to William B. Bankhead, June 24, 1936, in William B. Bankhead Papers, Alabama Department of Archives and History; "Statement and President's Report for the Year Ended March 31, 1936" (Typescript in Delta and Pine Land Company Records).

31. WPA, *The Plantation South,* 31; Gunnar Myrdal, *An American Dilemma* (2 vols.; New York, 1944), I, 269; Nelson, "Johnston, the New Deal, and the Cotton Subsidy Con-

The first stage in the consolidation of plantations was the wholesale eviction of tenants of all classes, especially sharecroppers. This process was protracted, but it seems to have been underway all over the South by 1934, the first full crop year following creation of the AAA. Some evictions occurred as soon as the program began in 1933, when one-fourth of growing crops were plowed under to reduce production for that first crop season. A white sharecropper's wife of Henry County, northwestern Tennessee, recalled that her husband "was still sheer cropping when the sign-up with the gov'ment come along." The landlord told them "he'd rented every acre of his [the tenant's] land to the gov'ment. He didn't say a word about our crops we was about middle ways of. The move jist came on us before we could plan for it." [32] Across the river in Mississippi County, Arkansas, the enormous R. E. Lee Wilson Plantation made the same decision for hundreds of sharecroppers in 1934. In black-belt Georgia, Arthur Raper discovered in 1934 that sharecropping had declined almost 15 percent since his previous visit in 1927, while wage labor had risen 14 percent. The same year the Coleman-Fulton Pasturage Company (the Taft Ranch) evicted its white and black sharecroppers in San Patricio County, Texas. Observers noted the phenomenon over much of the rest of Texas and Oklahoma as well. [33]

No one knows (or probably ever will know) how many evictions took place. No government official was responsible for counting, and those who tried to count were frustrated by difficulties in proving that multitudes of the wandering destitute were all former tenants thrown off their places because of crop reductions. USDA "liberals" and officials of the Southern Tenant Farmers' Union warned that the AAA would force thousands off the land, then declared that indeed many thousands had been evicted. A southeastern Missouri STFU officer wrote early in 1938, a full year before the celebrated roadside demonstration of stranded former sharecroppers, that there were "at least 10,000 people in Pemiscot County on starvation." [34] Trained social scientists who stud-

troversy"; WPA, Division of Social Research, *Landlord and Tenant on the Cotton Plantation*, by T. J. Woofter, Jr. (Washington, D.C., 1936), 55–56.

32. Ruth Clark, "Sorry Living," life history of Ella Paschall, November 17, 1938 (Typescript in FWP life histories files, SHC).

33. Mitchell to Sydney Olsen, April 11, 1936, roll 2, STFU Papers; Raper, *Preface to Peasantry*, 34; FERA, Rural Problem Areas Survey Report No. 62, Western Cotton Growing Area: San Patricio County, Texas (Typescript, January 11, 1935, in Record Group 83, National Archives), 1, 3. See also McWilliams, *Ill Fares the Land*, 247–48.

34. T. H. McConnell to Butler, January 6, 1938, roll 7, STFU Papers. See also Conrad, *Forgotten Farmers*, 47–48, 123–24.

ied three North Carolina tobacco counties could not be any more specific. Wilson County had 589 rural relief clients, Nash County about 300, Greene 269. Blacks outnumbered whites about two to one. Clients often told interviewers they were on relief because the "landlord could no longer finance family." Some destitute families on the rolls were not evicted tenants; yet the scholars were certain that relief agencies accommodated only a fraction of the poor. One of the social scientists speculated that there were ten thousand displaced tenants in the eastern North Carolina subregion.[35] Finally, an economist employed by the AAA itself conceded wide disregard for the agency's unenforceable subsidy-sharing rules. Norman Thomas and the Socialist party condemned the cruelty of evictions in his carefully documented tract *The Plight of the Sharecropper* (1934), and liberal southerners Will Alexander, Charles S. Johnson, and Edwin Embree conducted inquiries and published a devastating indictment of the New Deal's shortcomings in 1935, *The Collapse of Cotton Tenancy.*[36]

There is some evidence and considerable logic that evictions were not so widespread in the flue-cured tobacco belts as in the cotton country. Tobacco, known as a "thirteen-month crop," was much more labor-intensive than cotton. Landholding patterns in tobacco were different, too. There were more small-to-moderate-sized owner-operated units, and perhaps most important, machinery that might have made consolidation feasible did not yet exist. Therefore tobacco farmers and planters were less inclined to evict and more inclined to share subsidies to keep reliable tenants. In addition, North Carolina county agents usually distributed subsidy checks personally to tenants, not just to landowners, as in the cotton program.[37]

The decline of fragmented plantations, then, was most rapid in the cotton country, especially in black-majority areas. Although displaced tenants were not counted, there is strong corroboration for this view in the form of statistics on the demise of traditional tenancy and sharp increases in the employment of hired labor. In fact, the substitution of the

35. Gordon W. Blackwell, "The Problem of Displaced Tenant Farm Families—Wilson County," Blackwell, "The Problem of the Displaced Tenant Farm Family—Nash County," and T. J. Woofter, Jr., "The Problem of the Displaced Tenant Farm Family" (Typescripts, 1934, all in Tennessee Valley Authority Social Studies files, Box 25, RG 142, Atlanta Branch, NA).

36. See Mertz, *New Deal Policy,* 27–28.

37. Anthony J. Badger, *Prosperity Road: The New Deal, Tobacco, and North Carolina* (Chapel Hill, 1981), 92, 200–207, 209, 229; Pete Daniel, *Breaking the Land,* 110–33.

latter for the former constitutes a second stage, almost simultaneous with the evictions, in the evolution of neoplantations.

When the manager of the Taft Ranch evicted his sharecroppers in 1934, he hired Mexican daily and weekly laborers to replace them. Mexican migrants appeared in western Texas and Oklahoma cotton fields about the same time, and in August of 1937 they arrived to help pick the southeastern Missouri crop. Most cotton laborers were certainly not long-distance migrants, however, but local folk whose status had suddenly changed. This was Arthur Raper's impression in the Georgia black belt; it was also true of western Texas tractor drivers. During January, 1939, the STFU questioned almost three hundred families in southeastern Missouri about their status between 1937 and 1938. The survey revealed fifty-two fewer sharecroppers and fifty-four more day laborers, and no Mexicans were identified in the study.[38]

Sharecroppers, unlike share and cash tenants, had never enjoyed legal rights to land and crops. Indeed, legally sharecroppers had never been more than laborers, though in practice they were more settled than hired workers. They enjoyed "free" rent on their cabins, and they contracted with landlords for an entire crop year. Yet the virtual interchangeability of the two statuses is evident in nearly every surviving farm and plantation ledger before the New Deal and the age of evictions. Throughout the 1920s, for example, a small planter of Anderson County, South Carolina, recorded in his four sharecroppers' accounts not only debits for fertilizer and cash advances but credits for extra labor they performed—plowing his land, hauling timber, picking scrap cotton after the season. Down in Georgia, Arthur Raper was acutely aware of this slippery matter of status. Dependent people, he wrote, had "little choice but to occupy the tenure status the planters want them to. One year they will be wage hands—'Mr. George is doin' wages.' Another year they will be croppers—'Mr. George is halvin' 'em.'" In eastern Macon County, where cotton culture was leavened somewhat by peach orchards and asparagus fields, dependents actually worked in both capacities nearly every year. They raised small patches of cotton on shares, performed day labor during the winter pruning peach trees, some spring work in asparagus, picked peaches in summer and pecans

38. See FERA, Problem Areas Survey, San Patricio County; McWilliams, *Ill Fares the Land*, 247–48; McConnell to Mitchell, n.d. (*ca.* August 28, 1937), roll 6, STFU Papers; Raper, *Preface to Peasantry*, 152–54; "Texas Farm Workers Organize," *Sharecroppers Voice* (November, 1935) (copy on roll 1, STFU Papers); "Report on Relief and Farming Survey Made January, 1939" (Typescript, roll 10, STFU Papers.)

FIGURE 3
Tenants, 1920–1959,
and Hired Farm
Workers, 1935–1959
(in thousands)

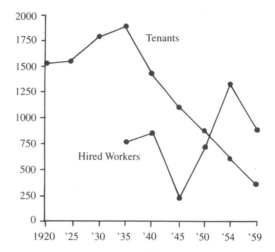

SOURCE: Censuses of agriculture, 1920–1959,
state tables.

NOTE: Enumerations include fourteen states—the
former Confederacy, West Virginia, Kentucky,
and Oklahoma.

as well as cotton in the fall. Many less diversified cotton planters employed the highly centralized "through-and-through" system, too, implying extraordinary supervision and a sort of sharecropping very much like gang labor. Here, mules were centrally barned, and all fields were plowed as one by crews; only then were fields laid off and divided among sharecropper families for individual attention.[39] Through-and-through crews were probably designated as sharecroppers. One may only wonder how the cotton-cropping, peach-picking dependents of Macon County, Georgia, were labeled by the Bureau of the Census. The distinction was precious, and the wave of evictions following the AAA squashed what remained of it.

The 1935 *Census of Agriculture* was the first to enumerate hired farm workers. Perhaps the massive expulsion of tenants during the pre-

39. Harold D. Woodman, "Post–Civil War Southern Agriculture and the Law," *Agricultural History*, LIII (January, 1979), 319–37; Kester, *Revolt Among the Sharecroppers*, 34–35; Sam Bowen Farm Records, 1921–1930, Clemson University Archives; Raper, *Preface to Peasantry*, 152–54. The Murphy Plantation in Jefferson County, Arkansas, is an excellent example of a "through and through" operation. See the John P. Murphy Store and Plantation Ledgers, University of Arkansas Library, Little Rock).

vious two years was a cause of the bureau's initiative. The count was haphazard, however, and probably grossly low. In 1935 and again in 1945 the census took place in January, after harvest. The 1940 count occurred the last week of March, during plowing in parts of the South but considerably before cotton chopping and tobacco resetting and weeding. In 1950 the count took place in April, still before the heaviest labor requirements. At last in 1954 the bureau settled upon the September–October harvest season and probably achieved something approaching an accurate enumeration.[40] Poor as the hired labor counts were before the 1954 agricultural census, however, they revealed the dramatic turnaround that signaled the beginning of the end of fragmented plantations. Figure 3 presents the figures as reported in the censuses, along with numbers of all classes of tenants for the entire region, through the 1959 census.

It is apparent from the censuses that the age of tenancy receded very rapidly after 1935 throughout the South. It seems obvious, too, that had not World War II production demands drawn from all classes of farmers, the hired workers graph line would have ascended steadily from 1935 to the 1954 apex. As the process did work out, hired workers equaled tenants sometime early in the 1950s, then virtually doubled them by middecade.

The end of the age of hired labor (the mid-1950s) signaled the consummation of the third stage in the development of neoplantations. Mechanization of plantations began modestly during the 1920s, then proceeded at an accelerated pace during the 1930s and especially the 1940s. Tractors, grain and corn combines, and finally cotton harvesters replaced many thousands of human workers. Yet until agricultural chemistry found ways to prevent the emergence of weeds or to kill them after emergence, many human hands, hoes, and some mules were still required. Despite such ingenious experiments as elevating tractors on stilts, machinery could not work well in high corn and cotton. During the 1940s federal funding and corporate and state experiment station research led to the development of preemergent weed killers, which were first marketed during the early 1950s. So as farmers of virtually all crops turned not only to capital-intensive machines but to chemicals, labor-intensive agriculture gradually died.[41]

40. This serendipitous methodology is confessed and described fully in *Census of Agriculture, 1954*, Vol. 1, *Counties and State Economic Areas*, Pt. 26—Texas, xvi.

41. Fite, "Mechanization of Cotton Production," 205–207. Tobacco was an exception. Tractors, mechanical stringers, and chemistry reduced labor requirements some-

An excellent means of dating and measuring the impact of mechanization on cotton production is the formula used by economists for the
average labor input (both skilled and unskilled) required to produce each
hundredweight of a commodity. In 1940, 33.82 hours (33.5 of them unskilled) were needed. By 1946 the figure had dropped dramatically to
24.57 (23.5 unskilled). The real plunge came between 1949 and 1952,
however: 20.7 in 1949 to 12.95 in 1950 to 10.04 in 1951 to 4.82 (only
3.0 unskilled) in 1952. In twenty rapidly mechanizing Mississippi delta
counties between 1949 and 1952, employment of unskilled agricultural
labor dropped by 71 percent. By 1957 the volume of such labor represented only 10 percent of the 1949 level.[42] The rise of machines and the
rapid decline of hired labor is also graphic in the surviving records of
the Thomas Hottel Gist plantations in eastern Arkansas. Gist began not-
ing fuel expenditures for his tractors, trucks, and automobile in 1945,
when he paid almost $1,000. In 1946 Gist spent more than $1,200, in
1947 nearly $1,800. Hired labor costs rose, too, from $2,607.79 in
1947 to $4,689.25 in 1948, to a high of $5,215.15 in 1949. Then, significantly, Gist paid only $2,427.80 for labor in 1950. All the while, as
chemicals obviated most hoeing and pushed out farm workers, general
prosperity and the cities of the nation pulled them. During the 1950s
nearly three million southerners left the region altogether. The exodus
exceeded even that of the wartime 1940s.[43]

In the heart of the cotton plantation country the demise of labor-
intensive farming and the rise of neoplantations proceeded somewhat
faster. Figure 4 presents the downward course of sharecropping (the
dominant form of tenancy there) and the tumultuous career of hired labor in ten black-belt and delta cotton counties that had black population
majorities in 1930.

---

what, but there was no "once over" harvester for flue-cured tobacco until 1970. The culture of burley tobacco is not yet mechanized. See Charles Kellogg Mann, *Tobacco: The
Ants and the Elephants* (Salt Lake City, 1975), 127–29. For insights on 1940s mechanization and early herbicides, I am also indebted to William H. Hawley II, who has farmed in
southwestern Ohio and eastern Indiana since 1946.

42. Arthur Ford, *Political Economics of Rural Poverty*, 29; Black Economics Research
Center, "Black Land Loss: The Plight of Black Ownership," *Southern Exposure*, II (Fall,
1974), 115.

43. See daybooks and ledgers, 1945–54, Thomas Hottel Gist Plantation and Business
Records, University of Arkansas Library, Fayetteville; Dodd and Dodd (comps.), *Historical Statistics of the South*, Chap. 9. *South* here means the same fourteen states represented
in Figure 3, minus Florida, which gained population for reasons having little to do with
agriculture.

FIGURE 4
Sharecroppers,
1920–1954, and Hired
Farm Workers,
1935–1959, in
Selected Cotton
Plantation Counties
(in thousands)

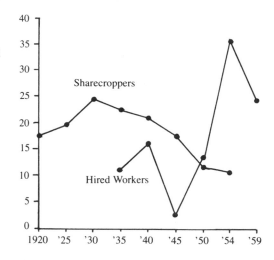

SOURCE: Censuses of agriculture, 1920–1959, county tables.

NOTE: The cotton counties are Macon and Sumter, Alabama; Crittenden and St. Francis, Arkansas; Sumter, Georgia; Tensas Parish, Louisiana; Noxubee and Washington, Mississippi; Edgefield, South Carolina; and Harrison, Texas.

Several differences between the experiences of these counties and those of the region (as represented in Figure 3) appear immediately: First, sharecropping peaked in 1930, not 1935, in the cotton plantation subregions. (This is true also of gross data of all classes of tenancy.) Second, there is no figure for sharecroppers in 1959 because the Bureau of the Census did not report them, and has not since 1954, when census officials decided that the institution had declined to insignificance. Perhaps, too, they were responding at last to the problem of defining status, which Arthur Raper had identified two decades earlier. Third, the number of hired workers exceeded sharecroppers during the late 1940s, not the early 1950s. And fourth, the number of hired workers in 1954 exceeded by more than ten thousand the peak volume of sharecroppers in 1930, whereas the apex of the hired worker graph line for the whole South did not approach the 1935 tenancy figure.

Some explanation of these differences can be inferred from the historical context as illustrated by a variety of examples from the black

FIGURE 5
Tractors in Selected
Cotton Counties,
1925–1959
(in thousands)

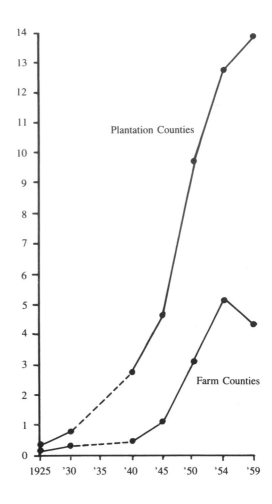

SOURCE: Censuses of agriculture, 1925–1959, county tables. Data for 1935 not available.

NOTE: The cotton counties with white majorities are Clay and Fayette, Alabama; Perry, Arkansas; Forsyth and Madison, Georgia; Sabine Parish, Louisiana; Covington and Tishomingo, Mississippi; Chester, Tennessee; and Trinity, Texas. In 1959 there were 11,090 farms in these counties with an average size of 134.1 acres, and the plantation counties sampled had 14,957 farms, averaging 215 acres.

belt, deltas, and elsewhere. Tenancy (especially sharecropping) began to disappear first on cotton plantations because landlords collected the bulk of AAA subsidies and thus, beginning in March of each year, had ready cash to hire laborers. Such cash, easier credit, and higher commodity prices also permitted planters to invest in labor-saving machinery and to accelerate the development of capital-intensive agriculture.[44] The process required more time—a lag of at least five years—outside the plantation areas. A comparison of the numbers of tractors on farms in the plantation counties with tractors in an equal number of cotton counties with hillier land, smaller farms, and white majorities reveals the planters' advantage and initiative.

The capitalization of plantations and farms devastated the old fragmented pattern of rural occupance. Hired workers during the 1930s were first housed in scattered tenant cabins. But gradually, from the 1930s into the 1960s, landlords demolished most of them, beginning with cabins standing in the way of machinery operations in enlarged fields. Gradually, too, the pattern of neoplantation occupance emerged: worker houses centrally grouped or spaced along a convenient plantation road with ready access to machinery and fields. The ultimate cotton plantation, the Delta and Pine Land Company, illustrates the profound changes in both occupance and production. During 1935–1944 the corporation maintained an average of 850 tenant houses. As early as 1947, 325 of them were vacant, awaiting destruction. Shortly, D&PL began to diversify, especially with soybeans (in the 1950s), then with rice as well (in the 1960s). On nearby Fallback Plantation in Bolivar County, fully 60 percent of the buildings standing in 1948 had been razed by 1955. Road mileage within the plantation had been reduced by 50 percent, too, to accommodate machine-driven operations in larger fields. The eastern half of Macon County, Georgia (the Flint River bottoms), was transformed almost as dramatically. In 1948 the area was still dominated by family-owned fragmented cotton farms and plantations, along with Flint River Farms, a federal resettlement project begun during the New Deal. In 1953 both cotton and fragmented occupance changed suddenly, when a large group of Mennonites from Virginia purchased about ten thousand acres and established dairies with cooperative credit and

44. On the rapid conversion from sharecropping to hired labor, compare 1935 daybooks with those for 1941–47 in the Gist Plantation and Business Records. The conversion is also evident in the records of the J. E. Little plantation in Faulkner County, Arkansas, and of the Frierson properties by the Red River in Caddo Parish, Louisiana. See ledgers, 1930–50, Frierson Company Records, Louisiana State University–Shreveport Archives.

marketing and when the Norris Cattle Company established barns, pastures, and feeder lots on ninety-five hundred acres. The Mennonites worked on thirty-five separate farms, but the Norris Cattle Company met all the criteria of a neoplantation.[45]

In hillier areas, such as Tate County in northern Mississippi, the evolution of neoplantations was slower. Of forty-two plantations examined there as late as 1960, only seven qualified as neoplantations. Three more were cash rented on what might be termed the middle western model. All ten of these were thoroughly mechanized. Three more remained in the classic fragmented form, with sharecroppers and all-mule power. The remaining twenty-eight were still in some transitional form of occupance, management, and power. Three were part-time sharecropper operations; four were through-and-through systems with tenant farms but centralized power; most were combination mule and tractor affairs with a variety of labor arrangements.[46]

Wherever and whenever neoplantations arose, cotton culture was diminished or abandoned. For decades, southern farm editors and agents of the Extension Service had appealed in vain for cotton crop reduction and diversification. AAA and PCA dollars at last produced change. Throughout the richer flatland, planters turned to dairying, beef cattle production, and alternative crops such as hay, grain sorghum, soybeans, and in the Mississippi Delta, rice. By 1959 there were only eleven counties in four southern states where cotton amounted to more than 50 percent of crops harvested.[47]

By the 1960s one might have found row-crop plantations with cotton,

45. USDA, AAA, "Farm Wage Worker Schedule" series, 1939 (Typescript copy in University of Arkansas Department of Agricultural Economics and Rural Sociology records). Charles Shelton Aiken summarized the relationship between machinery operations and housing arrangements (occupance) in "Transitional Plantation Occupance in Tate County, Mississippi" (M.A. thesis, University of Georgia, 1962), 67–70. See also Oscar Johnston, "Will the Machine Ruin the South?" (Typescript, 1947, for *Saturday Evening Post* article), and various annual reports for the 1950s and the 1960s, all in the Delta and Pine Land Company Records; Harry D. Fornari, "The Big Change: Cotton to Soybeans," *Agricultural History*, LIII (January, 1979), 245–53; Prunty, "Renaissance of the Southern Plantation"; Paul Fred Ries, "Rural Occupance Changes in Eastern Macon County, Georgia, from 1948 to 1967" (Ph.D. dissertation, University of Georgia, 1973), 1–4, 21–57, 130–65.

46. Aiken, "Transitional Plantation Occupance."

47. On the long campaigns for diversification and reduction of labor costs, see Thomas D. Clark, *Three Paths to the Modern South: Education, Agriculture, and Conservation* (Athens, Ga., 1965), 29–60. Examples of local production changes are Elbert O. Umstead, "History of Lonoke County" (Typescript, 1940, in FWP county history files, Arkansas History Commission), 53–54; Texas Agricultural Extension Service, "Annual

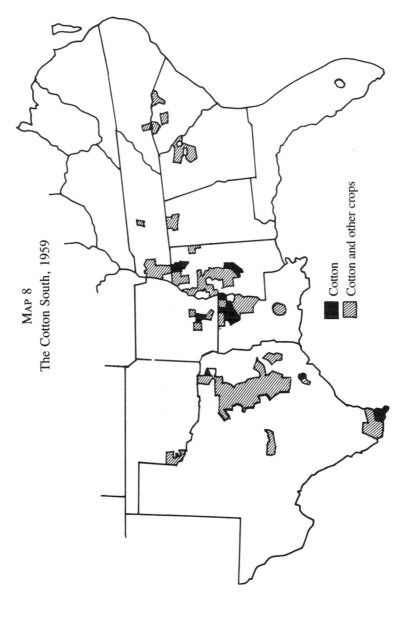

MAP 8
The Cotton South, 1959

Cotton
Cotton and other crops

SOURCE: *Census of Agriculture, 1959*, county tables.

soybeans, corn, and peanuts in parts of Georgia and Alabama; with cotton, soybeans, and rice in the deltas of Mississippi, Louisiana, and Arkansas, and in the Arkansas Grand Prairie. But many neoplantations had no row crops at all. Some specialized in pecans, some were huge dairies, many were enormous livestock plantations with feed grain fields. Most peculiar were woodland plantations. Often as large as ten thousand acres, they had small cash-crop fields (such as peanuts) and some pasturage, but most acreage was forested. The woodland neo-planter cut timber for income, but the estate's major function was as hunting preserve. There were ten such plantation preserves in three southwestern Georgia black-belt counties during the early 1960s. Much of Leon County, Florida (surrounding Tallahassee), and neighboring Thomas County, Georgia, evolved from fragmented cotton plantations into woodland neoplantations, as well.[48]

Cotton's move west to the level, irrigated lands of Arizona and the San Joaquin and Imperial valleys of California was already largely ac-complished by the end of the 1950s. The birthplace of factory-style ag-riculture, the West had demonstrated its superiority in machine cultiva-tion of cotton as early as the 1930s, as we have seen. When, following World War II, mechanical harvesters became available, westerners bought proportionately far more of them than did southern planters. The West had no boll weevils, either, and its ginned Acala lint was 5 percent longer and more uniform in quality than southern cotton.[49]

Report, 1940," 500, on change in the black-waxy land area; annual president's reports of the Delta and Pine Land Company; "Annual Narrative Report of M. F. Whatley, County Agent, Macon County, Alabama, Nov. 30, 1947" (Typescript in Alabama Extension Ser-vice Records, Auburn University Archives), on the cotton-to-cattle transition in the black belt; and Jack Temple Kirby, "Agricultural Souths, 1920–1960" (Paper read November 13, 1981, Southern Historical Association, Louisville).

48. Mealor, "Plantation Occupance Complex"; Clifton Paisley, *From Cotton to Quail: An Agricultural Chronicle of Leon County, Florida, 1860–1967* (Gainesville, 1968); Merle C. Prunty, Jr., "The Woodland Plantation as a Contemporary Occupance Type in the South," *Geographical Review*, LIII (January, 1963), 1–21; Sam B. Hilliard, "Bird-song: Biography of a Landholding" (Paper read September 23, 1983, History of Rural Life in America Symposium, Florida A & M University).

49. McWilliams, *Ill Fares the Land*, 17–20, 48–199, and *passim;* Harland Padfield and William E. Martin, *Farmers, Workers, and Machines: Technological and Social Change in Farm Industries in Arizona* (Tucson, 1965), 84–86; USDA, Farm Economics Division, Economic Research Service, Agricultural Economics Report No. 3, *Cotton Farms: San Joaquin Valley, California: Organization, Costs, and Returns, 1947–1950* (Washington, D.C., 1961), 1–3, 20; Moses S. Musoke and Alan L. Olmstead, "The Rise of the Cotton Industry in California: A Comparative Perspective," *Journal of Economic History*, XLII (June, 1982), 385–412.

EARLY ONE-ROW SPINDLE COTTON HARVESTER, MISSISSIPPI DELTA, *ca.* 1950s

Standard Oil Company of New Jersey Collection, Western History Collections, University of Oklahoma Library

By the early postwar era, then, major crop, organizational, and population changes had come to pass. The old pattern was broken. Except in a few especially suited places in the lower Mississippi Valley and in Texas, cotton was well on its way west; cattle and a variety of new

FIGURE 6
Tractors in Selected
Southern Cotton
Plantation Counties
and California Central
Valley Counties,
1925–1959
(in thousands)

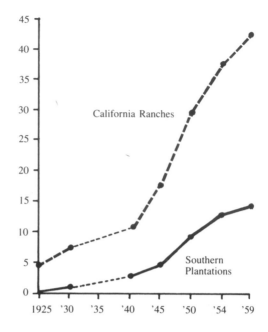

SOURCE: Censuses of agriculture, 1925–1959,
county tables. Data for 1935 not available.

plants had come east. The federal government continued to subsidize
bigness, and millions of the landless and near landless had been driven
from the countryside. Much structural change had not yet taken place,
however. The mechanization of flue-cured tobacco and of peanuts was
hardly underway, and the determination of an ultimate place for the millions of unskilled rural southerners who remained in the region would
be protracted. For all its impressive strides toward the agricultural factory model, the South merely crawled in comparison with other regions. In 1939, for example, 12 and 11 percent (respectively) of southeastern and delta farmland was broken by tractor power; by 1946 the
percentages had grown to 38 and 35. Yet in the corn belt in 1946 nearly
all land (92 percent) was broken by tractors. A comparison of tractor
power on cotton lands in the Mississippi Valley with the West also demonstrates the South's persisting disadvantage. In 1946 tractors broke
42 percent of Mississippi Valley land, 94 percent of the western turf.
Moreover, the high cost of new spindle-type cotton pickers—almost six

FIGURE 7
Cotton Acreage
Harvested in Selected
Southern Plantation
Counties and
California Central
Valley Counties,
1920–1959
(in thousands of acres)

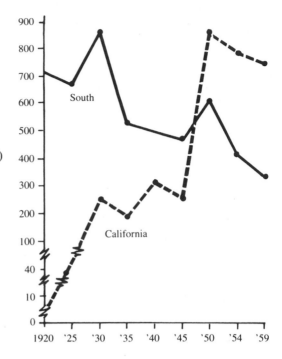

SOURCE: Censuses of agriculture, 1920–1959, county tables.

thousand dollars at the factory at the end of the 1940s—made southerners tardy in adopting these machines, too.[50]

Another reason for the southern lag was the persistence of what in
this brave new world was regarded as surplus population in the countryside—this despite decades of migration. In 1947–1948 a social scientist discovered on an Alabama black-belt plantation a thriving commissary where sharecroppers and hired laborers were still paid in scrip.
The owner-landlord had converted part of his properties to cattle production and a sawmill, but his cotton was still handpicked. As the plant
supervisor of this transitional estate told the investigator: "Most of the
work around here calls for strong backs and quick fingers. Cotton picking and chopping takes the most work. Them mechanical pickers out
West won't come around here for a long time . . . and when cotton out

50. Arthur Ford, *Political Economics of Rural Poverty,* 19, 39; Fite, "Recent Progress," 27.

West gets too tough for us to match we'll just stay with the cattle." As for the remaining peasantry, the boss did not "know what'll happen to all the niggers then. Guess they'll have to go North." [51]

So progress for the subsidized planters and pain and dislocation for the have-nots were hardly complete after the blitz of change brought about by the Depression and World War II. The social as well as economic aspects of this continued transition will be presented in later chapters.

51. Morton Rubin, *Plantation County* (Chapel Hill, 1951), 18–20.

It is almost sinful how I love these old acres here . . .
how I lay store by each inch of the land, each blade of
grass or grain it grows, how I believe there is no spot
in the universe so perfect, so dear, and so sweet as the
West Virginia mountains.
—A MOUNTAIN FARM WOMAN, *ca.* 1928

Mountain farmers haven't got no future—none at all.
Most of the land is give out, and they ain't no more
new land. . . . When these farms wear out, I guess the
National Park or the National Forests will take them
over and let the timber grow back. The old folks will
die about the time their land is give out, just as mine
has wore out. The young folks will have to live on
wages. . . . It may all be for the best.
—AN AGED GREAT SMOKIES FARMER, 1939

I like to load coal, or run a motor, and I refuse to farm;
the sun is too damn hot out there in them fields. I'll
just stick to mining; nothing suits me any better.
—A YOUNG HARLAN COUNTY, KENTUCKY, MINER,
1939

Chapter 3
Exhausted Colonies and Ruined Arcadias

WRITING ABOUT THE APPALACHIAN AND
Ozark highlands is fraught with danger. This was a different South,
without plantations, many black people, or a palpable Confederate
mystique. Vast, it nevertheless still seemed singular and simple. The
highlands remained hidden behind mountain fastness, serenely beyond
the modern world, primitive, clannish, violent, and beautiful. Late in
the nineteenth century outsiders discovered the highlands and began immediately to romanticize. Amateur and professional anthropologists,
folklorists, and musicologists described a folk so isolated they seemed
trapped in a time capsule from the eighteenth century or earlier, a
people without factories, who made everything they used with their own
hands and who sang "Barbara Allen" and other British ballads as in the
days of Elizabeth and James I. Fascination with such folks mounted at
the turn of the twentieth century, when writers of fiction joined the outland scholars. Best known is John Fox, Jr., a native of Lexington, Kentucky, who settled in Big Stone Gap in remote southwestern Virginia
and eventually published stories in national magazines as well as several
best-selling novels in which he dwelled upon living in nature, feuding,

and other quaint ways. *The Trail of the Lonesome Pine* (1908) was Fox's most famous effort.[1]

Romantic generalization has grown old but hardly ceased. As recently as the late 1960s Catherine Marshall, a writer of books with Christian messages, chose the early twentieth-century Great Smokies as the locale for her long novel *Christy,* which within a year of publication was reprinted fifty-eight times in paperback. The title character, a fervent nineteen-year-old, leaves her upper-middle-class home in Asheville, North Carolina, for missionary work as a teacher in the Cove over in Tennessee. Christy's youthful naïveté underscores the shock of her first encounters with the dirty, poor, superstitious, and diseased folk of the mountains. An older missionary and a local physician help her adjust, and Christy comes to accept the Cove people's virtues of stubborn independence and familism. Still, she strives to bring them knowledge, health, and a more loving Christianity to replace the stern, unforgiving, and feud-sustaining version they practice. This formula for preserving what is simple and virtuous while dragging the mountaineers into a religious and economic modern world had been conceived already by well-meaning reformers who encouraged the establishment of small businesses (such as furniture manufacturing) to provide the cash required in modern exchange, and Danish-model "folk schools," where youth would learn and preserve premodern arts and crafts.[2]

The folk school movement following World War I had produced the famous Highlander Folk School in Monteagle, Tennessee, and several shorter-lived ones elsewhere and had influenced romantic, radical colonies of artists and labor organizers at Black Mountain, North Carolina, and Mena, Arkansas. Much later, during the 1960s and 1970s, an ingenious high school teacher in the mountains of northern Georgia revived something close to the original Danish model as a means of English instruction. His highland students collected folklore and premodern crafts

1. The classic work, written by a missionary, is John C. Campbell, *The Southern Highlander and His Homeland* (New York, 1921). See also Jack E. Weller, *Yesterday's People: Life in Contemporary Appalachia* (Lexington, Ky., 1965). On mountain feuding, see James C. Klotter, "Feuds in Appalachia: An Overview," *Filson Club Historical Quarterly,* LVI (July, 1982), 539–55. On mythology and culture, see Henry D. Shapiro, *Appalachia on Our Minds: The Southern Mountains and Mountaineers in the American Consciousness, 1870–1920* (Chapel Hill, 1978); David E. Whisnant, *All That Is Native and Fine: The Politics of Culture in an American Region* (Chapel Hill, 1983); and Jack Temple Kirby, *Media-Made Dixie: The South in the American Imagination* (Baton Rouge, 1978), 39–41.

2. Catherine Marshall, *Christy* (New York, 1967).

from local elders. These projects led to publication of a magazine called *Foxfire*, then a series of books of the same title, which attracted national attention.[3] So a century after the first infatuation of outsiders with the southern highlands, the attraction of the supposedly isolated and pre-modern remained powerful. Yet all the folklore and music, the anthropology, fiction, newspaper cartoons ("Ozark Ike," "Snuffy Smith"), folk schools, and missionary work reflect more of urban people's yearnings for simplicity (and their irresistible urge to meddle) than of highland history and realities.[4]

Meanwhile, by the early 1930s, social scientists became interested in measuring socioeconomic problems in the mountain South to influence public policy formulation in the New Deal. Most important were Lewis C. Gray, an economist and historian with the Department of Agriculture Bureau of Agricultural Economics (BAE), who led a corps of able colleagues in Washington and fieldworkers across the country, and Howard W. Odum, head of the Department of Sociology at the University of North Carolina, whose many outstanding students included Rupert Vance, author of *Human Geography of the South* (1932). It was Gray and company who first formulated a map of Appalachia for the BAE's significant 1935 study *Economic and Social Problems and Conditions of the Southern Appalachians*. Odum consulted with Gray and adapted the BAE map to his famous 1936 opus *Southern Regions of the United States*.[5] In justice to Vance, Gray, and Odum, it must be said that

3. Rolland G. Paulston, *Folk Schools in Social Change: A Partisan Guide to the International Literature* (Pittsburgh, 1974); Martin Duberman, *Black Mountain: An Exploration in Community* (New York, 1972). On Commonwealth College in Mena, Arkansas, see H. L. Mitchell, *Mean Things Happening in This Land: The Life and Times of H. L. Mitchell* (Montclair, N.J., 1979), 50. On the northern Georgia enterprise, see Elliot Wigginton (ed.), *The Foxfire Book: Hog Dressing, Log Cabin Building, Mountain Crafts and Food, Planting by the Signs, Snake Lore, Hunting Tales, Faith Healing, Moonshining, and Other Affairs of Plain Living* (Garden City, N.Y., 1972); or another sample, Wigginton (ed.), *Foxfire 4: Fiddle Making, Springhouses, Horse Trading, Sassafras Tea, Berry Buckets, Gardening, and Further Affairs of Plain Living* (Garden City, N.Y., 1977).

4. This is a primary argument in both Shapiro, *Appalachia on Our Minds*, and Whisnant, *All That Is Native and Fine*. On cartoons, see M. Thomas Inge, "The Appalachian Backgrounds of Billy De Beck's Snuffy Smith," *Appalachian Journal*, IV (Winter, 1977), 120–32.

5. See Rupert B. Vance, *Human Geography of the South: A Study in Regional Resources and Human Adequacy* (Chapel Hill, 1932), 240–61; USDA, BAE and Forest Service, *Economics and Social Problems and Conditions of the Southern Appalachians*, by L. C. Gray and C. F. Clayton (Washington, D.C., 1935); Howard W. Odum, *Southern Regions of the United States* (Chapel Hill, 1936). On Odum's debt to the BAE, see Odum to Gray, October 18, 1934, in Southern Appalachian Study Papers, Box 140, RG 83, NA.

their versions of the highlands (especially Gray's) took notice of intra-subregional variety; but the sum effect of new scholarly attention to the subject confirmed the problematical tradition of homogeneity in mountain culture.

The first problem—and one with which subsequent scholarship has had little success also—is the map. Does southern Appalachia include all of West Virginia? (Odum placed the entire state in the Northeast.) Is western South Carolina part of the subregion? Does it extend southward all the way to Birmingham and southwestwardly into Mississippi? Do the western borders of the subregion reach to Lexington and Nashville? If the Virginia Blue Ridge Mountains belong in Appalachia, does the Valley of Virginia between the Blue Ridge and Alleghenies also belong there? The valley has always been rather prosperous farming country with a cash economy, urban centers, and good market transportation. Much the same is true of the Cumberland Plateau, the Valley of Tennessee, and several smaller river valleys. Then there is urban Appalachia, including Roanoke, Charleston, and Huntington, Asheville, Knoxville, and Chattanooga, and dozens of smaller cities—which were hardly poor, primitive, or isolated even at the dawn of the century.[6]

The precise borders of the highlands will ever elude scholars. If the subregion is perceived as a "problem" or a "culture area"—and it has always been so—then change in time produces an ever-changing map. The quest itself may be rather pointless, for Appalachia (as well the Ozarks) is in fact largely an abstraction. Appalachia in particular is too heterogeneous to be lumped into a coherent scheme. Yet the term *mountain South* persists in popular and scholarly parlance; so, despite great variations within the so-called subregion, it must still be conceptualized—at least in the beginning and with great care—in the singular. More important, there actually were and are some stark differences between the cultures of a great many highland southerners and those of the piedmont, plains, and delta residents.

If a terrible history of sprawling monoculture and economic colo-

---

On Odum's policy-making ambition as well as conceptual problems in *Southern Regions,* see Michael O'Brien, *The Idea of the American South, 1920–1941* (Baltimore, 1979), 60–69.

6. A survey of such questions is to be found in Rupert B. Vance, "The Region: A New Survey," in Thomas R. Ford (ed.), *The Southern Appalachian Region: A Survey* (Lexington, Ky. 1967), 1–8. On mapping, see also Karl B. Raitz and Richard Ulack, "Cognitive Maps of Appalachia," *Geographical Review,* LXXI (April, 1981), 201–13.

nialism had marked the lives of flatland and hill southerners since the
Civil War, highlanders were no less affected by the far-ranging minions
of the world economic system. While railroads, planters, and fertilizer
salesmen carried cotton and the cash economy to Dixie's hills in the decades following the war, most of the highlands remained remote. Then
some parts became the prey of extractive industrialists of another sort.
Toward the end of the century Collis P. Huntington completed his Chesapeake and Ohio Railroad across southern West Virginia, its western ter-
minus on the Ohio River in the new town named for the entrepreneur
himself. Huntington planned the C&O as an intercontinental link, fun-
neling North America's wealth through his shipyard and port at Newport
News, Virginia. Exploitation of natural resources in West Virginia was a
secondary benefit. Hardwood timber was the first resource. For count-
less generations semisubsistence-farming mountain men had earned
cash for taxes and a few store-bought luxuries by selectively cutting a
few trees from the ridges, snaking them with mule or horse-power to a
creek or river, then floating them down to permanent lumber mills in
such faraway places as Nashville and Lexington. Many of these same
native farmers throughout the South cut ties and sold them to railroad
companies as construction approached, subsistence farmers earning
small cash from the agents of the world system that would destroy their
simple economy of barter and work exchange. By about 1880 a great
timber boom got underway, spearheaded by large outside companies.
The C&O, then the Norfolk & Western, the Virginian, the Louisville &
Nashville, and other lines pushed spurs out from their trunklines to
serve such corporations as Champion Paper and Lumber of Hamilton,
Ohio. The lumber companies secured timber rights on ridges from landowners who, of course, did not cultivate such land and regarded the
cash as a bonanza. Champion bought many thousands of acres outright
(especially in western North Carolina) and later conducted scientific re-
forestation and restoration of cutover land. Most, however, practiced
the policy of cut out and get out. They laid their own rails and pushed
portable mills into the forests, cut, sawed, and moved on. Other companies operating on steep slopes built great wooden flumes to carry
water from damned mountain creeks and float logs to mills on level
ground. Sometimes agriculture was disrupted or destroyed for miles
around such operations. Rich cove land dried up, creek- and riverbanks
were changed. By 1910 the development of mechanized logging—Shay
locomotives, overhead cableway skidders, and larger and faster band-

saws—improved the efficiency of the lumber companies and hastened the ecological damage.[7]

Timber cutting in southern Appalachia reached its high plateau in 1909; that year 36 percent of all the hardwood harvested in the United States came from this subregion. A decade later the percentage was almost the same—35—but during the 1920s signs of depletion appeared. In 1929 the Appalachian share dropped to 31 percent, and many companies closed down or moved west to new fields. The great half-century boom was over even before the construction bust of the depressed 1930s. It is no accident that the movement to convert many of the cut-over swatches of Appalachia and the Ozarks (where a similar history transpired) to taxpayer-supported national parks and forests began at this time.[8]

The Appalachian coal boom began shortly after timbering got underway and closely paralleled its course to ruin. Large outside-owned mining companies arrived near the new rail lines of southern West Virginia in the 1880s, in eastern Kentucky shortly after 1900, and in southwestern Virginia and eastern Tennessee by about 1910. Before 1900 the unionized mines of Pennsylvania, Ohio, and Illinois supplied coal and coke to Great Lakes steel producers. Once the southern mines were opened—without unions—the producers, who often owned the mines through subsidiaries, shifted major supply orders to the South. Low wages and the superior quality of the southern seams led to overdevelopment of the industry as early as the 1910s, but war in Europe saved the day. Endless trains carried southern coal to the furnaces of Pittsburgh, Cleveland, and Gary, and down Collis Huntington's line to the seaports. Operators employed local labor at first. Many mountaineers were experienced in small, family-run "truck mines." Some were afraid of working underground, but most found cash wages irresistible and the work and pace agreeable. Most southern West Virginia

7. Emil Malizia, "Economic Imperialism: An Interpretation of Appalachian Underdevelopment," *Appalachian Journal,* I (Spring, 1973), 130–37. An excellent overview of the mountaineers' first experiences with industrialization is Ronald D Eller, *Miners, Millhands, and Mountaineers: Industrialization of the Appalachian South, 1880–1930* (Knoxville, 1982), esp. 91–112. See also David Allen Corbin, *Life, Work, and Rebellion in the Coal Fields: The Southern West Virginia Miners, 1880–1922* (Urbana, 1981), 1–24, which is very effective on the political and judicial framework of the rise of the coal industry. On preindustrial logging, see also William Lynwood Montell, *The Saga of Coe Ridge: A Study in Oral History* (Knoxville, 1970), 193–201.

8. USDA, *Economic and Social Problems,* 35; Eller, *Miners, Millhands,* 109–12.

mines had drift or slope shafts, not vertical ones with elevators. Workers could walk in, cut and load coal by themselves, have it weighed, and walk out when they pleased. There was little factory-style management discipline, and so, many miners found the work compatible with farming. Soon the numbers of native miners were utterly inadequate for the coal boom, however, and many thousands of migrants entered the mountains. Companies recruited flatland blacks from as far away as the Gulf States and shipped them in sealed railway cars to southern West Virginia (especially McDowell County) and to southwestern Virginia. Foreigners came, too. By 1910 there were already about seventy-six hundred Italian miners in West Virginia alone. The area around Boomer, in Fayette County, became predominantly Italian and Afro-American. Serbo-Croatians crowded Buffalo Creek in Logan County. Remarkable ethnic stews appeared in the mines of northern Alabama also, where Italians and Czechs worked with native whites and blacks.[9] Thus, well before American entry into World War I, parts of Appalachia bore little resemblance to the romantic picture of homogeneity and isolation.

By 1924 the coal boom was over in most parts of the mountains. The mines had been overproducing since 1919. A peacetime economy required less coal, and hydroelectric power had begun substantially to replace coal in the generation of electricity. Mechanization of coal mining, which had been proceeding rapidly since 1915, also had a permanent impact on employment. Then came violent strikes in the southern fields. By 1930 (as with the timber industry) there were widespread closings, and though some black and foreign-born migrants remained, most seem to have moved on. Natives were once more preponderant in mining and timber areas, but most were unemployed.[10] The age of industry was past. Modernization had extracted great wealth in natural resources, created temporary semiskilled employment, damaged the en-

9. Eller, *Miners, Millhands,* 128–75; Corbin, *Life, Work, and Rebellion,* 25, 38, 61–67; John W. Hevener, *Which Side Are You On? The Harlan County Coal Miners, 1931–39* (Urbana, 1978), 1–13. On white immigrants, see also William L. Giacomo, oral history of Virginia Ellen Perkins Giacomo, April 16, 1973, and Anna Laura Kovich, oral history of Joseph Anderson Kovich, n.d. (*ca.* 1975) (Microfilmed typescripts, both in Marshall University Oral History of Appalachia Collection [MUOHA]); Selena Cason, oral histories of John Sokira, July 24, 1975, and John Gioiello, August 7, 1975 (Both typescripts in Samford University Oral History Program, Birmingham).

10. Eller, *Miners, Millhands,* 155–75. On labor violence, see Corbin, *Life, Work, and Rebellion* on the Cabin Creek (1912–13) and Logan-Mingo (1919–22) struggles; and Hevener, *Which Side Are You On?* on the Harlan County strikes of the 1930s. The coal boom came late to Harlan and did not end until the onset of the Depression. See Hevener, *Which Side Are You On?* 9–10.

vironment, and wrought havoc with the semisubsistence economy. On the eve of the Great Depression, many highlanders had already forgotten how to live on the land. It is little wonder they became early welfare clients of the New Deal. A pathetic cycle was complete.

As mountain folk had sold, leased, or been swindled out of their woodlands beginning in the 1880s, the vast range so necessary to the self-sustaining mode of life began to shrink. As early as 1900, absentees—often from New York, Boston, Baltimore, and London—owned 90 percent of the land in Mingo and Logan counties and 60 percent of Boone and McDowell counties in southern West Virginia. Open ranging of hogs and cattle persisted into the 1920s in some places, but overall livestock production declined disastrously. By 1930, it is estimated, southern Appalachian hogs numbered only 39 percent of the 1880 figure. The effect of the alienation (and sometimes the destruction) of land was compounded by farmers' growing appetite for cash, whetted first by part-time employment, then forced by full-time specialized work that wrenched them away from farming altogether. Hillbillies became people without places, on the move, tied not to the cycle of farm work but to the vagaries of industrial opportunity. More southern West Virginia miners (78.8 percent) lived in company-owned housing than did miners in Pennsylvania's bituminous fields (50.7 percent) or in the eastern Ohio fields (24.3 percent) or those of southern Indiana and Illinois (8.5 percent). Southerners moved more often than northern miners, too. In 1923 more than 90 percent of northern miners had lived in the same place for at least five years, but in southern West Virginia only 26 percent of miners had enjoyed such stability. Thus had America's last self-sufficient folk become, like sharecroppers in the plantation areas, footloose and dependent. When the mines and mills shut down, many went north. Others, whose families still maintained farms, went home to overcrowding, to eroding ridges and spoiled creeks where the hogs no longer roamed.[11]

Southern Appalachia in 1930 presented a tragic portrait of postindustrial ruin and agricultural dislocation. New Dealers would attempt to measure and solve the problems. Economic and social surveys by the FERA, the BAE, the Forest Service, and the Tennessee Valley Authority (TVA), which survive in the National Archives, remain invaluable sources on the area at the end of its first industrial adventure. Yet significant parts of what is generally regarded as Appalachia were not touched

11. Eller, *Miners, Millhands,* xix–xxx, 162–63, 197; Corbin, *Life, Work, and Rebellion,* 4, 40–41.

MAP 9
Farming by Crop Type in Southern Appalachia, 1930

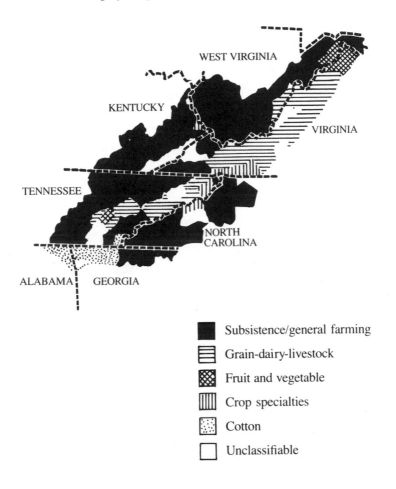

■ Subsistence/general farming

▤ Grain-dairy-livestock

▨ Fruit and vegetable

▥ Crop specialties

░ Cotton

☐ Unclassifiable

SOURCES: Charles Johnson *et al.* (comps.), *Statistical Atlas; Fifteenth Census: Agriculture,* county tables.

NOTE: Since the *Statistical Atlas* does not include West Virginia, I have classified counties in the southern and eastern sections of the state from the county tables of the census of agriculture. The Bureau of the Census used no such category as subsistence or self-sufficing but instead used general farming. So when a West Virginia county was classified as such and when acreage harvested was modest and livestock for sale were few, I have assumed it met Johnson's criteria for self-sufficiency. Several counties—for example, Logan, Webster, and Wyoming—had so little arable land, however, that they might have been unclassifiable and better represented in white on the map.

by mining or never became dependent upon the timber companies. Others remained so distant from rails or other transportation that something approaching a genuine self-sufficiency had survived.

At the bottom of the subregion as depicted in Map 9 there are several steep hill counties on the Tennessee borders of Alabama and Georgia and one in Tennessee on the Georgia and North Carolina line where small farmers had finally adopted the cotton culture of their piedmont neighbors to the south. Theirs was a poor existence, in most respects like that of the marginal-land hill parishes of northern Louisiana and the cut-over territories of Arkansas discussed in the first chapter. One county in southeastern Tennessee and several in northern Virginia and northeastern West Virginia were part of the fruit-vegetable South also described in Chapter 1. The Tennessee county (Rhea) specialized in truck crops and berries for the Chattanooga market. (Dayton, scene of the notorious "Monkey Trial" in 1925, was the principal town of Rhea County.) The Virginia and West Virginia counties grew apples primarily. Along the North Carolina border in southwestern Virginia, northeastern Tennessee, and nearby western North Carolina and in one eastern Kentucky county, farmers grew enough market tobacco and especially corn to be classified as crop specialists. Their culture resembled that of much of the row-crop flatland and hill South described earlier, but in the mountains crop specialists were far more likely to be white, own the land they worked, have no sharecroppers, and work with even less machinery than other southerners. They were also more likely to "live at home"—that is, to subsist on homegrown and homemade food and goods and to avoid the debt syndrome—than seaboard crop specialists. A larger area of this version of Appalachia—in Virginia (particularly the Valley), the eastern border of West Virginia (especially the Greenbrier Valley), and Tennessee—was grain-dairy-livestock country. Tenancy (sharecropping in particular) was very low, largely, no doubt, because broadcast small grains require so little labor compared to row crops such as corn. As in much of the Northeast and Middle West, farm families made do here with family labor, supplemented at harvest with a few hired hands, often youths from nearby towns.[12]

Those parts of the map that appear in white and black represent what

12. See county tables in Charles Johnson *et al.* (comps.), *Statistical Atlas of Southern Counties: Listing and Analysis of Socio-economic Indices of 1104 Southern Counties* (Chapel Hill, 1941), and for West Virginia, the county tables of the 1930 census of agriculture. On the differences between mountain and seaboard crop specialists, see Vance, *Human Geography of the South*, 247–48.

is conventionally assumed to be the "real" Appalachia, the parts lying in postindustrial ruins, and the remote, "primitive" homelands of semi-subsistence farmers. With the exception of white map spots that show urban counties—Knoxville and Chattanooga are readily recognizable—these are indeed the sections of the subregion most different from the cotton and row-crop South, and they deserve special exploration.

In 1930 most of the unclassified rural areas on the map were ripped-up, overpopulated mountain slums, their people abandoned by the sick timber and coal industries, their land inadequate for a return to subsistence farming. Wise County, in southwestern Virginia by the Kentucky border (once home to novelist John Fox, Jr.) is an example. In 1930 its population of 51,167—or 121.8 per square mile—was denser than any rural county in the state. The topography was rough, the soils shallow and unproductive. The Wise Extension Service agent estimated that hardly 5 percent of the county's land was arable.[13] Nearby Harlan County, Kentucky, scene of tumultuous coal strikes beginning in 1931, was similar. There Chester Mason, a native white man, had mined coal until his employers' seam played out in 1929. He then cash-rented a small farm near the settlement of Dayheit, attempting to feed his family of eleven on corn and vegetables. A milk cow and chickens helped, but Mason was seldom able to pay his rent or buy coffee, sugar, or clothing until the New Deal began. Then his eldest son went to a Civilian Conservation Corps camp and sent home twenty-five dollars each month, the family's entire cash income.[14] Webster and Wyoming counties, West Virginia, which appear as part of the subsistence area on the map, might well have been classified as nonagricultural. Experts wrote during the mid-1930s that only about 10 percent of Webster's and 15 percent of Wyoming's land was arable. The timber industry had entered Webster in 1885; coal companies had been a secondary employer. By 1930 neither offered more than part-time work; so the inhabitants had returned to rocky farms. Wyoming had been timbering country, too, until the Virginian Railroad arrived in 1907; then coal mining began also. In 1929

13. USDA, BAE, "Preliminary Report on Relief Conditions in the Counties of Buchanan, Dickenson, and Wise, Virginia, 1936" (Typescript in Land Tenure Section project files, RG 83, NA).

14. Lizzie Farmer, "Small Farm Renter," life history of Chester Mason, n.d. (1938 or 1939) (Typescript in "Our Lives" project files, WPA in Kentucky, Kentucky State Archives, Frankfort). See also Clarence F. Barnes, "Joined Union, Lost Job," life history of Mr. and Mrs. John Blevens, n.d. (1938 or 1939), *ibid.,* which portrays a hired farm worker in Harlan County, Kentucky. On the Harlan background, see Hevener, *Which Side Are You On?* 1–32.

the mines closed and, as in Webster, offered only occasional work; so the Wyoming folk, too, were stranded.[15]

There was little that was romantic about the subsistence areas of Appalachia by the end of the 1920s, except, perhaps, in one bizarre example that demonstrates again the extremes of variety within the subregion. This was Elk Garden, the estate of Henry Carter Stuart in southwestern Virginia. A nephew of the Confederate hero, J. E. B. Stuart, Henry Stuart served as governor of Virginia, 1914–1918, and built on his property the largest cattle operation east of the Mississippi. Elk Garden embraced 6 percent of all the arable land in four counties and included a coal mine and bank as well as Stuart's feed grain and livestock interests. Scores of year-round, specialized workers performed the labor and were paid in Stuart scrip accepted at his stores. A visitor once remarked that she had never truly understood feudalism until she saw Elk Garden.[16] Most folk in the subsistence areas on the map were dependent in different ways or struggled to maintain a semblance of the old isolation and independence.

We know a great deal about some of these, especially those people who by misfortune lived in mountain valleys later flooded by TVA dam projects. The federal government was obliged to compensate and help relocate the dispossessed. So while planning and construction of the dams proceeded, agents took careful inventories of property and surveyed communities. These papers have fortunately survived the families and communities. The Norris Dam area, involving five Tennessee counties north of Knoxville, is best known. In 1934 the Norris Basin (as it became known) in many ways resembled a collection of nineteenth-century communities. Settlements of a few homes, a store, and one or two churches were spaced every four to eight miles, a distance representing a maximum horse- or mule-drawn wagon ride of half a day for the most remote farm family. Store merchants arranged some farm marketing in Knoxville and handled some cash, but much of their business resembled the barter and work-exchange management common to Georgia's upper piedmont before the arrival of cotton and plantations. Churches were generally Baptist or Methodist ones unaffiliated with regional or national governance bodies. Rural folk attended the one near-

15. FERA, Rural Problem Areas Survey Report No. 18, Appalachian-Ozark Area: Webster County, West Virginia (Typescript, November 9, 1934, in RG 83, NA), 1, 3; *ibid.*, No. 15, Wyoming County, West Virginia (Typescript, November 6, 1934), 1, 3–4.

16. Charles E. Poston and Edward L. Henson, Jr., "Henry Carter Stuart: A Patrician Facing Change," in Edward Younger and James T. Moore (eds.), *The Governors of Virginia, 1860–1970* (Charlottesville, 1982), 196–97.

est, regardless of denomination, reflecting the dictates of poor roads and the absence of public transport. Farm tenants were statistically rare, and many of these, like northerners, were related to their landlords by blood or marriage. Tenants commonly kept gardens, cows, chickens, and fattened their own hogs, too—practices often not permitted in the row-crop plantation areas of the South. Much farm and home work was accomplished by "neighboring," the team sharing of harvesting and special projects such as building barns and slaughtering livestock.[17]

Samples of TVA inventories in Anderson and Campbell counties, Tennessee, illuminate the lives of these folk. There was a married, forty-four-year-old farm owner with six children at home. He owned seventy acres of which thirty were in crops of corn, hay, and tobacco; two mules, six cows and three calves, two hogs, eighty chickens; a wagon, harnesses, tools; a seven-year-old Chevrolet; no radio or phonograph. The TVA worker valued all the family's chattels at $969.50. A thirty-four-year-old married home and garden owner with four children at home had twenty acres of which half were woods, a one-acre crop of vegetables, no work stock or tools, a single chicken valued at thirty cents and no automobile. "This family does not even have enough furniture to list," scribbled the government agent, giving the total value of movable property as $40. A fifty-seven-year-old widowed farm owner with four children at home had ninety-two acres with thirty-one in crops of corn and tobacco and fifteen of the acres on level ground; one mule, one cow, three hogs, a hundred chickens; plows and harness; a foot-pedal-operated sewing machine; and no car. She told the TVA agent she did not want electricity on her new farm. A thirty-five-year-old married sharecropper with three children in a two-room house had planted thirty-five hilly acres in corn, half an acre in tobacco; he had no tools, no work stock, one cow, and a ten-year-old T-Model Ford truck valued at $25. The remainder of his property totaled only $125. A married, seventy-seven-year-old owner with one child at home had thirty-two acres, twelve of them level and planted in corn; one mule, two cows, a shoat, fifty chickens; plows and harness; a ten-year-old phonograph; no car: total valuation of chattels, $225. A married owner, age forty-eight, with one child and three other dependents had sixty-seven acres, twenty-five in general crops but no tobacco; two mules, three cows and two calves,

17. Michael J. McDonald and John Muldowny, *TVA and the Dispossessed: The Resettlement of the Population in the Norris Dam Area* (Knoxville, 1982), 33–38, 43, 91, 106–11, 118. Neighboring was common in West Virginia, too. See Lawrence Purdy Sommerville oral history, n.d. (*ca.* 1975) (Microfilmed typescript in MUOHA).

two hogs, eighty chickens, ten bee hives; plows, a wagon, harnesses, and tools, including a corn drill; a four-year-old Chevrolet auto, a piano, cook-stove, and phonograph—all valued at $1,238, excluding the land. A married renter with seven children at home farmed thirty acres of which half were in crops (primarily corn); he had two horses and a colt, a cow and a calf, three shoats and a sow, fifty-one chickens, plows, tools, harnesses, and a sewing machine but no car, radio, or phonograph. The agent assessed all this at $485.[18]

Not a one of these Norris Basin families had electricity. Few owned stoves for cooking or heat. All used fireplaces for heat, and most cooked in them as well. Nor did a single family have indoor water or a privy. Houses ranged from two-room shacks similar to tenant cabins in the cotton country to four-, five-, seven-, and even nine-room frame houses, some of them two-story. Inside, there were few books other than the Bible, few newspapers, and fewer magazines. Both tobacco and corn acreage had increased since the late-1920s, as farmers sought cash.[19]

The Norris folk were probably better off than most semi-subsistence highlanders. They lived in river valleys on land where there was no coal and few significant timber operations. They had continued to live at home—raise most of their own food—and avoided most of the cash economy and its specialization and dependency. Other rural people scattered about the sprawling subregion also escaped, for a while. One such family lived on 160 acres of land inherited from the husband's and wife's families near Jonesville in Lee County, Virginia, in the extreme southwestern part of the state. In their early forties (in 1939) with two children at home, they lived prudently and well with few modern conveniences and little cash. They raised vegetables and tree and ground fruits and kept milk cows, hogs, and chickens. For taxes they made a little tobacco. Each holiday season they sold some fruit in Jonesville and traded surplus cream and eggs to a dairy truck driver for coffee and sugar. They owned no automobile. The Blackshire family lived a similar existence in Putnam County, West Virginia, in the Kanawha Valley west of Charleston. They plowed only thirty-five to forty acres for corn and small grains but pastured Hereford and Angus cattle for sale and home consumption. Near the farmhouse was a garden, and the family kept milk cows, hogs, and scores of chickens and ducks. Every summer they canned vegetables and made sauerkraut. Other families combined coal

18. TVA, "Relocation of Families" files for Anderson and Campbell counties, Tennessee, RG 142, Atlanta Branch, NA.
    19. *Ibid.*

mining with general farming very successfully. Carl Fleischhauer of Braxton County, in central West Virginia, worked for thirty-seven years in a mine while he and his wife raised ten children on their hundred-acre farm. Mother and older children plowed, cultivated, and kept gardens and animals; father brought home cash for taxes, good tools, and store-bought things.[20]

People whose homes had lain in the path of the heavy resource extraction industries fared less well in 1930. Avery County, in northwestern North Carolina was a sad example. Between 1880 and 1920 the county's timber was cut out; then during the 1920s companies that mined iron ore and other minerals closed down. Avery's Extension Service agent persuaded many farmers to plant truck crops and establish nurseries (especially for rhododendron) for lowland markets, but by the early 1930s these markets were depressed. So in 1934 Avery County farms were primitive hoe operations with inadequate gardens and livestock, and 43 percent of all families received FERA relief. The semi-subsistence farm families of Laurel County, Kentucky, lived poor, too. In 1927 the BAE studied the incomes of 203 households in the county. There were considerable variations in cash available. Some families raised more money crops or earned more from outside work. Average annual living expenses for these large families, however, totaled only $688, and almost half this figure represented food used, nearly all of that homegrown.[21]

Many farmers around Mentone in the northeastern corner of Alabama, classified as cotton country by 1930, scraped existences from rugged ground and the ruins of extractive industry. Late in the 1930s a Federal Writers' Project interviewer wrote about "Dan Smith" (not his real name), who owned a small farm where he raised produce, selling surpluses from a tiny store he operated from his house. Smith carried some impoverished neighbors' accounts for years, allowing them to pay a little at a time. His wife took in the laundry of those who were better

20. Anne Davidson, life history of Beulah Handly, January 21, 1939 (Typescript in FWP life histories files, Southern Historical Collection, University of North Carolina [SHC]); Gerald Overby, oral history of Sherman Estal Blackshire, n.d. (*ca.* 1975) (Microfilmed copy in MUOHA); Carl Fleishhauer, "Cold Frosty Morning," in *Long Journey Home: Folklife in the South,* a special issue of *Southern Exposure* (Summer/Fall, 1977), 54–57.

21. FERA, Rural Problem Areas Survey Report No. 46, The Appalachian-Ozark Area: Avery County, North Carolina (Typescript, December 14, 1934), 1, 3–5, USDA, BAE, "Cost of Living and Population Trends in Laurel County, Kentucky" (Typescript, 63 pages, 1928), both in RG 83, NA.

off than the Smiths! "George Smith" (also pseudonymous) owned a twenty-acre farm near Mentone, on which he raised fruits and nuts and voraciously read federal and state agricultural bulletins, hoping to adapt and thrive. He hated cotton, he said. This Smith also operated a tiny coal mine with a pick, a shovel, and a mule. Other Appalachian Alabamians farmed and made illicit whiskey, or, as around Helena, they commuted from their rocky homes to part-time work in truck mines, shabby operations extracting leftover coal from mines abandoned during the 1920s by large companies. The work was dangerous, for supports were rotten and weak and mine mouths often caved in. Such work—along with a home garden and chicken yard—permitted many highlanders to keep their homes and avoid the terrors of migration.[22]

Such semisubsistence lives amid industrial rubble were so remote from turn-of-the-century portraits of Appalachian arcadias. Loretta Lynn, who spent her girlhood (late 1930s and early 1940s) in Butcher Holler, Johnson County, Kentucky, recollects the contrasts and contradictions within a tiny radius of the subregion. Butcher Holler was virtually inaccessible except by foot or saddle animal, but about four miles away was Van Lear, a company-owned coal town with stores and a movie theater. "Van Lear was another world," recalled Lynn. There, one Christmas when she was about twelve, she first saw electric lights at night. Once-a-month shopping and movie trips were almost always made during daylight, for the trip from the end of the paved road up the mountain to Butcher Holler was so difficult at night. The hard-surface town and mine roads gave way to a coal slag ("red dog") road topping, then "a dirt path leading alongside a creek, in the narrow space between two ridges." "As you walked up the holler," she remembered, "the path got steeper and steeper, with trees growing on both sides of you. You had this feeling of being all wrapped up in the trees and hills, real secure-like."[23]

The Ozark highlands present a smaller version of the problems confronting those who would generalize about Appalachia. The Ozarks are neither so high nor so rugged as much of Appalachia. They attracted timber companies but never mining operations on the eastern or middle

22. Covington Hall, "Mountain Merchant-Farmer," December 15, 1938, Hall, "Mountain Thinker-Experimenter," January 5, 1939, Hall, "Sam Cash, Farmer-Miner," December 4, 1938, Woodrow Hand, "Johnny Gates—Truck Miner," January 15, 1938 (Typescripts all in FWP life histories files, SHC).

23. Loretta Lynn with George Vecsey, *Loretta Lynn: Coal Miner's Daughter* (New York, 1976), 24–25.

western scale. Because their people were relatively isolated from the plantation South and because many Arkansans had migrated from the southeastern highlands, Ozark folk have seemed special and apart—except where, as in New Deal problem areas surveys, they were lumped with Appalachians. More typically, Ozarkians have been perceived as quaint, persisting well into the twentieth century with a culture if not unique, then about the same as Appalachia's. Ozark people, like the Appalachians, did remain outside the modern commercial world longer, so their handicrafts and oral traditions remained intact after much of the United States had become urban and industrialized and after the professionalization of anthropology and folklore studies, which focused on such places. The Ozarks, like the other highlands, then, have attracted scholars and romancers, virtually all of whom have been smitten with the beauty of the area.[24]

Much of this peculiar subregion, as it is usually mapped, lies in Missouri as well as in northwestern Arkansas. The Missouri part is excluded here for reasons historical and arbitrary: the Missouri Ozarks are well connected by rivers to the central and northern parts of the state, rendering them arguably less "southern" than other border areas of the South. (By contrast, the Bootheel of southeastern Missouri, on the Mississippi, was connected by that river and especially by its cotton-corn agriculture to the southern deltas below.) Settlers in the Missouri Ozarks were probably more ethnically diverse and northern, too. Map 10, then, presents approximately the northwestern quadrant of Arkansas, according to crop type by counties.

Northwestern Arkansas in 1930 resembled the southern rim of Appalachia. Benton and Fayette counties in the extreme northwest enjoyed relative commercial prosperity with their diversified grain-dairy-livestock and fruit-based economies. Marion County at the northeast and all the southern counties in the quadrant were poor places where cotton culture had been adopted on inhospitable land by farmers in need of cash. This is especially apparent in the southern tier of counties, through which the Arkansas River and many tributaries course. There narrow parcels of land supported small-scale cotton operations and influenced much of the economy of the broader area toward the cash

24. See Russell L. Gerlach, *Immigrants in the Ozarks: A Study in Ethnic Geography* (Columbia, Mo., 1976). A sample of scholarship as well as romance is Otto Ernest Rayburn, *Ozark Country* (New York, 1941). The premier Ozark folklorist was Vance Randolph. A small sample of his scholarship includes *An Ozark Anthology* (Caldwell, Idaho, 1940); *Ozark Magic and Folklore* (New York, 1947); and *Pissing in the Snow & Other Ozark Folktales* (New York, 1977).

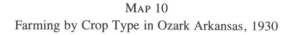

MAP 10

Farming by Crop Type in Ozark Arkansas, 1930

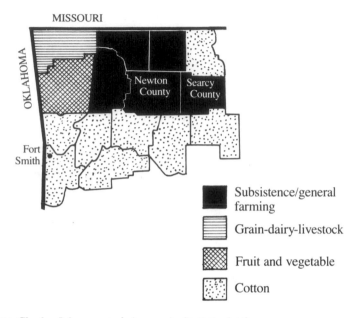

SOURCE: Charles Johnson *et al.* (comps.), *Statistical Atlas.*

nexus and dependency. Most of the farmers in the cotton counties probably lived humble, semisubsistence lives very much like those of the Alabama and Georgia mountaineers whose territories had also been recently invaded by cotton.[25]

Of the fifteen counties in the quadrant, only five were classified as self-sufficing in 1930. Except for the absence of the coal-mining towns and coal-ruined hills of Loretta Lynn's Johnson County, Kentucky, they seem very much like counties classified the same way on the map of Appalachia. Newton and Searcy counties are illustrative. Both were all white and dirt poor. Much of Newton was to become part of the Ozark National Forest, and by 1938 hardly one-tenth of its land was devoted to crops—some corn, small grains, a little tobacco and cotton. Diamond Cave near Jasper attracted tourists and some service employment; hunters and fishermen appeared occasionally; some timber companies and cooperages provided uncertain jobs. In 1935 the Searcy Extension Service agent reported that barely 50,000 of the county's 431,000-odd acres

25. See Arkansas tables in Charles Johnson et al. (comps.), *Statistical Atlas.*

were truly arable, but 200,000 acres were farmed. Even in this rugged area farmers harvested cotton on 10 percent of their land. During the 1920s many farmers had tried dairying with disappointing results because of inadequate markets. There was practically no industry either. By 1934 nearly all the small sawmills and stave factories were no longer operating. Most unlike the Appalachian South, all five Ozark Arkansas subsistence counties lost population between 1920 and 1930. Searcy's decline was most precipitous, 24.2 percent; Newton lost 5.7 percent.[26]

So Ozark Arkansas had begun before 1930 the first painful step toward adjustment: depopulation. There remained the problem of crop adjustment—elimination of cotton and reduction of other row crops and capitalization of cattle and feed-grain operations, which, in the new world of commerce that must embrace every farmer remaining, would be the future. The ruined and remote parts of Appalachia faced much more difficult problems. So many there had become dependent upon sick or dead industries, and during the 1920s their numbers had grown rather than declined. Kentucky counties with less industry and more traditional, semisubsistence families were no better off. Johnson County gained 17.1 percent during the 1920s, Knox 8.7 percent, and Laurel 6.5 percent.[27] New Deal welfare and workfare programs would ease the transition somewhat (just as Loretta Lynn recalled), but dramatic and traumatic transformation now seemed the only alternative to starvation or permanent dependency upon the government for most families. Frontier-style farming was doomed.

There is a cruel legend postulating the stupidity—and thus justifying the doom—of old mountain farmers. Supposedly lacking any notion of gravity or the effect of rainwash on their land, they were said to find it somehow convenient to plow crop rows up and down steep slopes. The story circulated widely by the 1930s and was employed by conservationists and agronomists both to condemn Appalachian farming practices and to illustrate the necessity for Department of Agriculture and Tennessee Valley Authority reform programs.[28] Conceivably some high-

26. FWP Newton County history files, Arkansas History Commission, Little Rock; FERA, Rural Problem Area Survey Report No. 35, The Appalachian-Ozark Area: Searcy County, Arkansas (Typescript, January 2, 1935, in RG 83, NA); county tables in Charles Johnson *et al.* (comps.), *Statistical Atlas.*

27. See county tables for Kentucky in Charles Johnson *et al.* (comps.), *Statistical Atlas.*

28. The historian Thomas D. Clark is one who helped disseminate this and other legends of southern farming practices. See Clark's *The Emerging South* (New York, 1961), 57–103, and *Three Paths to the Modern South: Education, Agriculture, and Conservation* (Athens, Ga., 1965), 81–90 and *passim.*

land farmer may actually have persuaded a mule or horse to drag a plow rig in such an improbable manner. More likely the legend illustrates the stupidity—or at least the condescension—of outsiders. Late in the 1930s an eastern Tennessee farmer with half a century's experience on the land explained agronomy in remote Appalachia plainly to a Federal Writers' Project interviewer: "I hear that some city folks say that we mountain farmers are so ignorant that we plow up and down a hill and that this causes the top soil to wash away. Not a bit of truth in that!" Neither he nor anyone he had ever known in Tennessee or in western North Carolina, where he had begun farming, had ever broken ground or formed rows that way. Such talk revealed "pure down fools," the farmer declared. "They ought to know that a horse can't pull a plow up a hill and a man can't hold a plow going down hill." Mountaineers, he argued, knew "all about terracing land to stop it washing. But it takes a team to throw up terraces and ain't many farmers up here owns more than one head of stock." Steep land would defeat a farmer fortunate enough to have a team, anyway. "One horse walks higher than his mate in throwing up ground for a terrace. The horses don't pull together, the harness gets broken." The old farmer knew the only workable system of row cropping on rugged terrain: careful cultivation of creekbanks ("cove land") for a few years while the loose soil lasted, then clearance of new cove land, and so on. "I bought five hundred acres when I first come to Tennessee so that I'd have plenty of new land later on," he reflected.[29] Such was the traditional system of the sparsely settled, semifrontier land the farmer knew as a young man in the 1880s. Considerably before the 1930s, when he spoke, population pressures on the fragile mountain environment had rendered this system no longer tenable.

Between 1900 and 1930 the populations of mountain counties in Appalachian states grew by 55 percent. (Nonmountain counties of the same states gained 33 percent.) Russell County, in southwestern Virginia, had 6,714 souls in 1830, and sufficient land to crop coves, range animals, and move on. In 1930 Russell's folk numbered 25,957. The median household size was 5.7, and there were only about two or two and a half acres of tillable land for each person in the county. Mining was virtually dead as an alternative employment, and poverty was "chronic," to use the word of a New Deal investigator. Yet, wrote the federal agent, there seemed to be "no tempering of the reproductive im-

29. Quoted in W. T. Couch (ed.), *These Are Our Lives* (Chapel Hill, 1941), 84–85.

pulse." Knox County, Kentucky, near Harlan, grew by only about 2,000 during the troubled 1920s, to a population of 26,266 in 1930. Then came a wave of mine closings and violent strikes, which shook the entire area of southeastern Kentucky. In 1932 a survey estimate set Knox's population at approximately 30,000, a growth in only two years about double that of the entire decade of the 1920s. This disastrous windfall of humans was owing not to a peculiar surge in the birth rate, but to the return to Knox of working-age adults who had lost their industrial jobs elsewhere. Many other Appalachian counties, already overcrowded with the unemployed, witnessed such augmentations also.[30]

This return of the natives, which seems to have begun before the end of the 1920s, exacerbated the pressures on the land and perhaps fed the legend of plowing up and down hills and ruining land through stupidity. For throughout the 1930s cropland and the number of farms expanded rapidly in the mountains. Farmers plowed cutover areas and converted ridge pastures to cropland. So the wilderness was further diminished out of grim necessity, not idiotic vertical plowing. As steep places came under the plow, leaching, washing, and serious erosion followed. The Norris Basin of Tennessee illustrates the syndrome in a nonmining area. In 1870 Campbell and Grainger counties had population densities of about thirty-five and forty-five persons per square mile. By the mid-1930s the density of the Norris Dam purchase areas of the counties was more than sixty per square mile. A 1907 Department of Agriculture study of Grainger County had already revealed a serious shortage of alluvial bottom and terrace lands, and corn production on ridge land was only five to thirty bushels per acre. Then during 1929–1934 young people thrown out of city work returned to their farm families for succor. Returnees were accommodated on the only land remaining—farther up the ridges.[31]

Semisubsistence mountain folk had always grown corn to fatten livestock before slaughter. Many had also grown a little burley tobacco for home use and sale. Now, in the Depression, farmers turned to corn and tobacco as cash crops, replacements for the public work that was no longer available. Landowners who established tobacco acreage before 1933 received permanent acreage allotments from the Agricultural Adjustment Administration. These guaranteed cash income each year for

30. USDA, *Economic and Social Problems*, 5; FERA, Rural Problem Areas Survey Report No. 45, The Appalachian-Ozark Area: Russell County, Virginia (Typescript, December 14, 1934, in RG 83, NA), 1; *ibid.*, No. 21, Knox County, Kentucky (Typescript, November 15, 1934), 1, 3.

31. Michael McDonald and John Muldowny, *TVA and the Dispossessed*, 74–75, 80–82.

the fortunate, but the allotments were very small, hardly adequate to support a family. In Lincoln County, West Virginia, tobacco crops served as collateral for credit at country stores even before the AAA allotment system was in place. During the Depression this practice apparently spread, along with conversion of increased corn production into illegal whiskey as well as into pork for sale. The daughter of a Norris Basin physician recalled that her father would be unpaid for months before corn crops were harvested. After local rustic distilleries had wrought their conversions, Kentucky bootleggers would drive down "and haul moonshine out by the carloads." Then "you'd know that so-and-so would be out before long to pay the doctor's bills." The Tennessee moonshiners "all had big families," the daughter recalled, and because so many "of them lived back on ridge places and . . . wanted to send their children to school," they mined the thin soils for more corn and cash.[32] Such adjustments to depression and overpopulation could not last very long.

The travails and slow progress of change in three remote Appalachian counties illustrate highland adjustments in the longer term. Logan County, in southwestern West Virginia, lay in the heart of the coal fields and never promised more than marginal farming. Johnson County, in eastern Kentucky, was similar, but with somewhat less rugged terrain. Both of these counties would no longer be classified as agricultural by the 1950s. Part of Sevier County, Tennessee (east of Knoxville), was subsumed by the Great Smokies National Park during the early 1930s. Much of Sevier is good, rolling land, however, which eventually became part of a much enlarged grain-livestock South. As early as the mid-1920s, however, all three counties were in dire straits. The growing populations of all three were at least 90 percent rural. Sevier had no coal or coal towns; so nearly all its country folk farmed. Logan and Johnson farms were virtually all located on dirt roads. There was one tractor in all of Logan in 1925, not a single one in Johnson; and hardly anyone bought commercial fertilizers. Nearly all farmers kept livestock and poultry, grew corn, and attempted to feed themselves. In Sevier about 350 farms were located by hard surface or gravel roads, but more than 2,800 stood by dirt roads. There were about two dozen tractors in the entire county in 1925, and almost a quarter of the farmers purchased commercial fertilizers, too; but Sevier farmers, like most Appalachians,

32. Gregory W. Cyrus, oral history of Sesco W. Sowards, July 8, 1974 (Microfilmed typescript in MUOHA). Quotation from Michael McDonald and John Muldowny, *TVA and the Dispossessed,* 32.

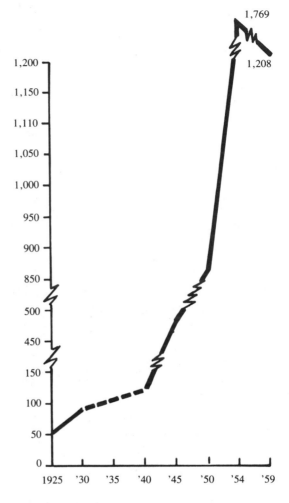

FIGURE 8
Tractors on Selected
Remote Appalachian
County Farms,
1925–1959

SOURCE: Censuses of agriculture, 1925–1959,
county tables. Data for 1935 not available.

NOTE: Counties included are Logan and Randolph, West Virginia; Johnson and Knox, Kentucky; Sevier and Campbell, Tennessee; and
Scott, Virginia.

also kept livestock and poultry for home use as well as for sale, planted
corn and vegetables, and tried to live at home. Tobacco was never significant in Logan and Johnson, but tellingly, Sevier farmers, with fewer
off-farm work opportunities and greater commercial farming potential,

FIGURE 9
Number of Farms in
Selected Remote
Appalachian Counties,
1920–1959
(in thousands)

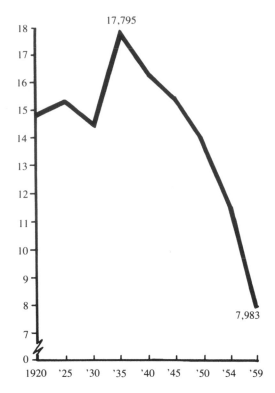

SOURCE: Censuses of agriculture, 1920–1959, county tables.

NOTE: Counties included are Logan and Randolph, West Virginia; Johnson and Knox, Kentucky; Sevier and Campbell, Tennessee; and Scott, Virginia.

turned to tobacco in droves during the mid-1920s. By 1929 one-fifth of them grew burley; by 1939 more than half.[33]

Sevier's resort to tobacco is no indicator of good economic health, of course, but rather the opposite. About 90 percent of the county's farmers continued to rely upon corn, too, throughout the 1930s. During these same years the number of work animals, as well as the number of

33. Data from county tables of the federal censuses of agriculture, 1925–59. The material on these counties is presented in detail in Sharon Edwards, "Transformation of Traditional Farming in Southern Appalachia: A Study of Agricultural Transition in Three Counties, 1925–1959" (Typescript graduate seminar paper, Miami University, November 11, 1983).

farms with draft animals, actually declined. Horses, which outnumbered mules, dropped from around 3,100 in 1925 to only about 1,800 in
1935, rising again to about 2,300 in 1940 before declining once more.
Mules, of which there were almost 2,900 in 1925, declined in numbers
throughout the 1930s and 1940s. In the meantime Sevier residents
bought few tractors before World War II. One must assume, therefore,
that many farmers either borrowed or rented others' animals or were reduced to cultivating with hoes. Both mules, which predominated, and
horses declined steadily in Johnson County, but not a single tractor was
recorded in the census until 1940—and then only one. In Logan County
farmers acquired more mules and lost or gave up horses during the early
1930s, then reversed the pattern during the late 1930s. Mules continued
to decline to insignificance, while the number of horses grew steeply to
a peak in 1945. Assuming that Logan draft horses were not expensive
purebred animals, their displacement of mules between 1935 and 1945
is probably an indicator of economic distress. Mules were always more
costly than scrub horses. Meanwhile, Logan farmers had acquired a
grand total of two tractors by 1940, eleven by 1945.[34]

Migration of surplus population, the paving of roads, electrification
of farms, and a variety of other modern factors gradually brought an end
to most semisubsistence agriculture, driving out those people unable to
capitalize operations and stabilizing farmers (especially in Sevier) who
were capable of specialized commercial production. The numbers of
tractors in Logan and Johnson began to grow during the 1940s and
climbed rapidly during the 1950s, although at the end of that decade
there still was not a tractor for every farm. In Sevier acquisition of tractor power was more rapid and complete. The number of farms and
acreage of cropland declined everywhere after 1940. In Logan and
Johnson there was more fallow cropland than harvested land during the
1950s. Of those farmers who remained, about 40 percent were buying
commercial fertilizers by 1954. In Sevier County the figure was about
85 percent, and approximately 80 percent of farmers were raising tobacco in the 1950s, while corn declined and cattle, poultry, and feed-
grain production increased.[35]

Map 11 reveals the striking changes wrought in the broader area
since 1930. Gone were self-sufficing counties. Many of these, including
Logan and Johnson, were now part of an enlarged territory where farm-

34. Censuses of agriculture, 1925–59; Edwards, "Transformation of Traditional
Farming."
35. Edwards, "Transformation of Traditional Farming," figures in appendices.

MAP 11

Farming by Crop Type in Southern Appalachia, 1959

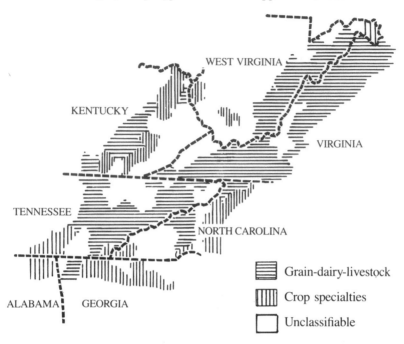

▤	Grain-dairy-livestock
⊞	Crop specialties
☐	Unclassifiable

SOURCE: *Census of Agriculture, 1959,* county tables.

ing was no longer a significant part of the economy. Others, such as
Sevier, had been transformed into grain-dairy-livestock counties. Also
gone were the scattered fruit-vegetable counties of Virginia, West Virginia, and Tennessee. In this category California and Florida producers
had triumphed in the new chain supermarkets, and though fruit and vegetable production actually increased overall in the subregion, grain and
cattle production became dominant in those counties that had earlier
specialized in fruits and vegetables for nearby urban markets. Gone, as
well, were the cotton-dominated economies of counties at the southern
rim of Appalachia. Some converted to grain-cattle operations, others
(especially those with more level land) to row crops such as corn and
soybeans. Many counties in northern Georgia, southeastern Tennessee,
and western North Carolina, and a few in eastern Kentucky and southwestern Virginia, also made the transition—like so many other American farms—to corn-soybean systems. Because level or gently sloping
corn land was so scarce in the broader region, however, most farmers

MAP 12

Farming by Crop Type in Ozark Arkansas, 1959

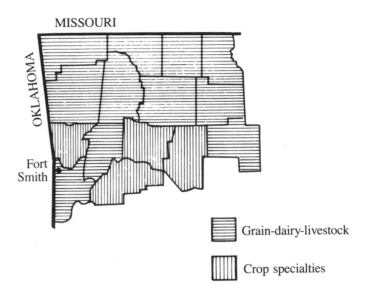

Grain-dairy-livestock

Crop specialties

SOURCE: *Census of Agriculture, 1959,* county tables.

finally quit clean-row production, the mainstay of overcrowded Depression farms and the sustenance of moonshiners and hog-raising live-at-home folk. Along with corn went hog production, culminating the second stage of the decline of this kind of livestock in the mountains, which began with the precipitous decline brought about between 1880 and 1920 by industrialization and the alienation of open rangeland. With so little corn for feed, by 1954 only about 16 percent of Appalachian farmers reported hogs and pigs sold. Forested slopes and grassy pastures erode little and support cattle well; so most counties in the subregion joined the great valleys of Virginia and Tennessee in feed-grain, cattle, and in some places, dairy operations.[36]

The other southern highlands—Ozark Arkansas—accomplished a similar long-term accommodation to the world of commercial agriculture. As Map 12 demonstrates, eleven of the fifteen counties in the

36. In addition to the county tables in the censuses of agriculture, esp. for 1954 and 1959, see Roy E. Proctor and T. Kelley White, "Agriculture: A Reassessment," in Thomas Ford (ed.), *Southern Appalachian Region,* 97, 99.

northwestern quadrant had grain-dairy-livestock economies by 1959. Only Benton County in the extreme northwest had had such a specialty in 1930. Washington County, just below Benton, had been a fruit-vegetable county in 1930, but like comparable spots in Appalachia, it lost out to interstate shippers from the year-round growing areas of Florida, Texas, and California. Newton and nearby counties were much given over to woodlands, especially the Ozark National Forest. Those farmers remaining had converted cotton and other row-crop land to pasture and feed grains. Of the southern tier of counties in the quadrant, formerly devoted to low-yield cotton production, four had converted to crop specialties, primarily corn and soybeans.[37] So like Appalachia, the mountains and hills of the Ozarks came to be almost indistinguishable in basic agricultural terms from most other humid parts of the nation. They were commercial and specialized, and they concentrated upon much the same crops as, say, Ohio and Illinois. By many specific indices, however, the highlands remained significantly different from both the Middle West and the neoplantation South.

Throughout the 1930s and 1940s the vaunted procreativity of the Appalachian folk continued without abatement. The subregion's population grew 18 percent despite substantial out-migration. The rural-farm population declined 14 percent, but this was not nearly enough to accommodate the lowered labor requirements of mechanized farming. (The national rural-farm population declined by somewhat more than 20 percent during these years.) So farms (as well as cities and coal towns) were relatively crowded with surplus humans. Following the streams of previous migrants became the only option for many of them during the 1950s.[38]

Farm sizes are another index. In the broader valleys and plateaus farms grew to average about 125 acres and more, but in more remote and rugged parts of Appalachia the net change between 1920 and the end of the 1950s was almost nil. During the early 1920s and again during the early 1930s farms shrank, probably through subdivision among relatives and because of hard times. After 1935 average farm sizes began to grow once more, but ever so gradually until the mid-1950s, when the typical farm at last expanded toward almost the same tiny size it had been in 1920. This poor cycle contrasts most dramatically with that of

37. County tables of the censuses of agriculture, esp. for 1959.
38. Proctor and White, "Agriculture," 87–88; James S. Brown and George A. Hillery, Jr., "The Great Migration, 1940–1960," in Thomas Ford (ed.), *Southern Appalachian Region,* 54–78.

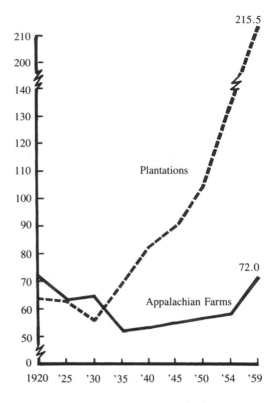

FIGURE 10
Average Farm Sizes in Selected Cotton Plantation and Remote Appalachian Counties, 1920–1959 (in acres)

SOURCE: Censuses of agriculture, 1920–1959, county tables.

NOTE: The cotton counties are Macon and Sumter, Alabama; Crittenden and St. Francis, Arkansas; Sumter, Georgia; Tensas Parish, Louisiana; Noxubee and Washington, Mississippi; Edgefield, South Carolina; and Harrison, Texas.

the cotton plantation areas, where federal subsidies and mechanization brought about rapid growth in average farm size after 1930.

Appalachia's nonfarm rural economy was also less stable than that of most other American subregions after World War II. Coal, the great employer of country folk, especially in West Virginia and eastern Kentucky, is emblematic. World War II provoked a new coal boom, which peaked in 1947, when 631 million tons were mined nationally. Annual production, to which the 3,255 mines of Appalachia contributed substantially, averaged about 200 million tons between 1944 and 1954.

After 1953, however, the coal market entered a period of wild shifts in demand and production. Generally, coal production declined. After 1950 railroads began to abandon coal-fired steam locomotives in favor of diesel engines. Indeed, diesels came to pull all coal trains from Appalachia to the Middle West and Atlantic ports. The great postwar surge in home building boosted sales in oil and natural gas furnaces, too, not coal burners. Hydraulic power turned more dynamos to produce electricity until the 1960s, when high demand obliged power companies to buy more coal again. All these difficulties were compounded by quantum strides in the automation of coal mining. Strip mining, the use of enormous bulldozers and shovels to remove the ground cover from seams close to the surface, dates back at least to 1920. During the 1950s strip mining became common in the Appalachian fields and elsewhere, and displaced many workers. Coal operators also developed so-called auger mining, a method of probing deeply into hills and mountainsides with huge drills, sixteen and twenty inches in diameter. When reversed, the drills, or augers, dropped coal in conveyors to trucks or trains. Few miners were required. Then, beginning in 1948, operators introduced continuous mining machines for deep mines. These fearsome contraptions, costing about one million dollars each, and guided by only one or two men each, performed virtually all the functions of mining—undercutting, drilling for blasting, and loading—which previously had required many men and many hours of labor. By 1957 there were six hundred such machines at work, producing close to 18 percent of all deep mine coal in the nation. Appalachia, home of so many slope and drift mines, had fewer of the behemoths than Pennsylvania and Illinois, but cumulatively, mechanization and shaky demand wrought more hardship in long-suffering southern Appalachia. In 1950 coal mining employed about 203,000 men in the subregion. By mid-decade the average number working daily was only about 120,000.[39]

World War II provoked a shorter-lived revival of the mountain lumber industry. By the 1950s the boom was over, and timber companies employed only thirty to forty thousand men, a mere 2 percent of all working people in the subregion. A few large corporations grew and harvested pine, factory-style, for paper production, but most Appalachian lumber operators were small, highly mobile, and offered only short-term or part-time work. Many such companies were obliged to work in

39. Robert F. Munn, "The Development of Strip Mining in Southern Appalachia," *Appalachian Journal,* III (Autumn, 1975), 87–92; Harold A. Gibbard, "Extractive Industries and Forestry," in Thomas Ford (ed.), *Southern Appalachian Region,* 103–10.

privately owned woodlands of modest size or to seek permits to cut timber from publicly owned forests.[40]

By the end of the 1950s the latter encompassed a huge portion of the southern mountains. In six states (West Virginia into northern Georgia), more than five million acres, or 8,419 square miles, lay in national forests, and state and county parks had also consumed additional territory since 1930. In fourteen mountain counties the United States Forest Service managed at least 40 percent of all the land in the counties. In another twenty-three counties the Forest Service controlled at least 20 percent of the land. The millions of people living in this "Appalachian Greenbelt" paid a dear price for their own and outsiders' privileges in the parks and forests. Residents, often descendants of late eighteenth- or early nineteenth-century homesteaders, were expelled when the parks were created, losing good farms as well as poor ones. Such publicly owned property then became tax exempt, in effect fixing the poverty of those remaining in the privately held parts of these counties. Personal property tax rates in these counties became considerably higher than in counties without parks or forests. By 1970 the counties in which 40 percent or more of the land was federally owned were among the least populous and poorest in the nation. Private resort development of land near the parks and forests had few positive effects and many disastrous ones for the natives. As developers bid land prices upward, locals who wished to remain as proprietors paid higher taxes. Wealthy newcomers' demands for better roads and public services drove taxes yet higher. New jobs were primarily in service occupations—menial, part-time, and low-paying. Nor did such new employment offset the subregion's deficit of jobs created by the great rollbacks in agriculture, coal mining, and timber.[41]

By 1960 the people of the highlands had made vast, painful adjustments to overcome the collapse of so much of their economy three de-

40. Munn, "Development of Strip Mining," 87–92; Gibbard, "Extractive Industries"; Si Kahn, "The Government's Private Forests," *Southern Exposure,* II (Fall, 1974), 132–44.

41. Kahn, "Government's Private Forests"; James Branscome and Peggy Matthews, "Selling the Mountains," *Southern Exposure,* II (Fall, 1974), 122–29; USDA, Economic Research Service, Agricultural Economics Report No. 69, *An Economic Survey of the Appalachian Region* (Washington, D.C., 1965), 41, 53, 67, and *passim.* See also Howard L. Gauthier, "The Appalachian Development Highway System: Development for Whom?" *Economic Geography,* XLIX (April, 1973), 103–108; and on the expulsion of natives to make way for a national park, Roy Carroll and Raymond H. Pulley, *Historic Structures Report: Little Cataloochee, North Carolina* (Boone, N.C., 1976), esp. 3–30. The Little Cataloochee community lay in Haywood County.

cades before. Millions of acres of land were abandoned. The shabby remains of semisubsistence life on remote family farms were abandoned, too, or mercifully executed at last by the manifold outside forces of the commercial world, its demands of efficiency and specialization, and the cash nexus. Tantalizing hopes of stable work in industries old and new were dimmed, if not dashed, by the vagaries of the world marketplace. The mountains were even more colonial than they had been, and the preeminent "solution" for these southern folk, as for so many of their brothers and sisters in the hills and flatlands, was not adaptation but migration.

Part Two

Modernization and Rural Life

We country folks ain't like you town folks. We don't
have to run to the store every time we get hungry. We
go to our smoke house for meat; to the hen house for
chickens an' eggs, to the cows for milk an' butter; send
our own wheat an' corn to the mill for flour an' meal;
have gardens an' orchards for vegetables, fruit; in
winter there's canned stuff, potatoes, plenty of cab-
bage, collards, turnips, an' our fire wood grows all
'round us. I don't see how you town folks live when you
have to spend money for everything, even dried beans
an' peas.
—A NORTH CAROLINA SHARECROPPER, 1938

The land lord dont al[low] tenent to hol[d] no hogs no
chickin, not a cow and no garden, no corn.
—AN EASTERN ARKANSAS SHARECROPPER, 1936

It has seemed at Possum Trot that the living go and the
dead return.
—HERMAN CLARENCE NIXON, 1941

Chapter 4
Folks, Communities,
and Economies in Flux

THE BORDERS OF VIRGINIA, KENTUCKY, AND
Tennessee meet in the ruggedly beautiful mountains around Cumberland
Gap. There native whites and a few migrants had farmed and mined
coal for generations. The gap, always an important transportation
point, had witnessed many changes before 1960: railroads and extractive heavy industries had made marks. But all the while most of the
local folk had also clung to traditional securities—the country home,
the little farm, the garden and animals—even as they ventured out to
mine and mill. Keeping and using the land and domesticated beasts were
prudent in an uncertain world, as well as very old habits. Then during
the early 1960s something quiet and very profound happened. It became
apparent, particularly to those returning to the gap after extended ab-
sences, that mining families and even farmers had abandoned their gardens, hen houses, and pigpens. Chain grocery stores had arrived and
won acceptance. Cash flowed, especially from the mines; hard times
seemed remote. So village and country folk at last gave up their old
culture of living at home in favor of living out of bags.[1] The phenome-

1. William B. Provine, author's interview, October 8, 1979, Oxford, Ohio. Provine,
now professor of history and biological sciences at Cornell University, moved to the Cum-

non of the pickup truck parked outside the Piggly Wiggly supermarket, now so common it provokes little comment, had materialized.

Self-sufficiency had been a way of life as well as an economic practice. Its abandonment occurred only gradually in the years following World War II. Nor was the resort to cash for food a uniquely southern phenomenon. This revolution in the elemental culture of country people affected every region, most noticeably the family farming sections of the Northeast and Middle West.[2] The demise of this way of life seems most poignant and ironic in the South, however, for there living at home had been the shibboleth and sacred solution among crusaders against poverty, monoculture, and the boll weevil for half a century. To county agents of the Department of Agriculture Extension Service, which had been founded in the South, keeping gardens and animals and canning and slaughtering for home use were gospel. Editors of such farm journals as the *Southern Planter* (Richmond), the *Progressive Farmer* (Raleigh and other cities), and the *Southern Cultivator* (Atlanta) eagerly joined the chorus. State legislatures appropriated funds for agricultural colleges that promoted self-sufficiency, and railroad companies sent teaching agronomists into the country in institute trains. The county agents, in particular, promoted living at home among the young, white and black. They demonstrated methods of improving corn yields to provide feed for swine, then organized pig clubs for community sharing and propagation of hogs. Black farmers celebrated home production during "Ham and Eggs" weeks at Fort Valley, Georgia, and other places. White farmers did the same at Auburn, Alabama; Starkville, Mississippi; and elsewhere. That the county agents, railroad officers, bankers, and professors also promoted commercial farming and focused their attention upon landowners with commercial potential adds another level of irony within the ironic defeat of the live-at-home movement.[3]

---

berland Gap with his parents during the early 1960s. The expression "living out of bags" seems to have been common throughout the region and was used in apposition to "living at home" or "out of the smokehouse and hen house." See Annie Ruth Davis, life history of SeeLula Demry, March 7, 1939 (Typescript in FWP life histories files, Southern Historical Collection, University of North Carolina [SHC]). Demry lived in Marion, S.C.

2. John L. Shover, *First Majority—Last Minority: The Transforming of Rural Life in America* (DeKalb, Ill., 1976).

3. On the origins and early history of agricultural education and the Extension Service, see Roy V. Scott, *The Reluctant Farmer: The Rise of Agricultural Extension to 1914* (Urbana, 1970); Jack Temple Kirby, *Darkness at the Dawning: Race and Reform in the Progressive South* (Philadelphia, 1972), 131–54; Earl W. Crosby, "Building the Country Home: The Black County Agent System, 1906–1940" (Ph.D. dissertation, Miami Uni-

The triumph of living out of bags is also a significant index to the arrival of what is vaguely called modernization. When country people leave self-sufficient or nearly self-sufficient farms to live in cities and work for cash to pay for housing and food or when they remain on the land but earn cash from off-farm work or they raise only cash-producing crops, we say they are modern. Their territories have become "developed." By this measure and others the South was modern and developed by about 1960. Not only was the little-cash life of living at home rare, but paved roads and automobiles, high-cost farm machinery and chemicals, and national credit and market institutions had smothered what had remained in 1940 of the small, community-centered world of exchange and country life. As we shall see in this and the next chapter, living out of bags did not appear suddenly or in all subregions of the South simultaneously. The beginnings of modernization, at the other end of our chronological spectrum, were ever so gradual and difficult to date precisely, too.

Before 1900 most of the United States consisted of island communities—towns, villages, or small settlements surrounded by farms. The settlements existed to serve the people of the countryside as markets for farm surpluses, as suppliers and repairers of tools, as mediums for processing and exchanging grain and other products, as centers of local culture. The island communities of the South were organized around a sort of grid, with small towns or settlements located close enough so a mule- or horse-drawn wagon might travel at most half a day to the nearest church, store, mill, or gin, and return. Railroads or riverboats may have transported cash crops such as cotton from these communities on to world markets, but life for country folks remained largely premodern. They saw little cash and maintained much of the local exchange system. To railroads and a few other modern influences Congress added the free delivery of rural mail in 1896. Carriers penetrated the most isolated places and deposited not only correspondence but the advertising bro-

---

versity, 1977). The bias of the Extension Service toward scientific commercial farming is evident in these sources, which concern the period from 1903 to about 1940, and in innumerable annual reports of county agents across the South in the 1940s and 1950s, which have been sampled. See, *e.g.,* "Annual Narrative Report of D. G. Sommerville, County Agent, Colbert County, Alabama, November 30, 1947" (Typescript) in Alabama Extension Service Records, Auburn University Archives. Sommerville wrote that the demonstration farmers in his work, with whom all extension "workers spend considerable time, are the leading farmers in the county from the standpoint of efficient production, soil building and net income."

chures of distant mail-order companies. At the beginning of Rural Free Delivery service farmers actually paid ten-cent fees to receive Sears and Roebuck catalogues and other such wonders. The products and the cash required to buy them must have struck important if unmeasurable blows against local cultures and premodern economies. Newspapers and magazines and traveling circuses and other entertainments also introduced outside cultural influences. Yet cumulatively such intrusions of outside markets and cultures did not outweigh local practices. Well into the twentieth century small watermills still ground corn and wheat for a percentage of the meal or flour (as in medieval and modern Europe) both in the highlands and in the river bottomlands of the upper and lower Souths. And when Tennessee Valley Authority surveyors and inventory takers arrived in the region, they found grids of country communities still far from the full grip of the cash nexus.[4]

Change—a term used synonymously in western culture with *progress* and *modernization*—occurs every moment. People usually become aware of deep changes only after the working out of many structural processes, and once it is recognized, change seems to have occurred suddenly. Modernization transpired this way. Its impact was most intense during the 1930s and 1940s in most parts of the South, but modernization began long before and it continues still. The phenomenon manifested itself in a variety of stages at various times over the subregions of the South. The cash nexus, machines, paved roads, and supermarkets appeared earliest in the most physically accessible places, latest in the most remote. This was a southern version of a process known to most of the peoples of the world. Similar transformations occurred earlier among the peasantries of western Europe, later in the so-called Third World.[5]

4. David J. Russo, *Families and Communities: A New View of American History* (Nashville, 1974), 1–3, 41; Roger L. Ransom and Richard Sutch, *One Kind of Freedom: The Economic Consequences of Emancipation* (Cambridge, Eng., 1977), 126–48; Wayne E. Fuller, *RFD: The Changing Face of Rural America* (Bloomington, Ind., 1964), esp. 287–314; Larry Hasse, "Watermills in the South: Retardant Institutions Working Against Modernism" (Paper delivered September 21, 1983, History of Rural Life in America Symposium, Florida A & M University); Michael J. McDonald and John Muldowny, *TVA and the Dispossessed: The Resettlement of the Population in the Norris Dam Area* (Knoxville, 1982), 33–38.

5. On the nature and speed of change in history, see David Hacket Fischer, *Growing Old in America* (Expanded ed.; New York, 1978), 100. On the end of local exchange peasant culture in France, see Eugen Weber, *Peasants into Frenchmen: The Modernization of Rural France, 1870–1914* (Stanford, 1976), 39–40 and *passim*. On the height and de-

Development, that other troublesome term, is not the same, actually, as modernization. In its most vulgar usage, development includes change through capital investment, and such investment overlaps an important stage of modernization. But development in the parlance of the international scholarly community of specialists means much more. It is a set of ideal social goals beyond finance. In the words of Dudley Seers, the British authority, development is "the realization of the potential of human personality." It aims to feed everyone; to eliminate unemployment, poverty, and inequality; and to secure political and economic independence. Modernization, on the other hand, has often widened class and income inequities, fixed many people in unemployed poverty, and bred economic and political colonialism. One may fairly generalize, then, that roughly between 1920 and 1960 the American South was modernized; it was not developed. Few regions or nations are.[6]

Following are portraits of four rather distinct Souths in the throes of those changes called modernization: the remote highland South (the Appalachian and Ozark counties classified as self-sufficient or rural-industrial in 1930); the more prosperous, white-majority areas that in 1930 grew fruits, vegetables, grain, beef, and dairy cattle; the poor South (also mostly white) on marginal land in the coastal plains and hills, which in 1930 was classified as self-sufficient or cotton producing; and finally the black-majority plantation South, the row-crop areas of 1930. There are exceptions within each South, which occasionally blur distinctions among the four; but generally speaking, different soils, crops, tenancy systems, income levels, and credit institutions made for noticeably different experiences as old ways slipped away and modernization first crept, then rushed in.

The remote highland South is the most distinctive and easily described. In 1930 it was the most "backward" part of rural America, dramatically lacking—even in comparison with the rest of the South—the infrastructures and amenities of farm business and life. Few country people had gasoline-powered machinery of any kind, electricity, indoor water, or telephones. Most notably they lacked automobiles. Poor folks

---

cline of cotton sharecropping in the lower Nile Valley, see Alan Richards, "Land and Labor on Egyptian Cotton Farms, 1882–1940," *Agricultural History,* LII (October, 1978), 503–18. The basic work on preindustrial village society is Peter Laslett, *The World We Have Lost* (London, 1965).

6. See Seers, "The Meaning of Development," *International Development Review,* XI (December, 1969), 2–6.

elsewhere, including cotton sharecroppers, owned cars. Highlanders did not because roads were too poor or lacking altogether.[7] The absence of paved roads until well into the 1940s and 1950s in such rugged areas meant they remained remote, and remoteness prolonged many aspects of traditional, premodern life.

As late as 1940 a team of sociologists found in eastern Kentucky (probably Laurel County) a grid of rural communities much like the frontier layout of the Norris Basin in Tennessee, described by TVA officials several years before. The Kentucky island communities were more remote, however, with more difficult topography and no market comparable to Knoxville nearby. Even as World War II raged, the Kentucky farmers followed an annual cycle very much like that of their forebears. In the winter they repaired buildings and fences; killed hogs, cured meat, and made sausages; cared for stock; and prepared tobacco seedling beds. Such work was easily accomplished; so men and older boys often left for public work, sometimes as far away as the industrial cities of southern Ohio, returning home for visits every third or fourth week. In March they would return for full-time farm work, plowing and manuring of coves and hillsides for tobacco, corn, and hay. In April they transplanted tobacco seedlings and planted hay, corn, and potatoes. May into July was cultivation time—suckering, weeding, and aerating tobacco and corn—mostly hand and hoe work. There were no machines for such tasks, and hillside fields were too steep and rows too narrow even for work animals. All members of the family over six years old took part. By the end of July crops were considered "laid by," having been hoed three times. Children had begun school early that month. Some of the older boys and men had left for public work once more. Remaining family members cut and stacked hay during late July and early August, then cut and split tobacco stalks. In September the heavy work of harvest and preparing for winter began. Men logged or "raised coal" with pick and shovel from a nearby hillside open seam for winter fuel. Families pulled fodder in the hillside cornfields and carried bundles down in their arms to fatten hogs for December slaughter. More corn was stored for winter feed. Men and boys dug Irish and sweet potatoes. Irish potatoes were placed in deep holes outside and covered with dirt to prevent freezing; sweet potatoes went into closets in the house or a "warm" building nearby. Meanwhile women and children picked the last vegetables from backyard gardens. There was little canning, even

7. See USDA dot maps on tractors, electricity, piped-in water, telephones, and automobiles on farms, 1930, in Record Group 83, National Archives.

though pressure cookers were widely available across the nation. Most beans were dried and stored. Now, too, families stripped air-cured tobacco leaves from the previously cut stalks and tied them into small bundles ("hands") for market. Some farmers hired trucks to haul these tiny crops to Lexington; others sold their tobacco below market prices to neighbors, who then managed shipment and sale of larger amounts of this one cash crop. Finally came hog butchering, curing, and sausage making, and the cycle began anew.[8]

Life in remote industrialized counties remained largely premodern, too, for those not living in the coal towns. Loretta Lynn and her family's existence in Johnson County, Kentucky, was more primitive than the idealized self-sufficiency of the family described above. And in Mingo and McDowell counties, West Virginia, large farm families lived by nearly impassable dirt roads with remarkably little cash. By the 1930s there was little local public work in rugged southwestern West Virginia; so older boys and men, as in eastern Kentucky, left for Ohio and elsewhere. The Depression had weakened the outside industrial sector, too, however, so these highlanders needed a cash crop. Instead of tobacco, the West Virginians grew more corn and made whiskey. According to a preacher–school teacher who lived in both counties, the rural folk never desired more than a continuance of self-sufficiency; so their moonshining operations were always small, never "any big money-making deals." The observer recalled that about 1933 a large family required only about $3.75 in cash per week, "because all they had to buy was flour, chewing tobacco, smoking tobacco, coffee, baking powders, saltlick, and the rest was raised right there on their little farm." So mountain men would cook a barrel of corn mash, run off about three gallons, sell those for $2.00 each in the coal towns, and have cash for nearly two weeks' store purchases. When the family needed more, they cooked another barrel.[9]

In fact tobacco and small amounts of corn whiskey were the only

8. Harry K. Schwarzweller, James S. Brown, and J. J. Mangalam, *Mountain Families in Transition: A Case Study of Appalachian Migration* (University Park, Penn., 1971), 11–18.

9. Loretta Lynn with George Vecsey, *Loretta Lynn: Coal Miner's Daughter* (New York, 1976), 3–25. On moonshining and self-sufficiency in Mingo and McDowell counties, see Guy R. Sutphin, oral history of Rev. Raymond Adkins, n.d. (*ca.* 1975) (Microfilmed typescript in Marshall University Oral History of Appalachia Collection [MUOHA]). Michael J. Galgano, oral history of Donivon Edwin Adams, September 19, 1974 (Typescript also in MUOHA), gives the perspective of a former state policeman on illegal liquor. On moonshining, bootlegging, and high liquor consumption in coal towns, see David Alan Corbin, *Life, Work, and Rebellion in the Coal Fields: The Southern West Virginia Miners, 1880–1922* (Urbana, 1981), 35–36.

cash-making alternatives to ever-more-distant public work for remote
mountain folk who wished to remain at home. Even tobacco was not an
alternative for those on the poorest land farthest from markets. Nor was
the corn-hog system of commercial (as opposed to subsistence) farming. Swine are propagated so easily. A sow is fat and mature for breeding at one year, and gestation for piglets is but four months. A good sow
might produce two litters of seven to nine each year. Theoretically, then,
a farmer owning a healthy sow and boar might possess and sell many
pigs and hogs after only a few years in the business. But he or she must
also have adequate corn or other feed, and reliable markets.[10] This system brought security and wealth to the Middle West in the nineteenth
century, but most highland farmers had neither sufficient corn land nor
markets. So throughout the 1930s and 1940s they patched together
modest livings from field, garden, tobacco patch, and still, making
petty cash and short-term credit purchases at tiny stores within the distance of a short wagon ride or a walk.

All the while this semiprimitive world was dying. Paved roads at last
arrived, along with the automobile. The little stores disappeared. Older
children, then entire families drifted away, usually out of the highlands
altogether. Those who remained lived by cash, the pickup truck, and the
Piggly Wiggly.[11]

The next most "backward" South lay scattered around the broader
region outside the mountains. Sociologist Arthur Raper called these
parts of this South he knew very well the white-land South for the light
tan or bleached appearance of poor, sandy soils. The term also describes most of the poor people on these lands, for even in Greene
County, part of Georgia's original plantation belt, which still had a black
majority during the 1930s, the disintegration of old cotton plantations
had had the effect of whitening the population. During the late 1910s
and early 1920s the boll weevil had devastated cotton production. Many
black sharecroppers left for cities, planters were ruined, and banks and
insurance companies took possession of much of the land. Poor whites
from outside—often from the mountains to the north—arrived to farm
what was left as cash or share tenants or small owners. They raised

10. On swine propagation, see Merrill K. Bennett, "Aspects of the Pig," *Agricultural
History*, XLIV (April, 1970), 223–35.
11. In addition to revelant citations in Chapter 3 above, see Clarence F. Barnes, "Con-
tented Merchant," life history of W. Z. Adams, n.d. (1938 or 1939) (Typescript in "Our
Lives" project files, WPA in Kentucky, Kentucky State Archives, Frankfort), on a Harlan
County country store that grossed $60–$80 per month.

cotton and corn, and tried to live at home while arranging credit with small storekeepers at crossroads or in Greensboro, the only town of size in the county. In the mid–1930s there was still not a paved road that traversed the width of Greene, even though the county lay between Atlanta and Augusta.[12]

Much the same poor existences, with poor roads, few automobiles (although more than in the mountains), and small local stores, were to be found before World War II in hilly cotton counties of northern Georgia, Alabama, Mississippi, and Louisiana, and over much of Arkansas from Little Rock westward. Relatively little cash changed hands in the sandy wire-grass coastal plains of the middle tidewater in Virginia or parts of the Carolinas, Georgia, Florida, Alabama, or Mississippi either. Many such flatland counties were classified as self-sufficient in 1930. Like older, used-up cotton counties (such as Greene, Georgia) and the newer, poor-soil hill cotton counties, much of the coastal flatland was ill-suited to commercial farming. Farms averaged somewhat larger than mountain plots or sharecropped fields, and tenancy, though high, did not include many sharecroppers. Because local tax bases were low, roads here were poor, too. The white lands had one advantage over both the remote highlands and the plantation backcountry: unpaved roads in sandy soil drained rapidly and were easily maintained with hand and mule power. Mountain and black-land soils turned into quagmires after rain or snow. Commercial-minded farmers might have traveled more easily to markets and chain stores before World War II—had there been such.[13]

An economic study of "developing" and "undeveloped" counties in the South Carolina–Georgia piedmont illustrates the distance between this "backward" South and nearby areas that were rapidly modernizing. The developing counties surrounded or had paved roads into small industrial cities such as Anderson, Greenville, and Spartanburg, South Carolina. By 1940, 13.1 percent of farm operators in these counties worked at least one hundred days per year off their farms. In undeveloped counties such as Gwinnett, Georgia, only 7.1 percent of farmers had so much public work. Another significant measure of difference is the percentage of farm products consumed at home. Self-sufficiency (or subsistence) was usually defined as 50 percent or more. Neither set of counties in the study met this criterion, but the farmers in

12. Arthur F. Raper, *Preface to Peasantry: A Tale of Two Black Belt Counties* (Chapel Hill, 1936), 12–13, 18, 178–79, 185–89.

13. *Ibid.*, 12–13, 18, on roads in "white" and "black" lands.

HARDSCRABBLE FARMER IN WHITE-LAND GEORGIA, *ca.* 1940
USDA No. 83-G-37961, National Archives

undeveloped counties consumed more home produce—33.7 percent—
than did the farmers of the modernizing counties—only 27.2 percent.
The more remote self-sufficient farmers had fewer all-weather roads and
more general stores, too.[14]

Bacon County, Georgia, in the wire-grass region above Lake Okefeno-

14. Anthony M. Tang, *Economic Development in the Southern Piedmont, 1860–
1950: Its Impact on Agriculture* (Chapel Hill, 1958), 68, 100, 105, 162, 164–65, 194,
and *passim*.

kee, was also white-land country without important urban centers. During the 1920s the cultivation of flue-cured tobacco had extended into the county, providing Bacon's first important cash alternative to cotton, which had never done well. Farmers had begun to deemphasize live-at-home practices in favor of cash when tobacco prices plummeted toward the end of the decade. New Deal allotments and commodity subsidies stabilized tobacco, but not sufficiently to bring about prosperity and a thorough market economy. Nearly everyone remained poor. The parents of Harry Crews, the essayist and novelist, hired laborers in 1935 at fifty cents each per day to chop corn, tobacco, and cotton on forty sandy acres the Crews family could not manage by themselves. Yet these farm-owning bosses were impoverished, too. They lived in a rude shack, carried in water, ate the plainest food, and worked like driven slaves on their own acreage. A poor black family that lived nearby was more like friends and neighbors than servants and clients, as in the plantation counties to the north and west. When Crews's mother (then divorced) returned to Bacon from factory work in Jacksonville, Florida, in 1942, she became a dirt poor employer once more. Buying another sandy farm, this one without a tobacco allotment, she hired a white man to plow and perform other heavy work. The Crewses and their workman gardened and slaughtered for home use, as before, worked hard, and lived simply, without an automobile. According to Harry Crews, few farmers had cars. Bacon had passable roads most of the year, but no cities and only one town of size, ten miles from the Crewses' farm. So the family seldom saw a store of any sort. Rather, for bolt cloth, candy, salt, coffee, and the repair and sharpening of tools, they relied upon an Orthodox Jewish peddler. Solemn, long-bearded and dressed all in black, the peddler appeared about once a month on the seat of a mule-drawn cart loaded with his wares and a grinding wheel. Crews's mother might spend ten or twenty-five cents in cash. Often the peddler accepted some hay for his mule, or a few eggs, in trade. Such peddling and exchange, dying out in the 1940s, had once been common over much of the South. That it persisted in Bacon County is a measure of the area's slow progress in modernization.[15]

King and Queen County, in the middle of Virginia's tidewater, presents another white-land variation. One of the oldest counties in the nation, King and Queen (about forty miles east of Richmond) had

15. Harry Crews, *A Childhood: The Biography of a Place* (New York, 1978), 36–37, 73–76, and *passim.* On Jewish peddlers elsewhere, see Rachelle Saltzman, "Shalom Y'All," *Southern Exposure,* XI (September/October, 1983), 28–36.

progressed from tobacco to wheat to a poor, sluggish live-at-home subsistence economy by 1930. It had no city, and the population was almost 55 percent black. About three-quarters of all adult males were employed in agriculture; approximately 71 percent of both black and white farmers were full owners, too; the tenancy rate was only 15 percent. A few substantial men such as J. H. Coulbourne owned extensive acreage, with wide fields, woodlands, and small sawmills. The great majority of King and Queen freeholders might have been mistaken for mountain farmers, however, had it not been for the gently rolling topography and the black skin of the majority.[16]

The southern end of King and Queen began to change before 1930. Just across the Mattaponi River (the county line) in King William County was the town of West Point, where the Mattaponi and Pamunkey join to form the York River. There the Chesapeake Corporation had established a pulp mill, which gradually expanded, hiring more and more country folk as workers. During the 1920s rural roads were so poor—mostly corduroy affairs, with pinelogs laid together perpendicular to the path—that rural people were obliged to migrate to West Point to work at the mill. By the late 1930s, however, a paved state highway ran northward from West Point through the communities of Shanghai, Little Plymouth, King and Queen Courthouse, and beyond. Now farmers might live at home part-time, while earning cash five, ten, or twenty miles away at the mill. The highway and the car became the media of this gradual movement away from the old subsistence world.[17]

James Furman Palmer, a small merchant-mechanic at Shanghai, ten miles above West Point, witnessed and served the transition. Early in 1937 he and his wife assumed operation of a combination country store, blacksmith and repair shop, and undertaking parlor. A son of the previous owner took the funeral business to West Point, and the Palmers transformed the remainder of the business into a store and Texaco service station. Later they acquired a fourth-class post office, as well. The Palmers began their store business with modern packaged items rather than the bulk and bolt goods associated with earlier general stores. (Large cheese wheels were an exception.) Their customers included the Coulbournes, their hired hands, and many small local farmers. Neigh-

16. Charles S. Johnson *et al.* (comps.), *Statistical Atlas of Southern Counties: Listing and Analysis of Socio-economic Indices of 1104 Southern Counties* (Chapel Hill, 1941), 253; Jack Temple Kirby, "Fumman, Go . . . Git That Wheel!" oral history of James Furman Palmer (my uncle), July 6, 1980 (Typescript copies in my and Mr. Palmer's possessions).

17. Kirby, "Fumman, Go . . . Git That Wheel!"

J. F. PALMER'S TEXACO STATION AND STORE, SHANGHAI, VIRGINIA, 1985

Photo by the author

borhood people ran weekly accounts and settled on Saturdays in cash. Furman Palmer repaired farm wagons, trucks, and tractors as well as cars on a drive-up rack outside the store. Most of the Palmers' business was auto related, however; they sold gasoline, oil, fan belts, and other auto parts. Gradually over the years (especially from the 1950s onward), their gas station business took greater and greater precedence over the store. When they stopped carrying ground coffee in cans in favor of two-ounce jars of instant coffee (about 1970), one might say that lower King and Queen was utterly transformed.[18]

White folk on other white land lived more precariously than the Crewses or the country commuters of King and Queen, especially during the 1930s. In the Coosa County hills between Montgomery and Birmingham, Alabama, lived a character whose occupation might

18. *Ibid.* Lower King and Queen farmers also developed truck crops for the growing West Point market. Farmers around Miami in Dade County, Florida, had similar experiences of combining off-farm work with truck and subsistence. See Walter A. DeLamater, "The Newton Family," life history of John Newton Blair, December 14, 1938 (Typescript in FWP life histories files, SHC). Around Mobile, Alabama, country storekeepers also did cash business with railroad section hands and lumber workers, a minor credit business complementing long-term debtors (at 8 percent interest). See Linda M. Jones, oral history of Everett L. Mays, March 16, 1975 (Typescript in Samford University Oral History Program, Birmingham).

ABANDONED SCHOOLHOUSE, HARMONY, GEORGIA, *ca.* 1940
USDA No. 83-G-41080, National Archives

have been hyphenated as squatter-sharecropper-fisherman-moonshiner-bootlegger. He worked spasmodically at crops (probably cotton and corn) on halves with his landlord but lived in a shack on land belonging to the Alabama Power Company. "They's supposed to charge three dollars a year" for rent, he told a Federal Writers' Project interviewer, "but they don't never come 'round to git any money. They jes' axes us to take keer of th' lan' an' watch out fer fores' fires." Much of the year he spent fishing for his own food and profit, but so many others did the same that the Coosa River and its tributaries could not support them. So he converted his corn into whiskey and peddled it up and down the Coosa to town middlemen.[19]

Marginal land in Florida was crowded with squatters before World War II, also. In Highlands County, above the Everglades, families survived in jerry-built shacks, raising and selling a few vegetables in towns nearby, hauling firewood in rusted cars with wooden seats and no tops, and hunting and fishing. In some ways like contemporary "Okie" mi-

19. Jack Kytle, "I'm Allus Hongry," in James Seay Brown (ed.), *Up Before Daylight: Life Histories from the Alabama Writers' Project, 1938–1939* (University, Ala., 1982), 118–27.

GETTING BY IN WHITE-LAND GEORGIA, *ca.* 1940. This family diversified its mule-farming operation by adding a gas station and store.
USDA No. 83-G-37960, National Archives

grants in California, they were motorized, however miserably, and some waited for harvest work. Florida squatters lived partway into a frontier existence, waiting for something to happen.[20]

The demographic chaos and economic bonanzas of World War II appear to have transformed most of the white-land South quite abruptly. Squatters, migrants, and marginal farmers suddenly found irresistible cash, either at home or more likely somewhere else, in cities. Farming on such land for the most part ceased, and as in much of the highlands, the country returned to forest.

A third South had the shortest and probably easiest road to modernization. This South included the fruit-vegetable and grain-dairy-livestock operators of 1930, plus farmers in cotton and other row-crop counties near cities, who abandoned the old staples early and found good cash markets for new crops. There was little white land in this South, and except for diversifying (or "developing") counties, populations were overwhelmingly white, tenancy rates were low, and possession of machinery (especially animal-drawn) was widespread. The grain-dairy-livestock lands of Virginia, Kentucky, and Tennessee were the heart of this South, which resembled the eastern Middle West in so many ways. Typical was the Traylor homestead of 150 acres between Cynthiana and Falmouth, Kentucky, above Lexington. About 100 acres were fine bot-

20. Barbara Berry Darsey, "Florida Squatters," December, 1938 (Typescript in FWP life histories files, SHC).

tomland, on which John Traylor grew corn, hay, and tobacco. The other third of the farm was hilly, and Traylor left that to pasture for his cattle and woods for fuel. A little farther north toward Cincinnati, in Pendleton County, Alvin King also farmed and lived frugally. He had 170 acres, but very little bottomland. King raised corn and tobacco for sale and kept his cattle fed with his own hay, like the Traylors. The family also gardened and slaughtered for home use, and Alvin King was judicious in sharing both work and profits with his sons, who were persuaded to remain in farming.[21]

A few grain-dairy farmers dwelled among row-crop farmers, too, of course. In eastern North Carolina near Morehead City, Alton Poe created a successful dairy farm following his combat service in World War I. Poe came upon hard times during the early 1930s, however. His barns became run-down, and debts forced him to exchange his purebred herd for mixed-breed cows. Yet living at home and frugal management—along with the nearby city market—helped him survive. Middle-sized, commercial-minded farmers around Orlando, Florida, coped with the Depression through cooperative marketing as well as frugality. Early in 1929 many of them joined the new Central Florida Poultry Producers' Co-operative Association (PPCA). Trucks belonging to the association picked up eggs from members, then packed and shipped them from Orlando. In 1930 farmers around Jacksonville formed a North Florida PPCA.[22]

Such resourceful (and lucky) farmers were to be found throughout the South, in the cotton country as well as the white valleys and hills and in Florida. When a farmer happened to live near a good market, wisdom, careful management, and hard work brought cash and family security during some of the worst of times. Throughout the 1920s and 1930s the *Progressive Farmer* published a regular feature on master farmers who triumphed over the boll weevil and low commodity prices. All the stories were no doubt true. One such success story was that of Daniel W. Wilkes of Dillon County, South Carolina. Wilkes raised some cotton and tobacco, like his neighbors, but during the 1930s he began to specialize in hogs for sale to Dillon and other nearby towns. Wilkes and his son raised their own corn for feed; Mrs. Wilkes and a daughter culti-

21. Fred Reinheimer, "Growing Good Crops," life history of John and Ida Traylor, n.d. (1938 or 1939), "Share in Crops Kept Boys on Farm," life history of Alvin King, n.d. (1938 or 1939) (Both typescripts in "Our Lives" project files).

22. Leonard Rapport, "Alton Poe, Dairyman," life history, November 21, 1938 (Typescript in FWP life histories files, SHC); "Poultry Cooperative Movement Sweeps Florida," *Florida Farmer*, XXXII (February, 1930), 1.

A Progressive Farmer (*left*) from Near Anderson, South Carolina, with His Extension Service Agent, *ca.* 1935
USDA No. 83-G-44562, National Archives

vated a garden for the family table. Like the Kings of Kentucky, the
Wilkeses shared profits with their children, too. "I'm smart," Dan
Wilkes declared. "I know how to keep my boy with me, by turning him
loose!" They had found "money in hawgs"; now the elder Wilkes succeeded in teaching "the children to love country life." Another South
Carolina farmer, near Spartanburg, was nearly ruined by the boll weevil
during the early 1920s. His county agent "preach[ed] diversification of
crops to me," the farmer recalled, "but my ears were filled with cotton."
The agent took the farmer to see a privately managed experiment with
peach trees, finally persuading the farmer to turn over ten, then more
acres of cotton land to orchards. The farmer agonized for five years
while the trees grew to peach-bearing maturity. Meanwhile neighbors
shipped a successful crop in 1925. The Carolina peaches ripened just as
the Georgia season ended, so they were easily disposed of in Spartanburg and many other cities to the north. The farmer shipped his own
first peaches in 1929. By 1939 he was planting only about ten acres of
cotton, plus Irish and sweet potatoes and a variety of other truck crops

for the nearby urban markets. He kept two mules, too, and had acquired his first gasoline tractor.[23]

Elsewhere in the cotton country farmers and planters also had the good fortune of choice. In 1928 a land company executive of Blytheville, in eastern Arkansas, reported a classic forked-road case from the new delta lands, cut over and cleared only a decade before. One pioneer family moved onto forty acres, planted a garden and orchard, and began to improve and increase their livestock. Before the end of the 1920s the farm had grown to a hundred acres, the mortgage was well secured, and the family borrowed no money for living expenses. They probably sold surpluses in the St. Louis and Memphis markets. Another farmer chose the other fork. He moved in with four mules and no other stock, going for bonanza cotton profits. Having no garden or meat for the table, this farmer borrowed for daily expenses, then was caught by the postwar collapse of prices. His farm was foreclosed in 1926. In 1928 he and his son sharecropped on others' land, and both his daughters had married croppers.[24] Such tales left the impression that farmers everywhere were masters of their fates.

Over in Madison County, Tennessee (surrounding Jackson), a bank cashier declared in 1928 that "diversified farming is strictly in style in this part of the country." He may well have meant that bankers, Department of Agriculture officials, and agronomy professors could easily perceive that diversification and establishment of contact with urban markets were good for everyone's business. In actuality, Madison County farmers in 1930 still harvested cotton on somewhat more than 50 percent of their cropland, and the tenancy rate stood at 65.6 percent.[25] Few of Madison's farmers possessed adequate property, other capital, or credit to face a forked-road decision. Theirs was cotton and cropper country, where owners were soon to be saved by the AAA, nearly everyone else abandoned. The fruit-vegetable and grain-dairy-livestock farmers of the South enjoyed advantages of location, tenure, and traditions that rewarded hard work, "scientific" farming, and modern marketing.

23. See "Master Farmer" clippings, esp. the 1928 file, in Howard W. Odum Papers, SHC; F. Donald Atwell, "There's Money in Hawgs!" life history of Daniel J. Wilkes, January 15, 1939, R. V. Williams, "John B. Culbertson," January 27, 1939 (Both typescripts in FWP life histories files, SHC).

24. C. G. Smith to Howard W. Odum, March 9, 1928, Odum Papers.

25. Simpson Russell to Odum, March 9, 1928, *ibid.*; Charles Johnson *et al.* (comps.), *Statistical Atlas,* 216.

They had choices. Most of Madison County's rural folks, like most of the denizens of eastern Arkansas, did not. They lived in quite a different world.

The largest of the modernizing Souths grew cotton and other row crops on sharecropped plantations and had black majorities. Here the problems and processes of modernization were most difficult and peculiar. Having been, in the classic sense, modern since their introduction into America in the seventeenth century, plantations had always been intimately connected with the world economy as suppliers and as clients of outside creditors. Paradoxically, inhabitants of plantation districts—especially tenants and laborers—were largely cut off from contact with cash and with outside cultural influences. Into the 1920s, at least, many of them dwelled in island communities superficially resembling those of the Norris Basin. Many farm owners and some tenants, even sharecroppers, lived at home in these districts. Most people here, however (one cannot be more precise), lived out of bags from the beginning, not as cash earners breaking out of island communities but rather as debt-bound dependents similar to West Virginia proletarians in company towns. From 1933 into the 1950s, nearly all sharecroppers and most share tenants were evicted or forcibly converted to cash laborers. This rapid, shocking method of modernization in effect substituted the federal government (as off-season welfare patron) and the impersonal national labor market for the insidious concoction of premodern paternalism and ruthless capitalist exploitation that had obtained on the fragmented plantations. Some former plantation dependents were able to continue farming for a while as diversified, live-at-home operators of some sort. Then most of those, unable to capitalize adequately, were obliged to give up agriculture for the cities and factories.[26] Yet others drifted only slowly or partway into the world of cash as part-time farmers or farm laborers, lumber workers, fishermen, and so on. Everywhere, both before and during this process of modernization, class differences and antagonisms plagued this South and, without doubt, hastened its end once the New Deal programs were introduced.

Planters were the lords of this sprawling creation. During the New Deal, federal researchers and policy makers defined a planter as owner of "a tract with five or more resident families, including the land-

26. Reference is made in particular to federal resettlement projects. See Donald Holley, *Uncle Sam's Farmers: The New Deal Communities in the Lower Mississippi Valley* (Urbana, 1975).

lord."[27] This definition, which avoided the snare of acreage as a criterion, went directly to the essential matters of power and dependency
that set the South apart from the Northeast and Middle West. Still,
planter-landlords were not equally powerful.

Samuel Wakefield Bowen of Anderson County, South Carolina, was
a small planter. During the 1920s (a decade for which his farm records
have survived), Bowen owned two farms: the Hamilton Place, which he
rented on shares to W. A. Miller (apparently a white man); and the Milt
Place, which he divided among four black sharecroppers and closely supervised himself. Miller grew cotton and corn on the Hamilton Place,
and Bowen charged him a commission for handling crops on the way to
market. Bowen apparently concerned himself little with Miller's affairs,
however. On the Milt Place the croppers grew cotton, corn, hay, oats,
and truck crops for the Anderson city market. The croppers also must
have maintained a substantial garden for the Bowens. For this labor, as
well as for ditching, hauling logs and firewood, and a variety of other
tasks, Bowen paid them in cash or entered credits beside the croppers'
names in his day books. Bowen had too few dependents to warrant operation of a plantation store; so his croppers bought clothing, coffee, and
a few groceries in town. Like most planters during the 1920s, Bowen
provided small cash advances against the value of growing crops and
additional labor. He apparently also had agreements with town merchants
to guarantee limited credit purchases by his croppers. The Bowen family
(husband, wife, two daughters) lived comfortably in a large house still
prized for its beauty. Their social lives were in the city of Anderson,
where they drove often in new sedans.[28]

During the mid-1910s many such middling or small planters of
northeastern North Carolina withdrew from active farming and moved
their homes to town. Up to this time they had used day laborers and
overseers. Now they finally adopted sharecropping because, as one
planter-turned-absentee-landlord put it, cropping allowed him freedom
from nagging supervision. The day-to-day operation of so much of this
cotton, tobacco, and peanut farmland was defaulted to thousands of the

27. WPA, Division of Research, *The Plantation South, 1934–1937*, by William C.
Holly, Ellen Winston, and T. J. Woofter, Jr. (Washington, D.C., 1940), xi.

28. Sam Bowen Farm Records, 1921–1930, Clemson University Archives. Additional
information on Bowen and his family is derived from Mrs. Fred L. (Mildren Ann Beatty)
Thackston (Anderson, S.C.) to the author, July 21, 1981, including copies of a note from
Annie Francis Clark (Anderson County auditor) to Mrs. Thackston, July 14, 1981,
and photocopies of tax records on the Bowen farms; and Joel Williamson to the author,
June 17, 1981.

black landless. One of the benefits to the coastal North Carolina share-croppers was freedom to use substantial plots of the land for gardens. Thus a woman recalled the 1920s and 1930s as the most blessed of times: "The landlords usually stayed in town; that's why you could always raise what you needed to eat. . . . We learned how to raise wheat and make our own flour, and we grew cane to make our own molasses. We could stay at home and grow our own food and be truly happy." By 1939 Carolina landlords, like those everywhere, had begun to evict tenants and consolidate and mechanize their farms. But for about a generation, their withdrawal had presented to the landless a remarkable opportunity to live at home while the whites enjoyed modern town and city life upon the earnings of the croppers.[29] Larger planters seem to have been more committed to supervision.

John Frederick Dugger of Lee County, Alabama (surrounding Auburn), exemplifies the rural upper middle class of the first half of the century. Dugger was born on a Hale County plantation during the Civil War and was educated in agronomy during the early 1880s. He then began an agricultural college teaching career that led him to Auburn, where he became the first director of the Alabama Experiment Station (1903–1921) and of the Alabama Extension Service (1914–1920). In the meantime he acquired 675 acres near the college town and undertook diversified farming operations with the help of a son and a number of sharecroppers. From incomplete records that survive, it would appear that Dugger, like Samuel Bowen, closely supervised and managed the finances (as well as refereeing the social relations) of his black croppers. Because his interests as early as the 1920s included a dairy and purebred beef cattle as well as cotton production, Dugger's scientific and commercial inclinations may well have led him to supervise croppers (and in the 1940s, hired hands) more closely than most planters. On such "progressive" plantations the majority of the population was thus separated from the modern commercial world. Dugger and his colleagues and neighbors, on the other hand, were well traveled, enjoyed town life, and each year might attend Farm and Home Week on the campus of the Alabama Polytechnic Institute (later Auburn University). In 1939 celebrants heard speeches by Edward A. O'Neil, another Alabama

29. The landlord (of Northampton County) is quoted in Bernice Kelly Harris, "Henry Calhoun Weathers, Landlord," March 1, 1939 (Typescript in FWP life histories files, SHC). The woman sharecropper (Bertie County) is quoted in Phaye Poliakoff, "Thought We Were Just Some Poor Old Country People," an interview with Alice Balance, *Southern Exposure*, XI (November/December, 1983), 30–32. Both spoke in the plural, as though the practice was widespread.

planter and president of the national Farm Bureau Federation, and by United States Senator Lister Hill. There were skits and plays from all-white groups representing various Alabama counties, tours of the experiment station, and many lectures, including one entitled "Tenancy Problems," delivered by an Extension Service district supervisor.[30]

Dugger was a poor man compared to Edward R. Alexander of Tuskegee. His mansion Grey Columns stands a short distance from the famous black college, from which Booker T. Washington and Thomas Campbell (a pioneer black Extension Service agent) had preached living at home to the peasantry of Macon County and beyond. Alexander's scores of black sharecroppers raised many bales of cotton from the 1920s into the 1950s under his patronage. His surviving plantation records are inadequate to determine whether Alexander maintained his own stores or diversified his crops. But the family's fortune was widely invested in holdings other than cotton land—a Tuskegee Esso station, the local railroad, the Birmingham Textile Company, Goodyear Tire and Rubber, Coca Cola, and various banks in Alabama and New York. Alexander was also a famous sportsman, a breeder of thoroughbred horses, hunting dogs, and gamecocks. A memorable black employee, reminiscent of Alex Haley's ancestor Chicken George, cared for the fighting birds. In July, 1936, while writer James Agee and photographer Walker Evans recorded the grim lives of Hale County white sharecroppers, Edward and Annie Alexander were consumed by the search for gold damask to match furniture in the mansion. Throughout the Depression they kept a chauffeur.[31]

William Alexander Percy's Trail Lake Plantation, near Greenville, Mississippi, in some respects resembled a huge, idealized antebellum estate. In 1936 Percy planted more than 1,800 of his 3,343 acres in cotton. Another 50-odd acres were in gardens, 50 more in pasture; the remainder was planted in corn and hay. Cabins scattered about Trail Lake housed 589 blacks in 149 families; 124 families were sharecroppers who received half the cotton they raised; 25 had their own work

30. Lee County and federal tax returns for 1925–26 and 1940–44, and correspondence in the John Frederick Dugger portion of the Dugger Family Papers, Auburn University Archives. See also copy of program, "Farm and Home Week" at Alabama Polytechnic Institute, July 31–August 4, 1939, in Walter Leon Randolph Papers, Alabama Department of Archives and History, Montgomery.

31. Business, tax, horse, canine, and gamecock materials in the correspondence and records of E. R. Alexander, Varner-Alexander Papers, Alabama Department of Archives and History. On Tuskegee, the Extension Service, and Hale County poverty, see Crosby, "Building the Country Home," and James Agee (with photographs by Walker Evans), *Let Us Now Praise Famous Men* (Boston, 1941).

stock and equipment, so were share tenants who received three-fourths of the cotton they harvested. Percy's cotton land yielded nearly a bale (about five hundred pounds of ginned lint) to the acre, better than the southern average at the time. So his tenants did relatively well. Percy calculated their "gross average income" (per family) during the mid-1930s at $491.90, with a "net" of $437.64. In addition they received "free" housing, water, fuel, pasturage (for those owning animals), and a garden plot. Gardens for croppers were as unusual in the delta as the incomes Percy reported. Many planters kept their own stores and forced their tenants to buy groceries there, but Percy was an extraordinary man. Scion of a line rich in cotton and land for at least three genera-tions, Percy was educated in the arts and by the 1930s was a well-regarded poet and critic as well as a planter. He gave serious moral as well as managerial attention to Trail Lake—the more so, it seems ob-vious, because of his awareness that his world was fast slipping away. In his famous memoir *Lanterns on the Levee* (published in 1941), Percy almost echoed George Fitzhugh, the eccentric champion of slavery who in the 1850s had compared industrial labor invidiously with the South's peculiar institution. "Our plantation system," Percy reflected, "seems to me to offer as humane, just, self-respecting, and cheerful a method of earning a living as human beings are likely to devise." He went on to describe his dependents with an ingenuousness that must have amazed even contemporaries: "I watch the limber-jointed, oily-black, well-fed, decently clothed peasants on Trail Lake and feel sorry for the telephone girls, the clerks in chain stores, the office help, the unskilled laborers everywhere . . . for their slave routine, their joyless habits of work, and for their insecurity." [32] Percy could not conceal his loathing for the im-personal and insecure modern world of commerce. If one cannot forgive him his self-interest in a fading plantation age, or the class and racial contempt for his dependents that he could not recognize in himself, one might at least credit the remarkable forthrightness of Percy's expression and his attempt to reify a nineteenth-century master-class ideal.

No such self-conscious moralism governed other delta and river val-ley estates. Consider, for example, the great J. E. Little plantation in Faulkner County, Arkansas, near Conway on a bend of the Arkansas River. From the 1910s into the 1950s Little kept an average of three hundred families—about half black, half white—on his bottomlands. The 1927 flood disrupted the plantation for several years, but on the eve

32. William Alexander Percy, *Lanterns on the Levee: Recollections of a Planter's Son* (1941; rpr. Baton Rouge, 1973), 279–80.

of the disaster and again by 1932, there were more than five hundred separate accounts kept in Little's commissary ledgers. Whereas William Percy thought he knew his croppers personally, Little's clerks and accountants assigned each cropper and laborer a number. In his tenant accounts, cash books, and labor books were recorded daily charges at the store, debits for fertilizer (croppers here and elsewhere were responsible for half the cost), credits for extra labor performed, cotton produced, and so on. During the 1920s, when planters elsewhere were making cash advances, Little issued coupon books in one-cent denominations, redeemable at his store. In Caddo Parish, Louisiana, on the Red River outside Shreveport, there were other sprawling properties managed in an impersonal, businesslike manner by salaried men on behalf of absentee owners. And Oscar Johnston, William Percy's neighbor and manager for British investors of the Delta and Pine Land Company, seems never to have pretended that D&PL was more than a successful business enterprise with decent working conditions for operatives.[33]

The largest plantations, crowded with dependents before the 1940s or later, did indeed resemble nineteenth- and early twentieth-century nonunionized factories. Managers, whether they were salaried or resident owners, were modern and efficiency-minded and paternalistic at once. Paternalism, indeed, often served the ends of efficiency, as was well understood and proclaimed by John Patterson of Dayton, Ohio, founder of the National Cash Register Company; by Matthew Verity of Armco Steel in Middletown, Ohio; and by Braxton Bragg Comer of Alabama, who was both a planter and a textiles manufacturer. Such industrialists spoke of employees as family, maintained corporate housing, and were ever mindful of operatives' welfare. The plantations seem least like the huge wheat farms of the Great Plains, which, well capitalized and mechanized from the start, supported tiny populations and presented few of the labor problems and practically none of the class relationships—or pretentious life-style—of plantations.[34]

33. J. E. Little Plantation Records, Arkansas History Commission, Little Rock. (The ledgers do not describe tenants by race. For this ratio I am indebted to Harry W. Readnour of Central Arkansas University, Conway, who repeated local tradition to me during an interview, May 20, 1982, in Conway.) See also the J. E. Cupples & Son Ledgers, 1921–33 (in William V. Robson Plantation Records), and Frierson Company Records, both in the Louisiana State University–Shreveport Archives; Delta and Pine Land Company Records, Mississippi State University library.

34. James Weinstein, *The Corporate Ideal in the Liberal State, 1900–1918* (Boston, 1968), 19–20 and *passim;* Kirby, *Darkness at the Dawning,* 142–43; Lawrence J. Nelson, "Welfare Capitalism on a Mississippi Plantation During the Great Depression,"

The daughter of a Lonoke County, Arkansas, planter recalled a girlhood in a big house east of Little Rock reminiscent of the Mississippi world Eudora Welty recreated in her novel, *Delta Wedding*. The Arkansas planter family was large, extended, and cared for attentively by two black cooks and a host of other servants who cleaned, washed, ironed, sewed, and repaired. Each resident of the manse, including children from about the age of ten, had a horse, which was groomed and fed by other dependents. Sharecroppers—forty to ninety families of them—lived on the place and grew cotton. During the 1920s and 1930s the planter kept 100 to 150 mules in a central barn (his daughter remembered), implying that the plantation was a through-and-through system in which croppers assumed work on their plots only after crews had plowed and harrowed broad fields. The father also used convict labor, and occasional escapes provided thrills for the white children. There was a commissary with a storekeeper, and a full-time manager for farming operations, assisted by straw bosses who supervised labor from horseback.[35]

During the late 1930s the Department of Agriculture Bureau of Agricultural Economics studied plantations in three Arkansas counties—Jefferson (Arkansas River bottoms), Miller (Red River), and Phillips (on the Mississippi). Statistics on the typical estate at that time permit several generalizations: plantations were large enough to support a life of ease for the planter class, mechanization was hardly underway, and the estates were still impacted with dependents. Plantations averaged more than a thousand acres, with about two-thirds under cultivation. Almost two-thirds of owners resided on their places and closely supervised the labor of tenant forces dominated by black sharecroppers. The typical plantation supported twenty-three families (in addition to the owner's), only three of which were white. In 1937, after four years of the New Deal, there had been but a 6 percent decline of resident families. Sharecropping had declined only slightly, but planters had converted or eliminated one-fifth of their share tenants, and numbers of wage laborers

---

Journal of Southern History, L (May, 1984), 225–50. (Nelson's plantation is the Delta and Pine Land Company.) Examples of business and life on north-central Oklahoma wheat farms are the Lyle L. Hogue Collection and the Clayton H. Hyde Collection, both in the Western History Collection, University of Oklahoma.

35. Rebecca Yarbrough, oral history of Mr. and Mrs. Robert H. Alexander, October 5, 1973 (Typescript in University of Arkansas Library, Little Rock). See also Eudora Welty, *Delta Wedding* (New York, 1945).

were rising. There were no tractors at all on thirty-three of eighty-nine plantations surveyed.[36]

A historian who studied plantations in eastern Arkansas (including Phillips County) for the year 1934, discovered that substantial incomes for planters were common. The average annual gross was $10,774, three-quarters of it from cotton. Typical expenses of $6,271 (for labor, ginning, feed, seed, and taxes) left an average net income of $4,743, representing a healthy 8 percent return on investment. Such earnings compared well with typical professional incomes at the time—for example, $3,300 for physicians, $3,500–4,000 for attorneys, and $2,600 for dentists. Planters could afford to take vacations and send their children to universities in the depth of the Depression.[37] So whether they moved to towns or remained actively engaged in supervision, planters were of the modern world. Their tenants, to varying degrees, were not.

Before most of them were driven from the land, southern tenants labored under a variety of contracts with their landlords. Tenancy was governed by state laws, but the statutes were vague and local judicial rulings over many decades had created an eccentric jumble of precedents and practices. Certain features can be easily generalized and illustrated, however. Most deals were made orally, were never written down, and extended for one year at a time. There were three broad categories of land use by nonowners: cash or "standing rent," a fixed amount of money or crop value; share tenancy, in which tenants usually paid one-fourth the cotton or tobacco (and often one-third of corn produced as well) no matter what the market price; and sharecropping, which almost everywhere meant payment of one-half of all crops as rent. Cash or standing rent was common in the North and rare in the South except in the mountains and the grain-dairy-livestock areas. Share tenancy was to be found everywhere in the South, but it was most common in hilly, white-majority areas. Sharecropping was called tenancy, but because croppers (unlike true tenants) had no legal rights to their crops or to make decisions of any sort regarding land use, it was actually a peculiar hired labor system. Owners of the best land, who grew commercial staples, preferred to retain control of their operations; so sharecropping was the dominant form of labor in the black belts and deltas. Black

36. USDA, BAE, "Land Tenure in Arkansas: Recent Changes in Farm Labor Organization in Three Arkansas Plantation Counties," by G. T. Barton (Typescript, December 22, 1938, in Land Tenure Section project files, RG 83, NA).

37. Donald H. Grubbs, *Cry from the Cotton: The Southern Tenant Farmers' Union and the New Deal* (Chapel Hill, 1971), 12.

folks' numbers were concentrated in these same plantation subregions after the Civil War, and three-quarters of a century later the typical southern cropper was still a black in the now enlarged plantation area. When blacks migrated and whites entered this area in numbers during the 1920s and 1930s, many of them became sharecroppers, too.[38]

Local crops and conditions created variations. In Southampton County, Virginia—cotton, tobacco, and peanut country in 1930—share tenants or croppers might have also had livestock agreements with planter-landlords. If the tenant cared for an animal, he or she received one-tenth the value at sale. If a tenant owned the animal entirely or in part, then up to one-half of the sale price went to the tenant or cropper. Fifty miles to the east, Princess Anne County, a truck-farming area close to Norfolk, was a different world. Sharecropping there was rare. Some tenants farmed general crops, especially corn, "on fourths" with landlords. Most tenants owned their own home plots and rented vege- table farms on the "one-third system" of crop payment for rent. In cen- tral North Carolina some share tenants turned over one-third of all crops, rather than the thirds and fourths common to the south. In Oktib- beha County, Mississippi, on the edge of the black belt, the Rice family wrote down by hand on plain paper contracts with illiterate black ten- ants that specified amounts of cotton and corn and sometimes poundage of hogs and turkeys to be paid in rent at the close of the season, from 1933 through the 1940s. J. D. Collins, for example, was to turn over two-fifths of his cut hay in 1933, and precisely 833 pounds of cotton (presumably unginned) and seventy-five bushels of corn. Collins and

38. USDA, *Agriculture Yearbook, 1923* (Washington, D.C., 1924), 507–600; Ken- tucky Agricultural Experiment Station Bulletin 418, *Legal Aspects of Farm Tenancy in Kentucky* (Lexington, June, 1941), 241–42; Lee J. Alston and Robert Higgs, "Contrac- tual Mix in Southern Agriculture Since the Civil War: Facts, Hypotheses, and Tests," *Journal of Economic History,* XLII (June, 1982), 327–54; Harold D. Woodman, "Post– Civil War Southern Agriculture and the Law," *Agricultural History,* LIII (January, 1979), 319–37; Ralph John Ramsey, "Criteria for Classifying Louisiana Tenants" (M.A. thesis, Louisiana State University, 1940); various Bureau of Agricultural Economics and Re- settlement Administration reports in Land Tenure Section project files, 1937–41, RG 83, NA. Examples of these studies, which correlate tenancy types to topography and soils, include BAE, "Report of the Kentucky Farm Tenancy Commission," September, 1941; BAE, "Types of Tenancy in Oklahoma (A Preliminary Report)," January, 1941; RA, "Land Tenure and Tenancy in Mississippi," by C. O. Henderson, May, 1937; BAE, "Types of Tenancy in Georgia," by J. C. Elrod, March, 1941; BAE, "Survey of Inter- views and Suggestions by Those Interviewed: Virginia Survey of Landlord-Tenant Rela- tions—June 17–30, 1939"; and BAE, "Land Tenure in Arkansas: I—The Farm Tenancy Situation," 1939.

other tenants fell short some years, so the Rices apparently converted the weight or bushel deficits into dollars at year-end prices and carried the debts into the next crop year.[39]

Whatever the variation in measuring rent, planters across the South sought to exploit croppers and share tenants, maximizing profits while sharing (especially with the croppers) as many of the risks of commercial farming as possible. A few planters, notably William Percy, disguised the hard edges of this system of business within an archaic world view of paternalism. More planters were forthright about the actual circumstances they made or inherited, and their surviving ledgers are brutally frank. For their part, tenants and sharecroppers understood the system and could explain it clearly, whether or not they had the advantages of education. A former northeastern Mississippi thirds-and-fourths renter declared, "Well, it's as much difference" between share tenancy and cropping "as night and day. If you sharecropping" the landlord "get half of it. And renting third and fourth, a bale of cotton come to a hundred dollars, you get seventy-five, he . . . get twenty-five, see. That's a great big difference."[40] A former cropper from Ripley saw advantages in sharecropping. Share tenants (or renters, as they were more often called) took too much risk during the 1930s and 1940s, his working decades, and often lost money. The widow of a Yalobusha County cropper elaborated. Life was too "hard on renters" when she and her husband began married life and labor during the Depression. Landlords did not furnish renters, and this young couple therefore failed to make enough cotton in their try at share tenancy. They had had to devote too much time to their garden, feed crops, and maintaining their stock and equipment. The modern world's cash nexus was to them a cruel trap. Falling to sharecropper status their second year was a relief from worry and the struggles of management.[41] Stuck in this lowest form of tenancy, hardly different from hired laborers, such sharecroppers sought to maximize their own day-to-day prospects in a world created to exploit them.

39. See USDA, BAE, interviews with E. A. Davis, Extension Service agent for Southampton County, n.d. (1940), and H. W. Ozlin, agent for Princess Anne County (Typescripts of both in Land Tenure Section project files, RG 83, NA); Stanley Combs, "A Pretty Hard Life," in John L. Robinson (ed.), *Living Hard: Southern Americans in the Great Depression* (Washington, D.C., 1981), 106–11; "Plantation" files in Nannie Herndon Rice Papers, Mississippi State University Library.

40. Lee Cayson, oral history, n.d. (*ca.* 1975) (Typescript in Mary Holmes College Oral History Program, West Point, Mississippi).

41. Hezekiah Braddock and Alberta Carothers, oral histories, n.d. (both *ca.* 1975) (Typescripts, *ibid.*).

Landlords, too, had their troubles. Sharecroppers and tenants did not share the bosses' proprietary outlook, and incessant skirmishing between the classes ensued. Landlords perceived croppers in particular as shiftless workers and poor managers, regardless of race. As described by an Arkansas planter late in the 1920s, a cotton cropper or laborer "has nothing, wants nothing, expects nothing, does not try to have anything, but does waste and destroy any and everything. He is wild for money, but when he gets it, it is not worth five cents on the dollar to buy his needs. That is for waste, his needs are bought on credit." [42] As for sharecroppers, they seem almost universally to have regarded their chief woe as lack of managerial authority. The twain never met. J. Marion Futtrell, governor of Arkansas during the early 1930s, complained of a tenant on his plantation "who not only took his share of the crop but a good part of that which belonged to me. He tore down nearly all the troughs in the barn. He took fencing and burned it up for both fire and cook wood and made a chicken house out of one of the best rooms in the house." When Futtrell ordered the troublesome fellow to leave, the tenant defied the governor to his face, but Futtrell prevailed. [43]

Arthur Raper observed another theater of the economic warfare in black-belt Georgia. There planters had abandoned commissaries before the mid-1930s and directed tenants to town merchants for furnishing. Merchants often had liens on crops in addition to the liens of land owners, and tenants took advantage of the tangle of claims and occasional lack of communication between planters and merchants. According to Raper, "there ensued a sort of grim game in which the landlord and tenant get all they can out of each other, the tenant carrying home all the provisions he can and the landlord furnishing as little as possible." Tenants proceeded upon the well-founded assumption that at settlement time late in the fall, they would see no cash; and sharecroppers, having no capital invested beyond labor, had nothing to lose. "The planter, on the other hand, puts up all the money and is saddled with the responsi-

42. Quotation from Rupert B. Vance, *Human Factors of Cotton Culture: A Study in the Social Geography of the American South* (Chapel Hill, 1929), 314. Another example of landlord contempt for white tenants is "From Poverty to Plenty," life history of E. W. Faucette, May 12, 1939 (Typescript in FWP life histories files, SHC).

43. On cropper perceptions, see the 1937 questionnaires on tenancy and poverty in Resettlement Administration, "Social Correlative of Farm Tenure" (Typescript, 1937, in Jefferson County, Arkansas, Series, University of Arkansas Department of Agricultural Economics and Rural Sociology records, University of Arkansas Library, Fayetteville). Gov. Futrell is quoted in Ernie Maddox to League for Southern Labor, March 20, 1936, roll 2, STFU Papers, SHC.

bility of seeing that the tenants' bills do not get too great and that he has a crop with which to settle accounts." [44] Raper was no apologist for landlords, however; he knew well that in this complex and crucial matter of accounts, tenants were decided underdogs.

There were across the wide South fair-minded men and women who were scrupulously honest, even indulgent, with tenants and sharecroppers. A few divided New Deal subsidy payments equitably, and it is difficult to imagine William Alexander Percy cheating his dependents at the store or at settlement over cotton weights either. Other planters and farmers who themselves had seen hard labor and want must have identified with the landless and resisted temptation. There was, for example, a white North Carolina farmer, aged about fifty-three in the late 1930s, who had begun with a horse and fifty uncleared acres, suffered a home fire and other misfortunes, including a mortgage, but who had struggled to build his holdings to about a hundred acres with four work animals. Two sharecroppers also worked on his place. He needed a gasoline tractor, but as he explained to a FWP interviewer, "One reason I don't climb no faster is because I'm honest with my sharecroppers, to the penny. There's ways a landlord can take short cuts and buy him tractors, but I never cared to own one that way." He took care to have croppers keep duplicate accounts, recording with him every cash advance and bag of fertilizer debited. "At the end of the year they can tell me how we stand from their book as good as I can from mine." Some padded croppers' accounts due, then robbed them of their corn in order to balance fraudulent books, the farmer declared. "Last year the colored feller that had a crop with me fell behind $36, but when he moved I let 'em take his share of the corn away with him. I say let 'em have the corn. You can't strip a man right down to the bottom like that." [45]

Among the thousands of letters, interviews, life histories, and oral histories of planters, farmers, and tenants of all classes that survive from the 1920s through the 1950s, hardly a handful relate such stories of fair practice. The spoken and written expressions of the landlord class are conspicuously silent on matters of account keeping and settlement. Without other evidence it is not possible to detect cheating in landlords' cash books or store accounts now, but errors in the pay of hired workers occurred so methodically, especially for black tractor drivers, that present-day auditors may conclude that systematic cheating

44. Raper, *Preface to Peasantry,* 161–73.
45. Bernice Kelly Harris, "Sharecropping's the Best," n.d. (1938 or 1939) (Typescript in FWP life histories files, SHC).

was widespread.[46] Documents from tenants, on the other hand, are filled with bitter reproaches not only against the system of tenure but against landlords' chicanery, bullying, mendacity, and voracious greed for money, no matter how small the denominations. Percy's class made a mockery of the term *gentleman,* which they loved so well, and discredited themselves before the class and the race they pretended to protect. Posing as premodern aristocrats, they lost credibility long before their fragmented plantations were depopulated and enclosed.

Planter-landlords gouged dependents in several ways. They maintained books on tenants' fertilizer and other debts that were not available to tenants' or others' inspection. When tenants did manage to keep books, landlords refused to accept discrepancies from their own or to submit to audit. They also prohibited tenants from marketing their own cash crops, insuring tenants' ignorance of actual credits at fall settlement. Where and when landlords extended cash advances as furnish, they charged usurious interest rates. Landlords who kept plantation commissaries charged higher prices to credit customers in addition to high interest charges on credit. Planters also not infrequently inflated the accounts receivable of share tenants who owned work stock and equipment to rob them of their chattels and reduce them to sharecropping. And some landlords, unbeknownst to tenants, mortgaged tenants' property as well as their own to bankers to have capital to raise crops *and* to practice usury on the tenants!

The career of "Jim Parker," a black North Carolinian, illustrates three variations of the account-keeping problem. Parker (a fictitious name used by a FWP interviewer) at first owned his own farm but lost that and his savings and went to sharecropping with a white landlord, "Tommie Stephenson." Stephenson provided Parker with mules and fertilizer and advanced supplies at his store to furnish Parker and his family of fifteen. Parker was ambitious to move back up the tenure ladder, so he bought a horse from Stephenson on credit. "That was the cause of our first misunderstandin'," said Parker. "Mr. Tommie charged the horse against my account that year, claimin' I didn't pay him, when I knowed I had. I lost it." Unlike most landlords, Stephenson permitted Parker to keep parallel accounts, "but the trouble was our books wouldn't run out together. I never went to school past the fou'th grade, but I learnt enough to keep up with my figgerin' and read right good." The "second

46. See, for example, labor account books for the late 1940s in Thomas Hottel Gist Plantation and Business Records, University of Arkansas Library, Fayetteville.

misunderstandin' with Mr. Tommie was over fertilize he charged against
me that I knowed I hadn't used. There was gettin' to be too much difference in our books." Parker endured Stephenson's accounting for ten
years before moving to another place. The next landlord did not permit
tenants to keep their own books, and "at the end of the year he had
enough fertilize charged against me to use on his whole farm, and I told
him so." [47]

In virtually every county of the South schools for blacks were miserable buildings, poorly equipped, with inadequate teachers and short
sessions. Among the results were illiteracy rates among black adults
usually twice as high as among whites. A Federal Emergency Relief Administration survey of relief families in cotton areas in 1934 revealed
that black heads of households were more than twice as likely as whites
to have "no schooling at all." Since one in four whites in the survey had
no education, the FERA survey implied that more than half of black
rural relief household heads were utterly without education and probably illiterate. [48] Such folks were usually fair game for crafty, manipula-
tive landlords.

Landlords kept cotton prices a mystery when they could, too. "We
are making an appealing for justice," wrote several Mississippi delta
sharecroppers to the Southern Tenant Farmers' Union in November of
1936. "We are closing our cotton crops. And are now ready for a settlement. We has gins our cotton but were not allowed to keep our compress
ticket" (which registered weights). "We are not allowed to see our
counts. Not allowed to ask any question what ever." [49] An Arkansas
cropper complained (also in November of 1936) that "the man" told him
cotton was nine cents per pound, but "when ive got out of de[b]t he just
give us 8 cents." [50] In Crittenden and St. Francis counties and elsewhere,
planters and their khaki-clad, pistol-bearing riding bosses collected
cotton from pickers and prevented their further involvement in the marketing of the crop. As a St. Francis cropper put it, the landlord "had a
man to way [weigh] our cotton," another to haul it, and he "would not

47. Bernice Kelly Harris, "Jim Parker Hopes Ahead," June 7, 1939 (Typescript in
FWP life histories files, SHC).

48. See county tables on schools, school years, and illiteracy in Charles Johnson *et al.*
(comps.), *Statistical Atlas;* and FERA and BAE, "Area Report: Survey of Rural Problem
Areas—Cotton Growing Region of the Old South," by Harold Hoffsommer (Typescript,
ca. 1934, in RG 83, NA), 10.

49. Ed Harper, Richard Cross, Will Cross, *et al.* to "Union Co—," November 16,
1936, roll 3, STFU Papers.

50. Fred Lewis to J. R. Butler, November 1, 1936, *ibid.*

let us go to the gin and woulden give us no seed ticket. No cotton ticket." When the croppers protested, the landlord began firing his pistol. "I got scared and run off." [51]

Share tenants were prize game because they had property that might be taken through fraud. An eastern Arkansan wrote in 1937 that his "account was padded to death this year padded not less than one hundred dollars, all this to hit the mark" his landlord-creditor was "aiming after." The landlord wished "to keep me from paying my honest debts and take approximately five hundred dollars worth of my belongings such as mules & tools and put me in the road." The tenant had good reason to fear the creditor and his allies, the sheriff and deputies. Too much complaining about padded accounts, "and the next thing for me will be beating or may be death." [52]

When sharecroppers were white, planters were hardly less determined to control marketing and the terms of settlement. The daughter of a Mississippi delta tenant recalled a dangerous confrontation with his landlord early in the 1930s. The white family had picked a wagonload of cotton and the father was preparing to drive to the gin, when "the landlord met him and told him to get down and go back to the field and keep picking." The cropper answered, " 'no,' he would take it." When the landlord moved toward the wagon, the father grabbed a heavy "glass jug that we used to carry our water in, and he told" the planter, "if he got up there he would knock him off . . . that he was taking that [cotton] to town." The landlord backed off, but the daughter reflected that this "was the last time" her father "made an effort . . . to carry his own cotton. He just give in, I reckon." Standing up for perceived rights was fraught with long-term as well as short-term danger, for "if you wanted to rent another plantation, well, the way you did had a whole lot to do with whether you could get it or not—a good rent." [53] Planters stood together and blacklisted such troublemakers.

Credit and interest arrangements plagued landlord-tenant relations all year, everywhere. About 1918 Ned Cobb, then a share tenant in Talla-

51. See C. J. Spradling (of Crittenden) to Butler, September 5, 1938, roll 9, and Willie North (of St. Francis) to Mitchell, April 27, 1936, roll 2, both *ibid.*

52. J. E. Johnson to Butler, November 24, 1937, roll 5, *ibid.* On physical intimidation and violence against tenants, see also H. L. Mitchell, *Mean Things Happening in This Land: The Life and Times of H. L. Mitchell* (Montclair, N.J., 1979), 18–19.

53. Quoted in J. Wayne Flynt, *Dixie's Forgotten People: The South's Poor Whites* (Bloomington, Ind., 1979), 68. Another example of landlord control of white tenants' lives and business is John L. Dove, "A Pile of Sawdust," life history of Lee Peake, November 30, 1938 (in Pontiac, S.C.) (Typescript in FWP life histories files, SHC).

poosa County, Alabama, discovered that his landlord had encumbered his mules, equipment, and other property with a town merchant. An illiterate, Cobb had made his mark on a note without understanding that he was making his own chattels collateral for the landlord's debts as well as his own. So in the late winter, upon paying his own debt and requesting his canceled note, Cobb was rebuffed by the merchant, who informed him the landlord-cosigner had not yet paid his part of the debt. "That was killin' to me," Cobb said, because "if he didn't pay . . . they'd come to me for it." The landlord "was the only one that could draw money" on the account, but Cobb and other tenant cosigners "were all responsible for what he owed." [54]

Country stores and plantation commissaries were the principal agencies of credit and chiseling. Crossroads stores were established throughout the expanding row-crop South following the Civil War. Merchants and planters who operated them received short-term credit for inventories from banks that charged high rates, then passed on these expenses of business and more to their rural customers. Accounting was new to the backcountry late in the nineteenth century, and it remained a mind-boggling mystery to the poor and uneducated who were obliged to do business on credit. Thus evolved early a cynical verse repeated all over the region for generations: "An ought's an ought / And a figger's a figger / All for the white man / And none for the nigger." White debtors of all tenure classes came under sway of the stores through merchants' or landlords' liens on their crops, but blacks of the lowest classes were more susceptible to manipulation and the abuses of the system. The classic country store, with bulk produce, tools, clothing, patent medicines, coffin hardware and linings—almost everything imaginable—began rapidly to disappear after World War I. The automobile, better roads, the appearance of chain stores in towns, the introduction of cash advances to tenants—all led to the modification or disappearance of the general store. The same pressures of modernization forced many planters to abandon commissaries, which had functioned much like stores. A New Deal study of 634 plantations in seven cotton states in 1934 revealed that 74.1 percent were without commissaries. Of those with commissaries, only 15 percent were compulsory ones—that is, tenants had the option of doing business elsewhere in most cases. [55]

54. Theodore Rosengarten, *All God's Dangers: The Life of Nate Shaw* (New York, 1975), 159.

55. Thomas D. Clark, *Pills, Petticoats, and Plows: The Southern Country Store* (Indianapolis, 1944), esp. 313–36. On automobiles, roads, town stores, and the decline of

Until planters acquired adequate capital directly or indirectly from the federal government, however, and until they finally disposed of most tenants, great dependent populations remained on the land, vulnerable to continuing extortion by methods old or modified. These included the charging of usurious rates on cash advances and the manipulation of prices and interest charges at updated stores and remaining commissaries. During the late 1920s and early 1930s, Arthur Raper found in Greene and Macon counties, Georgia, landlords and merchants charging 10 percent interest on advances for three and a half months. Four-month money cost 25 percent, and the actual annual rate was about 35 percent. Wide, careful federal surveys of plantations in 1934 and 1937 more or less generalized Raper's sample of two Georgia counties. Annual interest rates averaged about 37 percent both years across the cotton South. The federal researchers also found that this rate amounted to two to three times the interest planters paid banks for short-term credit. Near Blytheville, Arkansas, in 1937, black sharecroppers claimed "actual proof" that they were "being charged fifty percent [i]nterest on cash furnished" by their landlord.[56]

Commissary markups on goods remained outrageous through the 1930s. William R. Amberson of the University of Tennessee medical college in Memphis sampled prices of comparable items in eastern Arkansas plantation commissaries and in town cash stores. Twenty-four-pound sacks of flour cost 10.53 percent more, and four-pound cans of lard were sold for 12.5 percent more. A five-pound bag of sugar cost 34 cents in a commissary and 25 cents in a cash store, a difference of 36 percent. Commissary markups over cash store prices were usually most

country general stores, see also Rebecca Yarbrough, oral history of Alice Dortch Balch, March 25, 1974 (Typescript in University of Arkansas Library, Little Rock); Raper, *Preface to Peasantry,* 50–53, on the Georgia black belt; Katherine Palmer, "The Country Store," life history of Frederick and Lenore Moore, February 14, 1939 (Chatham County, N.C.), W. O. Saunders, "Isaac ('Big Ike') O'Neal," life history, n.d. (1938 or 1939) (Ocracoke, N.C.), and Saunders, "Business Is a Pleasure," life history of George A. Twiddy, January 12, 1939 (Elizabeth City, N.C.) (All typescripts, in FWP life histories files, SHC); Herman Clarence Nixon, *Possum Trot: Rural Community, South* (Norman Okla., 1941), 45–56, on the decline and ruin after World War I of Nixon's father's store in Alabama. The New Deal study is WPA, Division of Social Research, *Landlord and Tenant on the Cotton Plantation,* by T. J. Woofter, Jr. (Washington, D.C., 1936), 203. Eastern Arkansas seems to have been the center of continuing plantation commissaries. See Florence Smith to Mitchell, June 10, 1938, roll 8, STFU Papers.

56. Raper, *Preface to Peasantry,* 46; Gunnar Myrdal, *An American Dilemma* (2 vols.; New York, 1944), I, 247; Mrs. M. H. Barnes to Butler, September 2, 1937, roll 5, STFU Papers.

egregious on small items, such as one pound of salt pork (14 cents versus 11 cents, or 27.3 percent difference) and canned salmon (15 cents versus 12½ cents, or 20 percent). Cash and credit prices at a Woodruff County, Arkansas, plantation commissary in 1938 varied much more. Cash prices compare almost exactly with those charged at a one-price general store in Caledonia, eastern Texas, just outside the plantation subregion—eight pounds of lard, 80 cents; a loaf of bread, 10 cents; matches, 5 cents; baking powder, 10 cents, and so on. But the Arkansas commissary's credit prices on some of the same items soared—30 percent more for lard, for example, 80 percent more for a bushel of potatoes, 100 percent more for a sack of smoking tobacco, and 200 percent more for baking soda.[57]

The Delta and Pine Land Company, headquartered at Scott, Mississippi, attempted to achieve a measure of vertical integration through its plantation mercantile operations. During the 1930s corporate directors decided to have some croppers grow wheat. The company milled, bagged, and labeled the flour and stocked it in D&PL stores for sale (on credit) back to the croppers. Store managers were ordered to exclude the old brands from outside, but according to the store manager at Scott, there was a "rebellion" against D&PL flour. Customers liked their old brands and refused the assistance of the Bolivar County home demonstration agent (called in by the manager) in learning to bake the home flour. The head office still urged the distressed store manager to move the product, but he finally fed the flour to company hogs.[58]

Such defeats for the rural ruling class were hardly significant. The planter-landlords would lose power, in an important sense, only when the masses over whom they held sway were gone and both classes were utterly incorporated into the modern world of cash. Thorough capitalization of agriculture and depopulation of the countryside, in the meantime, required between twenty and thirty years. All the while, planters continued to enjoy not only managerial monopoly and credit controls but the advantages of access to governmental power in main-

57. Percentages calculated from William R. Amberson, "The Social and Economic Consequences of the Cotton Acreage Reduction Program," in Norman Thomas, *The Plight of the Sharecropper* (New York, 1934), 22. See also Ernest Williams to STFU National Office, June 18, 1938, roll 8, STFU Papers, on the Arkansas commissary; and daybooks and ledgers of the C. E. Sanford and Son General Store Records, Stephen F. Austin State University Library, Nacogdoches, Texas.

58. Bill Boyd, interview with J. L. Hatcher, n.d. (*ca.* 1975) (Audio tape of Delta and Pine Land Company Oral History, Mississippi State University Library).

taining control over labor until the end. In certain crises, planters' access to this power was demonstrated awesomely.

The terrible Mississippi River flood of 1927 is an example. Among delta planters from southeastern Missouri through Louisiana, hysteria reigned. Sharecroppers and laborers tied to estates by debt were dispersed to refugee camps on high ground miles from home. Planters feared not only for flooded fields but for the security of their investments and labor supplies. The Red Cross and especially the national guards of lower Mississippi states collaborated with landlords on every front of worry. Refugee labor (almost all black) was accounted for, fed, and effectively detained as close to home as possible. And labor recruiters from inland and the North were intimidated and run off, particularly by the Mississippi National Guard.[59]

The appearance of two ill-fated agricultural labor unions during the 1930s presented more challenges to planter-landlords. The Alabama Sharecroppers Union (ASU) was founded by white members of the Communist party, U.S.A., in 1932. Membership soared within a year to an estimated 5,500, virtually all black and non-Communist. The ASU attempted to organize and bargain collectively on behalf of farm laborers and to represent sharecroppers and share tenants in disputes over contracts, credit, and claims against tenants' property at settlement time. Still a rather shadowy organization—its officers used assumed names, and few union documents survive—the ASU gained one moment of national publicity as a result of a shootout between black union members and sheriff's deputies in Tallapoosa County. Ned Cobb fired some of the shots, wounded a county lawman, and went to prison for a dozen years. The union's very existence in black-belt Alabama reveals a certain amount of backbone among a peasantry theretofore silent, but the ASU was liquidated in 1935, and its membership had apparently dissolved before that. Perhaps the major significance of the episode is its demonstration of the effectiveness of planter-employers' alliance with county and state law enforcement and judicial institutions.[60]

59. Pete Daniel, *Deep'n as It Come: The 1927 Mississippi River Flood* (New York, 1977), 107–108.

60. See Rosengarten, *All God's Dangers*, 312–44, 393–94, 585–87; George B. Tindall, *The Emergence of the New South, 1913–1945* (Baton Rouge, 1967), 379–80; Mitchell to James E. Sidel, December 15, 1939, roll 13, STFU Papers, which gives an overview of union activity among farm tenants and workers; Thomas Burke to Mitchell, January 31, 1936, roll 1, STFU Papers. Burke was a member of the ASU executive committee.

The Southern Tenant Farmers' Union was more widespread, numerous, and well known. Founded in 1934 at Tyronza, Arkansas (northwest of Memphis), by two white Socialists, some black preachers, and a few sharecroppers of both races, the STFU tried to protect the landless from eviction and extortion in the wake of the New Deal's AAA program. Strongest in the deltas of northeastern Arkansas and southeastern Missouri, the STFU spread to eastern Oklahoma, Texas, and parts of Mississippi as well, claiming up to twenty-five thousand black, white, Indian, and mixed-race members. Like the ASU, the STFU organized local chapters, which demanded recognition from planters. The STFU went further, however, and staged several cotton pickers' strikes, one of which (in 1936) apparently gained minor wage concessions from landlords in Arkansas. By 1938 the union was practically dead, however. It could not stay the wholesale evictions and dispersal of its membership. Union jurisdictional and interracial troubles fractured what remained. But more spectacularly than the ASU's Tallapoosa shootout, the STFU was also broken by threats and violence from planters, their hired thugs and riding bosses, and local police. H. L. Mitchell, an STFU founder and its secretary-treasurer, did not exaggerate when he and Socialist party leader Norman Thomas declared that a "reign of terror" prevailed in Arkansas during the mid-1930s.[61]

The STFU files are filled with letters from frightened folks from Marked Tree, Blytheville, Truman, Earle, Round Pond, and dozens of other rural settlements. Outside Blytheville in the fall of 1937 a "Chamber of Commerce gang," wrote an eyewitness (without intending humor, it seems), stopped trucks loaded with cotton pickers and ordered them to work for no more than seventy-five cents per day.[62] "County officers" stood with planters and their hirelings armed with pistols, shotguns, and blackjacks outside country churches and other union meeting places. Sheriffs arrested a union organizer for "anarchism" and beat anyone within reach suspected of union activity. "Thangs is happening round hear," wrote a cropper from near Earle. A "planter got on me & tried to beat me up. . . . he cursed me for every thang . . . & hit me wonce." Resignedly he concluded, "You no that thar is no use of trying to get this law to do iney thang."[63]

61. See Mitchell, *Mean Things Happening,* 3–177; Grubbs, *Cry from the Cotton;* Howard Kester, *Revolt Among the Sharecroppers* (New York, 1936).

62. "Statement of Rellie Travis," n.d. (*ca.* October, 1937) (Typescript on roll 5, STFU Papers).

63. Hugh Nicholson to Butler, June 19, 1937, roll 4, and see Henry Burnett, deposition, October 13, 1937 (Typescript on roll 5), both *ibid.* See also (a small sample of anti-

Indeed. With few notable exceptions— for example, the jailing of a handful of planters for practicing peonage—"this law" protected the privileged, even to the point of extralegal vigilantism and violence. The South had no monopoly on the phenomenon. Throughout the years of the ASU's and STFU's losing struggles, local authorities (as well as town elites) in central and southern California sided openly with ranchers in disputes with unions of striking fruit, vegetable, and cotton pickers. Some of the battered California strikers were migrants from the Southeast.[64]

At least as significant, both in the plantation South and in California, was the support of federal authority. While local police participated in paramilitary actions against organized farm laborers, the national government subsidized the ascendancy of western cotton and the capitalization of large-scale southern agriculture, the final victory of the planters over their peasants. The impact of the AAA and its successors and of the Production Credit Association have already been chronicled. If anything, federal support for the cash nexus and the end of any remnants of premodern, subsistence rural life intensified after World War II. By the late 1940s nearly every important agricultural county in the lower South had a labor assistant to the Extension Service agent. His job was to instruct large farmers and planters in ever-more sophisticated ways to save labor in farm operations and management.[65] Such was the process of transforming a South modern in the original sense of the word into a modern world understood everywhere by 1950.

By then the southern island communities of 1930 were gone, save in those parts of the highlands not yet reached by paved highways. Gone also by the 1950s were the last of the semisubsistence local economies of the old era. Tractorization, other capital requirements of modern agriculture, and heavy migration obliterated entire communities. The young departed, as H. C. Nixon sadly wrote, and only the dead returned. Other, now-shrunken communities survived only as exurbs of cities within driving distance.

The big changes were probably easiest for rural folks who had already lived with cash and commerce for a long time—fruit-vegetable

---

union violence) W. B. Moore to Butler, May 26, 1937, roll 4, *ibid.*; Mitchell, *Mean Things Happening,* 3–177 and *passim.*

64. Pete Daniel, *The Shadow of Slavery: Peonage in the South, 1901–1969* (New York, 1972), 110–48, 170–92; Cletus E. Daniel, *Bitter Harvest: A History of California Farmworkers, 1870–1941* (Ithaca, 1981), 222–31.

65. See, *e.g.,* typescript annual narrative reports of county agents for 1947 in Ala-

and grain-dairy-livestock farmers, and diversified row-crop specialists fortunate enough to live near urban markets. They became the core of the southern family-farmer class of the postwar decades. Planters, too, survived and thrived. A sizable minority of them had moved to towns and cities well before World War II. The majority, with good automobiles, education, and social connections, had long been town oriented. The price planters paid for the rewards of neoplantation production—if one may call this a price—was loss of most of the masses they had ruled for so long. This is of course not an economic but a psychic price, and if we are to believe the planters who spoke out about tenant displacement and mechanization, few had regrets. Perhaps only romantics who gave serious humanistic thought to relationships between production and social organization—a few men such as William Alexander Percy—perceived the depopulation of the plantation South as a sad event.

Modernization wrought the most severe changes for those millions of plantation-belt landless, for highlanders, and for white-land southerners, black and white. For them there was no life-sustaining place left on the land. Many had no choice but migration. Others could either migrate or remain in the country, commuting to a city for work in something other than farming. As we shall see in later chapters, some migrants and commuters mourned the loss of local relations and the homier life of the semisubsistence economy, but most (especially black folk) were happy to be free of the oppression of the old system. No romantics were they.

---

bama Extension Service Records, Auburn University Archives; annual narrative reports (on microfilm) for 1947 for the Mississippi and Georgia Extension Services, Mississippi State University Library.

If maidens knew what good wives know
They never would care to wed.
—*PROGRESSIVE FARMER*, 1887

It's not nature to say if you will have children or not.
—A FLORIDA SQUATTER'S WIFE, 1938

It was always the women who scared me. The stories
that women told and that men told were full of violence, sickness, and death. But it was the women
whose stories were unrelieved by humor and filled with
apocalyptic vision. No matter how awful the stories
were that the men told they were always funny. . . .
But women would repeat stories about folks they did
not know and had never seen, and consequently, without character counting for anything, the stories were as
stark and cold as legend or myth.
—HARRY CREWS

Chapter 5
Women, Wedlock, Hearth, Health, Death

DURING SLAVERY NEARLY ALL BLACK FOLK
worked in the fields—women and children above the age of five, as well
as men. After emancipation, as the sharecropping system evolved, freedmen bargained for semiindependence, separate fields, and homes they
could manage themselves. One of their goals was to rescue their women
and small children from field work. Wives, mothers, and sisters would,
like white women nearby, remain in the home. For most, such hopes
soon proved futile. Not only did landlords supervise sharecroppers, but
an entire family's labor figured importantly in the acreage and soil a
cropper might "rent" for a year and, of course, in projected annual income. So free women and children marched off to chop and pick cotton
and to weed and pull corn and tobacco as before. Large families remained as economically important as ever, too; for theoretically, the
larger the labor force, the more production, the more earnings and security. And as the row-crop South expanded, life and labor for white
families came increasingly to resemble the sort of freedom blacks
had found.[1]

1. See Ronald L. F. Davis, *Good and Faithful Labor: From Slavery to Sharecropping
in the Natchez District, 1860–1890* (Westport, Conn., 1982); Roger L. Ransom and
Richard Sutch, *One Kind of Freedom: The Economic Consequences of Emancipation*
(Cambridge, Eng., 1977), 6–7, 232–36.

By 1930 the margin separating the lives of poor rural folks, black and white, was narrow. According to the United States Children's Bureau, almost 70 percent of white farmers' children in North Carolina were workers; 75 percent of black rural children worked. In Texas, where white families were predominant in cotton, 75 percent of all children aged six to sixteen were counted as laborers. Howard Kester, a white Christian socialist minister and antipoverty activist, reported seeing (probably in eastern Arkansas) "a two-weeks-old baby wrapped in quilts and laid in a furrow while the mother worked the cotton. I have seen mothers ready for child-birth still in the fields pulling at the soft white fiber." Arthur Raper recorded another scene of family labor (apparently white) in black-belt Georgia: "A mother left her tenant cabin with a baby in her arms, broke a sapling, carried it to the middle of the field, stuck it in the ground and tied her crawling child fast to it to keep him in the shade while she hoed." Nearby, Raper also noted, "was a thirteen-year-old boy with a hoe; he had been hoeing seven years." Because across the South blacks were proportionately more likely to occupy the lowest tenancy status, their lot remained harder than that of whites. Black women commonly worked as domestics in white homes, too—in addition to all their other chores—whereas poor white women in the country seldom saw outside domestic service.[2]

For girls of both races, childhood could turn suddenly into an adulthood of thankless drudgery. The eldest daughter of a white family of seven children in eastern Kentucky told a familiar story to an FWP interviewer late in the 1930s: "Mammy died when I was twelve years old. She laid her burden down and I took it up." The daughter not only cooked, washed, and cared for younger siblings, but worked in the family tobacco field as well. "I had to work awful hard, and pappy was so mean to me." After five years, at seventeen, she ran away and married, lessening her burden only momentarily.[3] A white North Carolina tobacco-cotton tenant's wife related another woeful tale of the shock of married life. "I fell in love with Paul when I was sixteen, and I married him against my parents' better judgment just before I was seventeen. He took me at once to the fifty acres that he had rented for the year, and the

2. Howard Kester, *Revolt Among the Sharecroppers* (New York, 1936), 45, 47; Arthur F. Raper, *Preface to Peasantry: A Tale of Two Black Belt Counties* (Chapel Hill, 1936), 29. The generalization is based upon typescript oral histories in the Mary Holmes College Oral History Program, West Point, Mississippi.

3. Hettie A. Dunn, "A Courageous Woman," life history of Fay Balleau Armstrong, n.d. (1938 or 1939) (Typescript in "Our Lives" project files, WPA in Kentucky, Kentucky State Archives, Frankfort).

second day after the wedding he put me in the cotton patch chopping cotton. I chopped ten hours that day." While she prepared their midday dinner in a steaming kitchen, her bridegroom told her she "might as well get used to it"; then he went "out in the shade and slept." [4] Another Carolina farm woman summarized a typical workday anytime between April and October for a woman not yet surrounded by children: "I was hollered out of bed at four o'clock and after I'd got the house cleaned up if I didn't go to the branch to wash, I went to the field to hoe. When I seen the sun get to noon I went back to the house an cooked dinner. Then when I'd hung my dishrag on the plum bush outside the kitchen door I grabbed my splitbonnet and took back to the cornfield." [5] Women in the throes of childbearing and -rearing often labored to exhaustion and despondency. A tobacco sharecropper's wife with children five years and nine months old declared, "I don't want to do nothing when I ain't working, except rest. I'm tired all the time lately and I reckon I've got a right to be." Tobacco culture compounded her weariness: "When you raise the stuff it's really 'backer all the time, pretty near all the year around." [6] Her contribution to all the tedious phases of making the crop was expected.

This is not to say all women suffered. Some were vigorous agrarians who loved heavy work and endless hours. A black domestic worker in Raleigh, raised in the country, deserted by her husband, and living in the poorest circumstances, stated disarmingly in 1939 that "work is de most pleasantest, comfortablest, thing 'tis in de whole world. I shore likes to work; allus did." [7] Another Carolinian (probably white) relished tobacco work. She bragged late in 1938, "I'm good at raisin' backer. I've broke land for backer, cotton, corn, oats and rye, laid off rows with stakes and without them, pulled plants from backer beds and set them out on acres and acres of land, wormed row after row" throughout the growth season, then "topped and suckered it, too." At tobacco barning and curing, she declared, "I'm as good or better than most men. The heat don't hurt me," and she could "grade 'bout as much as any man or

4. Mary A. Hicks, "Easier Ways," life history of Leonard and Bessie Warwick, July, 1939 (Typescript in FWP life histories files, Southern Historical Collection, University of North Carolina [SHC]).

5. Ethel Deal, "Maybe Some Day I Can Read to Myself," June 19, 1939 (Typescript, *ibid.*).

6. Tom E. Terrill and Jerold Hirsch (eds.), *Such as Us: Southern Voices of the Thirties* (Chapel Hill, 1978), 97–98.

7. Nancy T. Robinson, "If 'Tis God's Will," life history of Lula Garner, May 23, 1939 (Typescript in FWP life histories files, SHC).

GIRL'S WORK—GATHERING STOVEWOOD, *ca.* 1938
USDA No. 83-G-37947, National Archives

woman I've ever seen." [8] Blessed with robust health and free, apparently, from the care of small children, she made the most of life outdoors as a tenant's wife.

Younger siblings in large families, also, felt little of the ceaseless
pressure of responsibility that burdened the firstborn. A black woman
raised during the 1920s on a North Carolina cotton farm recalled (from
her home in New Jersey, late in the 1970s) that "I never did have it real
hard on the farm." Her assigned task of drawing water from a well without a pulley and crank was cause for complaint—"it wasn't no fun
drawin' water." But her older sister took principal responsibility for
washing, ironing, and cooking dinner. Helping her with these chores,
spring and fall work in the fields, and wintertime firewood gathering
were not onerous. Evenings, after supper and school lessons, she sat
"without a thing to do," watching the indomitable elder sister "piece
quilts, quilts, quilts." A white woman of Catawba County, North Carolina, gave the perspective of the eldest of an all-female brood: "It was

8. T. Pat Matthews, "The Wood Family," November, 1938 (Typescript, *ibid.*).

four girls in our family, and I was the oldest. I had to be boy and girl."
She planted, hoed, shocked wheat, and hauled hay, but plowed little, for
her father "never did think that was a woman's place." [9]

Other women among the rural poor had the good fortune to marry
strong, gentle men who treated them as beloved partners. One such was
the wife of Ned Cobb, the illiterate black denizen of Tallapoosa County,
Alabama, who struggled from sharecropper to share tenant to mortgaged small owner before his illustrious shootout with the sheriff's men
and prison. Mrs. Cobb was the bright daughter of a small landowner
who learned to read and write despite the nearly year-round field work
she performed on the family's farm. Cobb prized her literacy and good
sense. When they wed, he recalled telling her: "I'm married to you.
And I think my best business should be in your hands. If anybody
knows the ins and outs" of contracts, debts, and prices, "you are the
one to know." "She was," Cobb reflected, "in a way of speakin, the *eyes*
and I was the mouthpiece." So they survived most of the maneuvers of
crafty landlords and bankers and climbed the ladder of tenancy. Meanwhile Cobb also realized the postemancipation dream of keeping his
wife out of the field and in the house most of the year. Cobb even milked
their cows, keeping "the bucket out of her hands all except to bring
the milk in the house and strain it, prepare it for the family." Nor did
Mrs. Cobb do domestic work for whites. "I didn't want any money
comin into my house from that," Cobb said. Yet she did care for her
husband and their ten children, plus an eleventh child left by her dead
sister, while keeping the books and advising her husband on business. [10]

An unknown number of rural married women were coal miners. In
Kentucky, Alabama, and elsewhere in Appalachia they worked, usually
alongside their husbands, in small "contract" or family-run mines. Ethel
McCuiston of Walker County, Alabama, worked at night as a blaster
with her husband from about 1941 to the mid-1950s. When she began
her career with dynamite she still had a small child at home and kept
boarders as well. Usually she went underground three nights each week,
from seven o'clock in the evening until five the following morning. Returning home, she would "build a fire in the coal cookstove and boil me
a big kettle of water, and take a bath and clean up." Then she would

9. Audrey Olsen Faulkner, *et al.* (eds.), *When I Was Comin' Up: An Oral History of
Aged Blacks* (Hamden, Conn., 1982), 48; Jacqueline Hall, interview with Eunice Austin,
July 2, 1980 (Typescript in Southern Oral History Program, SHC [SOHP]).

10. Theodore Rosengarten, *All God's Dangers: The Life of Nate Shaw* (New York,
1975), 128, 280, and *passim*.

prepare breakfast for her boarders, clean the kitchen, make the beds, and feed the cows; about nine o'clock she would cook breakfast again, for her husband. At last, she said, "I'd go to the field, or do whatever I had to do. I never did need much sleep"![11]

Other women were sole heads of farm households at all levels of tenure. In 1939 two elderly white sisters had been successfully managing a diversified Alabama plantation of four hundred acres since late in the previous century. Black sharecroppers grew cotton, and a domestic and her daughter cooked and cleaned their house, but the sisters actively cared for swine and cattle, fruit trees, a large garden, and oversaw timber cutting and the marketing of cedar posts. In northeastern North Carolina an unmarried white woman owned a fifty-nine-acre "two-horse" farm, working about thirty acres herself and renting the other half on shares. Eager for independence from merchants and debts and wishing to live at home, she reduced the size of her peanut and cotton cash crops in favor of corn for her stock. Her only help was a black boy who lived on her place and did day labor. She apparently plowed, harrowed, and performed most heavy work herself. A black woman in Macon County, Alabama (near Tuskegee), lost a 40-acre farm in a divorce before World War I but recovered quickly during the war, raising cotton and living at home with the help of her son on another 40 acres. During the 1920s and 1930s she gradually acquired 140 more acres, supervised sharecroppers, studied agronomy at Tuskegee, benefited from New Deal subsidies, and emerged as a model for the tiny black rural middle class. A white woman near Saluda, North Carolina, also triumphed over personal misfortune. Addie Grimes (seventy-eight years old in 1939) raised six children, tenant farmed cotton, and worked in a textiles mill while her husband "drank himself to death." Finally she bought a small dairy and vegetable farm, which she worked with two daughters who remained at home. The three women raised virtually all their own and their dairy herd's food, and sold milk daily in Saluda.[12]

Like male farmers, most women who headed rural households across

11. Marat Moore, "Coalmining Women," *Southern Exposure,* IX (Winter, 1981), 42–47.
12. Terrill and Hirsch (eds.), *Such as Us,* 103–107; Bernice Kelly Harris, "Rosa Warrick, Farmer," March 21, 1939 (Typescript in FWP life histories files, SHC); Rhussus L. Perry, "Janey Gets Her Desires," in James Seay Brown (ed.), *Up Before Daylight: Life Histories from the Alabama Writers' Project, 1938–1939* (University, Ala., 1982), 169–75; Adyleen G. Merrick, "Women Have to Keep on Strivin'," life history of Addie Grimes, June, 1939 (Typescript in FWP life histories files, SHC).

the South were not owners but tenants of one sort or another. Some never married and sought places as sharecroppers from landlords who rented them twenty acres or less. Others assumed responsibility and the plow handles when their husbands deserted them. Others were widows who at various ages became farmers in the formal sense. Poor women with small children at home not yet ready for field work suffered particular strain and tension, especially if there were no relatives nearby to watch the children. And when New Deal crop reductions persuaded landlords to evict tenants, single women with families were not spared. An Arkansas widow and her eight children made eighteen bales of cotton in 1935, for example, but in 1936 they were homeless and desperate. A 1937 Southern Tenant Farmers' Union survey of eastern Arkansas union members in need of federal relief included few female-headed households—only about 5 percent of the total. But in 1930 women accounted for 12.3 percent of the Delta and Pine Land Company's largest store accounts (34 of 276). During World War II women took over the operation of farms throughout the nation, and southern landlords apparently turned to women as never before. Oscar Johnston of D&PL complained, however, that married women with husbands in the armed services often refused to work in the fields. They received from the government a fifty-dollar allotment per month for themselves, plus thirty dollars for a first child and twenty dollars for each additional child. A woman with two children thus had an undreamed-of monthly income of a hundred dollars. Women without uniformed husbands and, for whatever reasons, without wartime industrial jobs, however, remained as dependent as ever and prepared to take farms. By 1949 D&PL had fewer croppers overall, but a much larger ratio of women— 20.6 percent—keeping accounts at its stores.[13]

Examination of the intimate lives of rural folks is not easy and will never go very deep or be entirely convincing. In recent years scholars

13. See Helen Shuler, "Mattie Hammond Harrell," December 11, 1938 (Typescript in FWP life histories files, SHC); and Faulkner *et al.* (eds.), *When I Was Comin' Up*, 43–45, for examples of single tenant women and their trials. The Arkansas widow, Maggie McMarris, described her plight to the Southern Tenant Farmers' Union in a December 21, 1936, letter, roll 3, STFU Papers, SHC. Tommie Corvan to STFU, October 23, 1937, roll 5, *ibid.*, reported a case of an Arkansas landlord expropriating the chattels of a widow share tenant. See also typescript relief survey, 1937, roll 7, *ibid.;* and "Ticket Book Recapitulation" for stores (Typescript, March 31, 1930), "Statement and President's Report for the Year Ended March 31, 1944," and "Trial Balance" sheets for stores, March 31, 1949, all in Delta and Pine Land Company Records, Mississippi State University Library.

have discovered many remarkably explicit diaries and other documents of marriage and sexuality among the middle and upper classes on both sides of the Atlantic, but of the masses, who wrote down little and left less to research libraries, we know little. Whites and blacks appear to have shared what is usually thought of as a middle-class modesty, which forbade open discussion of intimacy either among adults or between parents and children.[14] Beneath this social surface there must have been much talk as well as activity. And as folklorist Vance Randolph discovered, there is a rich tradition of ribaldry among the lower classes. The most famous tale he collected, "Pissing in the Snow," relates the falling out of two Ozark neighbors. The father of a young girl forbids his friend's son from coming on his property because the boy has urinated in the snow, spelling his daughter's name, Lucy. "No harm," says the boy's father. "No harm!" yells Lucy's daddy, "there was two sets of tracks! And besides, don't you think I know my own daughter's handwriting?"[15] Such gems from the so-called inarticulate tantalize the imagination. One wishes there were more.

During 1938–1939 hundreds of interviewers paid by the New Deal's Federal Writers' Project (FWP) set out to collect the life histories of Americans, especially in the South. Experienced professional writers such as Bernice Kelly Harris, the North Carolina novelist, were given almost free rein to select subjects and structure interviews. Most of the writers were unemployed nonprofessionals, however, and most of them

14. On the middle and upper classes, see Peter Gay, *Education of the Senses* (New York, 1984), Vol. I of Gay, *The Bourgeois Experience: Victoria to Freud,* 3 vols. projected; Carl Degler, *At Odds: Women and the Family in America from the Revolution to the Present* (New York, 1980), esp. 249–78. On "Victorian" modesty, shyness, and abstemiousness among blacks, see Elizabeth Rauh Bethel, *Promiseland: A Century of Life in a Negro Community* (Philadelphia, 1981), 155–57; Faulkner *et al.* (eds.), *When I Was Comin' Up,* 26–29, 50, 119. On whites, see W. T. Couch (ed.), *These Are Our Lives* (Chapel Hill, 1939), 386–87; Gary Miller, oral history of America Jarrell, n.d. (*ca.* 1973) (Microfilm copy of typescript, in Marshall University Oral History of Appalachia Collection [MUOHA]); Mary P. Wilson, "I Don't Aim to Complain None Atall," life history of L. J. Fulham, June 28, 1939, Mary A. Hicks, "Self-Denial," life history of Peter B. Powers, February, 1939 (Both typescripts in FWP life histories files, SHC).

15. Vance Randolph (comp.), *Pissing in the Snow & Other Ozark Folktales* (New York, 1976), 37. In addition there is a tradition of libertinism among the poor. H. L. Mitchell, a well-known lothario, claims in his autobiography to have "made out" often as a teenager in rural western Tennessee. See Mitchell, *Mean Things Happening in This Land: The Life and Times of H. L. Mitchell* (Montclair, N.J., 1979), 15. In *Uptown: Poor Whites in Chicago* (New York, 1970), 25–28, Todd Gitlin and Nanci Hollander present the sexual adventures of "Ras Bryant," a one-armed wino, in rural West Virginia during the 1940s. I am not inclined to doubt Mitchell (a gentleman of my acquaintance), but as a rule I think it best to doubt anything men reveal about sex.

followed programmed questionnaires in their work. Among the subjects of interest to editor-bureaucrats were family sizes, birth control, and housing conditions.[16] Posing such questions often presented problems for both subjects and interlocutors. When white interviewer R. V. Waldrep asked a Franklin County, Alabama, black farmer about birth control, the black man responded in apparent shock, "You air gettin' mighty enquirin', ain't you?"[17] Yet he went on to give a response of sorts, as did most subjects. Women were usually more forthcoming when queried by other women. So a great many of the nearly sixteen hundred surviving southern FWP typescript interviews contain valuable if indirect and impressionistic information on the private lives of ordinary rural people. These, combined with more recent interviews, census data on population rates, scattered descriptions of housing (a subject bearing considerably on intimate lives), and a variety of published and unpublished accounts of birthing and birth control, provide valuable glimpses into secret worlds.

Next to China's, the American population growth rate in the nineteenth and early twentieth centuries ranks as a major phenomenon of modern history. Among Americans, southerners—and among them Appalachian whites and blacks everywhere—gave birth most often. Birthing was the major cycle of poor women's lives, especially. Urban and especially middle- and upper-class women had learned to space children and limit family sizes. By 1930 most of them had access to the services of private physicians and clinics, where they could receive accurate information, be fitted for diaphragms, or purchase spermicidal jellies and condoms. When city and town women gave birth they did so in hospitals with doctors in attendance, applying anesthesia. In the South and elsewhere after World War I rural women within reach of towns abandoned home birthing for hospitals and accepted the medical community's preferred mode of labor and giving birth in beds, with the mother on her back. As roads improved, too, doctors arrived to attend more rural births in homes, although into the 1930s female midwives, "granny women," often attended, too. The gradual, piecemeal demise of midwifery, indeed, paralleled other aspects of modernization in the region before World War II. Obstetrics became professionalized first in

16. See editor W. T. Couch's instructions and correspondence in the FWP life histories files, SHC, and similar documents in the "Our Lives" project files, and the Alabama Writers' Project files, Alabama Department of Archives and History, Montgomery.

17. R. V. Waldrep, "Luke Warn: He Ain't Talkin'," life history of Luke Warn, n.d. (1938 or 1939) (Typescript in Alabama Writers' Project files).

cities and towns, then in developing rural areas with paved roads near towns; the phenomenon appeared last in remote Appalachia.[18]

Before the Depression there does not seem to have been much interest among rural folks in limiting family size, and women accepted pregnancies as either blessings or fate. Tradition and strong economic pressures dictated many births for poor people. A Letcher County, Kentucky, father of five put it plainly about 1938: "What more could a man want? The more children I have the more land I can tend, the more money I can make." (He owned sixty acres and two mules.)[19] A decade earlier Rupert Vance had observed cotton landlords denying rentals to young, married would-be tenants on the ground they had no children or their children were not yet old enough to work. Much the same logic obtained in mill villages, too, where child labor was as significant as on farms. As Vance concluded, "Children thus may be said to cost the cotton farmer less and pay him more," rather as in slavery times.[20]

In remote places in the mountains, hills, and plains, southern women in labor sent for grannies and shooed husbands and older children out of doors. In the tiny all-black community of Promised Land, South Carolina, "the mens didn't have nothin to do with it," as one woman put it. Expectant mothers endured labor with only an occasional "sup of whiskey" and gave birth in a squatting position or "down on your knees."[21] During the summer of 1923 Mary Breckinridge observed much the same behavior among isolated mountain whites in Leslie, Knott, and Owsley counties, Kentucky. Breckinridge was a missionary public health nurse from the Bluegrass, who made her way through the railroadless and highwayless highlands on horse- and muleback. In 1920 the Kentucky legislature had authorized the licensing of midwives. County public health units were to provide instruction in hygiene and see that grannies carried bags of appropriate equipment, including silver nitrate for cleansing newborns' eyes. Breckinridge gathered avail-

18. James Reed, *From Private Vice to Public Virtue: The Birth Control Movement and American Society Since 1930* (New York, 1978), 225–39 and *passim*. See also Douglas DeNatale, interview with Mary Gattis, August 13, 1979 (Typescript tape index and notes, SOHP). Analysis is also based upon the interviews in the FWP life histories files, SHC, the "Our Lives" project files, and the Alabama Writers Project files; Bethel, *Promiseland*, 146–57 and *passim*; and other specific sources cited below.

19. Melvin Caudill, Jr., "The More Children, the More Land," life history of Kid Ingram, n.d. (1938 or 1939) (Typescript in "Our Lives" project files).

20. Rupert B. Vance, *Human Factors of Cotton Culture: A Study in the Social Geography of the American South* (Chapel Hill, 1929), 299–300.

21. Bethel, *Promiseland*, 146.

able delivery data for the previous year, and on her journey interviewed 53 midwives and observed some of their practices. In 1922 a grand total of 9 physicians had delivered 141 babies in three counties; midwives numbering 128 had delivered 824. All the midwives but one were white, all were native mountaineers, and their ages ranged from thirty to ninety (a median of fifty-seven). All were or had been married—overwhelmingly to farm owners—and all had given birth themselves. The average number of children among them was 8.5. Nearly all of the grannies over sixty were illiterate. Few had inherited their vocations from their mothers. Most had "gone about" with midwives while young, acquiring their learning by observation. None had the formal training professionals such as Breckinridge preferred. The midwives provided no pre- or postnatal care. Called to a labor, they calmed expectant mothers and prepared to catch infants from standing or kneeling mothers. Relatives of the mother or the grannies themselves often placed axes blade-up under the bed to "cut" postpartum bleeding as newly delivered mothers recovered. During delivery midwives made frequent vaginal examinations, first lubricating their fingers with pork fat or grease. Few carried the bags required by the 1920 regulations. Breckinridge's horror was barely concealed beneath the clinical style of her journal. She took heart that bed birthing was already becoming fashionable, however.[22]

In Carrboro and rural Chatham County, North Carolina, white women were served by a fabled black midwife, "Aunt" Hanna Degraffenreid, from early in the century until about 1930. Unlike the Kentucky grannies, Degraffenreid stayed on after deliveries to nurse mothers and children, for a week up to a month. In such relatively developed areas (Carrboro adjoins Chapel Hill and the University of North Carolina), physicians provided prenatal care from their automobiles or their town offices, and commanded at deliveries with assistance from midwives such as Degraffenreid. In Bynum, North Carolina, also Chatham County, Emeline Cotten was Degraffenreid's counterpart. From the

22. Mary Breckinridge, "Midwifery in the Kentucky Mountains: An Investigation," [1923 (?)] (Typescript in John C. and Olive D. Campbell Papers, SHC). As in Kentucky, midwifery was sanctioned by law in Arkansas during the 1920s. In 1947 new regulations required physician supervision. See Arthur English and John Carroll, "Midwifery in Arkansas," *Southern Exposure*, XII (February, 1984), 90. Dr. Julia Belk, a white physician practicing in western Tennessee around Jackson (*ca.* 1910–39) was amazed to find Gypsy women giving birth while squatting—implying that her poor black and white patients were already accustomed to bed birthing and modern obstetrics. See Ruth Clark, "Not a Lady-like Thing," life history of Dr. Julia Belk, in John L. Robinson (ed.), *Living Hard: Southern Americans in the Great Depression* (Washington, D.C., 1981), 230–35.

1890s until about 1905, she delivered babies alone; thereafter she assisted physicians.[23]

Another function of grannie women—although few would confess it—was as abortionists. Nineteenth-century middle- and upper-class women commonly obtained pills to induce abortions from physicians and pharmacists.[24] Rural and especially poor women consulted with midwives, who provided concoctions that varied according to local flora and what was available at country stores. In northern Alabama women drank a tea made from quinine, castor oil, and mistletoe (of all things), "berries, leaves, and all." In North Carolina an old granny woman advised an unhappily pregnant farm laborer's wife "to drink cotton root tea." The granny "swore that would knock it up, and it did but I liked to died."[25] There is no way of knowing how many such dangerous steps were taken to avoid childbirth. There is overwhelming impressionistic evidence, however, that southern women generally accepted pregnancy joyfully (at first, anyway) or stoically and bore children until they reached menopause or wore out and died.

There was, for example, a forty-nine-year-old white woman, wife of an utterly impoverished southern Florida squatter, who had given birth to fourteen children, one of them a mentally retarded girl. She told a FWP interviewer: "I never thought of trying to limit my family, even if I had known how [the retarded girl] would be. What could I have done about it? It's not nature to say if you will have children or not. People ought to take what comes and make the best of it; won't no one have more than they are bound to, anyway."[26] Another woman (apparently white also) expressed more despair than resignation: "Seems like all pore folks has is younguns. Then after they git here, you got nothing to keep them up." Her solution, and she well knew its tenuousness, was abstinence from sexual relations with her husband. "When my last baby

23. Valerie Quinney, interview with Mallie Ray, August 5, 1974 (typescript), Brent Glass, interview with John W. Snipes, September 20, 1976 (Typescript in "Series H"), both in SOHP. A legendary physician of Carrboro was Braxton Bragg ("Brack") Lloyd, mentioned in most of the "Series C" interviews in SOHP.

24. See Degler, *At Odds,* 227–48; Bethel, *Promiseland,* 157.

25. See Billy G. Mercer, oral history of Jessie Thrasher, November 12, 1974 (Typescript in Samford University Oral History Program, Birmingham) on northern Alabama; Couch (ed.), *These Are Our Lives,* 5–6, on North Carolina. See also Chlotilde R. Martin, "Midwifery Not What It Used to Be," life history of Lavina McKee, January 27, 1939 (Typescript in FWP life histories files, SHC), wherein a black Alabama granny denies she used "magic" teas.

26. Barbara Berry Darsey, "Lolly Bleu, Florida Squatter," November 29, 1938 (Typescript in FWP life histories files, SHC).

come, I had sich a time, I tole Sam when 'twas over, he could sleep in one bed and I'd sleep in the other. Well, she's two years old now, nothing's happened yet. I ain't goin' to say it won't though." [27]

It may have been easier for other husbands to take a more positive view, while sharing women's resignation to "nature." As a black Alabama farmer put it, "I don' min' tellin' you me and my wife we ain' never interfered with nature a-tall, and I reckon nature ain' overworked us. Eight kids ain't too many. When we get a kid, we want it an' it makes us know what we's working for." [28] And when an unpolished FWP traveler interviewed a crusty character in Harlan County, Kentucky, the following summary resulted: "He [the subject, father of many] believes it would be alright to limit the size of a family if he knew how, or what to do to prevent his wife from getting that way. But who in the hell is going to help a fellow stop that. . . . he says there is more fucking going on in Harlan County than any place in the world its size, no wonder there is a lot of kids. He says a big family just creeps up on [you] like, and before you know it you have a whole bunch of kids." [29] Even as men exchanged such rustic wisdom in the hills, there were 676 children under the age of five per 1000 women between the ages of fifteen and forty-four in the rugged subregions of Appalachia. (Nationally there were 391 children for 1000 women of childbearing age.) [30] This prodigious, impoverishing overproduction of highland children would persist for many years, but in other parts of the South the 1930s marked the beginning of change.

The 1933 New Deal plow up of one-fourth of the cotton, tobacco, and corn crops, along with the sustained program of acreage reduction thereafter, apparently shook southerners' confidence in large families for the first time. Widespread tenant evictions occurred as early as the winter of 1933–1934, and landless heads of households with large families apparently had problems finding adequate land to support themselves. "Big families is a drag and dead expense since the cotton acreage has been cut," said a white North Carolinian, wife of a sharecropper and mother of eight children, aged seven to sixteen. At the end of 1938 they had lost their place and were without prospects for 1939. [31]

27. Ethel Deal, life history of Jeannie Chambers, July 10, 1939 (Typescript, *ibid.*).

28. Waldrep, "Luke Warn."

29. Dewey B. Ison, "Life Story of Mr. Erwin Halcomb, Lynch, Kentucky," September 28, 1939 (Typescript in "Our Lives" project files).

30. USDA, BAE and Forest Service, *Economic and Social Problems and Conditions of the Southern Appalachians,* by L. C. Gray and C. F. Clayton (Washington, D.C., 1935), 163.

31. Bernice Kelly Harris, "Dona Balmer Male, White," January 10, 1939 (Typescript

Country doctors, accustomed to requests for abortion-inducing potions, recorded (albeit impressionistically) increased demand, and systematic birth control education at last was underway. The requisite changes in male physicians' attitudes toward women and birth began, as well. Work in a county health unit without doubt transformed many doctors. As one put it, "This broader field of service has changed some of my ideas that I thought were pretty firmly rooted. One was birth control." He had thought "it was wrong" and had lectured women asking for abortions "that we mustn't destroy life after its inception." Yet "after seeing so many frail women broken down from prolonged child-bearing with the end not yet in sight, so many helpless children neglected because their parents aren't able to provide even the necessities for them, I changed my mind." Birth control seemed then a grim necessity, as well as an easy moral alternative to abortion.[32]

Delivery of birth control information and devices and hygienic obstetrical care to the rural poor was another matter. The job was barely begun during the 1930s and 1940s, and with difficulty. The medical community was largely indifferent or hostile to such public services, and state governments pled shortages of revenues. So the first important initiatives in the South were private. Dr. Clarence J. Gamble, a medical researcher and heir to the Ivory Soap fortune, partly financed and supervised two pilot projects in Logan County, West Virginia, and in North Carolina, beginning in 1936 and 1937. In Logan the county medical board reluctantly agreed to permit Gamble to hire a public health nurse who would contact indigent rural families and distribute spermicidal jellies. Between 1936 and 1939 she reached 1,349 women, about half of Logan's fertility potential. In the three-year period their birth rate dropped 41 percent. Yet by 1939, when the program ended, 60 percent of the participating women had decided to stop using the jelly; most said they lacked confidence in its effectiveness. Meanwhile, in 1937 Gamble and his associates scored a coup with the North Carolina state Board of Health, winning its permission to conduct a similar program. Soon sixty-one of the state's eighty-one public health units were involved.

---

in FWP life histories files, SHC). See also Stanley Combs, "Liquor Will Ruin You," June 1, 1939, *ibid.*, the story of a white farm-raised, Wilson, N.C., plumber who with his wife had decided to raise only two children for economic reasons; and T. Pat Matthews, "Matthew Luke Matthews," n.d. (1938 or 1939), *ibid.*, on a childless black farm-owning couple in N.C. who attributed their success to lack of children.

32. Couch (ed.), *These Are Our Lives*, 273–74. See also Bernice Kelly Harris, "John Wesley Parker, M.D.," n.d. (1938 or 1939) (Typescript in FWP life histories files, SHC).

They distributed foam powder spermicides in most cases, jelly and diaphragms in about one-fourth, and occasionally condoms. The state director claimed the sixty-one cooperating units reached 70 percent of North Carolina's indigent women, but in 1941 an independent estimator concluded that hardly 4 percent (about 3,000 women) were actually participating. (There were only 4,291 women receiving assistance from clinics as late as 1950.) Absence of empirical tests of public health birth control instruction renders evaluation of Gamble's program difficult, too. In 1941 Gamble withdrew, and after some hesitation the state government agreed to continue the statewide program on its own. Modest as it was, North Carolina's action was a great breakthrough. In a short time six other southern states—Virginia, South Carolina, Georgia, Florida, Alabama, and Mississippi—followed suit. In Tennessee private physicians opposed appropriations for such purposes, fearing socialized medicine. But much of the region, at least, appears to have joined a national consensus that smaller families meant higher quality of life and that public funds might be spent to assist the poor in that goal, too. Public health clinics also exposed and began treatment and control of rampant venereal diseases, and during the 1950s prenatal care at last became available to virtually all women, regardless of class.[33]

Within their homes and among their families, women and men may or may not have been content. George Gallup, who began his scientific polling during the 1930s, did not reach such folks, and there remain for historians no reliable means of measuring happiness. Among the thousands of pieces of oral and written testimony from southern farm people during the first half of this century, there are assuredly scenes of satisfaction, security, sometimes bliss. The elderly white sisters who operated an Alabama plantation seem to have enjoyed life thoroughly. And Ned Cobb and his good wife made a happy home for themselves and their great brood, despite a multitude of external troubles. But the corpus of this large, if haphazard, collection of testimony contains far more instances of unhappiness, especially among women. Marriage was a cruel trap, motherhood often a mortal burden; husbands were too often

33. Reed, *From Private Vice to Public Virtue,* 225–39, 249–54; Couch (ed.), *These Are Our Lives,* 274. On the prevalence of syphilis, see also Carey McWilliams, *Ill Fares the Land: Migrants and Migratory Labor in the United States* (Boston, 1942), 172–73; "Midwife and Farmer," n.d. (1938 or 1939) (Typescript in FWP life histories files, SHC), the account of a black Alabama midwife who delivered infants from infected mothers. On the prevalence of prenatal care by the 1950s, see Mary Murphy, interview with Carroll Lupton, M.D., May 18, 1979 (Typescript in SOHP).

obtuse, unfaithful, drunken, and violent. The collective portrait is less of bliss than of pathos.

Some people—regardless of time or place—may have a peculiar capacity for strife and torment. Late in the 1930s, for example, there lived a family near Pineville, Kentucky, who suffered civil war without respite over a radio and dogs. The husband-father was probably the culprit. He loathed the radio, which made, in his words, "more noise than a barrel full of wild cats, jest growls an' grinds an' goes on." The wife-mother, on the other hand, could not bear his dogs and ordered him to get rid of them or depart himself, along with the curs. The husband thought this unreasonable. He owned, he reported, merely "thirteen in all, eight old hounds, four young puppies and a bird dog. Wish, by God, I had me two more good bred fox hounds." His solution to the family problem of noise was to trade the radio "off for an auger or somethin none of the family can't play." [34] Other families had far more serious problems.

Ned Cobb, for example, was a battered child. When he was only nine (during the 1890s) his father set him to plowing up sweet potatoes. Warm fall weather and swarms of gnats got the better of a child not yet large enough to handle such a task anyway. His father flew into a rage nonetheless, "got mad at me for that . . . picked me up by the arm . . . [and] wore out a switch nearly on me." Three years later Cobb's father considered the boy grown and set him to "plowin a regular shift," barefooted on rocky soil. Ned plowed under dissatisfied scrutiny, and never forgot his father's fearsome shouts of "Drop them britches. Drop them britches," whereafter he would use plow lines to blister his son's rear. [35] Southerners have ever believed in the efficacy of corporal punishment to correct their children's behavior. The elder Cobb was afflicted with a pathology, however, that neither his son nor his neighbors considered acceptable. Nevertheless, the wives and children were battered all too often, and there seemed no remedy for it.

A Kentucky mountain woman told a sadly familiar tale late in the 1930s. Her husband, so charming before marriage, turned out to be a mean drunk. "Tell you right now," she said, "if I had my life to live over again, I wouldn't marry no man. The sun ain't shined on the man's back that I would have." She dearly loved her children, the woman declared,

34. Everett Bishop, life history of Eugene Felton, n.d. (1938 or 1939) (Typescript in "Our Lives" project files).

35. Rosengarten, *All God's Dangers,* 15–17. On corporal punishment generally, see John Shelton Reed, *The Enduring South: Subcultural Persistence in Mass Society* (Lexington, Mass., 1972), 48–50, 53–55.

"but I've been through so much trouble in the twenty years that Bill and I have been married" that she would forgo motherhood rather than marry again. There was no economic alternative to her purgatory, however, so she remained.[36] Years later another Kentucky woman, escaping hard domestic work for romance at seventeen, married a deranged World War II veteran. "I found," she said much later, "there's worse things than being a hired girl." Hardly a fortnight after the wedding her husband began drinking and battering. Later, following the birth of children, things grew worse: "He would beat me, tear my clothes, set the curtains on fire. He broke my ribs, and my cheekbone three times. Once my eyeball was even out of its socket."[37] Another foolish teenaged bride, this one in North Carolina, married a tobacco tenant, not caring "a snap that he drunk and fought and had been in jail a time or two. I thought he'd stop it when I married him, but he got worse." Even in the frantically busy tobacco barning season the husband stayed in town or sat and drank from his jug in the kitchen. "If he wants to beat me or the children, he does, and that's all there is to it. He ain't got no mercy for nothing but mules and dogs." Yet for all his abuse, she concluded, "I love him better than most women love their husbands. I reckon women do love bad husbands better than they do good ones."[38] An elderly woman in western North Carolina had endured half a century of battering when she spoke in 1939, and there was no hint of such masochism. "Hell's a-yawnin' for such as Pap!" she pronounced. "He always knocked and beat me around." All eleven of their children had "done fell out with" him, including an afflicted thirty-year-old son whose injuries may have resulted from prenatal trauma. One cannot now know much of the cause or blame for the old couple's continuing strife, but the wife's report on the role of the police is sadly indicative of the helplessness of weaker people trapped with the pathological. "I've asked the law to help me," she said, "but when they come and get after

36. Clarence F. Barnes, "Never Marry Again," life history of William and Millie Hanson, n.d. (1938 or 1939) (Typescript in "Our Lives" project files).
37. Quoted in Dorothy Hall Peddle, "To Do What's Right," *Southern Exposure,* XI (March/April, 1983), 40.
38. Mary A. Hicks, "Backer Barning," life history of Ransome Jackson, July, 1939 (Typescript in FWP life histories files, SHC). For other instances of wives' tolerance of battering, child abuse, infidelity, and incest, see Hicks, "Easier Ways"; Susie R. O'Brien, "The Alexanders," October 20, 1938 (Typescript in FWP life histories files, SHC); Patty Dilley, interview with Hoy Deal, July 3, 11, 1979, (Typescript in SOHP); Couch (ed.), *These Are Our Lives,* 5–6, 35; A. G. M. "Nothin' But Trouble," in John Robinson (ed.), *Living Hard,* 31–41.

Pap, he just laughs and says, 'Why gentlemen, [she's] the mean'un. I beat her 'cause she just plain aggravates the life outen me.'"[39] During the 1940s one of Ned Cobb's daughters married a drunken chronic batterer, and Cobb, victim of his own father half a century before, mourned. His daughter suffered one humiliation after another. Once her husband took her out into the country, "made her pull off everything she had on but her underwear, and he beat her down over there. Again! Beat her down." But always, "she'd go back to him."[40]

The most outrageous misogynist in any of the 1930s interviews was a white logger from Taladega Springs, Alabama. Orphaned early and "given" to a farmer who abused and overworked him, the subject ran away to a circus at fourteen, sledgehammered his boss, then took up with a black moonshiner-carouser-gambler before settling finally in a logging camp. He lived successively with two women. The first died in childbirth; the second died after six children. "I tried batchin' it fer nearly a month" after the second common-law wife's demise, he said, "an' I weren't doin' no good at it." So one Sunday he went to the house of Nora and persuaded her to come home with him. Nora "never did take a likin' to" his "other woman's kids", however; so he decided he "had to get her up some of 'er own. . . . I allus did try to keep my women totin' a little bitsy baby. That keeps 'em from studyin' devilment." "Sometimes," the logger reflected, "I'd git drunk an' whale th' hell out-a her a time or two, but mostly I treated her as good as any woman ought'er be treated." Nora fared better than his previous women, he thought, "on account of her workin' to keep me in good humor," but she did not shake his credo on the nature and care of females: "A woman's like a dumb animal—like a cow or a bitch dog. You got to frail 'em with a stick now an' then to make 'em look up to you."[41]

Physical and economic intimidation, as well as fear for their children, trapped so many women in such situations. No wonder some behaved like dumb animals. Occasionally one struck back, however, quite literally. Such was a beleaguered wife in western North Carolina during the 1930s. Mary Green lovingly raised a calf, which a stranger offered to buy for three dollars. She could hardly bear to part with the animal, but she and her children needed clothes so badly she accepted the

39. Adyleen G. Merrick, life history of Samuel and Melinda Grumble, July 7, 1939 (Typescript in FWP life histories files, SHC).

40. Rosengarten, *All God's Dangers*, 450–51.

41. Terrill and Hirsch (eds.), *Such as Us*, 205–16.

money. Her husband immediately took the cash from her, however, giving a dollar each to his two loutish sons from a previous marriage and keeping one for himself. Women, he said, have "no need for cash money," whereas "men has got to have a little spendin' money on 'em in case of need." Mary reflected, "I reckon if Pap had stopped to reason with me instead of just walkin' off like he done I wouldn't a acted so ugly." But she burst into a rage, "run in the house and grabbed a gallon jar," put it in a cloth sack, and waited in ambush by the kitchen door. "Right thar I met Pap fair, and I just up and bashed him good over the head with that jar. When he drapped I got my dollar and went on to the fields to my hoein'."[42]

Divorce in the formal, legal sense was a luxury few poor people could afford, and in any case, they shared the belief of the middle and upper classes everywhere that marriage was sacred. Traditional morality thus conspired with poverty to bind marriage partners, whatever the quotient of unhappiness. Nonetheless folks split, usually without the assistance of the legal profession and the courts. In the Appalachian highlands, where public documents revealed virtually no divorces before World War II, New Deal social workers found a substantial minority of single-adult households. One partner, usually the husband, had simply decamped. Among blacks in the cotton belt, too, folks "didn't have divorces," as a native put it. "If there was a mistake, they tried to make it not a mistake." Otherwise, "the man just left and went north." When the FERA surveyed relief recipients in the cotton areas in 1933–1934, they found only 6 percent of white families and slightly more than 17 percent of black families headed by one adult, and these figures included widows and widowers as well as the divorced or deserted. However, according to the FERA, among all black families in the cotton South, only 30.5 percent were conventional ones with mother, father, and children together. The FERA calculated that 86.5 percent of white families were unbroken.[43] The significant difference between the races may well reflect the peculiarities of the subregion surveyed. Here, blacks were concentrated as sharecroppers; and though many whites sharecropped, too, they were more likely to be more secure tenants if

42. Adyleen G. Merrick, life history of Mary Green, July, 1939 (Typescript in FWP life histories files, SHC).

43. Bethel, *Promiseland,* 124; USDA, *Economic and Social Problems,* 162–63. See also FERA and BAE, "Area Report: Survey of Rural Problem Area—Cotton Growing Region of the Old South," by Harold Hoffsommer (Typescript, *ca.* 1934, in Record Group 83, National Archives), 10–11.

not landowners. Still, it is possible that blacks divorced informally more often than whites across the South.

The housing of rural southerners bore elemental importance to their lives, marriages, work, and health. Most of it was cramped and crude until well after World War II. There was wide variety, however, representing the economic status of occupants, subregional climate and topography, economic organization of the countryside, and historical periods of settlement. Many humble southern country folks, for example, dwelled in log houses of several styles as recently as the 1930s, 1940s, and later. Some were built between the two world wars; others were nineteenth-century frontier dwellings that had somehow survived fire and termites. In the mountains and in the piedmont and coastal plains of the upper South some log houses were two story. These were generally old houses originally built for families of relatively high status. During the first half of the twentieth century occupants of such buildings were occasionally of middling class, sometimes descendants of prominent pioneers; others were poor folk who rented or owned them because they had become run-down. In the lower South (South Carolina through the Gulf states) two-story houses were rare—except for frame or brick ones built by substantial landowners. Here log homes were frequently of the double, or open-hallway, frontier style. These were two- or four-room affairs set on short posts or stone foundations, with an open space in the middle from front to rear. Most had roofed porches with four supporting posts. On the black-belt nineteenth-century frontier, planters and their families often lived in one side of such houses, with a few black slaves in the other side, before fields were cleared and more imposing white housing could be constructed. The double houses became slave cabins, and after the Civil War, tenant houses. The open hallway permitted good air circulation in summer and penetrating frosty cold in winter. Double houses were also called dog trots because of the open hallway, where a dog might run through the house without touching anything. Early log double houses had wooden shake roofs. In the black belt foundations were often wooden, too, and chimneys were dangerous stick-and-mud columns, which often caught fire. Where there was natural stone (for example, in northern Alabama) foundations and chimneys were made of fieldstone or hewn rock. After about 1900 old shake roofs were frequently replaced with tin or tarpaper, sawn boards covered logs, and some black-belt cabins received stone or brick corner supports and chimneys. As late as 1940 farmers in Franklin County, Alabama, built new log houses and barns, but across the South many old log houses

CROPPER FAMILY IN THEIR OPEN-HALLWAY HOUSE, *ca.* 1939
USDA No. 83-G-37961, National Archives

decayed without refinements; and hardly any had glass or screens in windows, merely leaky wooden shutters.[44]

After 1900 a great many new double houses were built in the lower South. These were usually less substantial than log structures. Walls were constructed of corner posts to which horizontal boards were nailed; there were no studs. Roofs were tin more often than tarpaper-covered boards, for tin over uncovered rafters was cheaper. Rooms were usually unceiled and virtually never plastered or paneled. Such houses were almost invariably built by landlords for tenants. A black former sharecropper near Selma, Alabama, recalled life in such a place with grand sarcasm. He and his family "layed in the bed and seen the stars through the cracks in the house, and you could tell about how fair it was without going outdoors. But it was a healthy place to live 'cause you got plenty of air, didn't never get too hot. It wasn't hardly possible chance of

44. Physical descriptions of housing (except where otherwise noted) are based upon notes and photographs in the Roland M. Harper Collection, University of Alabama Library. Harper (d. 1962) was a geologist, botanist, soil specialist, and professor at the Universities of Georgia and Alabama. Between about 1905 and 1954 he took thousands of photographs of the southern countryside between Virginia and Arkansas, recording housing along with his main subject of interest, topography. Most of the pictures are too faded or poor in quality to reproduce, but they are an enormous asset to scholarship.

TENANT TRANSPORTATION AND PETS, NORTHEASTERN GEORGIA, 1941.
This automobile is parked in front of a house in which the landowner
once lived—now given over to tenants.
USDA No. 83-G-37949, National Archives

you catching a cold 'cause you didn't sweat in the house and go out and
hit the air. You was already cold in the house." [45] In parts of the delta and
black belt most affected by black migration during the 1910s and 1920s,
landlords apparently improved such jerry-built, well-ventilated housing
as they competed with other prospective employers for the first time.
The president of the Delta and Pine Land Company laid down such a
policy at a late-1921 managers' meeting: "We want to keep our expenses down as much as possible, but we must repair our cabins where
necessary and it is best to do this work before a tenant gets disturbed
and moves." [46]

The newer double houses and a great many single cabins in various
styles were not folk housing in the usual sense but industrial housing.
Migration notwithstanding, until World War II there remained a surplus

45. Debra Ann Burks, oral history of Allen Buster, November 29, 1974 (Typescript in
Samford University Oral History Program, Birmingham).
46. Typescript minutes of manager's meeting, December 2, 1921, Delta and Pine
Land Company Records.

of landless farmers in the South who vied for places, particularly in the newer delta lands. They took what housing was offered them, and it was poor. In the fall of 1927 young H. L. Mitchell left his home in western Tennessee to investigate farming prospects around Tyronza, Arkansas, and was shocked by the contrast. Accustomed to reasonably comfortable four-room cabins with vegetable gardens out back, Mitchell found two-room single houses "all made of green lumber, and the siding had warped in the hot delta sun." Landlords did not permit gardens, and "cotton grew almost to the door of the shacks." Windows were glazed— a sole improvement over older tenant housing—but doors sagged, and air, rain, and insects entered through roof and walls. The water supply for every two families "consisted of a three-inch steel pipe driven in the ground, with a hand pump attached." There was also a two-hole privy (uncleaned from the last occupancy) out back. Mitchell "decided to return to Tennessee where things were a little more civilized."[47] Almost a decade later Howard Kester observed in eastern Arkansas that landlords' mule barns were generally tight and well-constructed. Human housing had not improved. Nor had the problem of fuel been solved. The delta plantations had been laid out on forest land almost utterly denuded during the 1910s. Wood was scarce, and it was "a common sight," wrote Kester, "to see men, women, and children carrying wood on their backs from a distance of three or four miles." Schoolhouses were heated, but homes were often cold all winter.[48] In northeastern North Carolina one landlord accommodated sharecroppers in an innovative and grimly poetic manner. He converted old eight-by-fifteen-foot wagons into one-room shanties, sinking the wheels into field dirt for stability in wind.[49] Thus croppers, a notoriously mobile class, were moored for a time, during the late 1930s, while landlords collected federal subsidies and bought labor-saving machinery.

The bulldozing, rotting away, or firing of these and more permanent rural domiciles required twenty years and more after 1940, as most of the tenant population drifted or swarmed away. During the 1940s, on a black-belt Alabama estate about midway along the transition from fragmented cotton plantation to cattle-grain neoplantation, old housing crumbled slowly while the new emerged. Along the main plantation road stood new frame or cement block "bungalows" for the overseer,

47. Mitchell, *Mean Things Happening,* 17–18.
48. Kester, *Revolt Among the Sharecroppers,* 40, 43.
49. Bernice Kelly Harris, "Lawson Bennett: Sharecropper," October 29, 1938 (Typescript in FWP life histories files, SHC).

farm mechanic, and other specialists (all white men). These houses had four to six rooms with running water, plumbing, electricity, and central heating. A number of old log and cheap plank cabins had been razed, but some remained to house black croppers and farm laborers who drove tractors and picked cotton. The cabins were furnished from mail-order catalogues or with shabby pieces thrown out by whites. And they crawled with humanity. "Each room," wrote a visitor, "functions as sleeping quarters for adults and innumerable children. Old iron beds may hold as many as four or five persons, both adults and children if need be." Here, as well as the barnyard, was where southerners' sex education took place. "More fortunate tenants" had wood-burning stoves for cooking and heating. Most used fireplaces, as in the nine-teenth century and eons before that.[50]

Highland housing also presented a variety of folk, "modern," and industrial types. Some of the better and most commodious old homes were two-story log structures with glazed windows and huge kitchens, although few seem to have had indoor water or plumbing. There were many large, newer two-story frame and brick homes in the Virginia and Tennessee valleys; more were scattered about the smaller valleys of the Norris Basin and elsewhere. These often had modern conveniences. Farm homes in Augusta County, Virginia, in the Valley, for example, approached high national standards in 1934: 64 percent had telephones, 21 percent had electricity, water was piped into 28 percent; 16 percent had bathrooms with running water and toilets. Houses in more remote places were nearly as primitive as tenant cabins in the row-crop South, however. The USDA assessed the average house in Knott County, Kentucky, in 1934, at $340, but this figure was skewed by a few valued around $7,000. Some Knott County homes were assessed as low as $20. (The national average then was $1,207.) These and houses everywhere in remote Appalachia were never painted, were heated by fireplaces, had no water inside, and contained at least two persons per room. Parents and small children slept in one double bed together, older children all in another bed in the same room. Furniture was plain, often home-made, in contrast to cheap manufactured or handed-down furnishings in tenant cabins. Mountain cabins seem more often to have been ceiled, also, than tenant cabins in the plantation areas of the South. Inside walls were often tightly paneled with tongue-and-groove boards, too. Painted

50. Morton Rubin, *Plantation County* (Chapel Hill, 1951), 14–17.

floors—almost unknown in the lower South—were regarded as a characteristic of "nice" homes.[51]

Company housing in Appalachian coal camps and towns included one feature almost never found in poor folks' homes elsewhere, electric lighting. Because the companies required electrical power to operate loaders and other motors, they acquired their own generators or hookups with power utilities, then wired workers' housing as it was constructed. Quality of the housing varied according to the size of the company and of the coal seam being mined. Some housing was tight, warm, and well maintained, at least as long as the seam was rich. As seams played out and companies planned to move, housing was neglected. All were built close together (level or gently sloping land was scarce), were monotonously plain, and lacked indoor water. Outside, double privies served two families each. These were often cleaned by company crews once a year—a service included in modest rent charges. In southern West Virginia many companies favored the "Jenny Lind" style of industrial housing. Somewhat like newer sharecropper shacks, outer walls consisted of boards nailed vertically to squared framing, with no studs except at the corners. Narrow strips of wood were then nailed over the cracks, rendering a sort of Nordic façade that evoked images of Sweden in generous imaginations, and the houses were named for Jenny Lind, the melodic "Swedish Nightingale" who toured the United States during the nineteenth century. Jenny Linds were unceiled and usually lacked interior paneling or plaster; so, despite the wooden strips, they were leaky, drafty, and cold in winter. Most companies permitted renters to maintain gardens on steep, rocky ground, and to keep animals—another advantage over conditions in much of the row-crop South. Hogs ate the garbage, but inedible trash was usually strewn about the congested camps, making them uglier than the treeless delta of Arkansas.[52]

51. See USDA, *Economic and Social Conditions,* 137–40; Harry K. Schwarzweller, James S. Brown, and J. J. Mangalam, *Mountain Families in Transition: A Case Study of Appalachian Migration* (University Park, Penn., 1971), 10–11, 23–38; TVA, "Norris Project Family Living Study" (Typescript, 1934, in Box 28, RG 142, Atlanta Branch, NA). For an example of a comfortable two-story log house in Braxton County, W.Va., see Larry K. Lane, oral history of Edward C. Jackson, March 23, 1974 (Microfilm copy of typescript, MUOHA). See also Clarence F. Barnes, "Lonesome Widow," life history of Martha Baker, n.d. (1938 or 1939) (Typescript in "Our Lives" project files), which includes a description of a rude two-room log house in Harlan County, Ky.

52. See David A. Corbin, *Life, Work, and Rebellion in the Coal Fields: The Southern West Virginia Miners, 1880–1922* (Urbana, 1981), 9–10, 67–68; Lizzie Farmer, "Typical Miner's Family," n.d. (1938 or 1939), Clarence F. Barnes, life history of Harve

Home life in the cramped, crude housing of the rural South would be unbearable to those accustomed to privacy, modern conveniences, and high standards of cleanliness. Southern country folk hardly knew a life other than crowding, cooking from fireplaces or small stoves, washing clothes by hand in tubs outside, changing clothes once a week, and washing only one's face, hands, and feet (if that) before going to bed. Care of such homes fell to women, and some coped with these conditions better than others. About 1939 an FWP interviewer entered a Kentucky mountain home to find a haggard and distraught mother of five. "I mopped just before the kids came in," she said, "and when I saw them coming I ran with the broom" to prevent their retracking the floor. "Just as I opened the door Leon throwed a big mud ball and it bursted all over the place. I'll have to clean this up. . . . But you couldn't keep this place clean if you died trying." The visitor observed that the walls were covered with dirty hand prints and pencil marks, the floor with "dirt and dust," and sweet potato peelings were scattered around the fireplace.[53] In Highlands County, Florida, the "desolate two room house" of a family of white squatters resembled Erskine Caldwell's fictional *Tobacco Road* abode of Jeeter Lester and his filthy kin. Here the husband-father, like Jeeter a former cropper, dozed and dreamed and occasionally gathered firewood and stacked it in an old car for improbable sale in town. Awaking from a midday nap, he admitted an FWP interviewer into his yard: "Come right in, ma'am. I hain't had time to fix this here gate sinst I been a-living here, seems like. Don't pay no mind to them pigs a-sleeping on the steps; they'll run away soon's they see a stranger. Kinda nice havin pigs in the yard, fer they do clean up the scraps." The pigs had not cleared away "old tin cans, rags, bones, corn cobbs, and other debris," the visitor noted. Inside the house were a wife, six children, and to middle-class eyes and nose, amazing filth.[54] New Deal–era photographs of tenant cabin interiors reveal efforts to maintain cleanliness and homey comfort, however. Fire grates were clean-swept, beds were made, and kitchen tools and food were placed neatly on open

Dameron, September 18, 1939 (Both typescripts in "Our Lives" project files); oral history of Ted Miller, n.d. (*ca.* 1975) (MUOHA), which describes a Jenny Lind house.

53. Malta L. Miller, "Could Not Avoid Marriage," life history of Delia Elliott Derosett, n.d. (1938 or 1939) (Typescript in "Our Lives" project files).

54. Barbara Berry Darsey, "A Florida Squatter Family: Jason and Lily Iby," life history of W. B. Lundy, October 18, 1938 (Typescript in FWP of Florida files, University of Florida Library).

shelves. No doubt some of this order was staged for photographers; much apparently was not. Poor people who rented had little money or incentive to improve their dwellings, but they commonly decorated (and insulated) bare, gapped walls with newspapers and especially with magazine covers and old and new picture calendars.[55]

The quality of rural life was affected by the progress of paved roads, the acquisition of automobiles, and the proximity of towns as well as by class. Folks living far from towns on dirt roads lingered in something approaching premodern existence with little community contact other than at little churches and schools. Federal agricultural and home demonstration services were seldom evident here; nor were such "progressive" youth activities as 4-H or parent-teacher associations. "Society" was family, occasionally extended at country funerals, at church on Sundays when the circuit rider appeared to preach, or in one- or two-room schools where older children might spend part of the day instructing their own younger siblings. Farmers of any class—but especially those better off—were advantaged if they had cars and paved roads to towns. For them community was enlarged and not quite so personal. They were more likely to have telephones before the 1940s, to subscribe to newspapers and magazines, and to own radios. Paved roads spelled death for tiny churches, as farm folk drove off to growing congregations of their own denominations in towns. Consolidation of some schools paralleled changes in churches. Both institutions provided organized activities for youth and parents, too, and made Extension Service work more convenient and effective.[56]

Southern white Baptist churches during the early 1920s stood at the

55. See esp. the Farm Security Administration's photographs in the Library of Congress, and Walker Evans' pictures in James Agee, *Let Us Now Praise Famous Men* (Boston, 1941); Herman Clarence Nixon, *Forty Acres and Steel Mules* (Chapel Hill, 1938); Erskine Caldwell and Margaret Bourke-White, *You Have Seen Their Faces* (New York, 1937); Dorothea Lange and Paul Schuster Taylor, *An American Exodus: A Record of Human Erosion* (New York, 1939).

56. See USDA, *Agriculture Yearbook, 1923* (Washington, D.C., 1924), 579–80; USDA, *Economic and Social Problems*, 164; Raper, *Preface to Peasantry*, 227; Michael L. Berger, *The Devil Wagon in God's Country: The Automobile and Social Change in Rural America, 1893–1929* (Hamden, Conn., 1979), 43–44, 93–94, and *passim;* Loretta Lynn with George Vecsey, *Loretta Lynn: Coal Miner's Daughter* (New York, 1976), 52–53; USDA, BAE, "4-H Work in West Virginia," by T. L. Harris (Typescript, January, 1931, in RG 83, NA); Thomas Carson McCormick, "Stuttgart, Arkansas, Rural Organization Studies, 1933" (Typescript prepared for the USDA, in University of Arkansas Department of Agricultural Economics and Rural Sociology records, University of Arkansas Library, Fayetteville) and the FWP life histories files, SHC.

brink of these vast changes. Because the churchwide Sunday School Board surveyed its membership in 1922, there exists an excellent profile of this large institution just prior to the impact of roads, the auto, school consolidations, and migrations. The Board used concentrated populations of a thousand (rather than the federal Bureau of the Census standard of twenty-five hundred) to divide rural from urban occupancies; by this reasonable measure nearly 70 percent of all white southern Baptists (who then numbered more than two million) belonged to rural churches. A somewhat larger percentage (about 85) of Baptist churches were located in the open countryside; so presumably some Baptists were commuting from towns to attend services in 1922. Not quite a third of all rural pastors were full-time. In the entire state of Arkansas there were only fifteen full-time rural preachers. Almost 70 percent of all southern Baptist ministers were bivocational. Rural ministers on the average received $765 per year for their services, and seldom had paid-for residences. Urban Baptist preachers averaged $1,985 per year and lived in rent-free parsonages.[57]

Within a decade after the Baptist survey the blitz of change had been felt in rural churches of all denominations throughout the nation. Circuits of congregations served by the same minister were vastly reduced, church buildings were abandoned, and for the first time rural areas became overchurched in terms of skeletal congregations attempting to survive. Many parishioners, as we have seen, moved or drove to towns, but many rural folks were left churchless by the phenomenon. They could not identify with urban churches, despite a better-trained clergy and more extraworship activities, or they lacked cars and good clothes in which to attend. The latter reason applies, of course, to the poor.[58] The fate of a couple remaining in the country northwest of Nashville is illustrative. In their fifties with grown children, they had been Baptists all their lives until about 1930, when hard times and migration closed down their church. "Now we had nowheres to go to preaching," said the husband. At last a visiting Holiness preacher came around and per-

57. J. Wayne Flynt, "Southern Baptists: Rural to Urban Transition," *Baptist History and Heritage,* XVI (January, 1981), 24–34 (esp. 24–25). See also Lawrence F. Evans, "Story of a Minister's Family and Life," January 18, 1939 (Typescript in FWP life histories files, SHC). W. H. Evans, the minister, served 82 Alabama Baptist churches in a 40-year career; during the Depression he was paid about $47 per month.

58. Berger, *Devil Wagon in God's Country,* 127–34. On the lack of dress clothing as a deterrent to churchgoing, see Stanley Combs, "One of Them Might Be President," May 20, 1939 (Typescript in FWP life histories files, SHC).

suaded them they could worship at home by themselves.[59] Thus was a former community atomized. In northeastern North Carolina disintegration probably began earlier, when large landowners withdrew to towns (by about 1920) and left much of the countryside to tenants and sharecroppers. As a white Baptist minister described the situation late in the 1930s, "Many of the substantial families" had departed; thus "the congregation in many instances is more or less itinerant, constantly shifting." Withdrawal of those best able to support stable churches was compounded in North Carolina by consolidation of rural black schools. Schools as well as churches "made for greater community consciousness," observed the minister, "and any weakening of [the schools] . . . reasonably reacts on church life."[60] In black-belt Georgia consolidation of white rural schools was underway during the 1920s, simultaneously with the ravages of the boll weevil. So local schools as community centers disappeared just as cotton farmers of all classes fled. Country churches were the next institution to fall. Children bused to town schools developed associations that caused their parents to follow. Those with cars, in particular, soon changed church memberships to the large town congregations, even if they continued to live in the country.[61]

Black rural Georgians, ironically, were spared this disintegration of their communities for a time. Even as so many of them fled sharecropping and the boll weevil, their poor churches and schools survived. The schools were the key. White officials spent few public funds on them. Many black schools, indeed, were weird affairs built on donated land by neighborhood people who often performed upkeep and repairs on them as well. Some schools were still conducted in black churches as late as the mid-1930s. The taxpayers of Georgia paid teachers and provided some books and supplies. Most important, rural schools were not consolidated when the white system underwent "modernization." So while the schools remained, the churches thrived, too, albeit in straitened circumstances. Black ministers were poorly educated and extremely poorly paid. Arthur Raper discovered that black church members tried

59. Dean Newman, "The Hardest Unable Worker," in Robinson (ed.), *Living Hard,* 225–61. Many other country folks, particularly Holiness people, never affiliated with formal churches. See Berger, *Devil Wagon in God's Country,* 128–130; Malta L. Miller, "Don't Believe in Snake Handling," life history of Olivia Hinkle, n.d. (1938 or 1939) (Typescript in "Our Lives" project files).

60. Bernice Kelly Harris, "Richard Lloyd, Minister," January 17, 1939 (Typescript in FWP life histories files, SHC).

61. Raper, *Preface to Peasantry,* 350–54.

their utmost to protect their churches, however. Proportionately more blacks than whites contributed money to their churches, and considering financial ability, black contributions were probably sacrificial. So while the largest white churches came to be urban ones, the largest black churches remained in the open country, at least through the 1930s.[62]

As white, then black rural congregations thinned and finally disappeared, the ranks of the southern clergy apparently thinned, too, both absolutely and in proportion to the region's population. Ever-larger churches required fewer preachers. The part-time, bivocational ministers were most affected by the decline of rural life. A few hardy men actually began rural missions in the midst of the disintegration. One was John W. Lester. Born near Dadeville, Alabama, in 1908, Lester migrated to Detroit in 1927 and labored for a while in an auto plant. Responding to a "call" to preach, he moved again, to Chicago, and attended the Moody Bible Institute. Back in Alabama in 1934, Lester heard another call—this one from his father, who, after attending a rural funeral with no preacher presiding, challenged him to undertake a country ministry. Lester first served a circuit of four churches, which paid him a grand total of $285.13, barely covering his travel expenses. Later he went on to broader mission work in Kentucky and Alabama. Lester taught rural sociology at a tiny mountain seminary, founded churches for remote and abandoned poor folk, advised state Baptist conventions on rural church survival and development, and emerged finally as perhaps the South's foremost expert and spokesman for Christian rural life. He was the *Progressive Farmer*'s "Rural Minister of the Year" for 1949. Lester promoted the "Lord's Acre" scheme of tithing crop proceeds to country churches and developed a widely disseminated strategy for country ministers. Preachers entering rural communities (Lester wrote during the 1950s) needed first to build contacts with influential people whose services would most benefit rural folk and their churches. Who were they? The county Extension Service and Home Demonstration agents; the county forester, soil conservationist, and health department officers; vocational agriculture teachers and rural club leaders.[63]

Lester obviously accepted the irresistible force of modernization and

62. *Ibid.*, 49–50, 350–68.

63. Flynt, "Southern Baptists," 31–34; "Rural Minister of the Year" file, 1949, "Developing a Country Church" (Typescript, n.d. [*ca.* 1955]), both in John W. Lester Papers, Auburn University Archives.

attempted for forty years in effect to fight fire with fire. Among the poor and not-poor, he sought to make rural churches work through economic development as preached by the Department of Agriculture: modernize and capitalize to make rural communities prosper. Lester was heroic in his conservative devotion, and his career yielded many small satisfactions, but of course in the long run he was foiled. The dynamic of rural communities' enlargement into towns was indeed irresistible by 1934. And Lester's work and the towns alike had a paradoxical (if utterly predictable) effect upon the churches and especially upon the youth supposedly most benefited. Good roads, cars, and 4-H clubs tended to direct them away from farm life rather than cement them to the new, improved version promoted by the Extension Service. In 1927 the USDA, 4-H, and the Young Men's Christian Association surveyed 7,880 boys and girls in Virginia, Missouri, and Colorado about whether they liked farm life and village life. The questions implied another—whether they might prefer city life. About 95 percent of both boys and girls replied they liked farm life; 85.6 percent of the boys and 90.5 percent of the girls said they also liked village life.[64] The parents of black youths with little contact with agencies such as the Extension Service and YMCA were not so eager to have their children remain in the country. During 1936–1937 black farmers in Jefferson County, Arkansas, were polled about their aspirations for their sons. Would they prefer that the boys remain in farming, do something "other than farming," or were they uncertain? Of those with a stated preference, about 65 percent responded that they wished their sons to leave agriculture.[65] In time even better-off whites would follow. In 1955 the Southern Baptist Convention polled almost half a million white boys attending religious classes about their vocational ambitions. Agriculture came in seventh (about eighty-five thousand chose it) among thirty-one occupations listed, behind engineering, aviation, coaching, religious work, automotives, and science.[66] The three youth surveys are hardly parallel, of course, but they evoke the course of southern (and American) life between the 1920s and the 1950s rather well.

The physical appearance and well-being of southern rural folks also

64. USDA, BAE, "Attitudes and Problems of Farm Youth" (Typescript, n.d. [*ca.* 1928], in RG 83, NA), 20–21.

65. See Resettlement Administration, "Social Correlative of Farm Tenure" (Typescript, 1937, in Jefferson County, Arkansas, Series, University of Arkansas Department of Agricultural Economics and Rural Sociology records).

66. See "Vocational Plans of One Million Southern Baptist Boys and Girls" (Printed chart, 1955, in Lester Papers).

elementally reflect their cultures. During the 1930s this actually became a national issue, as well-meaning New Dealers and a variety of commercial sensationalists emphasized the most doleful conditions, and defensive southern publicists took exception. Georgia-born novelist Erskine Caldwell probably did more to initiate the controversy than anyone. His *Tobacco Road* (1932) and *God's Little Acre* (1933) presented a pantheon of grotesques—freaks, imbeciles, harelips, cripples—to a fascinated national audience. Documentary photographs of the time showed scrawny sharecroppers with running sores, rheumy eyes, and scarred hands. The historian Herman Clarence Nixon, son of an Alabama landlord-storekeeper and a well-intentioned agrarian himself, considered such portraiture grossly exaggerated. So he collected other photographs in a 1938 book he called *Forty Acres and Steel Mules,* which presented healthy-looking white and black southerners enjoying outdoor work and swimming holes. Caldwell's fiction was probably never intended as South-wide truth, although without a doubt many readers took it to be such. Caldwell's second wife, the famous photographer Margaret Bourke-White, consciously chose the poorest and dirtiest subjects for her pictures, going so far as to rearrange their home furnishings and pose the people before snapping her shutter. Other photographers, whether free-lancers or federal employees, tried to choose widely and portray much.[67] One is not obliged, of course, to choose between Bourke-White's southerners and those in Nixon's picture book. They were all real. What is required is perspective.

One generalization seems unassailable. Because of their climate and their poverty, southerners were less healthy than other Americans, and they looked it. Malaria, one of the three enervating "lazy" diseases peculiar to the Southeast, was well understood in the nineteenth century, but before World War II only limited progress was made toward ditching and draining mosquito-breeding pools from which the disease spread. Nor were poor folks' homes well screened against malaria-carrying mosquitoes. After World War II the pesticide DDT (now known to be dangerous in itself) was widely employed to control mosquitoes and other pests. Hookworm, another of the diseases that made southerners seem good-for-nothing, is an intestinal parasite common to barefoot people who step in feces containing worm larvae. Pellagra, the third of the lazy diseases, is a severe niacin deficiency common to folk who sub-

67. The controversy is discussed in Jack Temple Kirby, *Media-Made Dixie: The South in the American Imagination* (Baton Rouge, 1978), 56–63. See also William Stott, *Documentary Expression and Thirties America* (New York, 1973).

sist largely on corn. Both hookworm and pellagra were clinically described in the South early in the twentieth century, but despite the creation of public health units in nearly all the states by about 1920, little
progress was made in eradicating them. This was despite simple preven-
tative cures: sanitary privies and shoe-wearing for hookworm, balanced
diets (or in severe cases, niacin supplements not available until the
1930s) for pellagra. Such diseases tend to subside or disappear when
economic systems change and ways of life are altered fundamentally.
This was not to be for most southerners, especially for the poorest and
most susceptible, until the 1940s and afterward.[68]

Meanwhile generations of southerners from Virginia to the subhumid plains lived out shortened and uncomfortable lives. Outsiders
were invariably shocked at the sight of the most miserable. In 1907 Oscar Ameringer, the German-born Socialist editor who had spent much
of his youth in relatively prosperous rural Ohio, arrived on the Oklahoma cotton frontier along the Canadian River Valley. He could not
erase the images of white farmers more than three decades later, when
he wrote his autobiography. Everyone was "wretched dressed," he recalled, but Ameringer was most struck by the farmers' ill health and
premature aging: "I had come upon another America!" He "found
toothless old women with sucking infants on their withered breasts,"
women who were probably in their thirties. Others' hands were covered
with eczema. Children were "emaciated by hookworm, malnutrition
and pellagra," and young adults "had lost their second teeth before they
were twenty years old." Ameringer's second most vivid memory of
Oklahoma was of bedbugs in the homes of his hosts.[69]

Much later the writer Harry Crews gave another perspective on
southern physiques, this one of injuries rather than the ravages of disease and malnutrition. When Crews was a child during the early 1940s
in Bacon County, Georgia, he "became fascinated with the Sears cata-
logue because all the people in its pages were perfect." By contrast
"nearly everybody" Crews then knew "had something missing, a finger
cut off, a toe split, an ear half-chewed away, an eye clouded with blind-
ness from a glancing fence staple. And if they didn't have something

68. A useful overview of "southern" diseases is to be found in Thomas D. Clark, *The
Emerging South* (New York, 1961), 24–39. See also Daphne A. Roe, *A Plague of Corn:
The Social History of Pellagra* (Ithaca, 1973), which provides an international perspective
on that illness; and Elizabeth W. Etheridge, *The Butterfly Caste: A Social History of Pellagra in the South* (Westport, Conn., 1972).

69. Oscar Ameringer, *If You Don't Weaken: The Autobiography of Oscar Ameringer*
(New York, 1940), 229.

missing, they were carrying scars from barbed wire, or knives, or fish-hooks." Crews's stepfather bore scars from human teeth on his cheek; later a hog nearly bit off a finger. Crews himself suffered burns over most of his body when, about age five, he fell into a hog-scalding cal-dron.[70] Whether Crews's portrait of disfigurement is uniquely southern is problematic; one might reasonably imagine such mishaps in Ohio or Minnesota as well as in southern Georgia. The pathology Ameringer witnessed was hardly to be found north of the Mason and Dixon line, however.

Except for highlanders, southerners were overwhelmingly a corn-and-pork-consuming folk. Had the corn been leavened with other vege-tables, and had the pork been lean instead of fat, they might have been healthy. But tradition, ignorance, and especially economic circum-stances permitted in the main a diet only of "white" food—that is, fat pork; corn in the form of bread, or "pone," fried in pork grease; and molasses made from corn or sorghum. This diet was central to what Rupert Vance termed the "cotton culture complex," but it obtained to varying degrees outside the cotton-growing areas, too. During the late 1920s, Vance found, the "maize kernel" constituted 32.5 percent of all the food intake of southern blacks. The figure for whites (which Vance did not report) must have been near this. Among Tennessee and Georgia mountaineers corn made up 23 percent of total food consumption. Mountaineers had less corn land, as we have seen, and were more likely to have vegetable gardens and live at home. Still, highlanders' corn con-sumption was enormous compared with that of seventy-two sample "northern families of comfortable circumstances"—only 1.6 percent of intake.[71]

In fact, southerners of both races relished corn and pork and never apologized to outsiders. "We eat our hogs, fat-back and all," declared a North Carolina sharecropper in 1938; "I like fat-back." He went on to relate a tale of a campaigning politician who promised the electorate beefsteak if he were sent to Congress. "That kind er talk hurt him and lost him the precinct."[72] Convenience as well as necessity compounded preference. As a Carolina farm woman put it, "We et cornpone three times a day. . . . There was always something . . . even if it was samey." When asked about balancing food groups she replied: "Right diet? To

70. Harry Crews, *A Childhood: The Biography of a Place* (New York, 1978), 54.
71. Vance, *Human Factors of Cotton Culture,* 295–319, esp. 298.
72. William O. Foster, "Watkins Abernathy," October 22, 1938 (Typescript in FWP life histories files, SHC).

keep us healthy? Mmm—I never had no time to think about any right diet. My job was to fill empty bellies." [73] Yet another woman thought that pellagra "runs in our family"—this in 1939, a quarter century after the clinical description of the disease. She had been advised on diet by a city physician, but seemed somewhat confused about directions. Her ultimate dilemma was economic, however: "We eat the same things after the doctor told us to quit for the simple reason that we couldn't afford nothing else." [74] Such was the case in southern areas locked into the white-food syndrome.

Southerners who moved from live-at-home areas to white-food ones did understand the difference between balanced diets and fat, sweet, and starchy ones, and mourned their fates even if they could not articulate the nutritional deprivation that made them unhappy. Kathleen Knight, for example, moved with part of her family from northern Alabama to Cleveland, Mississippi, in the delta, in 1929. The land was flat and still covered with rich silt from the great flood two years before. There was no need for fertilizer, so the Knights hoped to make money cropping cotton on halves. But food, then illness, stymied them. Neither the landlord nor the sharecroppers wished to use land for vegetables: "If you had a garden down there you had to put it in skips of cotton or maybe part of your back yard," she remembered. So the people "just eat dried stuff— beans and things like that," especially fat pork and cornbread. Her mother's parents sent dried fruit and even collard greens to them through the mails, but her father came down with pellagra and the family finally returned to the Alabama hills, beaten by delta life and labor. [75]

The poor folk of the hills were objects of national sympathy, but they fared better than the poor of the old modern South, where the market crops grew in rows. Virtually all the people of the Norris Basin had gardens and milk cows as well as corn fields and hogs; and denizens of tiny farms and coal camps in southern West Virginia and the rugged parts of Virginia, North Carolina, and Kentucky almost always reported milk, butter, and vegetables in relatively bountiful quantities. A 1934 USDA study confirmed the existence of variety and balance in the mountain diet. There were problems, however; some families enjoyed surpluses of milk, for example, but others had too little or none. Nutritionists also

73. Deal, "Maybe Some Day I Can Read to Myself."
74. Mary A. Hicks, "A Waitress," life history of Eva Truelove, January, 1939 (Typescript in FWP life histories files, SHC).
75. Daniel Knight, oral history of Kathleen Knight, January 23, 1975 (Typescript in Samford University Oral History Program).

thought highlanders relied too much on finely ground cereals (cornmeal and wheat flour), which provided insufficient fiber, and there was inadequate canning and other preparation for winter.[76] Loretta Lynn's experience in Johnson County, Kentucky, confirmed the winter vegetable problem. "I can remember winters," she recalled, "when all we ate for weeks was bread dipped in gravy made of brown flour and water, and that was supper." Occasionally they had a treat, " 'coal miner's steak' — bologna." In the summer and fall the family had homegrown vegetables, and by midspring Lynn's mother would be gathering wild greens from hillsides to tide the family over until the garden produced. Her mother and brother also hunted opossums and squirrels while her father worked in the mines.[77]

The winter–early spring problem notwithstanding, hill folk came closest to the old ideal of living at home, and they must have enjoyed the considerable margin of advantage over the dependents of the commercialized rural South. The future of the South did not lie in realization of the live-at-home ideal, however, as we have already seen. During the 1940s, probably the last decade the USDA Extension Service paid serious lip service to self-sufficiency, county agents continued their chorus of dismay over the failure of farmers to grow enough food for themselves.[78]

So for decades, until they came to live out of bags from supermarkets and to rely upon the medical professions, rural southerners felt poorly and, more often than not, treated themselves. From the nineteenth century into the twentieth, they combined folk medicine with a variety of patented concoctions available in country stores. Until about 1903 the latter included unregulated opiates. Thomas D. Clark, the historian of the old stores, discovered records of poor folks' opium habits financed from their chicken yards; they traded eggs for tiny vials of the drug. Later, in North Carolina during the 1920s, there was a cocaine traffic among whites and blacks in rural areas as well as in cities; but one cannot be certain whether the usage was analgesic in the usual sense or an

---

76. Michael J. McDonald and John Muldowny, *TVA and the Dispossessed: The Resettlement of the Population in the Norris Dam Area* (Knoxville, 1982), 33–38 and *passim*. Food is also often discussed in the oral histories of the MUOHA, the FWP files, SHC, and the "Our Lives" project files. See also USDA, *Economic and Social Problems,* 153–54.

77. Lynn with Vecsey, *Loretta Lynn,* 45–46.

78. See typescript county agents' annual narrative reports for the decade in Auburn University Archives and those on microfilm in the Mississippi State University library.

"underworld" addition. More often southerners took laudanum, then aspirin-based pills and powders, and drank quantities of liquor to deaden pain. As late as the mid-1930s peddlers of bizarre remedies still crowded into county seats on court days, hawking their wares. Arthur Raper observed Georgia salesmen of "herb" potions capable of curing "all the diseases known to man." One, a white man in blackface hoisting a huge snake above his head, sang strange ballads until he attracted an audience sufficient to pitch his Bitter Root Pain Remover. Folks also mixed many homemade nostrums for pain and constipation. Teas, especially, were boiled from roots of wild and domesticated plants. Folk medicine seems to have waned rapidly after about 1920, along with conjuring and traditional superstitions. Still, white and black women "talked fire" from burned hands and applied opossum grease to deaf ears well after World War II. A North Carolina physician, impatient for payment from country people during the 1930s, sent bills marked with skull and crossbones. He claimed this always worked.[79]

Tobacco—usually thought of as a pernicious habit—was probably southerners' great drug of choice. Pipe smoking was common among men and women in the nineteenth century and remained so well into the twentieth. Cigars gradually gave way to cigarettes between 1900 and 1920. Poor folks bought cloth bags of loose cigarette-cut tobacco (at five cents per bag) in the 1920s and 1930s and rolled their own. Chewing tobacco and snuff almost defined rural southerners well before the 1930s, however. Plug and powdered tobacco had been marketed since long before the Civil War to the entire nation. But by World War I most Americans moved to towns and cities and away from the expectorating tobacco habits. Not so, rural southerners. Travelers not accustomed to the lumped lip or swollen jaw invariably remarked on country southerners' near universal affection for the pinch and chewing plug. Margaret Bourke-White bribed subjects for her photographs with snuff, declar-

79. See Thomas D. Clark, *Pills, Petticoats, and Plows: The Southern Country Store* (Indianapolis, 1944), 236–37; Jesse F. Steiner and Roy M. Brown, *The North Carolina Chain Gang: A Study of County Convict Road Work* (Chapel Hill, 1927), 156–61; Raper, *Preface to Peasantry*, 283–84. Oral history interviews contain many references to folk medicine and superstition. See, *e.g.*, Couch (ed.), *These Are Our Lives*, 383–84; Gail Hatton, oral history of Dr. Donald Hatton, July 22, 1973, Ruby Morrison, oral history of Charles R. Knightstep, October 27, 1973 (Both typescripts in MUOHA); Harris, "John Wesley Parker, M.D." In an interview with John W. Snipes, September 20, 1976 (typescript in SOHP), Brent Glass mentions "sheep ball tea" (made from sheep manure and used as a cure for measles) and other mysteries still employed in North Carolina during the 1920s and later. My maternal grandmother, a South Carolinian (1884–1969), conjured burn pains from victims' hands with mumbled secret words.

ing, "They seem to live on" it and religion.[80] What she and other outsiders seemed not to realize was that tobacco dulled the pain of hunger
and aching teeth and gums, while providing a pleasant, gratifying sensa-
tion in the mouth.

In fact, tobacco use (particularly snuff and chewing) was an important part of folk medicine that survived the passing of most other rituals
and superstitions. A black woman raised in Virginia during the 1920s
recalled a debilitating childhood illness. Her recovery was slow because
of vomiting. A "doctor" called in by her mother recommended "a little
snuff on a broom straw," placed on the tongue in the morning to settle
the stomach. She recovered and dipped snuff the rest of her life. In West
Virginia, Alabama, South Carolina—in every subregion—boys and
girls of both races took up chewing or dipping because their parents enjoyed it or to relieve toothache. Tobacco even played a merciful role in
childbirth. When an expectant mother had labored long and seemed unable to muster strength for a climactic push, midwives might "quill" the
exhausted woman. Granny Lewis, a beloved midwife of Burlington,
North Carolina, was a noted practitioner of quilling well into the 1930s.
Placing a bit of snuff in one end of a sipping straw, and carefully timing
natural contractions, the midwife could blow the snuff into a woman's
nostril at the right moment, inducing a great sneeze and—voilà—the
baby! Where there was not pain to soothe or infants to quicken, chewing, dipping, and smoking provided blessed oral gratification.[81]

The habits were not unlike the supposedly southern phenomenon of
geophagy, or dirt eating. Actually devotees did not eat dirt but merely
kept lumps of loess or clay in their mouths, perhaps sucking from time
to time. The taste and feel of just the right moist lump of home soil gave
immeasurable satisfaction.[82] Such were the modest medicines and small
pleasures of Dixie's folks, which helped them endure.

At the end of life's comforts and travails inevitably comes death.

---

80. See Joseph Clarke Robert, *The Story of Tobacco in America* (New York, 1949);
Raper, *Preface to Peasantry,* 43–45. Quotation from Stott, *Documentary Expression,* 233.

81. See Faulkner *et al.* (eds.), *When I Was Comin' Up,* 64 (the Va. case); Maude Cain,
life history of Julia Rhodes, n.d. (1938 or 1939) (Typescript in FWP life histories files,
SHC) (on an Ala. girl); and Gary Miller, oral history of America Jarrell (on a Boone
County, W.Va., girl). My own maternal grandfather began chewing tobacco in Williams-
burg County, S.C., at the age of seven (in 1886) because of a toothache. Mary Murphy reports on Granny Lewis' quilling in her interview with Carroll Lupton, M.D., May 8, 1979
(Typescript in SOHP).

82. Robert W. Twyman, "The Clay Eater: A New Look at an Old Southern Enigma,"
Journal of Southern History, XXXVII (August, 1971), 439–48.

Among the poor, as late as the 1920s across the rural South the occasion was still marked in traditional ways. At night, usually, the "death owl" came to roost, and if it quivered, someone died. Then families or friends would wash the body of the deceased, rub the chest and abdomen in salt or turpentine, dress it, lay it out in a homemade coffin with hardware from a general store, and await neighbors and relatives. A mule-drawn wagon carried the coffin at last to the cemetery, survivors trailing behind. There had been no embalming. The only "professional" services rendered were those of a minister—if indeed one was available.[83]

By the late 1930s such a ritual was hardly to be seen any more. Another aspect of modernization had taken place. The profession of embalming and funeral management, well established in cities by the 1890s, had at last reached country folks. Paved roads to towns, the automobile, then the motorized hearse accomplished this particular process. Traditional burial insurance societies (especially among blacks) enabled humble folks to pay for such professional services. Much of tradition remained, to be sure. Funerals black and white were emotional and profoundly religious, and usually took place in churches. (The "funeral home" service came later.) Nor did modernization end differences in ethnic customs. Blacks preferred Sunday funerals and usually kept bodies "out" longer so larger funeral crowds might gather from distant places. Embalming and cosmetology facilitated this. And black funerals also often included the participation of "flower girls," a feature whites deemed appropriate only at weddings.[84]

Whatever the style, modernized funerals became *de rigeur*, and younger people eager for a new sort of respectability shunned the old ways. Old people who, for whatever reason, happened to prefer traditional funerals, did not always have their wishes fulfilled. A black woman recalled the death and burial of her mother's father, an eighty-eight-year-old preacher, in rural Virginia during the 1930s. They heard of the old man's death, and by the time they arrived at the grandparents'

83. Sara Brooks and Thordis Simonsen, "You May Plow Here," *Southern Exposure,* VIII (Fall, 1980), 61. See also oral history of Mary Johnson, May 8, 1977 (Typescript in Mississippi Department of Archives and History, Jackson); Faulkner *et al.* (eds.), *When I Was Comin' Up,* 68–69, on a Virginia funeral during the 1920s; and more broadly on burial traditions, Thomas Clark, *Pills, Petticoats and Plows,* 260–74.

84. On the evolution of southern undertaking, see Charles R. Wilson, "The Southern Funeral Director: Managing Death in the New South," *Georgia Historical Quarterly,* LXVII (Spring, 1983), 49–69. On white and black customs during the 1930s, see Grace McCune, "You Have to Get It While They're Crying," n.d. (1938 or 1939) (Typescript in FWP life histories files, SHC). The interviewee was a black embalmer in Athens, Ga., who was trained by whites and knowledgeable in the preferences of both races.

house, "they done carried Granddaddy to the funeral home and had him embalmed and brought him back to the house," then on "to the church that he preached at." As a "hearse rolled up in the yard, a storm broke out. Granddaddy told them before he died don't take his body on no hearse, take him to church on horse power, but they didn't do that." Why not accede to a dying man's desire? "They say it looked bad."[85] Many years would pass before many folks might again see dignity in the traditional country funeral. Then, of course, affectation played the style in reverse, as when mules drew the coffin of Martin Luther King, Jr., a man city born and bred, down Atlanta's Auburn Avenue in the spring of 1968.

---

85. Faulkner *et al.* (eds.), *When I Was Comin' Up*, 78.

A mule will walk all day, straight as a plumb line, setting his feet down only inches from young corn, corn that might be less than a foot high, and he'll never step on a plant. A horse walks all over everything.
—HARRY CREWS

Then I says to myself, "Why, hell, Jim, you got to live somehow," so I went to work for a fellow stilling, hired out to help him make outlaw whiskey.
—A NORTH CAROLINA MOONSHINER, 1939

It would be a pleasant thing to believe the South is to achieve regionalism as a folk movement. . . . we have seen the peasantries of Denmark and Ireland recreated, as it were, in a new economy, a new culture, and a new state. . . . But nowhere [in the South] is there genuine regional renaissance or a genuine folk movement; neither Ireland nor Denmark is being duplicated in Dixie.
—RUPERT VANCE, 1932

Chapter 6
Men, Mules, Moonshine, Music— Destiny

MANY SOUTHERN FARMERS LIVED WITH MAchinery long before gasoline-powered tractors, trucks, cotton harvesters, and combines appeared in numbers. Some had hay balers, corn and cotton planters, pesticide sprayers, a large variety of contraptions—all pulled by work animals. So country people, especially the men, lived with wrenches, screwdrivers, gears, and grease two or three generations before they had to become accustomed to the clatter of valves and the smell of exhaust fumes while working in the fields. Powered machines, like everything manufactured with interchangeable parts, assume eccentric personalities, too. Tractors, trucks, and automobiles "behave" in certain ways and require special human psychological traits, as well as technical expertise, to perform well. Yet the passing of animal power from agriculture meant a profound change in culture. Not only were multitudes displaced from rural life by machines, but life for those remaining changed fundamentally. Timing of the cycle of farm work remained about the same. But now one labored in din and dust (not to mention debt) undreamed of before. Fuel replaced fodder. Accounting supplanted estimation. Farmers became mechanics who worked sitting down. And those who lived through the transformation never overcame the feeling of loss especially of the *company* of an animal. For most

FARMERS' PARKING LOT BEHIND MAIN STREET, HARMONY, GEORGIA, 1941
USDA No. 83-G-37932, National Archives

southerners that animal was the mule—preeminent source of farm power, factotum of regional symbolism, and one of the most interesting creatures ever to walk this earth.[1]

The mule is, of course, a hybrid animal, the fruit of a jackass and a mare. Mules have gender—there are he-mules (also called horse mules) and she-mules (mare mules)—but they cannot reproduce themselves. Among Europeans the Spanish were the most fond of mules and the most prominent mule breeders and exporters. Their mules tracked Central and South America long before the king of Spain presented a fine stud jack to George Washington, which the general named Royal Gift. Washington became a major American promoter of the mule, and his and others' enthusiasm caught on particularly in the South. No one quite knows why, but during the early nineteenth century mule breeding and work grew with the first great cotton kingdom. The mule population

1. On agricultural mechanization and the loss of contact with animals in the U.S., see John L. Shover, *First Majority—Last Minority: The Transforming of Rural Life in America* (DeKalb, Ill., 1976). On the South, among many sources, see Theodore Rosengarten, *All God's Dangers: The Life of Nate Shaw* (New York, 1975), 253, 556–57, and *passim;* and the oral histories (on audio tape) at the Arkansas County Agricultural Museum, Stuttgart.

grew again after the Civil War, as cotton culture expanded once more. The American mule population reached its peak during 1900–1925, however, with the last great expansion of cotton culture into new Mississippi Valley delta lands and into Texas and Oklahoma. In 1900 there were 2,480,000 mules in the South; in 1925, 4,465,000. Thereafter the numbers declined, at first slowly, then (after 1940) very rapidly.[2]

Mule power always correlated closely with cotton culture; so the population was concentrated in the lower South. There, in 1925 more than two-thirds of all draft animals were mules. Louisiana, with its sugar and rice staples, was an exception; horses were favored there. Grand Prairie, Arkansas, rice planters used some mules, but like most farmers working boggy land, they preferred bigger-footed horses. In the upper South 65 percent of North Carolina's draft animals were mules; tobacco farmers favored them as much as cotton growers did. But the remainder of upper South farmers used as many horses and oxen as mules; the range of mule-powered farms was about 30–60 percent. Mules were a distinct minority among draft animals in Kentucky and Virginia, except in Virginia's cotton and tobacco counties and the potato- and truck-cropping Eastern Shore, where growers also favored mules. Mules have often been associated with black people as well as with subregions. The prevalence of mules in cotton culture in the lower Mississippi Valley, where about 84 percent of farmers (of all tenures) were black, presents a high correlation between mules and race. In the new Texas and Oklahoma prairie lands, however, blacks made up less than 10 percent of mule-driving farmers, and they were barely 40 percent of North Carolina's cotton and tobacco farmers. Overall, blacks (who were about a third of the southern population during the 1920s) made up about half the farm population in the heavy-density mule subregions of the South. So the human experience with the animals was rather well shared by both races.[3]

An irony of the southern association with the mule is that for most of the long ascendancy of the creature in farming, most mules were bred outside the region. This is yet another aspect of the South's colonial experience but perfectly logical, too. Mule breeding requires space and grasses. Valuable cotton land would not be devoted to this or any other sort of husbandry. The great Missouri River Valley in central Missouri

2. Robert Byron Lamb, *The Mule in Southern Agriculture* (Berkeley and Los Angeles, 1963), 1–5, 42–51. Lamb's South includes Missouri and excludes West Virginia.

3. *Ibid.*, 49–51, 74; J. M. Spicer, *Beginnings of the Rice Industry in Arkansas* (N.p., 1964), 83–84.

was perfect. So the plains breeders of Missouri supplied most of the mules who broke the piedmont clay during cotton's vast expansion during 1870–1900. Tennessee and Kentucky breeders were important secondary sources. All three of these states continued to export mules during the first quarter of the twentieth century, but Texas took honors as the largest breeder after 1900. Texas mules worked at home, however, in the new lands, although some were shipped to delta farmers in the East, too.[4]

An additional irony is that Missouri farmers—and to a lesser extent, Tennessee's and Kentucky's—shunned mules for work in favor of horses. Conversely, lower South farmers generally spurned horses and persisted in working mules while their prices rose, both absolutely and relative to horse prices. After 1870 mules always cost more than ordinary horses. The differential ranged from $10 to $50, but was often much more. Mules averaged about $120 in 1910, $150 in 1920. In depressed 1930 the typical price dropped to around $60, but it rose again to above $100 in 1940 and about $140 in 1945. Fine two- to six-year-olds cost $200 and more. Harry Crews's impoverished stepfather paid $60 for a horse in Bacon County, Georgia, about 1940, because he could not afford a mule, the equivalent of about nine months' income.[5] So there must have been excellent reasons for southerners, the poorest of American farmers, to work the costlier beasts. Hence a wonderful, generations-long mules-versus-horses debate, which reveals so much of southerners' old rural culture and their powerful affection for mules.

Northern farmers seem not to have been impelled to defend their use of horses. When I have pressed older men and women in Ohio and Indiana, they usually produce one plain, practical argument. Their soils are mainly a heavy, gray clay that retains water. Horses' larger hooves are less likely to sink and mire. Southerners had logical arguments, too, but because mules were considered peculiar by outsiders, mule men often moved beyond empiricism in defending their beast of choice.

4. G. K. Renner, "The Mule in Missouri Agriculture, 1821–1950," *Missouri Historical Review,* LXXIV (July, 1980), 433–57; Peter Chew, "If Mules Are 'Born in a Man,' It's for Life," *Smithsonian,* XIV (November, 1983), 98–108, esp. 107.

5. Renner, "Mule in Missouri Agriculture"; Lamb, *Mule in Southern Agriculture,* 24; Harry Crews, *A Childhood: The Biography of a Place* (New York, 1978), 32. Farm records and account books for the early 1920s in the C. E. Sanford and Son General Store Records, Stephen F. Austin State University Library, Nacogdoches, Texas, confirm Lamb's average mule prices for the time. Another Texas mule trader, of the 1930s and 1940s, reported selling "them as high as $400.00 a pair, $275, $300.00." See "Buck Rushing—Horse and Mule Trader," *Loblolly,* IV (Winter, 1977), 29.

MULE SHEARING IN ALABAMA, 1930s. Clipping sensitive ears necessitated holding the animal's head motionless with rope and stick.

ACES Photo Collection, Auburn University Archives

Broadly, the promule arguments were seven: (1) Mules live longer than horses. (2) They are more resistant to diseases. (3) They withstand heat better. (4) Mules are stronger. (5) They eat less. (6) They are more sure-footed in crops. And (7) mules are smarter and more easily trained for work. Some of these generalizations were true, others false; and elaboration of most of the arguments was based more on tradition and prejudice than verifiable science.[6]

First, mules probably did (and do) live longer than horses. In the Mississippi River delta lands early in the twentieth century mules worked only about six to eight years. But many mules have been known to live past the age of thirty, even forty, and perform at least light work until near the end. Closely related are the disease and heat arguments, both of which may also have been true. During World War I United

6. For example, the Beckett family of Oxford-Millville Road, Butler County, Ohio, who still breed and work Belgians on their farm. The promule argument is a composite of discursive summaries in Lamb, *Mule in Southern Agriculture,* 27–29, 83; and Chew, "If Mules Are 'Born in a Man,'" 105–106. The following analysis is based upon these sources unless otherwise noted.

States army veterinarians found that horses were six times more susceptible to diseases than mules, and widespread impressionistic evidence
exists that mules thrived in the pest-ridden lower South, where horses
suffered. That the Spanish, then southern Americans, preferred mules
and worked them in tropical and semitropical climates, may have prevented a fair test of horses' powers to withstand heat. Lower South
farmers always rested mules at midday during the summers, too, and
were careful to replace evaporated water. Nonetheless in the hot, humid
lower South mules seemed to fare better than the relatively few horses
working nearby.[7]

It is unlikely that mules are stronger. First, mules are smaller and
lighter. The heaviest he-mules weigh about eleven hundred pounds, the
largest draft horses around seventeen hundred pounds. Such horses or
yokes of many oxen broke the plains of Illinois, Iowa, and beyond, turning over with great steel plows deep-rooted prairie grasses. One cannot
imagine mules performing such feats of strength. Whether mules are
stronger than horses "pound for pound" is not resolvable, except in
meaningless animal-to-animal contests. The matter of animal size relates closely, of course, to the argument that mules eat less. Naturally
the smaller creature consumes less fodder.[8]

On the surefootedness of mules southern farmers were effusive in
their praise. According to this argument, mules' generally smaller feet
were guided by nimbler musculature. "Most everybody preferred a
mule to a horse," declared a Texas farmer, "so they wouldn't get their
stuff stomped on." In the 1970s an elderly Texan still worked a mare
mule, Old Mandy, in his large garden. "I work right up the fence with
her almost. She'll sidle up there, she knows how to kind of push that
plow at the right time. She can almost turn on a dime."[9] To say that
mules' muscles as well as smaller feet made them less clumsy seems
rather absurd, considering the complex steps and strides of which
horses are capable. When southerners such as the old Texan bragged on
their mules' surefootedness, they were actually describing a kind of
cognition rather than physical instinct. Mandy's real virtue was that
"she *knows* how." Thus we arrive at mules' most important characteristic, their superior intelligence.

7. On withstanding heat in Texas, see "Marvin Wolfe—Mules," *Loblolly,* IV (Winter,
1977), 49–51.
8. An example of the fallacy that mules eat less (absolutely, as opposed to relatively) is
"Copeland Pass—Mules," *ibid.,* 55–56.
9. "Gus Davis—Mules," *ibid.,* 60.

A mule was easily broken and trained with the use of plowlines for guidance and only occasional light whipping. With a horse, as Harry Crews put it, "you had to come to some understanding with him, which most men did not seem able to do." Crews's stepfather was a rare fellow, willful and cruel enough to break a cheap horse and compel it to plow corn and tobacco without harm to crops or man.[10] Luckier farmers had mules with steady, sweet dispositions, and "sense," as one admiring owner stated, "plenty of it." Mules learned human commands so easily, southerners said. "When you want him to turn to the right you tell him, 'Gee,' and when you want him to go to the left you tell him, 'Haw.'" Mules learned much more, too. A Panola County Texan recalled a "little . . . mouse-colored mule" that responded to the farm dinner bell every morning about eleven o'clock. "She'd hear that dinner bell ring. If we were headed away from the house that mule walks just real slow. But when you got to the end of the row and turned back to go towards the house, you better get ready to walk because that mule was gonna walk your legs off coming back. . . . She knew that dinner bell was quitting time."[11] According to Ned Cobb, mules ate less than horses not because of their smaller size but because of good mule sense (there being no such thing as horse sense) or at least a God-given temperament of restraint. "A mule won't overeat hisself if he's used to getting plenty to eat. But you better not fool with no horses thataway. A horse will overeat his stomach. . . . it's nature for em to do it." Cobb thought horses fundamentally unsuited to farm work, intractable, restless against discipline. Mules, on the other hand, he considered elementally compatible with humanity. They are, he reflected, "kinder and more willin to work than a horse. . . . You can't trust a horse. . . . It's known: better to have you a mule out there than a horse because that mule goin to bow when you call him and your business will pick up."[12]

Hardly ever does one find in the lore of southerners the stubborn mule. Rather, from Virginia into the southern plains, the reliable temperaments and fine intelligence of mules were legendary. It is no wonder that they accompanied highlanders into coal mines, too. They hauled in timbers for ceiling supports and pulled out carts loaded with coal. As engines came to mechanizing mines, mules disappeared, but they continued to work with men and women in small mines until well after World War II. Thus some of the richest mule stories emerge from south-

10. Crews, *A Childhood*, 32.
11. "Rudolph Marshall—Mules," *Loblolly*, IV (Winter, 1977), 40.
12. Rosengarten, *All God's Dangers*, 556.

ern West Virginia as well as from Alabama and Texas. A retired Mingo County miner recalled (during the 1970s) the marvelous wisdom and endearing personality of an "old gray mule" he drove for years. "I didn't have to tell him which place to go into or anything. . . . he knew it . . . just like a man." When there was a delay at work, waiting for a shift change or the restoration of power during an outage, his mule "lay down and really rested; you would be really surprised how smart he was. . . . he was a real pet." Hardly lazy either, the old gray "could run pretty fast, a good runner," the former miner recalled. And he went on to declare that he had seen other mules "walk the railroad ties and not step off a one. Even walk across a trestle on those ties." [13]

The involvement of mules in the daily lives of southern rural folks was so intimate and consuming it seems quite impossible to measure or overestimate. Without a mule a farmer must take a poor horse—an awful fate—or without either one, become a sharecropper, losing in effect one-fourth the income potential of a landless farmer with animal power. But sharecroppers, too, of course, lived with others' mules every day. They plowed and harrowed behind them, hitched them to wagons on Saturday for the trip to town, hitched them up again on Sunday morning for a ride to church. Ned Cobb, reminiscing during the early 1970s about almost three-quarters of a century in the fields, recalled every mule he had worked since boyhood—its sex, name, color, weight, age, personality, characteristics at work alone or in tandem, hauling timber or plowing cotton. Some were "horses," some "mares," some tan, others brown, white, gray, almost black. A few were sullen but persuadable; some were frisky; some were heroic workers. Cobb understood that his and his family's well-being rested on their endurance, but he cared for his mules with love for more reasons than crude practicality; they were his pride and nearly like people. "Twice a day if I'm plowin, mornin and night, I'd brush and curry my mules," he said. "Keep my mules in a thrifty condition, keep em lookin like they belonged to somebody and somebody was carin for em." The mules reciprocated. "Mule love for you to curry him; he'll stand there just as pretty and enjoy it so good. . . . He feels good to be clean just like a person do." Cobb spoiled his mules on feed, too. Many farmers fed

13. Oral history of Ted Miller, n.d. (*ca.* 1975) (Microfilm copy of typescript, in Marshall University Oral History of Appalachia Collection [MUOHA]). On other mules in coal mines, see Benny Hendrix, oral history of Luther V. Smith, November 24, 1974, J. Wayne Flynt, oral history of Lloyd V. Minor, August 20, 1974 (Both typescripts in Samford University Oral History Program, Birmingham).

their work stock field corn, but when Cobb put his mules to use in diffi-cult timber hauling one winter, he used part of his wages to purchase "that number one timothy hay. . . . Best hay ever I heard of or fed my stock. . . . Well, my mules dearly loved it." So much, indeed, that "they got to where they wouldn't eat corn raised on my farm so I bought it for em regular." [14]

Like Cobb, every mule man studied the creatures carefully for physi-cal characteristics to match soils and crops and for personalities. Ac-cording to a white Texas farmer, for example, one should avoid mules with prominent noses "tapered from about his eyes down," for such "Roman noses" indicated meanness, a rare condition easily avoided. One should instead seek an animal "broad across the forehead. They're more intelligent than straight headed mules." For steady work and long life a mule's body should be "tight, made like a little barrel," and set on short or average-length legs. A mule's body should not be "too high off the ground," the Texan averred. As for sizes and weights, "light land, like sand" called for "a little mule that weighed six or seven hundred pounds. . . . If you had bottom land, heavy land, you would get bigger mules." [15] Changing farms often indicated changing mules to suit differ-ent soils, and trading ensued with at least as much drama and risk of chicanery as was associated historically with horse trading. As with horses, mules' teeth usually reveal age; so naturally, elaborate tech-niques for disguising worn teeth were devised. Rustic mule dentists spe-cialized in the fraud. Their problem was to restore, usually with special files, the little trenches ("cups") at the tops of mules' teeth. Old mules wore down the trenches while eating, rather rapidly if they fed off sandy ground, masticating abrasives with corn or hay. By the age of ten most all mules became "smooth-mouthed" (no visible cups), then progres-sively buck-toothed. Not much could be done about this. Judgments about mule flesh then became profoundly subjective—appearance of the coat, gait, head position, and so on. In Bacon County, Georgia, the ultimate test of a strange mule for sale concerned its digestion. "A fart-ing mule is a good mule" served as gospel. [16]

Good mules' notorious flatulence pervaded folklore and humor. Plowing behind a "farting mule" promoted great height in boys, who stretched and jumped to avoid foul exhausts. [17] And there is a story, set

14. Rosengarten, *All God's Dangers*, 253, 556–57.
15. "Marvin Wolfe—Mules."
16. Crews, *A Childhood*, 149–50.
17. Heard by the author while serving in the U.S. Army, 1956–59, and at other times.

on a farm near Spray in north-central North Carolina by the Virginia line, probably during the 1910s, wherein a mule disrupts a funeral. A certain white farmer "believed in buryin' his own close to his house." Gravestones for a first wife and a daughter stood in the yard already; now "neighbors had come to help put pore Miss Mattie [a second wife] away, and the buryin' had got along as far as lettin' her down in the grave" with plowlines. The bereaved husband "was kneelin' thar by his second wife's grave when of a sudden come the sound of a mule not far away eatin' and poppin' off gas. Hit sounded awful loud comin' into the quietness that had settled round the open grave." While everyone else continued to kneel, the solemn husband arose and tied the mule to a tree beyond earshot. The storyteller, in agony suppressing laughter, held herself until safely away, off in the woods.[18]

The very existence of mules sometimes provided sad demonstrations of the worst in human nature. Ned Cobb recalled the tension of keeping watch over his team and wagon at church. "I think about how roguish some folks is that go to church, they just go for devilment." Cobb would "stand where I could keep my eyes on my wagon and that team of mules. I knowed how some of em was. They'd even take your food out of your wagon, slip it out if they could and give it to their own stock."[19] Some mules (perhaps all with Roman noses) were evil natured themselves. But more often, especially in the memories of folks who lived through the era of mechanization and most deeply sensed the loss of association, mules reflected and nurtured by example the best in humankind. Such was the memory of a Texas mare mule bought with a mate about 1930. The mate died and the mare mule pined. "She wanted a pal so bad," recalled her owner, "that she took up with the cows. She would follow the cows, that's all she had to stay with. And wherever they went she went too unless you put her in a lot so she could not get to them. We kept her about 20 years. She came to be a kind of family keepsake."[20] The demise of the mule is a great debit against the presumed benefits of the modernization of agriculture.

Moonshining (the production of untaxed liquor) and bootlegging (sales of the liquor) are also southern folk experiences to be reckoned with seriously. Traditional American images of these shadowy occupations bifurcate. Moonshiners were lank Kentucky mountaineers who op-

18. Ida L. Moore, "Hester," November, 1939 (Typescript in FWP life histories files, Southern Historical Collection, University of North Carolina [SHC]).

19. Rosengarten, *All God's Dangers,* 472.

20. "Ezra Harris—Mules," *Loblolly,* IV (Winter, 1977), 27.

erated stills on forested ridges or deep in deserted coves mainly for their
own and friends' delectation. Thus they escaped their stern religion and
exercised historic contempt for civil authority. Other moonshiners (although this bucolic name is hardly used) and virtually all bootleggers
were Yankees, often foreign-born and always slick gangsters, who ma-
chine-gunned each other on mean urban streets during the Prohibition
era.[21] Both popular images describe actual types, but the former is too
limited both geographically and in attribution of the cause of lawbreak-
ing; the latter captures but a brief and exceptional part of the history of
illegal liquor manufacturing and marketing.

Honest, God-fearing American farmers converted corn and other
grains into whiskey long ago, and they continue. At first the practice
was a practical necessity forced by frontier conditions, especially the
absence of decent market roads. Such was the case at the end of the
eighteenth century in western Pennsylvania, when corn farmers staged
the ill-fated Whiskey Rebellion against Treasury Secretary Alexander
Hamilton's onerous excise tax on liquor. Thereafter isolated people with
little cash persisted in making small amounts of whiskey for home use
and sale. As the modern cash nexus grew closer at various times in various places, rural folks in particular found liquor a convenient and necessary means of coping with rising taxes and other costs of what is euphe-
mistically called development. We have already seen how highland
farmers and out-of-work miners turned increasingly to corn culture and
whiskey making during the hard times of the 1920s and 1930s. That the
collapse of mountain lumber and coal industries and the onset of the
Depression coincided with national Prohibition made moonshining and
bootlegging all the more logical as a strategy for coping with misery
and overpopulation. And just as country people took their liquor-
making skills and habits to coal camps, migrants to textiles towns also
cooked whiskey for succor. During the mid-1930s a physician making
house calls in the squalid Piedmont Heights section of Burlington,
North Carolina, saw a man distilling spirits on his kitchen stove. Another factory hand sold corn whiskey from his mill village shack, hiding
his supplies under the house next to the chimney base. No adult (including the police) could squeeze into the crawl space, so the bootlegger's
four-year-old son did the fetching. Thus were rural ways adapted to urban scenes. Years before Congress passed the Volstead Act, southern
states had adopted their own legislation outlawing liquor. So distillers

21. See Herbert Asbury, *The Great Illusion: An Informal History of Prohibition* (New
York, 1950); Eliot Ness with Oscar Fraley, *The Untouchables* (New York, 1957).

and purveyors had worked in a risk-filled environment, with jail as well as social ostracism as ever-present dangers. Urban moonshiners and bootleggers may well have been more vulnerable. When national Prohibition was repealed in 1933, every southern state retained some form of liquor control (including continued prohibition), too; so as Yankees celebrated the return of booze and real beer, the southern tragi-romance continued.[22]

Moonshining seems to have been almost exclusively the province of males. Women cooked indoors, men out (unless they lived in towns). Thousands of preachers condemned liquor. Some women drank it nevertheless, but men were primary as both clandestine makers and consumers. "In most rural communities," said a young Raleigh plumber and former tenant farmer in the late 1930s, "people make and drink their own corn whiskey." At eighteen he "could make the stuff" and did, while his comrades watched "for the law."[23] For him running a still was his heritage, an adventure and a passage to manhood. Men who did not acquire trades made whiskey well past the age of eighteen to feed their families when farming went bad and no other employment presented itself. A Hendersonville, North Carolina, man's career is illustrative. "Roy Corn" (as a wry interviewer called him), a white man born about 1899, spent two years in federal prison before World War I on a liquor conviction. Already married as a teenager, he did not see his first child until she was about two years old. During the 1920s he tried to go straight, but his little farm yielded little cash, he had no cow, and his children needed milk. So back to "blockading" he went, in partnership with a black man who had taught him this particular craft. Corn was bitter that folks in the liquor traffic were deemed lazy, wealthy, and corrupt. No "enemy of society" was he, Corn declared. His business was small, and like every other moonshiner-bootlegger he knew in 1938, he converted corn in order to survive.[24] Another North Carolinian told a similar story. Crossing the Great Smokies into Tennessee early in the

22. Ian R. Tyrell, *Sobering Up: From Temperance to Prohibition in Antebellum America, 1800–1860* (Westport, Conn., 1979); Andrew Sinclair, *Prohibition: The Era of Excess* (Boston, 1962). Scenes of moonshining and bootlegging in Burlington are related in Mary Murphy, interview with Carroll Lupton, M.D., May 18, 1979 (Typescript in Southern Oral History Program, SHC [SOHP]). On prohibition movements and administrations in the South, see Dewey W. Grantham, *Southern Progressivism: The Reconciliation of Progress and Tradition* (Knoxville, 1983), 160–77 and *passim*. See also Norman H. Clark, *Deliver Us from Evil: An Interpretation of American Prohibition* (New York, 1976).

23. Pat Matthews, "From Tenant Farmer to Plumber," n.d. (1938 or 1939) (Typescript in FWP life histories files, SHC).

24. Frank Massimino, "Roy Corn, Blockader," December, 1938 (Typescript, *ibid.*).

century, he ran out of money and "couldn't find a job to save my life." Becoming desperate, he finally reasoned with himself: " 'Why, hell, Jim, you got to live somehow,' so I went to work for a fellow stilling." Like Corn, Jim worried over breaking the law and religious teaching: "Folks will say, 'Oh, I wouldn't do such as that.' Well, maybe not. I did. I was hungry and needing a place to stay." [25]

No doubt some makers, sellers, and imbibers of corn whiskey felt no qualms and made no defenses. A decrepit fellow from the marshlands of Dare County, North Carolina, told a federal interviewer in 1939: "Since I got no 'count, there aint nothin' in the world gives me such pleasure as lying around out here in the yard with a jug o' likker and takin' a drink when I feel like it. I lay out here sometimes until bedtime." One comfort seemed to breed others, too. "You'd be surprised at the wimmen that come around here after dark lookin for a drink. I always accommodate 'em." [26] More often, one senses from surviving testimony, liquor men were torn between necessity (not to mention comfort and profit) and formal morality. A Raleigh bus driver's story of his moonshiner father's funeral is a poignant example. The father died on a Christmas Day (about 1930) after working at his still in freezing rain. His religious wife had pleaded with him for years to stop; now he was dead and she grieved without reproach. Their sons took it upon themselves to arrange the funeral. Finding little money in the house, they loaded a car with whiskey and sold it in town, then purchased a casket, burial suit, and a spray of flowers. The deceased properly laid out, the boys "went back to my mother's uncle's house and asked him to preach the funeral. He is a Holiness preacher and that's the way Mother wanted it, but he refused to preach the funeral . . . [or] have the body brought into his church . . . remarking that such as Sam Askins would pollute God's house." The future bus driver "cussed him worse than I ever cussed a stubborn mule or a broke-down car." So the moonshiner was buried in "an icy downpour" by friends, "with no sermon, no song, no prayer or music, and only one pitifully small design of flowers to cover the red clay." That day the brothers "promised each other solemnly that we'd starve and see our families starve before we'd fool with whiskey and be dumped in our graves like cows." [27]

25. Adyleen G. Merrick, "Street Sweeper and Tonic Maker," life history of Thomas Sizemore, June 8, 1939 (Typescript, *ibid.*).

26. W. O. Saunders, ". . . And Set Me Up a Hell-Buster," life history of John W. Twiford, June 4, 1939 (Typescript, *ibid.*).

27. Mary A. Hicks, "The Head of the Family," life history of N. G. Blake, March, 1939 (Typescript, *ibid.*).

Selling moonshine seems to have been the occupation of women almost as much as men, particularly in towns and cities. Usually operating out of their own homes rather than speakeasies, bootleggers no
doubt made modest amounts of money with relative ease, but they faced
great risks. Any unknown customer might be a policeman or his in-
former, and raids on bootleggers' homes were common. There is no
way of establishing how many bootleggers were cynical profiteers or,
like so many country moonshiners, torn with conflict over the morality
of their livelihood. It is certain that both sorts existed. A marvelous example of a female mountebank originates from Salisbury, North Carolina, where a pious magistrate related the following about 1939: On the
evening before the trial of a bootlegger the magistrate attended a church
revival. At the service appeared a distraught woman, wailing for for-
giveness and eager to accept the faith. The judge himself prayed over
her in public. On the following day, as he remembered, "I called the
case," and "up stepped a lawyer, and with him as the defendant was the
poor little woman that had been prayed over by me the night before."
With her "were about eight children of assorted sizes and sexes—
mostly female." As the case was presented, "they all begun to cry and
yell and go on so, we could hardly hear the testimony." The woman's
attorney described her as a poor widow with "many mouths to feed and
how hard it was to get food honest durin' hard times and how the only
thing a poor woman could do at home, where she had to stay and take
care of her children to earn a penny, was to sell a little liquor." The final
straw was her public conversion the evening before, witnessed by the
magistrate himself. So smitten by overwhelming evidence of both guilt
and redemption, he "refused to bind her over." Only later, from the
furious arresting officer, did the kindly judge learn that this had been
the lady's fifth offense, that only one of the bawling children was hers
(the others having been "borrowed for the occasion"), that she had been
married and divorced (not widowed) five times, and that "she owned
one of the best farms in the upper part of the county and had good income from her tenants." Her considerable capital all derived from selling corn whiskey.[28]

Such brash charlatans were probably rare. More typical in all likelihood was another woman who sold liquor from her home in Humboldt, in western Tennessee above Jackson. Owner of a small bungalow,
she was unable to get public assistance for her wheelchair-bound, polio-

28. William E. Hennessee, "The Magistrate," life history of Clarence E. Fesperman,
n.d. (1938 or 1939) (Typescript, *ibid.*).

stricken son or for a crippled former husband for whom she also assumed responsibility. So from a moonshiner she bought about twenty
gallons of whiskey each week at two dollars a gallon, selling it for fifty
cents a pint (a 50 percent markup). Six days of every week her home
was open to customers—90 percent of them men—who came to her
door. She measured each pint from a pitcher, keeping her stock hidden,
so that if the police arrived, she could pour out its contents quickly and
rinse both her sink and pitcher while her former husband slowly opened
heavy door locks. This way she earned on the average thirty dollars per
week, a modest but decent living for the 1930s. The money also allowed
her to keep an automobile, which she used for Sunday escapes from her
clients. She never went to church, the bootlegger told a FWP interviewer, but she was nonetheless "a religious woman" and refused to sell
booze on the Sabbath. Driving about with her two cripples, she listened
to hymns on the radio.[29]

Bootlegging enabled the Humboldt woman to retain her home and
care for two dependents in material comfort approaching that of the
middle class. The mountebank of Salisbury achieved (at least in material terms) the status of the upper class. One cannot be sure, but the
great numbers of bootleggers in the South probably remained poor, like
the mill hands of Burlington. There in 1933, many large families tried
to exist on weekly incomes as low as twelve dollars. Making and selling
whiskey permitted survival and hardly more. One wonders, too, at the
poor competing with the poor in the liquor business and whether the
moneyed of Burlington were sufficiently numerous as customers to tide
them over until better times arrived.[30]

Shadowy and incompletely documented as moonshining and bootlegging will ever remain, there is evidence that sheds considerable light
on the business, moonshining in particular. Beginning in 1920 federal
enforcement of national Prohibition got underway, and the commissioner of internal revenue was charged with reporting the activities of
Treasury Department agents in their war on liquor. The commissioners'
annual reports included counts of only those stills discovered by agents,
along with gallonage of confiscated spirits. There are no estimates on
undiscovered stills and gallons of liquor that escaped the revenuers.

29. Della Yoe, "A Hard, Mean Business," life history of May Clark, in John L. Robinson (ed.), *Living Hard: Southern Americans in the Great Depression* (Washington, D.C.,
1981), 208–14. See also an earlier draft, Della Yoe, "Clare Garber," December 19, 1938
(Typescript in FWP life histories files, SHC).

30. Murphy, interview with Lupton.

Over a period of forty years, however, the IRS reports yield interesting comparisons of moonshining in the states and certain trends that demonstrate the persisting southernness of the illegal traffic.

North Carolina, for example, led the nation in numbers of illicit stills for many years. In 1920 agents seized 3,104 Tar Heel stills. Virginians and Georgians lost more than 2,000 stills each, and South Carolinians and Alabamians lost more than 1,000 each. West Virginia, by contrast, had only 176 stills confiscated, Kentucky 387. Mountaineers were probably not preeminent among moonshiners. The trans-Mississippi states of Arkansas, Louisiana, Oklahoma, and Texas had but a few stills. After 1920 (when 12,135 stills were seized in fourteen southern states) the total number of stills in the region and the nation declined substantially. From 1921 through 1930 agents seized only about 5,000 stills per year in the South. In 1927 the region's confiscated stills fell below 50 percent of the nation's for the first time, too; and in 1930 southern stills seized were only 30 percent of the nation's. Nonetheless, North Carolina, Virginia, and Georgia still led the nation, with Alabama, Tennessee, and occasionally Kentucky following at respectable rates.[31]

When agents seized southern stills they almost always confiscated less liquor than at nonsouthern stills, however. In 1920 the average number of gallons at southern stills was only 3.27. Through the remainder of the decade, average gallonage increased markedly, as southerners, like other Americans, responded to the great Prohibition market for illegal spirits. In 1921 gallonage per seized still jumped to ten, in 1923 more than fifteen, in 1924 above twenty, and in 1929 somewhat more than fifty. By contrast, nonsouthern distilleries were large operations. A comparison of North Carolina with New York is illustrative of the extreme. In 1920 revenuers confiscated 4,796 gallons of whiskey at North Carolina's 3,104 stills, but 25,965 at only 46 New York stills. In 1925 North Carolina's 319 stills had 3,732 gallons. New York's 46 had 20,564. By 1929, when southern moonshiners had increased per-still production, agents seized 20,924 gallons at 326 North Carolina stills,

31. Treasury Department, Internal Revenue Service, *Annual Report of the Commissioner, 1920* (Washington, D.C., 1920), 189. Citations for the annual reports through 1925 are the same, with pages as follows: (1921), 174; (1922), 181–82; (1923), 181–82; (1924), 186; (1925), 173–74. Report for 1926 not available. For 1927–30, see Treasury Department, IRS, *Annual Report of the Commissioner of Prohibition, 1927* (Washington, D.C., 1927), 84; (1928), 88; (1929), 100; (1930), 110. *South* (as elsewhere in this book) includes fourteen states: the former Confederacy, plus West Virginia, Kentucky, and Oklahoma. Aggregate data is from tables on pages cited.

but 167,148 gallons at 377 New York operations. For some reason Georgia stills (at least those seized) always produced more than North Carolina's, and Georgia stills came to outnumber North Carolina's, too, by the end of the 1920s.[32]

After four years (1927–1930) in which southern stills numbered less than half the nation's, in 1931, two years before repeal of Prohibition, southern moonshiners once more emerged as America's premier illicit distillers. The absolute number of southern stills leaped, too, from 2,420 in 1930 to 14,321 in 1931 (or 67.1 percent of the nation's). In average gallonage confiscated, however, nonsoutherners maintained clear superiority until 1938, when southerners for the first time lost more than half the country's seized liquor. After the repeal of Prohibition the number of stills in the South dropped, varying from about 8,300 in 1938 and 1949 to 12,300 in 1937 and almost 12,000 in 1955. But the trend after the early 1930s was toward virtual moonshine monopoly for the South in both stills and production. Monopoly is normally defined as a 90 percent or better share of market. In 1942 southern stills seized passed this figure; in 1948 gallonage confiscated in the South exceeded 90 percent of the nation's for the first time.[33] Figure 11 illustrates the region's role in moonshining, in relation to the nation.

Several generalizations, then, appear reasonable from cautious analysis of the federal data as well as scattered personal testimony. First, moonshining was and remained an east-of-the-Mississippi phenomenon. Within this broad area, five contiguous states—Virginia, the Carolinas, Georgia, and Alabama (plus Tennessee, periodically)—were the focus of federal enforcement and probably of production. Moonshining also appears to have been as common (if not more so) in the piedmonts and coastal plains as in the mountains. Second, southern blockaders were always small-time operators. After gallonage confiscated passed

32. Treasury Department, *Annual Report of the Commissioner*, 1920–25, 1927–30. In 1930 southern stills averaged 131.20 gallons, no doubt an anomaly.

33. Treasury Department, Bureau of Industrial Alcohol, *Statistics Concerning Intoxicating Liquors, December 1931* (Washington, D.C., 1931), 86–87; (1932), 136–37; (1933), 93–94; (1934 report not available); Treasury Department, IRS, *Annual Report of the Commissioner, 1935* (Washington, D.C., 1935), 151–52; (1936), 167; (1937), 150; (1938), 159; (1939), 167; (1940), 172; (1941), 175; (1942), 174; (1943), 185; (1944), 188; (1945), 196; (1946), 207; (1947), 201; (1948), 222; (1949), 218; (1950), 224; (1951), 233; (1952), 246; (1953), 128; (1954 data not tabulated by states); Treasury Department, IRS, *Statistics Relating to the Alcohol and Tobacco Industries . . . 1955* (Washington, D.C., n.d.), 65; (1956), 65; (1957), 77; (1958), 75; (1959), 81. Regional data aggregated from tables on pages cited, as before.

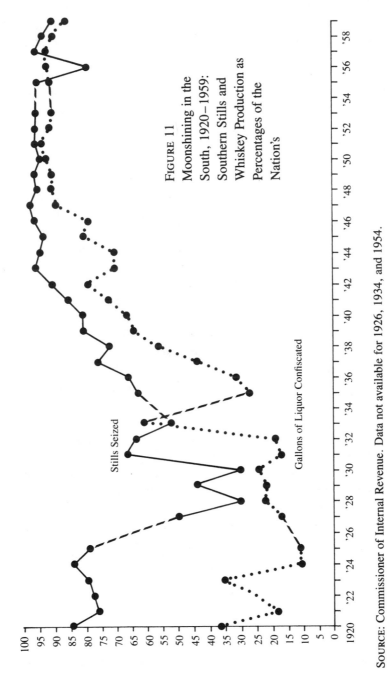

SOURCE: Commissioner of Internal Revenue. Data not available for 1926, 1934, and 1954.

NOTE: South here is the former Confederacy, plus West Virginia, Kentucky, and Oklahoma.

FIGURE 11

Moonshining in the South, 1920–1959: Southern Stills and Whiskey Production as Percentages of the Nation's

Stills Seized

Gallons of Liquor Confiscated

50 per still in 1929, the figure fell off rapidly once more to 22.75 in 1931, up to 32.84 in 1933 (the last year of national Prohibition), then downward once more to 17–23 gallons per still for the remainder of the 1930s. As southern stills and gallonage achieved national dominance in the 1940s, the average number of gallons seized with stills dropped further, to 14.33 in 1942 and down as low as 9 and 6 gallons. During the 1950s, when agents raided about ten thousand southern stills each year, gallonage seized was typically 14 or 15 per still. This figure was much greater than the 3.27 gallons of 1920, yet still smaller than in the national Prohibition era and tiny in comparison with northern and western stills before 1933. A third generalization is actually a guess, based upon the foregoing, that during the 1940s and 1950s moonshining continued to be primarily an enterprise of the poor. After 1920 federal agents never found as many as 12,135 stills again, although during the mid-1950s the figures came close. Relative to the region's increased urban and decreased rural populations, however, the absolute decline of stills seems significant. Poor country folk, typical moonshiners, were driven from rural areas by New Deal era enclosures and mechanization, then lured away by wartime service or industrial opportunities. The persistence of southern moonshining, however reduced, probably indicates several things: a sizable population of the rural poor still on the land, the intractability of tradition, the survival of a considerable demand for the taste of homemade corn whiskey, and of course, continued southern state controls over or prohibition of liquor.

All this means there was little abatement of the preoccupation of federal, state, and local law enforcement officers with the makers of and traffickers in illegal booze. Struggles between sheriffs and cooperating federal revenuers, on the one hand, and moonshiners and bootleggers, on the other, ripped communities, divided families, and caused more than a little bloodshed. Conceivably some blockaders and sheriffs' deputies (perhaps young men) thought the conflict a grand adventure, superior to hunting squirrels or bear. Most of the men and women involved were determined, businesslike, and probably scared. Of Mississippi's early experience with statewide prohibition (1910s), a former delta deputy recalled: "Them days was hard times, yes, yes. I went through a whole lot in them days. The people was mean and killed one another." He remembered racial troubles, a white mob taking two black prisoners from jail and lynching them, but worse was the constant hunting for stills and shootouts with moonshiners. In those times the deputy commonly carried a repeating rifle and a couple of pistols.[34] J. E. McTeer, young sheriff of Beaufort County, South Carolina, during the late 1920s, related in his autobiography incidents with overtones more of Dodge City or Tombstone than the sleepy Low Country. McTeer, too, engaged in shootouts in the dark woods, but most frightening was a face-off with a hunting companion who happened also to make whiskey and sell it from his country store. The moonshiner finally sent a message to McTeer: "The next time you come to Bluffton, come prepared. I mean it." McTeer was obliged to answer the challenge. He drove into an empty street (all knew of the challenge) and burst into the store with gun in hand. Luckily for both men, the moonshiner had imbibed too much of his own corn squeezings and sat asleep in his chair, his pistol resting in his lap.[35]

The perspective of those on the wrong side of the law was frightened and grim, too. In all likelihood for every still raided—in the federal reports, from as few as 1,673 to as many as 14,321 a year—at least one man went to jail. The value of barrels, copper tubing, and other apparatus, and a great many automobiles was all lost, too. Liquor making was dangerous and costly to people least able to afford being caught. A destitute North Carolinian explained this well in 1939: "These here clothes I got on is all the clothes I got. They is so slick with dirt I guess I smell like a pole cat." Lacking any other means of making money, he would make and sell whiskey again, he said, but "the law" was too "hot." "I done seen the inside of them places where they keep law breakers. I ain't hankerin' to go back."[36] Men in prison, he well knew, could not help their families, missed their children's growth, lost wives and property, and endured regimes of work and humiliation so cruel it is surprising more were not deterred from breaking the law. Yet the lure—and the pressing need—of cash remained too great.

Moonshiners and bootleggers were not the only southern felons to be sent to prisons, of course. But as poor people, they were typical, as has ever been the case. Over the years prisoners formed a minority of many thousands; so something of the experiences of jail are appropriate here. Serious felons and repeat offenders went to central state penitentiaries,

34. Oral history of W. H. Haynes, February 26, 1973 (Typescript in Mississippi Department of Archives and History, Jackson).

35. J. E. McTeer, *Adventure in the Woods and Waters of the Low Country* (Beaufort, S.C., 1972), 38–39.

36. Mary P. Wilson, life history of Henry Durham, July 12, 1939 (Typescript in FWP life histories files, SHC).

where they were locked up and heavily guarded, and executed with great frequency. Kilby, the maximum security prison of Alabama, had a fearsome reputation. Ned Cobb, the Alabama Sharecroppers' Union man sent to jail during the 1930s, never served there but shuddered, years later, at reports of Kilby he heard many times through the prisoners' grapevine: "Kilby—that weren't nothin but a slaughter pen, strop men till the last breath gone from em, then they commenced settin em in the lectric chair." [37] A white drunk, moonshiner, and knife fighter sent to the West Virginia penitentiary in 1941 presented a perspective of quite a different central state institution in Appalachia: "They had dormitories just like the army, you know, army camp. Just exactly the same difference. Nice place, all right—recreation, ball games, pitch horseshoes, and oh, a lot of stuff you could do for pleasure." Segregated blacks and whites formed baseball teams, which played each other, the prisoners betting cigarettes on the games. Guards were no trouble, and the mountaineer, whose standards were admittedly low, was enthusiastic about prison food: "And boy, you talk about eatin. They piled everything on. . . . get anything you wanted. [38]

Comparable extremes were experienced in the state prison farms. Early in the 1920s Virginia's prison farm was "reformed"—its guards militarized and disciplined; its crop, livestock, and dairy operations modernized under expert administration; and its prisoners given improved clothing, food, and medical attention. [39] At the Alabama farms at Spignor and Wetumpka, Ned Cobb found hard work and stern discipline but excellent food and housing. "Every bit of the food we et come off of that farm" in Spignor, he recalled. "That farm was doin better, accordin to the yield, really, than the farms out here at home. And the prisoners was eatin better, in a way, than folks was on the outside." At Wetumpka, where he raised food for white women inmates incarcerated there, Cobb "couldn't have asked for better quarters. The buildings was tighter, warmer, than any house ever I lived in." [40] Lower South prison farms resembled slave plantations in outward appearance. Stern discipline and

37. Rosengarten, *All God's Dangers,* 397. Brief reference to Kilby's terror from a former white inmate is to be found in Jack Kytle, "A Dead Convict Don't Cost Nothin'," in James Seay Brown (ed.), *Up Before Daylight: Life Histories from the Alabama Writers' Project, 1938–1939* (University, Ala., 1982), 106–17.

38. Quoted in Todd Gitlin and Nanci Hollander, *Uptown: Poor Whites in Chicago* (New York, 1970), 21–22.

39. Jack Temple Kirby, *Westmoreland Davis: Virginia Planter-Politician, 1859–1942* (Charlottesville, 1968), 101–102.

40. Rosengarten, *All God's Dangers,* 367, 384–85.

high work productivity were the rule, and prisoner−field hands were overwhelmingly black. William Faulkner described the regime at Parchman, Mississippi, during the 1920s so well in his long story "Old Man." Yet though a prison may be a plantation, prisoners were in important ways not slaves. They were criminals, bound for punishment, living as single men rather than in families; and there was an endless supply of them. Thus daily treatment for prisoners was seldom restrained; the punishment principle usually ruled. This was certainly true at the notorious prison farm in Arkansas during the 1930s. A white gambler, confidence man, and former inmate explained: "They [the guards] start out in the morning on them quarter mile rows of cotton or corn and call off one of the boys and say, 'If you ain't the first man through [hoeing] this row we'll help you a little before you start the next one.' And then to another man they say, 'If you don't beat him through we'll give you some inspiration.' So both of 'em fly in and work like mad, but one of 'em is going to be laid down on his belly and whaled with a leather strap at the end of the row." [41] If such a field hand were disabled through beating, his replacement came cheap.

Most southern felons did not serve in central penitentiaries or on state farms, however, but in county road gangs. During the 1920s the population of North Carolina's county penal systems was double that of the state's central prison, and this seems to have been typical of the entire region before World War II. Road gangs of men bound in leg irons and chains have long been associated with the South, and properly so, but before 1900 chain gangs existed in eighteen nonsouthern states, too—including New York, Indiana, Michigan, Illinois, Iowa, the Dakota Territory, Colorado, and California. Such gangs were the primary means of maintaining county roads. For a variety of reasons—the growth of humanitarian outrage at balls and chains, weather too harsh for year-round outside work—chain gangs disappeared everywhere outside the South except in Arizona and Nebraska. By the 1920s county road work of prisoners was state supervised (and perhaps less harsh) in Virginia and Maryland. In Louisiana only about one-sixth of the state's parishes maintained chain gangs. In West Virginia hardly a quarter of the state's prisoners worked on roads. In Florida (until the early 1920s) and Alabama (until 1928), counties were permitted to lease their prisoners to private contractors, who hired their own guards and worked

41. William Faulkner, *Three Famous Short Novels: "Spotted Horses," "Old Man," "The Bear"* (New York, 1961). Quotation on Arkansas from Walter Rowland, "A North Little Rock Thief," n.d. (1938 or 1939) (Typescript in FWP life histories files, SHC).

convicts at some sort of production. The chain gang or some version of the county road camp remained supreme in southern penology into the 1940s and 1950s nonetheless. Everywhere inmates were overwhelmingly black. In North Carolina (a white-majority state) in 1926, blacks outnumbered whites two-to-one. In black-belt Georgia, county inmates were virtually all black. Most inmates were young men (under thirty-five). In North Carolina (during the mid-1920s) Prohibition violations sent the typical (39 percent) white prisoner to the chain gang; larceny (25 percent) was the second most common crime. Among blacks larceny was the first-ranking felony (31 percent), Prohibition offenses (24 percent) were second. County judges had wide discretion in determining whether felons should be sent to work on the roads or incarcerated elsewhere. There is considerable evidence from North Carolina that when roads were in need of repair, judges supplied the labor.[42]

Sheriffs and deputies were eager to cooperate, for in many states county law enforcement officers were compensated not in fixed salaries but through fees, "according to how much arrests and subpoenas and warrants" they accomplished, as one deputy explained. This particular officer assured himself an adequate income by lurking about at funerals, auctions, political meetings, and barbecues, where he invariably uncovered furtive drinking and, especially at the latter two types of gatherings, open fighting. "Almost any gathering where people git together may mean you can pick up a fee."[43] Thus men went off to the chain gangs.

County penal facilities varied from place to place, but not so widely as central penitentiaries or prison farms. The West Virginia moonshiner quoted above saw the inside of more than thirty county jails between the late-1930s and the 1950s, but he seems never to have worked on the roads. He merely sat in surroundings he considered crude but tolerable. Over most of the region, road work predominated, and the great majority of inmates lived in conditions between degrading and horrible. Alabamian Ned Cobb spent much of his prison time in road camps around the state. Accommodations were comparable to poor tenant shacks—not so good as prison farm housing—and food was monotonous and seldom well prepared. But as long as one obeyed guards' orders, life was safe and endurable. Cobb was fortunate not to have been jailed in

42. Jesse F. Steiner and Roy M. Brown, *The North Carolina Chain Gang: A Study of County Convict Road Work* (Chapel Hill, 1927), 4–6, 16–17, 103–104, 125–35; Arthur F. Raper, *Preface to Peasantry: A Tale of Two Black Belt Counties* (Chapel Hill, 1936), 291–99.

43. W. T. Couch (ed.), *These Are Our Lives* (Chapel Hill, 1939), 300–301.

ROAD CAMP PRISONER CAGES, WAKE COUNTY, NORTH CAROLINA, 1919
North Carolina Division of Archives and History

the 1910s or 1920s—in Alabama, Georgia, North Carolina, or else-where—for over much of the South before the 1930s road gangs did not live like all-male groups of sharecroppers; they were caged, mobile crews. Before the availability of trucks to move convicts conveniently from one work site to the next, many counties used "movable pris-ons"—four-wheeled wagons, about eighteen to twenty feet long, six to eight feet wide, and eight feet high. Over the wagon bed was con-structed a large cage, usually of iron, sometimes of heavy wood. Tar-paulins were rolled and tied to the roofs, to be let down in inclement weather. In such contraptions about eighteen men slept, on three levels, with insufficient room to sit upright. Heat was supplied by a small stove in the front end; light came from a kerosene lantern hung from the ceil-ing. A pail of drinking water, a dipper, and a "night bucket" completed the furnishings. In Greene County, Georgia, about 1934, Arthur Raper found a four wheeler (as cages were called there) employed as a perma-nent dormitory. After supper prisoners were marched to the rig. "Here they are taken off the big chain, but never relieved of their iron ankle bands and shackles." There was no stove; the tarpaulins were merely rolled down in winter. "An open tub under a hole in the floor serves all sanitary purposes." This particular cage had continued in such service more than a decade after it had last been drawn behind draft animals or a truck.[44]

Cages and permanent camps alike were pestholes, especially before the expansion of public health services during the 1930s and 1940s. During the 1920s inspectors from the North Carolina state Board of Public Welfare reported horrifying conditions in a county camp. They found two tubercular black prisoners bedded in a cage; another sick man lay in an old house nearby. "No sleeping garments are provided them. They have on regular convict stripes. The third man has running syphilitic sores on his legs. The tubercular patients have no receptacles to expectorate in, consequently they use the ground, the floor of their cage, and anything that is convenient." Since neither cage, old house, nor kitchen was screened, flies swarmed over all. The kitchen was located close to the cage with the expectorating tuberculars, and meat was left outside on a woodblock to collect flies, dust, and whatever else might happen upon it. "The filth of the bedding and the sleeping quarters," wrote the inspectors, "is indescribable." One patient, sick for a month, said he had received "no clean bedding" the entire time.[45]

A rare humanitarian aspect of southern penology before World War II was unofficial sanction of private visits from spouses and friends of the opposite sex. This practice is well documented in Alabama and probably prevailed elsewhere as well. Ned Cobb, always the carefully spoken gentleman, explained his experience: "When I went off to prison I was a able-bodied man, my wife was an able-bodied woman, and we lost nearly all our nature activity. I taken it pretty hard at the start." But after he established a record of obedience in road camps and prison farms, he was permitted weekends at "home on parole," or if a road camp was near enough, "she was comin to where I was." According to Cobb, "nature-privilege weren't given to us, exactly, by the officers at the prison." "These places"—vacant outbuildings—"was available, though, and they wouldn't try to keep the prisoners out of em. . . . they left it up to you." So Cobb would take his mattress and his wife to a shed or storehouse. Prison became endurable.[46] A white Alabama road camp guard also has testified that during the 1950s and 1960s, the washhouses of permanent camps were used every other Sunday for conjugal

44. Gitlin and Hollander, *Uptown,* 22–23; Rosengarten, *All God's Dangers,* 410–22 and *passim;* Steiner and Brown, *North Carolina Chain Gang,* 55–60; Raper, *Preface to Peasantry,* 298–99.

45. Steiner and Brown, *North Carolina Chain Gang,* 78–80.

46. Rosengarten, *All God's Dangers,* 422–23.

visits. Authorities also tried to assign trustworthy prisoners to camps close to home to facilitate such contact. In the larger institutions where long-term prisoners were kept, however, wives and girl friends (or men for female inmates) were not permitted private visits, and as has ever been the case, sodomy prevailed. Incorrigible bad men in the lower South were called "gators." Gators were also often "tush hogs" (a curiously Yiddish-sounding expression) who dominated and sexually exploited young, effeminate prisoners called "gal boys." [47]

Southern prison guards' toleration of prisoners' sexuality seems remarkable in light of an otherwise unblemished record of brutality. In the main guards were country men, like their charges, and perhaps they extended their lifelong kindly regard for lower animals and their instincts to human prisoners. Before their professionalization (not until the 1950s in Alabama and many other states), guards were white men, scarcely above the felons they managed in education, intelligence, ability, and morals. Never trained in any formal sense, most were local political appointees, friends or family of a clerk, sheriff, judge, or guard boss. Or they were recruited off farms near road camps because of their vigorous youth, size, reputation for meanness, and skill with tracking dogs. Some were stern but fair men who believed in heredity as destiny and in righteous deterrence by means of swift corporal punishment. But many if not most were not only violent in their official functions but drunkards, moonshiners and bootleggers (often in league with convicts), and whoremongers. The public seemed largely indifferent to this peculiar caste and their brutality. All prisoners were to be punished (more than rehabilitated), anyway; and since most of them were black, racism compounded a vicious public attitude. Even then, North Carolina county gang guards and bosses were commonly fired for malfeasance and convicted for Prohibition violations, pandering, theft, and murder. Discharged guards not actually sent to prison themselves usually took similar positions in other counties, however. [48]

Some of the worst guard brutality on record took place before 1930 in convict-worked coal mines and in road camps around Birmingham in Jefferson County, Alabama. The account of one former guard bespeaks the economics as well as the racism of the system. A white man who escaped the poverty of the hill country by accepting this position with a

47. Ray A. March, *Alabama Bound: Forty-five Years Inside a Prison System* (University, Ala., 1978), 26, 119.
48. *Ibid.*, 1–84, on Oscar Dees, a burly native of Mobile County, Ala., who became a prison guard in 1931; Steiner and Brown, *North Carolina Chain Gang*, 81–85.

private contractor, he learned his mission on the job: "I got my first trainin' at handlin' men when I's watchin' them convicts," he related. "They was a bad crowd, an' I had to be bad with 'em. I hadn't been thar two weeks when I got atter a buck nigger 'bout how he was buildin' a scaffold that keeps th' roof [of the mine] from fallin' in; and he sassed me. They'd done told me never to take nothin' off them bastards, so I jes' went over to him an' nearly beat his brains out with my club. That nigger wasn't able to dig no more coal for a long time." There "wasn't no pamperin'" of prisoners in the contract mines, he said. Guards were instructed "to shoot quick as hell if anybody got rough, or tried runnin' off. They said they was lots more whar these come from, an' that when you knocked one of 'em off it was no worse'n killin' a hog or a cow." Still, guards lacerated prisoners' backs with whips far more often than they killed them.[49] Another white man recalled a career managing Jefferson County gangs who shoveled rocks for local road repairs. Prisoners were always blacks, serving terms up to twenty-seven months, usually for theft. Yet penalties for infractions of rules were Draconian. These included bread and water for three days following a first offense. Then came whipping, with the convict lying face down over a barrel. Another was the "dog house"—confinement in a cage overnight, chained in the standing position, after a large dose of salty hot water so the prisoner would defecate down the backs of his legs. "Hosing" meant a beating with a three-feet long rubber pipe that would not "break the hide." "Bull-tonguing" was an extreme lashing with a leather whip consisting of three eighteen-inch long layers of leather, designed to "tear him up."[50]

Sheriffs, their deputies, and jailers across the South—but especially in the black belts and deltas, it seems—were less imaginative in terrorizing their short-term prisoners. They were almost as brutal, however, commonly using gun butts, clubs, and blackjacks to subdue or intimidate their charges. The horrors of life in county jailhouses are almost as legendary as the chain gangs. Blacks in particular felt the terror here, too. Louis Johnson, for example, was an elderly man jailed in Osceola, Arkansas, in 1939 for the crime of "night-riding." He had tacked up Southern Tenant Farmers' Union posters! In June he wrote, "This is a hard place. I am a fread all the time that someone is going to

49. Kytle, "A Dead Convict Don't Cost Nothin'."

50. John Earnest, oral history of Eugene Herbert Moore, November 16, 1975 (Typescript in Samford University Oral History Program). Moore worked at one of six all-black prisoner camps. There were three white camps, as well, but unfortunately I have found no accounts of treatment in these.

hurt me." One man had already been blackjacked to death. "The Laws [police] is so hard on the Prison[er] Easpecial the colard [colored] one—they are Beating and lashing all the time." In July, Johnson wrote, "These laws treat us Negro so Bad here something need to be done about it [be]cose some of these Laws outer be in jail" themselves.[51]

One of the saddest tragedies of southern history is this brutalization of the poor by men of the same or very similar origins and class. Racial fears and antagonisms (a subject to be treated in the next chapter) played an enormous role in dividing the poor and near-poor against each other. Southerners who bossed, bullied, whipped, and sometimes even killed men and women of their own color and class perhaps evoke most strikingly the nature of the region's cruel systems of penology and plantation production. Such men are hardly unique in history. The term *compradore*—a native collaborator-servant of imperial masters—derives from China in the age of European colonialism and has been used to describe similar people around the globe. Southern compradores, whether prison guards or plantation overseers, were in all likelihood men who accepted without question a political economy into which they were born and who grasped opportunities of advancement when they appeared. Such opportunities came usually to white men. Sons of small farmers, tenants of some station, or unskilled working-class townsmen, they took up guns and clubs to get ahead. Many of them, for a variety of reasons, often including racism, identified positively with a repressive system and with planter-landlords. Personal power is a motive to be reckoned with, too. Prison guards' life-and-death options we have observed already. On great black-belt and delta plantations riding bosses and straw-bosses, as they were known in Arkansas, wore khakis, broadbrimmed hats, and usually packed pistols strapped to their waists. Having received permission from sheriffs (with planter intercession) to carry arms, they became "pistol-totin' deputies" ready for extraplantation official duties as well. Black men had no opportunities to serve as prison guards, but in Georgia's southwestern black-belt counties about a tenth of plantation overseers were black. They bossed all-black labor forces. Unlike white overseers, who were (according to Arthur Raper) "distant tenants," black bosses were usually lifelong acquaintances of planter-landlords or trusted tenants from the estates where they worked.

51. Louis Johnson to J. R. Butler, June 17, July 6, 1939, both on microfilm roll 11, STFU Papers, SHC. Among many other examples of brutality and law breaking by Arkansas local police to be found in the STFU Papers, see copy of STFU press release, April 16, 1939 (roll 11), on the Crawfordsville (Crittenden County) town marshal.

Black overseers (like antebellum slave drivers) usually worked with their own hands, too, unlike the mounted whites. Yet in the early 1920s at least one white Georgia planter armed black assistants who (themselves under death threats) helped him enslave, then murder black laborers. And in eastern Arkansas during the 1930s there was at least one black riding boss, a man called Bob, mounted and armed, on the R. E. Lee Wilson plantation near Osceola.[52]

One is at a loss to discover, then, a southern folk who shared some broad sense of history, class consciousness, cultural cohesion, or mission. To be sure some segments of the region's rural population did—most notably organized coal miners and members of radical tenant farmer organizations. Most southerners might best be described, however, as less a folk than a *folksmasn:* this is an excellent Yiddish term which means (in Irving Howe's explanation) that people "responded more to the urgencies of their experience than to any fixed idea"; there was "no 'principled' reason" behind their actions.[53] The southern *folksmasn*—white and black; small landowner, cash tenant, share tenant, sharecropper; living at home or out of bags; spread over a vast area including perhaps eight crop-tenure system subregions—had little region-wide coherence beyond several manifestations of poverty and dependency. Most of their experiences organically and logically fragmented them. *Southerner* is a rather pernicious abstraction when closely examined; it confuses understanding of these people's heterogeneity, a matter that goes beyond race. The destiny of the southern "folk," then, is actually no issue. It is raised here because a variety of activist intellectuals asserted the existence of a singular white folk and, in so doing, caused conceptual and other mischief not yet completely undone.

Because the highlands were the last southern subregion to succumb to the modern cash nexus, Appalachia (and to a lesser degree, the Ozarks) attracted waves of outside, upper-class folklorists, musicologists, philosophers, and writers of cultural travelogues and fiction. Possessed of arrogance, religious mission, scholarly curiosity, and

52. On the social origins of white prison guards, see March, *Alabama Bound;* Steiner and Brown, *North Carolina Chain Gang.* On overseers and riding bosses, see Raper, *Preface to Peasantry,* 107–109; H. L. Mitchell, *Mean Things Happening in This Land: The Life and Times of H. L. Mitchell* (Montclair, N.J., 1979), 18–19. On the armed black Georgia bosses, see Pete Daniel, *The Shadow of Slavery: Peonage in the South, 1901–1969* (New York, 1972), 110–31. On the black Arkansas riding boss, see the Henry Rover and Mary E. Hicks depositions, both June 23, 1938 (Both typescripts, roll 8, STFU Papers).

53. Irving Howe, *World of Our Fathers* (New York, 1976), 62–63.

sometimes a foreboding dissatisfaction with the course of their own worlds—as early as the 1890s they began, as David Whisnant puts it, a systematic program of "cultural intervention." This meant (among other things) the establishment of settlement and folk schools, little academic bunkers where mountain traditions and handicrafts might survive the blitz of modernization; folklore societies dedicated to collecting and printing preindustrial tales; missions to collect "genuine" folk songs and segregate them from corrupted modern ones; and the staging of folk music festivals to celebrate as well as preserve the "authentic" voice of the people.[54]

Such intervention did bring benefits to the natives. Mountain parents were eager to have more and better schools, and they donated land and helped build folk schools and sent their children to the flatland teachers. The folklore societies of West Virginia, Virginia, Kentucky, and North Carolina flourished, published, and joined amateurs and professionals ultimately in some constructive ways. So too did the labors of the ballad collectors—John C. and Olive Dame Campbell, Evelyn Kendrick Wells and Maud Karpeles, the English scholar Cecil Sharp, and many others— add to the sum of knowledge. And despite their frequent confusion about the authentic, the musicologists in particular remain useful, through their record keeping and travelogues, in helping scholars to date the gradual passage of isolation and the intrusion of outside cultural influences. Cecil Sharp, for example, observed in 1916–1917 that tradition was "being rapidly killed in its prime by industrialism." In 1917 Wells and Karpeles toured widely in the mountains and discovered what they regarded as fine natural music everywhere except in resort hotels and (ironically) missionary settlements. Following a 1955 retracing of the 1917 tour, Karpeles wrote, "The region is no longer a folk-song collector's paradise, for the serpent, in the form of the radio, has crept in, bearing its insidious hill-billy and other 'pop' songs."[55] Of course the

54. David E. Whisnant, *All That Is Native and Fine: The Politics of Culture in an American Region* (Chapel Hill, 1983), 13 and *passim*.

55. *Ibid*, 7–8, 11, and *passim*; Kenneth Clark and Mary Clark, *The Harvest and the Reapers: Oral Traditions of Kentucky* (Lexington, Ky., 1974), 63–64. As late as the mid-1930s the New Deal also subsidized scholarly searches for the "folk" of Appalachia. See TVA and Civil Works Administration, "Folklore and Folkways in the Blue Ridge and Cumberland Plateau Sections of Tennessee," by William E. Cole and Urban Anderson (Typescript, 174 pages, May 1, 1934, in Record Group 142, Atlanta Branch, National Archives). Cole and Anderson (University of Tennessee sociologists) were concerned with superstitions and concluded, "It is apparent . . . that the few remaining credences are rapidly falling into disrepute, and that the well-organized mass of beliefs possessed by our grandfathers is almost forgotten." (p. 19).

radio had been around for more than three decades in 1955, and the phonograph (also well known in Appalachia) was even older. The collectors' observations nonetheless help bracket chronologically the period of most intense change in musical styles and instruments, 1910–1930.

Much of the remainder of cultural intervention in the highlands was bizarre and paradoxical. At the settlement and folk schools, outland instructors promoted British and European dancing never known on the North American continent. Crafts teachers from outside insisted upon textiles and pottery designs marketable in New York and Boston but foreign to the hills. Musicologists abominated guitars, mandolins, and banjos, insisting that folk performers use dulcimers. When dulcimers could not be found in the mountains, folk schools promoted dulcimer making and flatlanders taught highlanders to play them and to sing "real" mountain music. Without doubt the most perverse cultural interventionist of all was John Powell, the famous composer and conductor from Richmond, who became a promoter of the White Top Folk Festival (1931–1940) in remote southwestern Virginia. Powell's own tastes and expertise were classical. His interest in the folk derived from his extreme racism. An organizer also of the Anglo-Saxon Club of America, Powell had been a successful lobbyist for Virginia's 1924 "racial integrity law" (which toughened old legislation against racial intermarriage). Thus Powell looked to the hills to arrest the decline he saw in "Aryan" culture.[56] Several folk schools and folklore organizations survive to this day and interest in preindustrial music and other artifacts persists, but systematic cultural intervention was a shambles (if not a joke) before World War II. The interventionists created goals and coined terms that aroused interest far beyond the hills, however, and raised interesting if inconclusive debate about the folk, particularly during the 1930s and early 1940s.

Other scholars have written well about southern intellectuals' interwar *angst* over their beloved region. Editors, essayists, poets, social scientists, historians, and novelists were all preoccupied with tradition and change induced by industrialism and urbanization. More of them assumed the existence of homogeneous white and black "folks" than attempted carefully to define them and assess their relationships to the times. The Agrarians of Vanderbilt University, who in 1930 published *I'll Take My Stand*, were not cultural interventionists but eccentric reactionaries who condemned the city and factory and ignorantly celebrated

56. Whisnant, *All That Is Native and Fine*, 56, 64–67, 79–80, 93, 101, 168–69, 183–88, 237–46.

an idyllic rural tradition. W. J. Cash, the North Carolina journalist and author of the brilliant and influential volume *The Mind of the South* (1941), projected throughout the region as a homogeneous model the highland and western piedmont poor to middling whites from whom he himself sprang. Cash's southerners were glandular, God obsessed, hedonistic, and doomed by their "savage ideal," a blind passion akin to totalitarianism, which separated them from blacks in their own predicament, shunned intellectual discipline, and emphasized orgiastic religiosity to the exclusion of reason and program. Ben Robertson, another writer and native of South Carolina's western piedmont, wrote in a vein similar to Cash's about a people one or two social strata above Cash's southern folk. In *Red Hills and Cotton* (1942) Robertson described his clan of upland planters: "We are farmers, all Democrats and Baptists—a strange people, complicated and simple and proud and religious and family-loving, a divorceless, Bible-reading murdersome lot of folks, all of us rich in ancestry and steeped in tradition and emotionally quick on the trigger." [57] Unlike Cash, Robertson forthrightly labeled his memoir by specific subregion and insisted upon the differences and antagonisms between the piedmont and low country. This was rare among popular writers.

In the academy it was the great sociologists of the University of North Carolina who most self-consciously and carefully sought the southern folk. From the late-1920s into the 1950s and after, Howard W. Odum, Rupert B. Vance, Arthur F. Raper, and others conducted research, wrote articles and books, and attempted (especially Odum, the master grantsman) to harness a scholarly concept of regionalism to state and federal governmental programs. Odum, the great founder of regionalism, failed both as definer-conceptualizer and as would-be policy maker. [58] Both Odum and his colleagues succeeded splendidly in establishing the varieties of political economies and subcultures existing within the South, however. I myself am deeply indebted to the Chapel Hillians for this accomplishment. Odum was undone, paradoxically, be-

57. Ben Robertson, *Red Hills and Cotton: An Upcountry Memory* (New York, 1942), 7. In addition to Whisnant, see the scholarly works of Michael O'Brien, *The Idea of the American South, 1920–1940* (Baltimore, 1979); Richard H. King, *The Southern Renaissance: The Cultural Awakening of the American South, 1930–1955* (New York, 1980). See also Twelve Southerners, *I'll Take My Stand: The South and the Agrarian Tradition* (New York, 1930); W. J. Cash, *The Mind of the South* (New York, 1941). For excellent critical evaluations of Cash, see C. Vann Woodward, "White Man, White Mind," *New Republic,* CLVII (December 9, 1967), 28–30; David Hackett Fischer, *Historians' Fallacies: Toward a Logic of Historical Thought* (New York, 1970), 219–20.

58. See Michael O'Brien, *Idea of the American South,* esp. 70–93.

cause he insisted upon scholarship and policy for *a* region containing discrete folk*s* with problems not subject to the same solutions. Odum's colleagues were not ambitious policy makers and were seldom ensnared in such conundrums. Among them Rupert Vance most forthrightly approached the problem of "folk" in his invaluable *Human Geography of the South* (1932). Here he blasted the romantic dreams of the cultural interventionists. "It would be a pleasant thing to believe the South is to achieve regionalism as a folk movement," Vance wrote. But the region's "traditionally inarticulate [in the intellectual sense] peasantry" was rapidly evolving into an "inferiority-conscious proletariat." The South's "aristocracy" provided no leadership. Perhaps Vance hoped that the academy and government might save the day, but his tone was pessimistic: "Neither Ireland nor Denmark is being duplicated in Dixie." [59]

Had Vance had available to him in 1932 William Alexander Percy's 1941 memoir, *Lanterns on the Levee,* he might have despaired even more of the South's planter class and intellectual elite. Vance no doubt well understood the sad history of the elite's exploitation of the poor, black and white. He may not have been prepared for Percy's arch contempt for the white masses: "The poor whites of the South: a nice study in heredity and environment. Who can trace their origins, estimate their qualities, do them justice? Not I." But indeed he tried. "The present breed is probably the most unprepossessing on the broad face of the ill-populated earth. I know they are responsible for the only American ballads, for camp meetings, for a whole new and excellent school of Southern literature. I can forgive them as the Lord forgives, but admire them, trust them, love them—never." Percy thought the white masses "intellectually and spiritually . . . inferior to the Negro, whom they hate." Later, in certainly his best remembered rage, Percy recalled a political crowd in 1912 who defeated his father in favor of the redneck rouser, James K. Vardaman: "I looked over the ill-dressed, surly audience, unintelligent and slinking. . . . They were the sort of people that lynch Negroes, that mistake hoodlumism for wit, and cunning for intelligence, that attend revivals and fight and fornicate in the bushes afterward. They were undiluted Anglo-Saxons. They were the sovereign voter. It was so horrible it seemed unreal." [60]

It is not suggested here that Percy spoke for his class. Yet he was

59. Rupert B. Vance, *Human Geography of the South: A Study in Regional Resources and Human Adequacy* (Chapel Hill, 1932), 508–509.

60. William Alexander Percy, *Lanterns on the Levee: Recollections of a Planter's Son* (1941; rpr. Baton Rouge, 1973), quotations 19–20, 149.

arguably the most articulate and artistically gifted among them. His services to the white "folk" were neither solicited or profered. Percy was at
least frank in his bigotry and wrote but once, in his memoir, of his contempt. His urban, upper-class contemporaries, who promoted industrial
growth for the region, were probably more insidious and more repetitious
in their low characterizations of the white masses. Yankee manufacturers,
they advertised, should move south because displaced farmers were
available, cheap, and "docile"—that is, ununionized and untrouble-
some, a dependable new *Untermenschen* not unlike romanticized plantation slaves of old.[61] Next to Percy and the industry hunters, indeed,
the cultural interventionists in Appalachia seem almost harmless.

It was to their work, in fact, that Vance referred when he held up
Ireland and Denmark as unattainable models for the South. The folk
schools were founded upon a late nineteenth-century Danish model,
which thrived still in the twentieth. Among school founders in the
South, Olive Dame Campbell of Massachusetts was most dedicated to
defining and preserving southern folk culture after such European examples. Before establishing the John C. Campbell Folk School (named
to honor her late husband) in Cherokee County, North Carolina, in
1925, Campbell toured and studied intensively throughout Scandinavia.
Among many European variants of folk schools, she chose the most romantic and conservative, one that did not presuppose systemic change
in the political economy of the region. So the Campbell School sponsored a modest cooperative dairy, which succeeded for a while, and a
handicraft guild to promote and market woven and carved objects from
the institution. In her own time Campbell's strategies withered and her
goals were subverted. Students and their families migrated. Those remaining performed Danish dances. By the late 1940s the school drifted
aimlessly, a succession of new directors searching pathetically for useful-
ness. What had been missing from the start was understanding and acceptance of historical realities. Denmark, Ireland, and other nations
where peasant cooperatives, folk schools, and folk renewal had taken
place had all undergone some form of political upheaval. Common
folks and intellectuals together, and with great difficulty, had built new
societies upon the ruins of old ones. Campbell and other interventionists
were hardly prepared to break eggs and make omelettes.[62] The South
was not a separate nation, anyway, but a collection of colonies inside the

61. James C. Cobb, *The Selling of the South: The Southern Crusade for Industrial
Development, 1936–1980* (Baton Rouge, 1982), 96–212 and *passim.*
62. Whisnant, *All That Is Native and Fine,* 102–179.

United States. Its intelligentsia (broadly conceived, in the old Russian sense) were hostile to the semiwashed masses. The folk were a *folksmasn*. So Rupert Vance, an intellectual in the narrow American sense, was correct in pronouncing the entire enterprise hopeless.

Yet even as Vance despaired, even as the interventionists went astray, southern folks were busy fashioning several regional voices that had not existed before. They were musical ones. Neither local, nor "folk" in Cecil Sharp's sense, this music was modern and commercial, popular, and still organic and genuine to common people. Sharp, Wells, and Karpeles had been infuriated by the new hillbilly music, and they, John Powell and a host of other upper-class cultural arbiters tried in vain to squelch it. In fact, this music, which synthesized traditional and outside forms, was evolving rapidly some years before Sharp first came to America to collect ballads. The music was a cultural by-product of the ending of mountain isolation, that enlargement of community that proceeds with modernization. Free delivery of mail brought catalogues from Chicago offering cheap guitars, mandolins, and banjos. Better-off families—such as Jean Ritchie's in Perry County, Kentucky—also possessed Sears and Roebuck record players as early as 1905. Much later Ritchie became a singer and champion of "pure" old time songs, but she and her siblings were nurtured on a much wider selection of Americana delivered by new technology. So it was not only in the mountains but throughout the rural South, among blacks as well as whites, that music expanded geometrically during the first two decades of the new century. In the flatlands, however, people had moved so often, exchanging instruments and styles as frequently as addresses, that no barrier of cultural purity stood in the way of continued synthesis and finally, vast popular "discovery." The appearance of disk recording and the radio brought a veritable explosion of popularity to such music. The coincidental existence of an urban market for things primitive and folk magnified the commercial effect.[63]

So throughout the 1920s agents from New York recording companies scoured the South. In Bristol they found the Carter Family, in Atlanta Fiddlin' John Carson, and delta bluesmen in New Orleans, Blind Lemon Jefferson in Dallas, and so on. Hillbilly and "race" record industries were born, and before the end of the decade national stars had appeared from the southern outback—Vernon Dalhart, then Jimmie Rodgers; and Jefferson, Josh White, and Huddie Ledbetter ("Leadbelly"). Commer-

63. *Ibid.*, 93, 95; Bill C. Malone, *Southern Music/American Music* (Lexington, Ky., 1979), 28–69.

cial radio stations were established in southern cities as early as 1922, and they eagerly presented such performers as well as local talent. WSM in Nashville began in 1925 a "barn dance" show, which evolved into the Grand Ole Opry, which in turn brought hillbilly performers (a few of whom were black) together from throughout the South. No comparable radio program existed for the various black musical styles, but in recording studios and in bars and clubs in New Orleans, Memphis, St. Louis, Chicago, New York, and many other places, they played for appreciative audiences of both races and exchanged influences upon each other, synthesizing country, delta, Texas, Memphis, and many other styles of singing and playing.[64]

Rapid electronic expansion of southern musical communities did not simplify the music. Styles, in fact, multiplied and varied even more, as rustic musicians from Tennessee heard Hawaiian crooning and ukeleles, as Mississippi whites heard Mexican-Texan, as North Carolina bluesmen and -women heard Blind Lemon Jefferson and Bessie Smith. Still, I will suggest here that the "inarticulate" southern "peasantry" and "proletariat" (as Rupert Vance termed them) had at last become articulate to everyone. They spoke in at least two, perhaps six or more "languages"—black country and urban, white highland, flatland, Cajun, and "Tex-Mex." But all were recognizably southern and were heard at home, nationally, and even abroad (especially the blacks). These southern folks seldom articulated a programmatic political message. They sang about God, death, sex, liquor, prison, and home. Economic conditions and power relationships in the rural South permeated many lyrics until the 1950s and even later, however. Blacks referred to "the man"; whites to hard times and a cruel landlord "down on Penny's farm." And nearly all addressed migration in one way or another—moving to the textiles mills, loss of homes and kin, the lure and entrapment of "city lights."[65]

So paradoxically, on the threshold of its death, the old mule-powered, overpopulated rural South acquired a powerful vocality. What good such

64. Malone, *Southern Music/American Music*, 50, 58; Malone, *Country Music, USA: A Fifty-Year History* (Austin, 1968), 41–42, 55–58, 84–88; Harry Oster, *Living Country Blues* (Detroit, 1969); William Ferris, *Blues from the Delta* (Garden City, N.Y., 1979). On white Mississippi community singing, *ca.* 1910–30, and the evolution of a professional country singer, see oral history of J. P. Wright, July 30, 1972 (Typescript); and hear the oral history of Roy Alford, August 12, 1975 (Audio tape), both in the Mississippi Department of Archives and History, Jackson.

65. Malone refers to a few "political" songs by whites in *Country Music, USA*, 139–44. On black singers' references to rural life and migration, see, *e.g.*, Ferris, *Blues from the Delta*, 3–9.

voices did for the people is difficult to say. It certainly did not arm them politically in defense of their old homes. Many seemed all too happy to leave the country. Southern wailing and yodeling on the radio marked them as hayseeds and primitives to many urban natives, North and South, too. The middle-class denizens of Detroit and Chicago would be well prepared to brand any working-class southern migrant with the pejorative "hillbilly." There seems little doubt the music was a comfort to the folks, however. Of that, and religion and tobacco, they had considerable need.

No niggers at all live here, not one.
—A WHITE TENNESSEE MOUNTAINEER, *ca.* 1939

Negroes have funny names for things. . . . They have a language all their own.
—A WHITE ALABAMA BILL COLLECTOR, *ca.* 1939

For many years the Boss Class has succeeded in keeping the two races divided, and at the same time robbed both the Negroe and the white equally. . . . There are no "niggers" and no "poor white trash" in the [Southern Tenant Farmers'] Union.
—H. L. MITCHELL, 1935

I know all about the rich white man; what he wants [*i.e.,* money] it's wrote all over his face. But I don't know how to take poor white people.
—NED COBB, *ca.* 1970

Chapter 7
Black and White, Distance and Propinquity

AT THE END OF WORLD WAR I THE STRUC-
ture of farm tenure, the distribution of white and black farmers among the tenure classes, and the geographical spread of the races remained much as in the 1870s and 1880s in the South. Whites still owned an overwhelming preponderance of farm land. Whites who were not owners were cash or fixed renters or, more likely, share tenants. This last status, as Arthur Raper put it, was "historically a white institution" developed to accommodate mule- or horse-owning hill folk who lacked land. Blacks were to be found among the planter class, small owners, and all sorts of renters, but the great bulk of them were sharecroppers. "Cropper farming," declared Raper flatly, "is a Negro institution." Half a century after emancipation, the poorest of black southerners still lived among the wealthiest of whites in the plantation districts. There, to a considerable extent, race and class correlated well. Beyond the black belts and deltas, however, into the sandy white-land subregions, the hills, and finally the mountains, the black population thinned and virtually disappeared. Both tenants and sharecroppers were more likely to be white, and large, wealthy farmers were rare. Where blacks were so few there was hardly opportunity for "racial relations" per se, but rather an attitude or ideology of exclusionism among whites that more closely re-

sembled that of the rural Middle West than the southern plantation areas. Southern rural race relations, then, were governed by class and geography and produced more variety than many observers have conceded. After 1920, too, there were substantial changes in the geographical distribution of the races and racial occupance of tenure statuses. By the 1940s and 1950s old economic and social structures had become so undermined that continuance of traditional white dominion was no longer possible. What occurred during these decades amounted to a sort of prerevolution in race relations that not only prepared the way but made possible the "Negro revolt" and human rights movements of the 1960s.[1]

So much of the South was always a white man's country, in a literal demographic sense. In Harry Crews's home county of Bacon, in sandy southeastern Georgia, blacks were only 15.4 percent of the population in 1930. Of the hardly 1,100 black Baconians, fewer than 100 were full owners of farms. School-age black children numbered only 383, and they, too, were impoverished, by per-pupil public expenditures for education only one-sixth of that spent for white schools. Yet there were no lynchings in Bacon during the first three decades of the century, and Crews's recollections of relations between his own impoverished, small-farm-owning family and a neighboring black family (apparently non-owners) were of cordiality and cooperation. Small children played together color-blind, but adults adhered strictly to the etiquette and rhetoric of white supremacy.[2]

In the highlands black folk were hardly to be seen, except in some rich river valleys and in coal-mining settlements. Mountain counties of eastern Tennessee had tiny black populations in 1930—Blount, for example, 8.4 percent of its total; Washington, 6.1 percent; Green, 3.3; and Sevier only 1.0. Out in the Ozarks of Arkansas, in a block of four counties—Boone, Marion, Newton, and Searcy—there was not a single black person in 1930.[3] Many, perhaps almost all, whites preferred such a white environment. About 1937, for example, a poor farmer of New-

1. Arthur F. Raper, *Preface to Peasantry: A Tale of Two Black Belt Counties* (Chapel Hill, 1936), 148–49. Generalizations on tenure and geographical distributions are based upon *Census of Agriculture: 1959*, Vol. 1, *Counties and State Economic Areas*, Pts. 24–37, p. 6 of each part, which recapitulate tenure and race since the census of 1920.

2. Harry Crews, *A Childhood: The Biography of a Place* (New York, 1978), 50–60 and *passim*. Data from Charles S. Johnson *et al.* (comps.), *Statistical Atlas of Southern Counties: Listing and Analysis of Socio-economic Indices of 1104 Southern Counties* (Chapel Hill, 1941), 87.

3. Charles Johnson *et al.* (comps.), *Statistical Atlas*, Arkansas tables.

ton County, Arkansas, an eccentric Socialist and would-be organizer for the Southern Tenant Farmers' Union in the Ozarks, wrote to union headquarters offering timber-cutting jobs to two men. He felt obliged to specify white men, he wrote, "not that I have anything against a man just because his skin is Black But this is a white county."[4] The Tennessee mountains, almost as white as the Ozarks, had a longer history of settlement, some experience with slavery, and perhaps a fiercer commitment to the exclusion of blacks. A white woman related her rural community's demographic story to a Federal Writers' Project (FWP) interviewer about 1939. At that date Big Ivy had "not one" black. "Old Squire Irby Brazeale's pappy used to own three or four niggers back before the Confederate War, but the Klux ran them all out. Never been back since then." Subsequently the inhospitality of Big Ivy's white denizens had intimidated even would-be passers-through. "Why, let a nigger start from Oak Springs to Sand Hill, he will cut around through the crosstimbers or go away over to Zama and circle back before he'll pass through Big Ivy." The woman acknowledged, however, that a few landowners wished for black laborers, wanted to "lay hands on nigger help to crop on the shares or hire on the place." But there were no takers: "You can't get them to come in noways at all."[5]

The southern mountains had rural classes and tenancy, but the spectrum in most places was narrow. Familism, self-sufficient farming, and the ethic of hard work prevailed in practice and in the formal value system. Rugged topography had forbidden plantations, large black populations, great agricultural wealth, and a class-racial system that emphasized paternalism, dominance, manipulation, and exploitation. Highlanders were clannish democrats who—despite occasional lapses, wishing for black sharecroppers—preferred to exclude blacks. They understood that blacks were poor and vulnerable to manipulation; so highlanders in effect wished to avoid both economic and moral temptation and contamination. They were, like most white northerners, aversive racists, in contrast to the dominative racists of the piedmonts and flatlands.[6]

4. Stephen C. Seys to STFU (J. R. Butler), n.d. (*ca.* June, 1937), microfilm roll 4, STFU Papers, Southern Historical Collection, University of North Carolina (SHC).

5. [Ruth Clark (?)], "Talking Is My Life," n.d. (1938 or 1939) (Typescript in FWP life histories files, SHC).

6. Harry K. Schwarzweller, James S. Brown, and J. J. Mangalam, *Mountain Families in Transition: A Case Study of Appalachian Migration* (University Park, Penn., 1971), 11–18. See also Pierre L. van den Berghe, *Race and Racism: A Comparative Perspective* (New York, 1967), esp. 25–37, on the aversive-dominative scheme for classifying racists.

Blacks lived in greatest numbers and in closest proximity to whites in the plantation districts and nearby counties, especially in the lower South. In 1920 black proportions of populations ranged from the neighborhood of 38–42 percent in Georgia, Alabama, and Louisiana, to 51–52 percent in South Carolina and Mississippi. Delta and black-belt black populations were far greater—63.5 percent, for example, of Edgefield, South Carolina; 67.2 percent of Macon, Georgia; 74.2 percent of Dallas, Alabama; and 85.8 percent of Tunica, Mississippi. This was also the land of the sharecropper. Of 335,037 black croppers in fourteen southern states in 1920, 221,513—or about two-thirds—lived in five lower South states. There were only 87,838 white croppers in these states.[7] White planters and merchants and their riding bosses and clerks and all their families lived in veritable oceans of black folk. Their sharecropping system of labor implied considerable personal supervision, thus almost daily interracial contact. Outside the black belts and deltas, in other row-cropping areas such as Virginia's and North Carolina's cotton, tobacco, corn, and peanuts counties, significant numbers of blacks and whites lived and labored in close proximity, too, as bosses and hands, fellow tenants, and neighbors. Much of the southern countryside, then, was in a literal sense racially integrated throughout the age of segregation.

De jure neighborhood segregation was, in fact, always an urban affair. During 1910–1913, as the "progressive" movement reached its legislative zenith, southern state legislatures and city councils elaborately ordered urban residential patterns, attempting to eliminate awkward interracial fringes between racial neighborhoods, while fixing long-standing de facto boundaries. As this peculiar reform was being completed, Clarence Poe, young publisher and editor of the *Progressive Farmer,* raised a cry for rural neighborhood segregation. The son of a Chatham County, North Carolina, yeoman farmer, Poe was an agrarian and self-taught intellectual who feared for the future of rural life. Fol-

---

For background on northern aversive racism, see Leon F. Litwack, *North of Slavery: The Negro in the Free States, 1790–1860* (Chicago, 1961). Harrison and Washington counties, in southern Indiana, are illustrative of middle western exclusionism in the twentieth century. Before World War II whites in both county seat towns prohibited blacks from living in town. Information from informal interviews with elderly citizens of Corydon (Harrison) and Salem (Washington), *ca.* 1967–75.

7. State percentages calculated from population tables in Donald B. Dodd and Wynelle S. Dodd (comps.), *Historical Statistics of the South, 1790–1970* (University, Ala., 1973). County percentages (from the 1930 census) are from the tables in Charles Johnson *et al.* (comps.), *Statistical Atlas;* sharecropping data from *Census of Agriculture, 1959.*

lowing a 1912 tour of Britain and the northern Continent, where he observed prosperous farm villages with many cooperative enterprises, Poe
concluded that only a vast reordering of the southern countryside's scattered occupance pattern could save the region from ruin. He would
bring southern farmers together in well-managed villages. Before that
tall order might be fulfilled, Poe reasoned, the rural South must become
rigidly segregated. Only then would whites feel "safe" and blacks be
free to develop their own "racial life." Poe's inspiration here was South
African. During his trip abroad he had interviewed Maurice S. Evans of
Durban, Natal, a world-renowned "expert" on race relations and an
early proponent of a policy that much later became known as *apartheid*.
Using the podium and his newspaper columns, Poe campaigned for two
years (1913–1915) for rural segregation. He failed miserably. His
scheme was too vast and perhaps implied totalitarian execution. Politicians with well-earned reputations as white supremacists thought it bizarre. Blacks attacked it, as did other white farm editors. Most important in Poe's defeat, however, was probably the opposition of landlords
who shuddered at the thought of losing their black laborers. As a Mississippian wrote to Poe: "We cannot get along without the blacks. The
day comes when they are segregated, I want to go with the negro." [8]

So there was to be no *apartheid* in the huge expanses of the South
where the great majority of the people lived. To what extent de facto
integration prevailed, in the absence of Poe's or some other scheme of
segregation, is problematical. Schools were separate everywhere. So
were churches, social clubs, and cemeteries. In the deltas and black
belts, with their oceans of blacks and relatively few whites, there was
such a preponderance of one race that a chasm existed between the
races, a chasm much deepened by class, which amounted to a sort of
segregation perhaps more profound that the urban format. But the term
segregation misleads here, for segregation means the absence of propinquity, and of that there was much in the plantation subregions.
Whites and blacks shared country stores and commissaries, gins and
warehouses, the roads, and recreational resources. And there was ever
the boss-hand, creditor-debtor relationship, close and personal but of
course laden with both class and racial distance and hostility. In the row-
crop piedmont districts, where class and caste differences were not so

8. Jack Temple Kirby, *Darkness at the Dawning: Race and Reform in the Progressive
South* (Philadelphia, 1972), 24–25; Kirby, "Clarence Poe's Vision of a Segregated 'Great
Rural Civilization,'" *South Atlantic Quarterly*, LXVIII (Winter, 1969), 27–38. Quota-
tion from the *Progressive Farmer*, November 8, 1913, p. 36.

great and where more whites lived in circumstances approximating those of most blacks, there existed a bewildering variety of human relationships that almost confound attempts at generalization. After 1915, and especially after 1920, when the black exodus began anew, the deltas and black belts came increasingly to resemble the whiter piedmont and its more complex racial relations. "In the disastrous period 1920–1930," observed Rupert Vance, referring to the boll weevil's ravages and poor staple prices, "the evidence is unmistakable that when Negro tenants fled from the blighted cotton area to the refuge of northern industry, white tenants crept in to take their places." [9]

The proportionately greater black migration to cities meant over time, then, a growing complexity in race relations over much of the region. In 1920 there were 226,386 white sharecroppers in the South, only 87,838 in five lower South states. Twenty years later, despite mechanization and conversion of so many croppers to wage hands, there were 240,915, with 100,525 in the lower South. In the meantime 335,037 black croppers (221,513 in the lower South) shrank to 298,507 (and 200,357). [10] So as the region—along with the ranks of the poorest farmers—grew whiter, traditionally "black" status was assumed by whites, rendering the last two decades or so of the old tenure system fraught with tension and confusion. Race nonetheless remained of paramount importance to the region's economic order and social behavior until the old rural system utterly collapsed during the 1950s and 1960s. But before the end of the 1930s, as we shall see, the whitening of the plantation districts tended to expose the colorless class basis of that old order.

Meanwhile in the plantation districts, the forces of tradition and the hard fact of blacks' predominance as sharecroppers persisted. Landlords overwhelmingly preferred the humble, voteless sons and grandsons of slaves as laborers until blacks were virtually all gone. A North Carolina planter with access to and experience with both races was frank in stating his preference in 1939. "A white tenant has his notions of running a farm and is less amenable to suggestions," he began. "I can say . . . 'Go hitch up the horse' when I want a horse hitched . . . to a negro . . . and I can't to a white man." Once a white tenant working for him "was such a know-it-all I soon had to get rid of him. He was a good

9. Vance quoted in Howard W. Odum, *Southern Regions of the United States* (Chapel Hill, 1936), 493.
10. *Census of Agriculture, 1959.*

farmer, it's true, but right or wrong the landlord should govern," he declared. "Negroes are more loyal."[11] Managerial power, of course, was the issue. White managers preferred the most powerless dependents when they could get them. Ned Cobb, a black Alabama farmer, recalled a telling incident from Tallapoosa County during the 1940s. A white landlord inquired of Cobb if he knew of a suitable family looking for land. Cobb recommended a white family, and the landlord responded (as Cobb quoted him), "Aw, hell . . . I don't want no damn white man on my place." Cobb reflected, "That teached me fair that a white man always wants a nigger in preference. . . . How come that? How come it for God's sake? He don't want no damn white man on his place. He gets a nigger, that's his glory. He can do that nigger just like he wants to and that nigger better not say nothin against his rulins." Whites, on the other hand, "won't take that . . . off another white man."[12]

Some blacks—one cannot say how many—accepted this station with apparent equanimity. Well into the twentieth century, plantation district race relations sometimes resembled those of the mythic antebellum era, with dependents clinging to paternal planters for security and arbitration. During the 1930s, for example, an elderly North Carolina tenant reflected on the parade of fellow blacks to northern cities. "Lot of colored people moved up North lately," he told an FWP interviewer (a white man). "They makes more wages but pays higher rent. Some of the rich folks like to work 'em until they's through with 'em. When they is out of work a Northern man won't even give 'em a meal. What's the good of calling you 'mister' if they won't give you work and won't help you when you's hungry?" So, he concluded, "I tell 'em they can go to Chicago or Detroit, wherever . . . but I'm er-staying right here." The landlord's "place is home ter me."[13] Black croppers and resident hired hands throughout the plantation districts either accepted or tolerated constant planter-landlord interference in their personal lives, too, from the breaking up of boisterous Saturday night parties to arbitration of family disputes. As late as 1945 an elderly woman on J. F. Dugger's plantation near Auburn, Alabama, appealed to Dugger to use his power to force

11. Bernice Kelly Harris, "Henry Calhoun Weathers, Landlord," March 1, 1939 (Typescript in FWP life histories files, SHC). For an exceptional North Carolina landlord, who preferred white sharecroppers, see Harris, "Jackson Bullitt, a Small Landlord," March 11, 1939 (Typescript, *ibid.*).

12. Rosengarten, *All God's Dangers*, 511–12.

13. William O. Foster, "Staying Right Here," in John L. Robinson (ed.), *Living Hard: Southern Americans in the Great Depression* (Washington, D.C., 1981), 101–105.

her husband to abandon another woman and cease "treating me like a dog." [14] Even Ned Cobb, never deluded by the fraud of white paternalism, was grateful at least once for upper-class imperiousness. Around the turn of the century, when young Ned was being introduced to all-day work and his father's cruel lashings, a white man "stood up there on the road and looked at my daddy beat me up." The man reined his mules and asked Cobb's father: "What you beatin on your boy so bout this morning?" He was not satisfied with the elder Cobb's excuses and finally threatened him: "He's your boy. He's your boy. But there's a law for the way you beat him up." So Cobb, now an old man himself, conceded: "There's some of these white people in this country done better than others; they'd take up against the wrong thing." [15]

Such concessions, much less the North Carolinian's profession of respect for landlord paternalism, were rare. Much more common among surviving testimony of plantation-area blacks are bitter statements about the order of economic relationships, which demonstrate their recognition of race and class as one. An Arkansas sharecropper bluntly told a white FWP interviewer: "De landlord is landlord [*i.e.,* white], de politicians is landlord, de judge is landlord, de shurf [sheriff] is landlord, ever' body is landlord, en we ain't got nothin'." [16] A Mississippi delta tenant spontaneously used "white people" to describe his oppressors and "people" to describe the oppressed in 1939. "The white people is robin the people sore bad," he wrote to the Southern Tenant Farmers' Union. [17] In 1937 the New Deal Resettlement Administration conducted an interesting poll among black and white men of all tenure classes in the Arkansas River cotton plantation county of Jefferson, surrounding Pine Bluff. Jefferson's population was about 58 percent black (in the 1930 census), and the county's overall tenancy rate was 86.3. And less than a third of white farmers were full farm owners; so Jefferson was crowded with tenants and croppers of both races. The Resettlement Ad-

14. Lillian Glance to J. F. Dugger, April 10, 1945, and see May 17, 1945, both in Dugger Family Papers, Auburn University Archives. See also Debra Ann Burks, oral history of Allen Buster, November 29, 1974 (Typescript in Samford University Oral History Program, Birmingham), which are the recollections of a self-described "white man's nigger" in the black belt of western Alabama; Rebecca Yarbrough, oral history of Alice Dortch Balch, March 25, 1974 (Typescript in University of Arkansas Library, Little Rock), wherein Balch describes her husband's role as policeman and referee among black dependents.

15. Rosengarten, *All God's Dangers,* 22–23.

16. Walter Rowland, "Ain't Got No Screens," June, 1939 (Typescript in FWP life histories files, SHC).

17. Zero Mumford to Butler, December 26, 1939, roll 13, STFU Papers.

ministration pollsters found little solidarity among blacks and whites when it posed this question: "What *class* of people do you think is worst off?" A few black respondents answered in terms of class—renters, croppers, or laborers. Most, however, gave racial responses—colored or colored people. Why? In spaces provided for elaboration on the questionnaires they wrote, "Not getting equal rights," "Inadequate pay," and "They don't get justice". White respondents of all classes usually gave class answers. Four white landlords wrote "negroes," meaning renters or croppers; and rationalized their being "worse off" with "shiftlessness" or "bad management". A black landlord wrote "colored people" because of both "low wages" and "thriftlessness".[18]

About the same time a thoughtful black sharecropper in eastern North Carolina was able to express class conflict in economic terms alone, denying a place for race. White men with whom he "had made crops," he said, always "treated me like I was a man. It's sharecroppin' that's wrong. . . . Half ain't enough for the labor a sharecropper puts into a crop. Everything he's got's invested—his time and strength and health." Landlords, on the other hand, charged as interest on advances "ten cents to the dollar . . . a good return for their investment, but we sharecroppers don't get no interest on ours. Livin' on another man's land, takin' his orders about a investment that's half ours, subject to get movin' orders any time, and havin' to accept a settlement we know ain't right. . . . No, I wouldn't sharecrop if I didn't have to." [19] It may be significant that the black man's words were spoken to a white woman, his interviewer, who happened also to be the wife of a landlord. For the denial of a race-class correlation is unconvincing, especially when he recited his experiences with the capriciousness and dishonesty of landlords. Black Mississippi former croppers who spoke to black interviewers during the 1970s virtually all agreed that white landlords cheated them at settlement times because they were black. In 1939, too, a Holmes County, Mississippi, cropper wrote to the Southern Tenant Farmers' Union that a landlord forced him "to sign a release of my cotton benefit lien . . . because of my color." He was "afraid to object"

18. Resettlement Administration, "Social Correlative of Farm Tenure" (Typescript, 1937, in Jefferson County, Arkansas, series, University of Arkansas Department of Agricultural Economics and Rural Sociology Records, University of Arkansas Library, Fayetteville), my italics. Census data for 1930 from Charles Johnson *et al.* (comps.), *Statistical Atlas*, 62.

19. Bernice Kelly Harris, "No Pleasure in Nothin'," in John Robinson (ed.), *Living Hard*, 116–21.

to his new landlord (now holder of the lien), because of his "past brutality in the treatment of the negro. . . . he may decide to have me 'strung up' if I make trouble for him." [20]

Ned Cobb well understood the system's class and racial resemblance to slavery. "White man made hisself a law" to tie blacks to the land in service to whites, he said. Wealthy landlords used political power over sheriffs to "protect" blacks from imprisonment, only to intimidate and exploit them themselves. "The sheriff come on a white man's place messin with the colored folks. . . . that man would call the sheriff's hand in a minute. 'That's *my* nigger—' . . . landlord had power over the sheriff and he'd talk his big talk in defense of that nigger. How come it? Because that's *his* nigger." When Cobb declared elsewhere in his long memoir, "*all* God's dangers ain't a white man," he referred to the boll weevil, a scourge he battled much of his long farming career. Yet the burden of Cobb's recollections of three-quarters of a century of rural life in Alabama was that *most* of black folks' burdens were indeed white men of the upper class. Cobb thought paternalism a cruel joke: "Every landlord ever I had dealings with tried to euchre me." Perhaps the sorriest commentary on plantation district race relations ever heard anywhere is Cobb's comparison of life as a prison inmate with life as a "free" man dealing with landlords and merchants. "I safely could say, them white people at Wetumpka [prison] treated me better than any of their color have treated me on the outside." Inside, he was unavailable for commercial exploitation, but "outside they raised figures against me in place of wire." [21]

More widespread and profound documentation of black-belt and delta blacks' reaction to upper-class whites lies in the records of the massive black exodus and blacks' willful alienation from farming and rural life. Helplessness and the awful social and economic immobility of the black poor taught lessons over three generations that are not yet forgotten. In 1939 a sixty-two-year-old cropper near Seaboard, North Carolina, summarized much of his people's experience in retelling his own. "My daddy, after freedom," he said, "spent his life sharecroppin', movin' round from place to place, and died not ownin' a foot o' ground. I aimed to do better'n that, but looks like I ain't made much improve-

20. See the Mary Holmes College Oral History Program typescript interviews, all with former sharecroppers and renters, West Point, Mississippi. Quotation from Dan Pace to STFU, February 18, 1939, roll 10, STFU Papers.

21. Rosengarten, *All God's Dangers,* 354–55, 235 (my italics), 408–409.

ment on his record. He eat and wore clothes; that's about where I am now." [22] Migrants without land in the South departed with little regret, more often with relief and glad hearts. Migrants with land sold it, or they parceled it among many remaining relatives, who in turn sold or lost what little remained of their stake in the region. By 1970 a black southern farmer of any sort was almost as rare as a black middle western farmer. Of all Ned Cobb's children, only one remained on hard-won land in Alabama. Most blacks, as Cobb explained, hated farming because of its association with racial and class oppression: "They has once in days past made crops under the white man's administration and didn't get nothin out of it." So the black man "don't want to farm today regardless to what he could make out there; he don't want to plow no mule—that was his bondage and he is turning away from it. He huntin for a public job, leavin the possession of the earth to the white man." [23]

Those blacks who did own southern farms seldom enjoyed the peace and independence associated with freeholding. In the first place, acquisition of substantial acreage of prime land was next to impossible for them. Whites with capital arrived on such land first, then usually refused to sell to rare blacks who might somehow possess the price. Still, there were many black farmers. Ironically, most lived in the lower South's plantation districts, where they acquired small parcels, often mere homesteads with large gardens. As late as 1940 such black "farmers" actually outnumbered white owners in the black-majority cotton belts. Blacks usually obtained land in one of two ways: Being known and trusted by a white patron, they were given or permitted to purchase a piece of land in recognition of their or their families' long service to a landlord family; or like some new white landowners of the 1920s and 1930s, blacks moved into eroded, weevil-infested land as planters abandoned it. Such black hardscrabble farmers usually had a modest stake of capital earned elsewhere; now they plowed it into farms with little promise, even though acreage was usually much larger than the homesteads of local folk well connected to whites. The desire of landless blacks for land and their willingness to make extreme sacrifices in order to get it are pathetically expressed in spoken testimony and so many

22. Bernice Kelly Harris, "Jim Parker Hopes Ahead," June 7, 1939 (Typescript in FWP life histories files, SHC).

23. Rosengarten, *All God's Dangers,* 563, and on Cobb's farmer son, see 463, 488, 575–76. On the general matter of blacks' alienation from farming and their loss of land, see Leo McGee and Robert Boone (eds.), *The Black Rural Landowner—Endangered Species: Social, Political, and Economic Implications* (Westport, Conn., 1979).

letters written in pencil on cheap paper to the Southern Tenant Farmers' Union. As Ed King, a southeastern Missouri cropper, wrote in 1938, all "i wants is a Home and 40 acres of Land and a Pair of good Mules." He was "a Poor Man," he explained, "homeless and Landless. . . . i am longing for my own Home i am a Colared man." [24]

Living in an area where planters owned nearly everything, King may well not have realized how difficult life was for black farm owners. As Ned Cobb testified, most of the dangers were associated with race. Bankers, merchants, ginners, salesmen—almost all whites—regarded black owners as well as renters and croppers as fair game for cheating. Blacks with sufficient land to become landlords themselves were often poor ones, too, least able to furnish tenants adequately (because their own credit sources were white men), and owning the lowest-yielding rental land and the shabbiest tenant cabins. Occasionally black landlords were as avaricious as whites in their dealings with tenants of their own race, too. [25]

Among poorer people black and white, in the plantation districts and piedmonts, there existed as many situations of human relationships as there is surviving testimony. Lee Carey, for example, was an enterprising black man who practiced the risky business of horse and mule trading in rural western Kentucky throughout the first four decades of the twentieth century. He "always made money," Carey said about 1939, "speculatin' stock and hoss swappin'." As was ever the case in his profession, customers sometimes returned to him, furious over alleged misrepresentations concerning certain beasts. When such customers were white men, Carey knew he was in jeopardy. This fact alone characterizes the sad condition of Kentucky blacks. But Carey survived and prospered on guile, using whites' bigotry on his own behalf. "I'm just a poor old Negro," Carey would protest, "and can't be molested. I know you are a good white man." Whites always "fell for that stuff," he re-

24. Raper, *Preface to Peasantry,* 112–13, 118–19, 122–23, 129; Rosengarten, *All God's Dangers,* 246. Data on ownership in the cotton belts from *Census of Agriculture, 1959.* Quotation from Ed King to STFU, September 3, 1938, roll 9, STFU Papers.

25. Rosengarten, *All God's Dangers,* 519, 521 (on a black landlord), and *passim;* oral history of Maggie Burnett, n.d. (*ca.* 1976) (Typescript in Mary Holmes College Oral History Program), on black landlords' poor credit capabilities. See also Elizabeth Rauh Bethel, *Promiseland: A Century of Life in a Negro Community* (Philadelphia, 1981), 206–10; Len Day, oral history of Annie May Bankhead, November 26, 1974 (Typescript in University of Arkansas Library, Little Rock), on small black farmers' struggles during the 1930s.

ported.[26] In Pineville, Kentucky, in the eastern mountains, however, two of the poorest families to be found in the state lived in an old warehouse divided into two units. One family was white, one black; and though both were known as raffish folk, they seemed to have coexisted in relative harmony. Over in the marshlands of eastern North Carolina, a white FWP interviewer encountered the following scene in June of 1939. John Twiford, a white small farm owner, former moonshiner, and occasional WPA worker, sat in the shade with a jug. A young black man, a neighbor, approached casually, stopping to take up a stick and kill a water moccasin in a ditch. Reaching Twiford's shade, he asked for the loan of the white man's mule and plow. Twiford had already loaned out the mule, so the black man accepted the plow. But first he asked, "Cap'n . . . aint yo all goin' to give me a drink?" Twiford responded, "There's the jug, nobody aint stoppin' ye." Then the younger man inquired, "Got a glass for me to drink out uv?" out of respect for racial etiquette more than sanitation. Twiford answered, "Hell no, I aint got a glass to drink out uv myself. What ails you, bein' so damn particular; kaint you drink out o' a bottle?"[27] Whether this wonderful exception proves the violated rule of racial etiquette or such vignettes were common is impossible to say.

Blacks' recollections of integrated rural life in the South are mixed with memories of helpful friendship and bitterness at the limits imposed by the region's racial rules. A woman from north-central Florida recalled her father and their white neighbor: "They farmed together and was right around together for fifteen or more years. . . . Papa would help him, he would help Papa. Course you couldn't go in they home and sit down, but then some [whites] were better than others."[28] Another woman, raised in eastern Virginia during the 1920s, recalled, "Peoples was all mixed up in St. Michaels, white and colored." Even though schools were separate, she had a white friend of the landlord class, a

26. Kattye Orr, "Where Water Was Hot," life history of Lee Carey, n.d. (1938 or 1939) (Typescript in "Our Lives" project files, WPA in Kentucky, Kentucky State Archives, Frankfort).

27. Floyd C. Combs, "Bill, He Likes His Likker," life history of Bill and Alice Kiel, n.d. (1938 or 1939) (Typescript, *ibid.*). Quotation from W. O. Saunders, ". . . And Set Me Up a Hell-Buster," life history of John W. Twiford, June 4, 1939 (Typescript in FWP life histories files, SHC).

28. Quoted in James N. Eaton, "The Impact of Religious Beliefs and Training on the Racial Attitudes of Elderly Afro-Americans," *Bulletin* of the Center for the Study of Southern Culture and Religion, Florida State University, V (March, 1981), 3–4.

year older and a grade ahead, who studied with her and helped her. When the black girl's friends and siblings taunted the white girl—"that old white cracker"—the black girl defended her. Later, as the girls became adolescents, they drifted apart. A black man recalled a violent altercation between himself and a Georgia country store clerk about 1920, when both were teenagers or young adults. The white man demanded that the black stack boxes a certain way out of doors on a cold, rainy night after quitting time. The black fellow refused, and the white threatened, "we'll go together." He jumped, and they did—"went down between the wagon and the store, tied up just like snakes." The young black man won the fight, he said, along with the white's respect: "He found out that I was a man to be 'fraid of, and a man who believes in right." As old men in the 1970s, he declared, they were "still good friends." Yet, that the black man referred to his former white antagonist as "Mister," and the white man addressed him by his given name, and that the black man was proud he could return to his home town and "walk the front street" instead of sneak in back alleys may tell something of broader significance.[29]

Poor black and white farmers who performed free-lance winter logging work labored in proximity, using their own teams, and sometimes earned mutual respect and affection. At corporate timber camps, however, employees were usually segregated by race, the whites given skilled work in the woods and mill yards, blacks the lower-paid work of felling trees and sawing lumber to length.[30] The races made frequent contact in the mills and woods, however, and there is little wonder that rivalry and resentment sometimes became ugly. During the 1910s, for instance, a young white Mississippian went to work on the skidders— small engines that pulled cut logs from the woods—in Smith County between Jackson and Meridian. The young man was less than an exemplary worker, and he admitted as much years later. One day "the foreman put a nigger out there" to work with him, as the white fellow related the story. He was even less prepared for interracial work rivalry than hard work itself, and the black man compounded the awkwardness of the situation by informing the foreman that the white youth was loafing. The black fellow "talked pretty rough," the white man recalled,

29. Audrey Olsen Faulkner *et al.* (eds.), *When I Was Comin' Up: An Oral History of Aged Blacks* (Hamden, Conn., 1982), 75–76, 86–87.

30. See Rosengarten, *All God's Dangers,* 182, 184, and *passim;* Baynard Kendrick, "Florida's Perpetual Forests" (Typescript, 1967, in University of Florida Library), 68.

still outraged more than half a century later at the black's temerity; so he "hit him with a axe handle." In this case of poor men's interracial violence it was the white who was punished; the foreman fired him. But the white man went on to a long career as an engineer in logging company locomotives in southern Mississippi and never relented from his pathological racism. As an old man (in the 1970s) he still enjoyed telling tales of blowing his train whistle in order to disturb dogs and black people, whom he considered comparable: "A hound dog and a nigger's got a fear just alike, you know. There's [a] certain thing about a whistle, make a dog howl and make a nigger go crazy." [31]

That whites of poor and middling circumstances often brutalized black folk has been established already. As prison guards, sheriffs and deputies, riding bosses, and town and country bully boys, they fell to every opportunity to behave like beasts in order to demonstrate their belief that blacks were less than human. The agricultural crisis of the 1930s and the activities of blacks in the Southern Tenant Farmers' Union in the Mississippi Valley delta country provided, as we have seen, too many opportunities to count. [32] Modest New Deal subsidies also provided at least one poor white the opportunity to attempt extortion from a poor black man, in effect copying an old practice of the white upper classes. In 1938 the black man, a tenant or cropper near Helm, Mississippi, borrowed $15.00 from a white laborer, against the expectation of the black's "government check." When the payment arrived, the black man discovered that his creditor wanted 50 percent interest. The debtor was $1.50 short, and the white laborer threatened to shoot him on sight! A year later, as the frightened debtor reported, "I happen to meet him in Leland and he call me and ask me is I got his money and call me a lot of bad name and reach for his gun and his wife grab his hand and I run on." It is hardly surprising that the fugitive sought advice not from his local sheriff but from a black vice-president of the STFU. [33]

The most pathological examples of lower-class white behavior toward black people almost invariably derive from the lower South. Scholars and many sensitive observers of the southern interracial scene

31. Oral history of Jim Kennedy, October 27, 1976 (Audio tape in Mississippi Department of Archives and History, Jackson).
32. See, for example, Henry Johnson, affidavit, October 28, 1939, G. B. Mayberry to H. L. Mitchell, November 23, 1939, Butler to Henry Wallace, November 25, 1939, all on roll 13, STFU Papers, which document more anti–black violence in Mississippi and Arkansas.
33. Major McNeal to F. R. Betton, December 17, 1939, *ibid.*

have often argued that extreme racism logically emanated from whites living among the most blacks.[34] Another confirming test is perusal of fifteen hundred–odd FWP interviews (many of which concern race in some manner) from the late-1930s, as well as approximately a thousand other oral histories of elderly southerners, conducted during the 1970s. Among FWP life histories of Kentucky and North Carolina whites, for example, one generally finds restraint and allegiance to an ethic of decency (albeit, with condescension) toward black folk. Lower-class whites believed as strongly as the upper classes that one should say "colored person," not "nigger," and enforced the rule in rearing children. Many interviewees violated the rule, themselves, but its existence seems significant. The FWP's collection of South Carolina interviews is markedly different. It is entirely possible that the selection of subjects, serendipitous as always in the project, merely happened to yield expressions of arch racism from all classes of whites, all of whom addressed a white female interviewer. But happenstance reinforces a conventional and logical view. Lower South whites, surrounded by black folk, were more preoccupied with race and belligerent in championing white supremacy. The following vignette, related by a South Carolina landlord, may capture much of the generalization. The planter recalled an incident from his school days. "Twenty or thirty" boys on their way to class "decided it wasn't right for the niggers to walk the same foot logs as us" when crossing a creek. So they "picked up sticks and old pieces of wood . . . around the woods and lined up on the foot logs to wait for the niggers. We told them that these foot logs belonged to the white people and if they wanted to get on the other side of the creek, they would have to wade the water." The black children fought back, "pulling up lightwood stumps to throw at us. . . . Oh, we had war there for a spell, but we made them niggers wade that water before the fight ended." The white man seemed grandly gratified with his recollection.[35]

There are, of course, exceptions to all rules and generalizations. Ned Cobb reported an interesting one from his own experiences with the

34. See, for example, W. J. Cash, *The Mind of the South* (New York, 1941); V. O. Key, *Southern Politics, in State and Nation* (New York, 1949).

35. See the FWP life histories files, SHC; the "Our Lives" project files; the Marshall University Oral History of Appalachia Collection (microfilm); and the small collections of white FWP life histories at the Alabama Department of Archives and History, Montgomery; at the Arkansas History Commission, Little Rock; and at the University of Florida Library. Quotation from Annie Ruth Davis, "Mr. John Black's Experiences on the Farm," life history of Wilbur White, December 27, 1938 (Typescript in FWP life histories files, SHC).

white classes in Alabama. In 1950 he was raising a six-bale crop of cotton and needed chopping help. "A white gentleman and his wife and his wife's sister came to me—poor people—and they wanted to work." Cobb accepted them, but was embarrassed and not a little frightened that his white laborers addressed him as "Mister." "They come from this country and still they called me 'Mister.' I felt that if their color, their race, heard em call me Mr. . . . they'd hate *me* for it." Cobb asked them to address him familiarly, but they "wouldn't do it." Later Cobb reflected on the behavior of the white classes, and his summary may well capture a simple and profound truth of both the upper and lower Souths. Upper-class whites—"the big white ones"—he said, were interested in but one thing, money: "it's wrote all over his face." But at the end of a long life, Cobb declared he did not "know how to take poor white people. There's some of em won't stand a nigger at all; and there's some will go along with him to an extent. But they seemed to have always thought they was a class above the Negro." This puzzled and confounded Cobb even in his extreme age. "And what are *they*? What are they? Dough faces! Raw-gum chewers! There's been many a white man as well as Negro that's been undertrodden. But I just can't loosen up to em; I can't lead em in the lights of nothin." [36]

Whites closest to blacks economically lived on the battleline of white supremacy and most in conflict with the economic logic of class solidarity. Like upper-class whites, their children might play innocently with black children in the integrated countryside. But at a certain age, a parting of friends inevitably came, usually in adolescence, with sexual maturation and the beginning of courtship. Meanwhile adults prepared youth for the eventual partings, with stern if only occasional lessons in racial etiquette. At about age five Harry Crews referred to a prosperous local black farmer as "Mr. Jones." An aunt corrected him; he must say "nigger Jones." Young Crews absorbed the message without reflection at the moment but soon made the connection that his beloved playmate, Willalee, was also a "nigger." [37]

Interracial sex remained a powerful taboo. Blacks appear to have disapproved of it as much as whites, but whites seemed to make more of miscegenation's economic and political implications for black advancement. Blacks saw their own women's accessibility to white men as yet another arena of racial exploitation. In actuality, by 1920 there was

36. Rosengarten, *All God's Dangers*, 477–78, 512–13.

37. See Faulkner *et al.* (eds.), *When I Was Comin' Up*, 75–76; Crews, *A Childhood*, 58.

probably little black-white sexual activity, and interracial marriage was against the law everywhere. The great age of miscegenation was the late seventeenth and early eighteenth centuries, when the bulk of the American mulatto population was born in the upper South. The mixing of mulattoes and blacks probably accelerated on the antebellum cotton frontier of the lower South. During this time the domestic slave trade fed large numbers of light-colored slaves from the upper South into the Southwest, where they mingled with darker slaves brought westward from the eastern Carolinas and Georgia. Then during Reconstruction the process continued, as a mulatto elite from the North moved into the lower South to assume positions of leadership and to mix with a leadership drawn from both dark and light freedmen. By the 1880s, a long period of aversive racism marked by public ideologies of "racial pride" among both whites and blacks began, continuing until well after World War II.[38]

Still, in the second quarter of the twentieth century, as throughout the ages where folks of different colors have met, some mixing occurred. Afro-British "conchs" from the Bahamas settled in the fishing village of Riviera, Florida, above West Palm Beach and confounded local people. Some were so white, with blond hair and blue eyes; others appeared completely African. School officials finally declared conch children white—even the darker ones—but adults were excluded from other public facilities patronized by whites. One may reasonably doubt if adult whites were successful in persuading their children to shun the blond, blue-eyed conch children. No documentation of young conch–local white mixing has been discovered, but certainly a perfect situation for miscegenation existed. Perhaps more interesting were the "Portuguese" who lived in a colony of three to four hundred on either side of the state line between southeastern Virginia and northeastern North Carolina. Dominated by two clans, the Waltons and Wiggins, the "Portuguese" were considered mulattoes by neighboring whites, thus Negroes. But these swarthy folk refused to be "colored" and organized their own school and hired a white teacher.[39] By 1939, when a FWP interviewer traveled in the colony, paved roads had ended the swampy isolation of the "Portuguese"; so one may wonder again if surrounding whites were

38. Joel Williamson, *New People: Miscegenation and Mulattoes in the United States* (New York, 1980), 5–59, 76–94, and *passim*.

39. Veronica Huss and Stetson Kennedy, "The Riviera Conchs," November, 1938, Bernice Kelly Harris, "Rosa Warrick, Farmer," March 21, 1939 (Both typescripts in FWP life histories files, SHC).

successful in maintaining their taboo against these people. It seems doubtful, for the "Portuguese" were too few to maintain a separate, distinct culture; and the policing of sexual contacts has ever been defeated.

In Wake County, North Carolina, during the 1930s, there lived a racially mixed couple whose story resembles an antebellum romance. Richard Medlin was the son of a Confederate veteran. His wife, Mimi, was the illegitimate daughter of an illegitimate daughter. Her grandmother had been a spoiled belle who fell in love with her slave coachman and gave birth to his child. Thus Mimi was one-fourth African and a pariah in the white neighborhood. Medlin defied them when he married her about 1900, but his family was helpful, supplying them with a log cabin on the Medlin property. The Medlins raised fourteen children, but were obliged to educate them at home because the white school board would not admit children who were one-eighth black, and the Medlins would not send them to the black school. Meanwhile the family worked hard, lived at home, and gradually became one of the most prosperous in the county. White acceptance came gradually. They were admitted to membership in a white church, but neighbors still resisted contact between their own and the Medlin children. Nevertheless, by the end of the 1930s all had married whites, although most had left the region.[40]

Another sort of antebellum formula romance existed in northwestern Tennessee during the same years. Here a white planter kept a common-law black wife, who bore two children and operated the planter's store with shrewdness. (The planter was illiterate.) When the planter died about 1938, she apparently inherited his property and continued to run the store and direct the work of hired laborers, including whites. To protect herself—or perhaps merely because she preferred to do so for non-economic reasons—she also "took up with another white man."[41]

Most interracial sex that did take place probably remained unrecorded. Affairs that lasted more than a few weeks were no doubt known, but not much discussed in public. Ned Cobb, however, remarked on two scenarios in Alabama that may have obtained elsewhere. The first concerns coerced sexual relations. At the Wetumpka women's prison and other penal institutions during the 1930s and early 1940s white guards used black female inmates. As Cobb put it, a guard "would take them

40. Mary A. Hicks, "The Medlin Family," life history of Richard and Mimi Medlin, November, 1938 (Typescript, *ibid.*). Medlin may not have been the family's real name; FWP interviewers often invented names for subjects.
41. Life history of William A. Maynard, May 30, 1939 (Typescript, *ibid.*). Maynard was a white cotton picker on the plantation.

colored gals out from the prison department . . . and take a chance with some of em." (Cobb also reported that a fellow inmate, a black man, "would holler and raise the devil" when he witnessed the abuse. Cobb thought him "a brave nigger, in his way, and a bit of a fool." The man was transferred.) The other scenario concerned affairs between white women and black men on the outside. Cobb thought such liaisons were not uncommon, although he did not imply they were widespread. Cobb disapproved and observed that white women often betrayed dark-skinned lovers. "Whenever a white woman, if she's been foolin with a nigger, as soon as she finds out that she's in a little danger of bein found out, she gon to jump up and squall and holler." As a consequence, "Nigger's burnt up then. . . . Been doin it for years." [42]

Another arena of interracial sex was the prostitute-client relationship, but this is most difficult to document. I am aware of only one bit of testimony from a rural area. The subject was a white prostitute of near Paris, Tennessee, who with her mother had served black clients. Having once contracted a venereal disease from a dark-skinned man, she averred, "I don't take niggers, leastways not many, and then they've got to be yaller niggers." [43]

Public commentary on interracial sex seems to have been rare after the 1910s, when an age of brutal race-baiting by whites waned with the establishment of de jure segregation. That miscegenation continued to prey upon southern minds, white and black, is apparent not only in Ned Cobb's recollections but in a Macon County, Georgia, scene Arthur Raper witnessed during the fall of 1934. A minstrel show came to the town of Oglethorpe. Whites sold tickets and announced the acts, but the troupe was composed entirely of Negroes, including light-skinned women. All wore blackface, with lips painted white. The mixed-racial audience sat segregated by a narrow aisle. At the end of one of the skits a mulatto girl tells a boy: "Why don't you know who I am; my daddy's the largest planter in Georgia." The next skit was timed so close to this line that there was no opportunity for the audience to react. They sat, mute and apparently stunned. The troupe had pushed to the very brink of toppling taboos, then rushed on before whites might become hostile. The troupe cleverly balanced other comedic commentary on lower South race relations, too. In another skit a Florida preacher received a call to Americus, Georgia, but the high sheriff beat and jailed him, then

42. Rosengarten, *All God's Dangers*, 400–401.

43. Nellie Gray Toler, "Bessie Mae Boatwright," December 8, 1938 (Typescript in FWP life histories files, SHC).

returned him to Florida. The preacher's son asked his father, "Do you 'spose the Lord knows how the white folks at 'mericus Georgia, treat us niggers?" The father: "Yes, son, he knows, but just don't give a damn!" Immediately the stage went dark, and a woman struck a match, peered into emptiness and declared in the best jim crow tradition, "Now, that's a good one on them niggers; they must a thought I had my razor wid me!" Now there was a pause, and Raper heard laughter from both sides of the aisle.[44]

The remarkable combination of tension, danger, and mirth during the Oglethorpe minstrel show may be a metaphor for the gamut of feelings and conventions of rural and small town race relations. Raper and others observed another area that serves well, too. This was the southern field and stream, where the two races pursued their passions for hunting and fishing. Upper-class whites have ever hunted with black guides, and this arrangement often led to warm affection and mutual respect, even though white condescension inevitably colored such relationships. J. E. McTeer of Beaufort County, South Carolina, for example, hunted his native swamps and woods throughout the 1920s and 1930s with a legendary black man named Sammy Robinson. McTeer admired Robinson's knowledge of animals and the forest and his great physical strength: "If he killed a deer on the drive, he would have it strung over his shoulders in a flash and keep right on driving the hounds." McTeer's "greatest fear" was that a stranger might shoot Robinson when he appeared, "like a wraith, out of the woods." Robinson called McTeer "Daddy." Each year at the onset of hunting season McTeer would find him, and Robinson would declare, "Daddy, I been da look for you." McTeer would respond, "Well, here I is; you call me Daddy still I see. How do you think I have such a pretty son?" And Robinson would come back, "Go 'way man, you is all we Daddy."[45] Thus Robinson maintained a certain dignity and expressed affection, while recognizing the essentially paternalistic class relationship between himself and McTeer.

Arthur Raper, a trained observer of human behavior and a racial liberal, saw more in Georgia. There, as over much of the South, practically all rural land not posted by clubs was open to hunters of both races. Blacks might hunt on white-owned land if they were "known" or "recognized." Occasionally, Raper wrote, the "two races . . . hunt to-

44. Raper, *Preface to Peasantry*, 292–94.
45. J. E. McTeer, *Adventure in the Woods and Waters of the Low Country* (Beaufort, S.C., 1972), 26–27.

gether," but "more often they do not." Yet "by day and night in the open fields and in the woods and swamps," black and white hunters encountered each other in pairs and small groups. These armed meetings of the races were usually for the purpose of claiming killed game—often a confusing matter, for animals might run some distance after being shot. Potential danger was avoided by adherence to an important custom of long standing: "the game, no matter who kills it, goes in good spirit to the one whose dog was first on the chase." Raper did not write of black hunters' reasons for honoring the code, but white hunters blended bigotry with their adherence: "Any white hunter who would make a practice of killing and keeping the game which a Negro hunter's dog was chasing would be teased and laughed at unmercifully by his fellow white hunters." As for fishing, Raper observed that some places on riverbanks were "reserved by mutual agreement for the whites," but that "along most streams, he who gets there first is ceded the rights to the bank." [46] What emerges from these practices is a portrait of a sort of rural etiquette that seems to have prevailed when white-black relationships were not clearly of the boss-servant kind. The hunters' code of game claiming preserved peace and at the same time lent itself to whites' notions of their superiority. White monopolies or turn taking at riverbanks accomplished about the same ends. These were the ways "integrated" rural folks managed the sharing of recreational resources and a great deal of the rest of their social lives.

Throughout these decades—the 1910s past World War II—life and race relations may have seemed static to casual observers. Blacks remained so poor and oppressed. The code and institutions of white supremacy seemed so strong that whites seldom bothered with old rituals of voluble tribute. Yet all the while the very structures that sustained jim crow were crumbling, and some of the outward forms of observance showed strain. The two most elemental causes of a prerevolution in southern race relations have already been named in different contexts: massive migration, especially of blacks, and the collapse of fragmented plantations along with their black-majority sharecropping system of labor. Migration quite simply removed four and a half million black folk from the southern scene and system. There were profound political effects, as well. In the North and West migrants encountered racial discrimination, but Democratic organizations generally welcomed their numbers as voters. By the 1940s white mayors and congressmen in the

46. Raper, *Preface to Peasantry*, 396–97.

North had become beholden and emerged as national advocates of equal rights. Mayor Hubert Humphrey of Minneapolis championed anti-jim-crow planks in the 1948 Democratic convention platform, and President Harry Truman not only accepted them as policy but sponsored color-blind social programs and ordered desegregation of the armed forces.[47]

In many parts of the North and West black southerners mingled with white southern migrants. Occasionally, blacks were rudely reminded of home, for some of the whites did not respond to the North's ways with equanimity. During the 1930s, for instance, a white Floridian returned from auto work in Detroit partly because he could not tolerate public integration. "If I'd a-staid up there I'd a-had to kill a whole passel of niggers," he declared. "Them Yankee niggers haint gotta bitta manners. Why, the black sons-o-buzzards ull set right down by a white man, in a street or any place." He was twice arrested "up there for kickin' the tar outa niggers."[48] Not all white migrants reacted thus, however. A young West Virginian in Chicago during the 1960s declared that blacks had "just as much right as I've got. . . . Color just goes skin-deep. They been done so damn dirty." Living in the North had changed his heart, he said. "They're O.K. I'd just as soon work with a nigger as work with a white person."[49] More interesting, perhaps, is the testimony of an older white man in Chicago about 1965. "You know I'm from North Georgia," he said, "and they hate the Nigras." But his grandfather had taught him "not to low-rate any nationality, any race of people." The old man's righteousness was based upon biblical teaching and the fact that blacks both worked for him and lived as neighbors nearby. So in Chicago the grandson followed the same injunction.[50] The variety of working-class white reactions to northern interracialism reflects not only the variety within southern white racial ideology and practice but an ambiguity in racial relations everywhere, which was doubtless heightened by ongoing change.

The collapse of fragmented plantations and the sharecropping system also had results at first ambiguous. Race relations probably worsened, even as the means to improvement were being found. The hallmark of

47. August Meier and Elliott M. Rudwick, *From Plantation to Ghetto: An Interpretive History of American Negroes* (New York, 1966), 219–20.

48. Lindsay M. Brown, "'Jaydy' Abbin, Florida Adventurer," n.d. (1938 or 1939) (Typescript in FWP life histories files, SHC).

49. Quoted in Todd Gitlin and Nanci Hollander, *Uptown: Poor Whites in Chicago* (New York, 1970), 226.

50. *Ibid.*, 181–83.

upper-class white racial ideology and behavior in the plantation districts was paternalism. Blacks had little choice but to accept and exploit as best they could this particular white rationale for their power over labor. Few blacks seem to have been deluded about how paternalism served the landlords' interests, however; and occasionally (as, for example, with the management of 1927 Mississippi River flood refugees), whites made the mockery in paternalism quite transparent. The coming of the New Deal farm subsidy and rural relief programs made a shambles of paternalism. The federal government's role in the capitalization of large southern farms and plantations and in the conversion of tenants and croppers into wage hands, has already been detailed. An additional federal bounty to landlords was the government's assumption of an important traditional paternal duty—provisioning dependents during midsummer lay-by and winter off-seasons. Agents of the FERA observed the phenomenon throughout the cotton belt in 1934. One wrote from Richland Parish, Louisiana, at the end of that year: "As in certain Mississippi counties, the landlords are using the relief rolls as a means of escaping the necessity of providing for their tenants during the off seasons, a practice which the relief authorities of the locality find it impossible to resist." Elsewhere FERA workers reported that tenants, croppers, and wage hands eagerly accepted federal help in lieu of landlords' credit. Black and white dependents alike understood not only that government handouts carried no interest charges but that bureaucrats, despite all their shortcomings, treated them with more dignity. So, inadequate as FERA (then WPA) relief was in the face of massive hardship, the New Deal dealt devastating blows to a system already weakened by depression.[51]

Landlords' avarice in laying claim to New Deal subsidies without sharing with tenants may have been a more important factor in the demise of paternalism, for subsidies to the relatively well off were more common than welfare for the poor. Whatever respect and prestige planters may have retained into the 1930s were dashed by greed both petty and grand. It is impossible to measure precisely the personal and psychological impact of middle- and upper-class actions—evicting dependents or bullying them into signing over government benefits—but from

51. FERA, Rural Problem Areas Survey Report No. 47, Western Cotton Growing Area: Richland Parish, Louisiana (Typescript, December 17, 1934, in Record Group 83, National Archives), 4. See also FERA and BAE, "Area Report: Survey of Rural Problem Areas—Cotton Growing Region of the Old South," by Harold Hoffsommer (Typescript, *ca.* 1934, *ibid.*).

the founding of the Southern Tenant Farmers' Union in 1934 until the onset of World War II, the union's files filled with bitter reports and complaints. Some of these have already been related here in other contexts, but two more will illustrate black contempt well earned by white men who belonged to the class that had so recently paid lip service, at least, to paternalism. A sharecropper near Round Pond, Arkansas, had laid by a cotton crop early in July of 1938, when his wife died. The next day he laid her to rest, but in his absence his landlord found an excuse not to share the crop with him. The cropper explained the sequence: "My wife died on the 8 of July. I Bered her on the 9. An Bee cause I did not go to work when I come from the Grove he drove me off the Place. An I could not Even get change clothes." [52] Half a year later a southeastern Missouri landlord evicted a black family of thirteen. According to the husband-father, the landlord had been blunt in his explanation: "I had to move because the man tole me to move he say . . . if any gravy [*i.e.*, subsidies] was in the boat he was going to sop it his self." Day labor at seventy-five cents to a dollar a day, part of the year, was utterly inadequate to support such a family. They needed to live at home and feed themselves, but as itinerants, the father pointed out, "we can't have hogs, cow are [or] nothing . . . what am I to do [?]" [53] Before the new age of the federally supplied cash nexus, when land was cheap and large families were in high demand, paternalism (not to mention self-interest) would have dictated that such people would find a home on a white man's place. Never again. One wonders what became of this family. The long-term benefits of the demise of white paternalism probably did not occur to them. Bitterness toward the white race as well as the landlord class were immediate, however.

A less sudden but in all probability equally profound cause of change in racial relations was the automobile. Its appearance in the countryside all over the nation created pressures for better roads, which encouraged more cars and more travel and ultimately transformed fundamental relationships between rural areas and towns and cities. Americans worried about the effects of automobiles upon human civility and morals, too. As early as the 1910s magazine and newspaper editors made much of

52. Hays Perry to Butler, August 2, 1938, roll 5, STFU Papers.
53. Rufus Lark to STFU, February 2, 1939, roll 10, *ibid.* Operation of the tobacco program was an exception, once more. Black tobacco tenants in North Carolina voted in referenda on crop-restriction programs. In some cases they accompanied white landlords and followed their instructions; in others they voted independently without incident. See Anthony J. Badger, *Prosperity Road: The New Deal, Tobacco, and North Carolina* (Chapel Hill, 1981), 225.

the demise of roadway courtesy and rural amenities. Cars frightened farm animals, causing horses and mules to rear and overturn wagons, goods, and people—even though farmers often used the same animals to pull cars from axle-deep mud. Slow-moving animal-drawn wagons might be conveniently halted so drivers might offer rides to country pedestrians, who could readily identify drivers on uncovered seats anyway. Writers thought it too easy for fast-moving, anonymous motorists to speed by, ignoring and offending their neighbors.[54]

In the biracial South these sticky matters were rendered more so by color and extreme class differences. Arthur Raper observed the appearance of autos in the Georgia black belt during the 1920s and again in the mid-1930s, and though he understood that certain rural amenities would disappear, Raper the racial liberal became an enthusiastic champion of the car. "Only in automobiles on public roads do landlords and tenants and white people and Negroes of the Black Belt meet on a basis of equality," he wrote. If the auto ultimately provided "a basis for a new morality . . . based upon personal standards rather than upon community mores," then Raper cheered the change. "This type of morality," he declared (meaning personal autonomy in a classless and colorless new society), "is more fundamentally democratic than anything the world has known." The upper classes never ceased to complain that the poor foolishly purchased cars in good years instead of farming equipment and land. Raper understood the truth of this charge, too, but defended croppers and tenants in psychological terms: "The feel of power, even in an old automobile, is most satisfying to a man who owns nothing, directs nothing, and while producing a crop literally begs food from his landlord." Since by 1935 it was clear that most rural folks were bound either for mechanized farms or for cities and factories, Raper thought cars had practical utility, also. Poor country car owners were "becoming 'machinery wise'" doing their own repairs, and thus were preparing to depart the old, silent world of animals and hoes. In Greene and Macon counties about two-thirds of white renters and more than half of white croppers owned cars about 1935. Among blacks about half of renters and around 40 percent of croppers had them.[55]

54. Michael L. Berger, *The Devil Wagon in God's Country: The Automobile and Social Change in Rural America, 1893–1929* (Hamden, Conn., 1979), 71–72 and *passim*.
55. Raper, *Preface to Peasantry,* 174–75, 86–87. Curiously, in the all-black community of Promised Land, S.C., there were only 2 cars among about 200 families before World War II. Most of the families owned farms and put capital back into real property, apparently. See Bethel, *Promiseland,* 228.

Raper did not formally consider the potential for racial antagonism in auto ownership. When whites, in particular, were somehow excluded from this "new morality," and blacks happened to have cars, ugly resentments were magnified. This scenario was heightened during the New Deal, when substantial federal welfare and workfare programs added a volatile new ingredient to the formula. Here began the legend of the welfare Cadillac. The wife of a South Carolina renter, with four mules but no car, vented her resentment upon a FWP interviewer toward the end of the 1930s. "This government work is holding us all down from making what we ought to on the farm these days," she said. (Her husband chafed at acreage restrictions on his cotton and tobacco.) She hated the WPA even more, for it was "feeding the niggers and they're wasting their time away" when farmers needed their labor. Meanwhile her family had "no way to go nowhere 'cept in the wagon, while the niggers drives automobiles."[56] So the democratic virtue Raper saw in car ownership obtained only when both races participated. Yet, because whites of all classes owned cars more often than blacks, perhaps it is reasonable to assert that white resentment was not so important as the democratizing benefits Raper proclaimed.

All considered, the effects of the auto on racial harmony were ambiguous. At best the proliferation of the machines built upon a few fair, color-blind customs that already existed, then began the obliteration of the oppressive "community mores" that ruled the countryside. Turn taking without respect for color or class, for example, had obtained at store counters and at cotton gins for generations. Social groups usually congregated by color at both business establishments, but when business was to be conducted, folks assembled to be waited upon in mixed lines. When those lines moved slowly—which was always the case at gins during the fall—blacks and whites could not resist conversation. Ned Cobb recalled "waitin our turns" at a Tallapoosa County, Alabama, gin, where "white and colored . . . [would] talk about crops and how much more we had at home and how much we done ginned and what the cotton was bringin that year." Turn taking was readily applied to the order of business at filling stations when autos appeared. The difference was the absence of personability, especially after cars with enclosed seats became universal. Talk might occur only with attendants, unless unhurried drivers chose to leave their steel bunkers and loiter. The impersonal, colorless democracy of the car was most effective when the

56. Annie Ruth Davis, "The Skippers," life history of Mr. and Mrs. Willie Marlowe, n.d. (1938 or 1939) (Typescript in FWP life histories files, SHC).

machines were in motion. Every driver, barely visible behind glass, frame, and wheel, had his or her right to the right side of the road, by law, no matter what his or her shade or tenure.[57]

More certain and unambiguous signs of the disintegration of the old racial system were the sudden appearances of radical unions representing tenants and farm workers. First came the Alabama Sharecroppers' Union, which aimed to protect small farmers and share tenants from the expropriation of their property by creditors and their law-enforcement allies and to bargain collectively on behalf of croppers and wage laborers. The rank and file were apparently virtually all black men, most of them among the most powerless folks of the black belt. The union accomplished little and was dissolved by 1935, but its brief and occasionally violent history reveals black backbone in the heart of Dixie, where none was thought to exist.[58] Yet even ephemeral protest is also a sure sign that irreparable fault lines had begun to widen across the surface of the old racial system.

Far more remarkable and important to interracialism was the Southern Tenant Farmers' Union. Like the ASU, the STFU failed to make substantial gains for the rural poor. The union's several cotton-pickers' strikes wrought more hardship on members than planters. Its attempts to stop tenant evictions were fruitless. And the union had no more success in guiding New Deal farm policy than did the AAA liberals. But the STFU was longer-lived than the ASU; its membership included blacks, whites, Indians, and Mexicans—perhaps as many as twenty-five thousand of them in six states; it attracted sustained national attention and such influential supporters as Eleanor Roosevelt and Norman Thomas; and many STFU members survived to participate in the post–World War II equal rights movements, linking the Depression-era protests with more recent and successful ones.[59]

The STFU was born poor and idealistic. In 1934 a group of eighteen black and white farmers, preachers, and Socialist small businessmen organized the union at Tyronza, Arkansas, in the cotton plantation country northwest of Memphis. The sparkplug of the group was Harry Leland Mitchell, always known as Mitch, a young white man who owned a tiny dry-cleaning business. Mitchell was a sharecropper's son,

---

57. Rosengarten, *All God's Dangers,* 196–97; Raper, *Preface to Peasantry,* 275–91.

58. Rosengarten, *All God's Dangers,* 312–44, 393–94, 585–87; George B. Tindall, *The Emergence of the New South, 1913–1945* (Baton Rouge, 1967), 379–80.

59. See Donald H. Grubbs, *Cry from the Cotton: The Southern Tenant Farmers' Union and the New Deal* (Chapel Hill, 1971).

H. L. MITCHELL IN HIS MEMPHIS OFFICE, 1938
Photo by Dorothea Lange, courtesy of H. L. Mitchell

born near Halls, in western Tennessee. He managed to attend high
school, was influenced by a supporter of Eugene Debs, and read some
Marx and a serendipitous collection of old American Socialist tracts. So
while pressing planters' pants in Tyronza, as Mitchell fondly remembered, and witnessing the suffering of the landless in the aftermath of
the New Deal's first Agricultural Adjustment Act, he began to discuss
protest with local folks. The STFU spread rapidly up into the southeastern counties of the Missouri Bootheel. A few western Tennessee
farmers joined, as well. Later (about 1935–1936) the union spread
through the poor cotton country of eastern Oklahoma, where membership strength became second only to that in Arkansas. Texas organizers
established locals in eastern and south-central counties, although the
union never really took hold there. And in 1939, as the STFU virtually

disappeared in Arkansas, Missouri, and Oklahoma, there was a surge of interest among black sharecroppers in the Mississippi Delta.[60]

The STFU leadership and rank and file were a remarkable ideological as well as racial concoction. Mitchell and his business neighbor, Clay East (owner of a filling station), were Socialists. So were others, apparently all of them white men and women, both at the Memphis headquarters and scattered about the Arkansas and Oklahoma countrysides. The Socialists added a wonderful self-conscious radicalism to southern rural culture, and the southern rural folk also had much to offer socialism. Early in 1936 Charles McCoy, a privy cleaner of Truman, Arkansas, announced May Day plans to Mitchell: "The comrades are talking of haveing [a] fish fry at my place May day. So if we have this dinner it will be coffee fish and corn bread. if wee work it out i will let you no would like to have you come and bring some good speakers." [61] At least two white Communists—Al Murphy (also known as Albert Jackson) and Thomas Burke, former leaders of the Alabama Sharecroppers' Union— also took minor roles in STFU affairs. More numerous, however, were homegrown Christians, including many black Baptist ministers who spoke for people without rigorous formal ideologies who urgently wanted justice from landlords and the New Deal, then land for their own. The Reverend Owen H. Whitfield, a tenant on a plantation near New Madrid, Missouri, and an STFU officer, was a dynamic and charismatic spokesman for the landless black masses. There was always potential conflict over ultimate aims within such a coalition. Mitchell and other articulate Socialists understood the irresistible dynamics of capital and scale in commercial agriculture and from time to time made plain their ultimate preference for collectivism. The New Deal Resettlement Administration and Farm Security Administration experimental farm cooperatives for the rural poor seemed a proper model. But pressure from the black and white rank and file forced the Socialists to retreat to a simple slogan, "Land for the Landless," and to gloss over deep differences over objectives. Meanwhile internal unity was also preserved for a while by the friendly interest and support of the union by Christian

60. See H. L. Mitchell, *Mean Things Happening in This Land: The Life and Times of H. L. Mitchell* (Montclair, N.J., 1979), 11–45 and *passim;* various membership lists and organizers' correspondence in the STFU Papers. The disarray of Arkansas and Oklahoma locals is evident in form letters and reports on microfilm roll 13. On the weakness of the Texas branch, see the correspondence of organizer J. E. Clayton, *e.g.,* Clayton to Mitchell, June 21, 1938, roll 8.

61. Charles McCoy to H. L. Mitchell, March 19, 1936, roll 1, STFU Papers. On McCoy's occupation and background, see Mitchell, *Mean Things Happening,* 37.

socialists such as Howard Kester and Ward Rodgers (white ministers) and Charles S. Johnson and Arthur Raper (liberal black and white, respectively, academic sociologists).[62] Such men were at least symbols of synthesis.

For four years or so, too, ideological and racial stress were minimized by a joyous movement culture within the STFU, which amounted to a binding spirit of brother- and sisterhood among union members. They were all so poor. Most locals never handled so much as $10.00 per month. Typical was the treasury of the Tomato, Arkansas, local at the end of January, 1938: there was $2.70 cash on hand and a debt of $2.00. Yet in times of crisis the poor could be depended upon to gather pennies and nickels and donate them to strangers. During the Missouri highway demonstrations early in 1939 officers of the Earl, Arkansas, local wrote to Memphis headquarters: "Find incloes $5.00 . . . to aid Brothers and sisters in Mo it is all we able to give . . . as we are share cropper and money is hard to get now." They also shared danger from planters, their gunmen, and sheriffs' men. Headquarters staff sent all correspondence to members in unmarked envelopes, and even the union's president, J. R. Butler, was once kicked down the courthouse steps in Forrest City, Arkansas. STFU folks were also elevated by their class consciousness, which, in the heart of the plantation country, was color-blind. H. L. Mitchell became an evangelist for racial equality: "There are no 'niggers' and no 'poor white trash' in the Union," he wrote in 1935. A. B. Brookins, a black Baptist minister, accommodated union audiences, mixed both racially and ideologically, with the greeting: "Brothers and sisters—and *comragies!*" And in the country near Blytheville, Arkansas, in 1937, Mrs. M. H. Barnes, the articulate secretary to Local 322, organized a children's group to teach, among other things, "cooperation between individuals and races."[63]

62. See Mitchell, *Mean Things Happening*, 171–73, 179–180, and *passim;* O. H. Whitfield to Mitchell, January 10, 1938, roll 7, Mitchell and Butler, "Supplement to Southern Tenant Farmers' Union Statement on Farm Tenancy," addressed to the Arkansas State Tenancy Conference (Typescript, October 10, 1936, roll 3), [J. R. Butler (?)] to Donald Henderson, January 31, 1939, and Henderson to Mitchell, January 28, 1939, both roll 10, all in STFU Papers. See also Howard Kester, *Revolt Among the Sharecroppers* (New York, 1936). Charles S. Johnson and Arthur F. Raper served as trustees (along with liberal theologian Reinhold Niebuhr) of the STFU Delta Cooperative Farm in Mississippi. See "Memorandum of Agreement Between Delta Cooperative Farm and Albert Day, Covering the Year 1939" (Typescript, n.d. [*ca.* November 30, 1938], roll 9, STFU Papers).

63. See monthly reports for locals for 1938, Armster Davies and Will Strong to Butler, January 28, 1939, both roll 10, and see Evelyn Smith (STFU office secretary) to Donald Henderson, March 2, 1938 (on secret mailings), J. R. Swinea, J. W. Vincent, J. F.

The STFU's movement culture was formalized by secret ritual and strident anthems. Socialists addressed each other as comrade, but had no difficulty adapting to a churchly brother or sister when in company with preachers and their followers. "Brother" became the official address of men in the union's *Ritual*, distributed early in 1938, along with the advice that the pamphlet be locked away when not being studied. "Signs and Signals" were necessary "to protect members of the Union, who are constantly hounded," and to assist in discriminating "between Union and non-Union persons." To call a brother, for example, one should "extend the right hand, palm up, close fist slowly. Repeat three times at intervals of about 1 minute." The sign of distress was "right hand raised just above the head, palm opened with thumb in palm." A brother recognizing distress "will advance and drawing the index finger across the throat . . . [offer] the right hand, thumb in palm." Distress might also be signaled by handclapping or the firing of pistols or guns three times. The *Ritual* was vigorously promoted by Edward Britt McKinney, a bald, hyperbolic black preacher from Marked Tree, Arkansas. McKinney was a former follower of Marcus Garvey, the ill-fated Jamaica-born black nationalist of the 1910s and 1920s; and McKinney remained a strong advocate of racial pride. But white STFU members, hardly less fond of secret ritual than black lodge members, seem to have accepted and enjoyed McKinney's handiwork, too. The troubadour of the STFU was John L. Handcox. A black former sharecropper and barely educated, Handcox had a generous disposition and poetic soul, which combined to synthesize traditional religiosity and Socialist class consciousness. He was the author of "Mean Things Happening in This Land," the union anthem, which Mitchell adopted as the title of his autobiography many years later: "There are mean things happening in this land / (repeat) / But the Union's going on / And the Union's growing strong / For there are mean things happening in this land." Handcox also wrote "Roll the Union On" (sung to the tune of "Polly-Wolly-Doodle")—"If the planters in the way / We're goin' to roll it over them / Goin' to roll it over them / . . . Goin' to roll the Union on"—and he adapted such spirituals as "Go Down, Moses" and "No More Mourning" to STFU messages of solidarity and hope.[64]

Hynds, A. T. Riley, and Jack Cunningham (the attack on Butler) (Typescript depositions, October 9, 1937), Mrs. M. H. Barnes to Mitchell, August 23, 1937, all roll 5, Mitchell to Nathan Wiley, November 21, 1935, roll 1, all in STFU Papers. A. B. Brookins quoted by Mitchell in conversation with the author, October 30, 1984, Oxford, Ohio.

64. STFU *Ritual* (Ca. February, 1938, roll 7, STFU Papers). See Grubbs, *Cry from*

E. B. McKinney
Photo by Howard Kester, courtesy of H. L. Mitchell

Union leaders and many of the rank and file made valiant efforts to create and keep interracial balance and equity. National offices were disproportionately held by whites. J. R. Butler and Mitchell served as president and secretary-treasurer, respectively, throughout the 1930s. But vice-presidents and several other executive board members were always black men. E. B. McKinney, then F. R. Betton, were influential vice-presidents who often sallied forth to reassure all-black locals in

---

the Cotton, 67–68, on McKinney's background; song lyrics (Typescript, roll 3) and printed program for the 1938 convention, roll 7, both in STFU Papers. On Handcox, see also Mitchell, *Mean Things Happening*, 111–12.

Arkansas, Missouri, and Mississippi. The union was also dedicated to integration as a means and symbol of unity and defiance of the landlords who wanted the poor to divide along racial lines. Annual conventions featured mixed-racial seating for business and meals. In 1938 the union was evicted from Community Hall in downtown Little Rock because of this. Groups of locals staged integrated picnics, too. Of one of these in southeastern Missouri in 1936, John Handcox wrote: "Every body had a plenty to eat and it were not serve to us white & colored but as a big family dinner." [65] E. B. McKinney, head of the all-black local at Marked Tree, Arkansas, once invited a neighboring all-white local to meet in the blacks' lodge hall, the only building available to accommodate large groups. The whites accepted, and one later remarked to Mitchell, "You know, that nigger's got more sense than any white man here." [66] Where locals had mixed-racial memberships poor men and women tried to balance their corps of officers at least as well as the STFU headquarters model. A white man from near Earle, Arkansas, wrote to Mitchell in 1937, "We elected one negro, name Will Johnson a wage hand from Luther Wallins Saw Mill" to an office. Both Johnson and the white correspondent were sadly "ignorant," he wrote, begging for "some Litature" to help the integrated leadership serve their membership: "[We] kneed to learn." [67] At Hillhouse, Mississippi, the STFU established the Delta Cooperative Farm, and union instructions to the manager specified that "he will especially respect the relations between Negroes and white persons." The Oklahoma branch of the union, led by a flamboyant Cherokee cotton farmer and would-be Democratic politician named Odis Sweeden, achieved a wonderful balance in the STFU's most ethnically diverse subregion. In 1938 Sweeden announced that a new Oklahoma state commission had been formed. The commission consisted of three whites, three blacks, two Indians (Sweeden and another man, a Choctaw), a man who was half Anglo and half Cherokee, and a Mexican. [68] It is no wonder that such efforts at racial conciliation—combined with Socialist idealism—led the union the same year to declare its opposition "to the idea of war, good or bad" and to condemn congressional appropriations for battleship construction when

65. C. A. Stanfield to Mitchell, February 26, 1938, news release on Community Hall (Typescript, n.d.), both roll 7, and John Handcox to Mitchell, September 28, 1936, roll 3, all in STFU Papers.

66. Grubbs, *Cry from the Cotton,* 67–68, quotation 68.

67. C. J. Spradling to Mitchell, April 24, 1937, roll 6, STFU Papers.

68. "Memorandum of Agreement: Between Delta Cooperative Farm . . . 1939"; Odis Sweeden to Mitchell, September 24, 1938, roll 9, STFU Papers.

INTERRACIAL STFU GATHERING, COLT, ARKANSAS, 1936
Courtesy of H. L. Mitchell

there was such need for money at home "for the constructive purpose of
reestablishing the landless farmers of the nation upon the soil." [69]

The union and its movement culture promoted assertiveness among
the poor who, despite a certain tradition of rural radicalism in the
region, had been meek. This seems especially true among blacks.
Lettered women such as Mrs. M. H. Barnes held many locals together.
Men began to fight back against the powerful. Early in 1936 Jim Ball, a
black cropper and secretary to the St. Peters local in Crittenden County,
Arkansas, resisted when deputy sheriffs broke into a union meeting at
his church. For disarming a shotgun-bearing lawman, Ball was sen-
tenced to seven years imprisonment by what union officials called a
"planter picked" jury. Owen Whitfield's rise to prominence was mete-
oric. From a tenant on a Missouri plantation, then an FSA client, he
became a spokesman for the poor, pursued by politicians and the press.
Early in January, 1938, he wrote to Mitchell about his impending meeting with the governor and state social security administrator in Jefferson
City, "trying [to] get something started to get food for the People and
tent[s] for the 400 families that are to be evicted in the next few days."
And "Oh say!" he continued, "the Editor of the St. [Louis] Post Dis-
patch came down to see me last Wednesday. We went to the court

69. See copy of 1938 convention resolutions, roll 7, *ibid.*

EVICTED TENANTS, CROSS COUNTY, ARKANSAS, 1936
Photo by Howard Kester, courtesy of H. L. Mitchell

House. Called in all the big Shots & Planter[s] & relief workers and had a 3 hours Press conference, and did I tell em?" Whitfield exulted, "Well, I am going places and doing things Where a Negro has not been allowed." [70]

Sadly, by the time Whitfield's fame approached its zenith, the STFU had begun to disintegrate as a grass-roots movement. Persisting evictions further impoverished members already hardly able to pay modest dues. Evictions and union strikes also scattered the membership and disrupted the locals. In 1937, desperate for help, the STFU became part of the Congress of Industrial Organization's (CIO) United Cannery, Agricultural, Packing, and Allied Workers of America (UCAPAWA), which, under the presidency of Donald H. Henderson, was already busy among California packers and farm workers. Henderson, a former lecturer in economics at Columbia University, had great zeal but little practical grasp of farm laborers' situation and hardly any sense of the peculiar southern system. He and his staff clashed with Mitchell's office and endangered STFU members by sending out loads of union correspondence in envelopes marked with the union's return address. (Many of the rank and file lived on planters' property and received mail there.) That

70. See "Planters Railroad Union Men to Prison" (Typescript press release, February 21, 1936), and copy of Ball's printed appeal of his sentence, both roll 1, O. H. Whitfield to Mitchell, January 10, 1938, roll 7, *ibid.*

Henderson was a Communist made matters worse. Socialists such as Mitchell and Butler came to fear a take-over. In 1936 Mitchell had barely escaped death while visiting Commonwealth College in Mena, Arkansas, when a deranged STFU member fired five or six shots at the secretary-treasurer. Now Mitchell suspected the would-be assassin had been a red agent, and his animosity toward Henderson became obsessive. The UCAPAWA connection also fractured the STFU's movement culture. Preachers who had tolerated Socialists loathed the less flexible CIO reds, and in turn, Henderson and his associates encouraged dissident blacks to challenge the Memphis headquarters' authority and jurisdiction.[71]

The STFU had never been free of racial stress. As early as the spring of 1935 the white leader of a Cross County, Arkansas, mixed local attempted to separate the races and form two chapters. G. E. Ferrell, a black member, fought the move: "I don't think this is right, I believe as we started this organization together we ought to go that way," lest the poor fall into the landlords' trap of division and conquest. Ferrell won the day, and the white separatist was expelled from the union. Other mixed locals had similar strife, with whites, especially, always ready to expel blacks and go it alone. Whites frequently argued with Mitchell that a separate union for each race would enhance recruitment among whites. But most locals were in fact already monoracial. In 1937 headquarters received fifty-five completed membership questionnaires from an equal number of Arkansas locals. Only eighteen had biracial rolls, and nearly all these had but one or two members of one race, with the great bulk of the other.[72] This may merely reflect residential patterns, but black union people remained suspicious that they were bearing virtually all the initiative, inconvenience, and risks in interracialism. Mrs. M. H. Barnes wrote from Blytheville that same year, "It is going to be absolutely necessary to take drastic measures in order to convince especially white union members to stand faithfully by their obliga-

71. See Cletus E. Daniel, *Bitter Harvest: A History of California Farmworkers, 1870–1941* (Ithaca, 1981), 279; Mitchell, *Mean Things Happening,* 94–97, 164–170, for assessments and background on Henderson, UCAPAWA, and the Mena gunfire. On the matter of UCAPAWA mailings, see Evelyn Smith to Donald Henderson, March 2, 1938, roll 7, STFU Papers. On Mitchell's hatred of Communists, see Whitfield to Mitchell, February 28, 1939, roll 10, *ibid.,* in which Whitfield responded to Mitchell's warnings of red subversion: "But must i ask every person i meet what his politics are?"

72. Quotation from G. E. Ferrell to Howard Kester, May 21, 1935, roll 1, STFU Papers. On white restlessness and rejection of interracialism in Cross County and elsewhere, see correspondence on rolls 1 and 2, *passim.* The completed questionnaires are on roll 6.

tions." From Charleston, Missouri, John Handcox wrote exasperatedly: "I'm up against a hard point. It seem like all the white members have lost all interest in the union. . . . The Colored people seem to be pushing forward and the white backward." And despite the noblest of intentions, too, the Delta Cooperative Farm in Mississippi maintained de facto separate housing for its worker-residents.[73]

Serious racial rifts appeared in 1938. E. B. McKinney, the former Garveyite, circularized black locals, inviting them to form a separate union under his leadership. McKinney was encouraged by Claude Williams, a Communist; Mitchell and Butler smelled a conspiracy, and the STFU executive board expelled both McKinney and Williams. A union convention later readmitted McKinney without his rank as vice-president, but the wounds never healed. McKinney was disconsolate, and trust was not restored. As a black rank-and-filer from Tyronza wrote to Mitchell, "the split" caused "members to fall out and cant get them to Work. . . . the Peoples has scattered." [74] The stage was thus set for a spectacular incident that both showcased emergent black leadership and effectively killed the STFU.

Early in December, 1938, word got out that southeastern Missouri landlords, rather than submit to a federal ruling that tenants' shares of subsidies were to be mailed directly to tenants, had decided in concert to evict their tenants on January 10, 1939, and convert to wage labor. Such mass evictions had occurred before. Owen Whitfield (then second vice-president of the STFU) and Al Murphy (a founder of the Alabama Sharecroppers' Union) began to plan a protest demonstration. Whitfield dutifully sent a letter outlining the plan to STFU headquarters in Memphis, but J. R. Butler, more than once before a hapless fellow, either lost or ignored Whitfield's message. When the evictions came and about 250 cropper and tenant families (approximately eleven hundred people) poured onto U.S. Highway 61 in January, the STFU as such was surprised and embarrassed. For arguably this pathetic roadside show, in which the national press covered the plight of families camping in the open during the dead of winter, was the most dramatic demonstration ever of the cruelty of both the plantation system and federal policy. One of the demonstrators got a letter through to Memphis. The landlords

73. Mrs. M. H. Barnes to Mitchell, August 23, 1937, roll 5, John Handcox to Butler, February 19, 1937, roll 4, Sam H. Franklin, Jr., to Butler, May 28, 1937, roll 3, all *ibid.*

74. See Evelyn Smith to Norman Thomas, August, 23, 1938, roll 8, Mitchell's form letter to all locals, September 29, 1938, roll 9, both *ibid.;* and Mitchell, *Mean Things Happening,* 159–62. Quotation from Mid Hayes to Mitchell, February 1, 1939, roll 10, STFU Papers.

"said thay was gone to work thay land by day labor," he wrote, "an . . . now thay want to give 75[cents] & $1.00 a day we cant make no living at that price." So "We had to move . . . out on the highway and . . . dont think or dont see where we can support our familys." [75]

Meanwhile Donald Henderson moved into the demonstration at the northern end of Route 61, farthest from Arkansas and STFU influence, and claimed credit and direction of the affair for UCAPAWA. Whitfield withdrew to St. Louis and conspiracy. Actual leadership along the highway apparently devolved upon an able STFU local officer named Booker T. Clark, a black man. It was he who probably deserves most credit for directing the flow of donated tents, blankets, food, and clothing that poured in from the Arkansas brethren and from other sympathetic people around the nation. The FSA established a camp-cooperative in the area, which accommodated several hundred of the homeless. Most of the demonstrators remained adrift or squatted in Missouri towns and cities, swelling ghettoes. [76]

By this time Memphis leaders had decided to secede from UCAPAWA. Whitfield called upon Missouri locals to decide between the two, preferring a separate Missouri union under Henderson's auspices. Butler, Mitchell, and F. R. Betton scolded Whitfield, who seemed to be replaying the McKinney secessionist role. Whitfield felt caught in the middle of a nasty jurisdictional dispute not of his own making. "I am really sorry these things are happening," he wrote, "because i know i am going to get all the blame." [77] Whitfield may indeed have been ambitious, and his secessionism had racial as well as ideological overtones: the Missouri locals were overwhelmingly black, and Henderson's Communists stood behind Whitfield.

The climax came in Memphis. Henderson called a meeting designed to throw out Butler, Mitchell, and Betton. Mitchell and company packed the Beale Street hall with hostile Arkansas supporters. Henderson, surrounded by bodyguards, railed against them and the STFU leadership, who had absented themselves for the moment. When Butler and Mitchell finally appeared, violence threatened. Then Mitchell dramatically called upon the crowd to walk out, leaving Henderson and his men

75. Mitchell, *Mean Things Happening,* 171–80; Louis Cantor, *Prologue to the Protest Movement: The Missouri Sharecropper Roadside Demonstrations of 1939* (Durham, N.C., 1969), 63–65; Ike Tripp to STFU, January 26, 1939, roll 10, STFU Papers.

76. Mitchell, *Mean Things Happening,* 179–82; Cantor, *Prologue to the Protest Movement,* 84–94.

77. Whitfield to Betton, February 27, 1939, and see Whitfield's circular letter to STFU locals, February 24, 1939, both roll 10, STFU Papers.

without an Arkansas union. They did, retiring to a labor hall three blocks away. There the Reverend A. B. Brookins proposed (as Mitchell remembered) "a committee to go seize Don Henderson, take him to the foot of Beale Street, where he, Brookins . . . would baptize Henderson in the Mississippi River, and make a Christian of the UCAPAWA president." The motion was not acted upon.[78] At best it reaffirmed the old spirit of toleration between preachers and Socialists, which had never included the reds.

The STFU and UCAPAWA survived separately for some years, both shells of their former selves. Former Missouri demonstrators lodged in the FSA camp remained affiliated with UCAPAWA into the 1940s and during the war staged a strike for higher wages from the government under union auspices. The STFU became an American Federation of Labor affiliate, changed its name, and sent Mitchell off on a long career as a farm worker organizer throughout the country.[79] The union's significance for rural race relations, meanwhile, was enormous if hardly neat and conclusive. The STFU's integrationism, always weak and stressful, nonetheless forthrightly challenged the law of the South and the custom of the nation. Mitchell's and others' survival and consistency as integrationists is a strong link between the STFU and integrationist organizations of the 1950s and 1960s. UCAPAWA, like so many Communist-led CIO unions of the 1930s, was mischievous and conspiratorial but, despite its faults, provided at least as good a springboard for black assertiveness and leadership as the STFU. Certainly the logical tensions between interracialism and black power, which destroyed several interracial organizations during the late 1960s, were well demonstrated three decades earlier, in Memphis, Truman, Blytheville, Marked Tree, Lilbourn, and dozens of other southern places, where sharecropping and paternalism died, with long-lasting implications.

78. Mitchell, *Mean Things Happening*, 179–180.
79. *Ibid.*, 181 and *passim*.

Part Three
Exodus

[Rural parents'] sons and daughters come to manhood
and womanhood, depart the farm and are lost to them
in some distant community. . . . They have established
no permanent home, their kith and kin are scattered far
and wide.
>   —A SMALL-TOWN GEORGIA BANKER, 1914

Being poor ain't easy nowheres, but it's a sight better in
the city than on a farm.
>   —A FORMER TENANT FARMER'S WIFE,
>   KNOXVILLE, *ca.* 1939

Industry is not only setting past errors right, but it is
determining Southern culture for the present and
future.
>   —BROADUS MITCHELL AND GEORGE SINCLAIR
>   MITCHELL, 1930

Chapter 8
Migrants in the Homeland

IN 1920 THERE WAS HARDLY A SOUTHERN
state in which the population was not at least two-thirds rural. Louisiana's fell slightly short, at 65.1 percent. Florida's was the least rural of all, at 63.5 percent. The populations of both Carolinas, Mississippi, and Arkansas were more than 80 percent rural. The first statistically urban southern state was Florida, which by 1930 had undergone rapid growth and urbanization, leaving only 48.3 percent of its people in the country. All the other southern states maintained rural majorities into the 1940s and later, however, even though their cities grew inexorably. In 1940 Georgia's population was still 65.6 percent rural, Alabama's nearly 70 percent, Kentucky's 70.2, West Virginia's 71.9, North Carolina's 72.7, South Carolina's 75.5, Arkansas' 77.8, and Mississippi's 80.2. During the 1940s and 1950s came the most dramatic transformations, and by 1960 most of the South was urban at last. Using the new definition of *urban* (adopted by the Bureau of the Census following the 1940 enumeration), which included unincorporated places of twenty-five hundred or more people, along with city "fringes" not yet annexed, only six of fourteen states had rural majorities in 1960. The majorities had been much narrowed since 1940, too: Arkansas, 57.2 percent rural; Kentucky, 55.5; Mississippi, 62.3; North Carolina, 60.5; South Caro-

lina, 58.8; and West Virginia, 61.8. Florida's rural population, mean-while, had shrunk to 26.1, Louisiana's to 36.7, Oklahoma's to 37.1, and Virginia's to 44.4. Texas, remarkably, had outdone Florida and become the least rural of the southern states, at only 25.0 percent.[1]

During the same forty-year period the region lost 1,532,793 farms. The net loss of rural population, 1920–1960, was 1,330,771, but this figure misleads; six states—Louisiana, Florida, South Carolina, North Carolina, Virginia, and West Virginia—gained rural population even while losing farms. A "rural" net surplus of approximately a million and a half people in effect slipped through cracks in the Bureau of the Census' definition of *urban*. The other eight states lost 2,910,474 rural people over the four decades. A better perspective of the human dimen-sions of southern urbanization might perhaps be gained by assuming that each 1920 farm household consisted of five persons—a modest es-timate. Then, by 1960, we could guess that nearly eight million farm folks had disappeared from the countryside. This amounts to a major event in southern history. It is also remarkable in comparative perspec-tive. The capitalization and enclosure of southern farmland was more dramatic and chronologically compressed than that in the Northeast and Middle West. Northern farms were always relatively well mechanized and not so overpopulated; so the social disruption of the rural South in so brief a time seems particularly intense (and traumatic). In terms of its revolutionary effects on agriculture and humanity, the southern up-heaval was at least the equivalent of the principal phase of the English Enclosure Movement of the last four decades of the eighteenth century.[2] The nature of the structural changes in southern agriculture has already been discussed. In this chapter and the next we shall try to account for the millions of people who left southern farms during these decades.

One must first understand that much of the South's farm population had long been very mobile. From the end of the Civil War southerners with and without the means to own land gravitated westward to new

1. Data from state population tables in Donald B. Dodd and Wynelle S. Dodd (comps.), *Historical Statistics of the South, 1790–1970* (University, Ala., 1973).

2. Calculations from state population and farm tables, *ibid.* On shortcomings of the federal censuses, see Liston Pope, *Millhands and Preachers: A Study of Gastonia* (New Haven, 1942), 51–54. Pope showed that Gaston County, N.C., had a number of mill vil-lages with populations under 2,500 that were classified as rural. See also John L. Shover, *First Majority—Last Minority: The Transforming of Rural Life in America* (DeKalb, Ill., 1976), *passim*, for the U.S. perspective; G. E. Mingay, *Enclosure and the Small Farmer in the Age of the Industrial Revolution* (London, 1968); C. S. Orwin and C. S. Orwin, *The Open Fields* (Oxford, 1967), 161–69, on the persistence of enclosure after the movement in England.

MOVING DAY FOR A CROPPER FAMILY. A boy is ready with the loaded truck.
USDA No. 83-G-41126, National Archives

delta and plains lands. And in old and new lands alike the tenant and sharecropper classes moved often, seeking better soils, crops, housing, communities, and especially better landlords. In 1922 about two of every ten American farmers changed locations. (This figure includes 27.7 percent of tenants and 6 percent of owners.) In eight cotton states, however, the rate was 30–40 percent. White sharecroppers were particularly mobile, moving about every year. Data gathered by the Cotton Section of the AAA revealed that a large percentage of the landless had changed places six or seven times since undertaking farming. Some families had lived on as many as fifteen different farms. White share tenants and croppers were still more mobile than blacks. A 1934 Federal Emergency Relief Administration survey of sample counties in cotton areas found that nearly all black cropper families remained on the same land virtually all their lives. Whites moved much more, usually short distances. The FERA no doubt exaggerated the stability of blacks, for in 1936, in Greene and Macon counties, Georgia, the average tenure on farms of black share tenants was 3.7 years, and of black croppers only 2.8. Still, white tenants and croppers stayed put for somewhat shorter periods: 2.9 and 2.4 years, respectively.[3] So it is no wonder that frequent moving settled into the consciousness and humor of the lower classes. The itinerant life, they said, affected the behavior of their chickens. In 1939 a white New Bern, North Carolina, mail carrier gave his version: "My daddy," he said, "moved around so much that Mama used to tell him that every time the chickens heard a wagon they would set down in the yard and cross their legs to be tied."[4]

Huge numbers of such itinerants left farming altogether before World War II. Others, and an unknown number of small owners, spent these years drifting between farming and other work. The family of a white North Carolina farm owner was reduced to day labor, for example, after the father bought an expensive Buick in 1922, then had bad luck with crops and mortgaged the farm. By the end of 1923 the farmer had become a guard at a prison farm. A dozen years later, the daughter who related the story was working as a waitress in Raleigh. A black Mississippian (born in 1898) never left the country but shifted from nonfarm work to farming and back again in a long career. During the 1920s he cooked on a "quarter boat" operating between Vicksburg and Memphis, then went to sharecropping for the Delta and Pine Land Company. After the Depression he continued with D&PL as a day laborer and handyman. A white man, probably born about the same time, moved back and

3. USDA, *Agriculture Yearbook, 1923* (Washington, D.C., 1924), 590, 595. AAA and Georgia information from David Eugene Conrad, *The Forgotten Farmers: The Story of Sharecroppers in the New Deal* (Urbana, 1965), 13–14. See also FERA and BAE, "Area Report: Survey of Rural Problem Areas—Cotton Growing Region of the Old South," by Harold Hoffsommer (Typescript, *ca.* 1934), "Area Report: Western Cotton Growing Area," by Z. B. Wallin (Typescript, November 14, 1934), both in Record Group 83, National Archives.

4. Mary M. Phillips, "Contracting the Mails," life history of Thurmond Bennett, February 8, 1939 (Typescript in FWP life histories files, Southern Historical Collection, University of North Carolina [SHC].

forth from farming, too, in northwestern Tennessee and southwestern Kentucky. Orphaned very young, he was a child farm laborer in Tennessee before World War I and received no formal education. During the 1920s he cut ties for railroads, but after 1930 demand for ties declined, and he returned to agricultural day labor and sharecropping—and raising ten unschooled children.[5] Another white family's history (during the 1920s and 1930s) shows the almost dizzying interchangeability of farming and mill work as occupations of restless, driven people: "We were married in Lake Mill," the odyssey began. "We stayed there about a couple of years, then we farmed about a year. Then we went back to the cotton-mill and stayed about two or three years. Then we went to Woodburg and farmed for a year and a half. Then we went back to Lake Mill and worked about six months and then we moved to Smith County to this mill and stayed here for about five years." This was the family's longest tenure anywhere, for "in the spring we moved back to the Lake Mill and stopped there until Christmas. Then we took to farming for three or four months. We went back to the Hampton Mill and worked about two weeks and then moved to the Triffen Mill and stayed there two years. Then we moved back here."[6]

The state of Florida, always a magnet for migrants, seemed bursting with the itinerant poor during the 1920s and 1930s. Bill Griffin, for instance, sold his Alabama cotton and corn farm and tried growing vegetables in Highlands County during the 1920s. He failed and in 1939 was working as a contract pruner of corporate-owned orange trees at fifteen cents per tree. Bob and Anne Franklin, both from successful Alabama cotton-corn farming families, married and began to plant the old staples in 1919. The boll weevil drove them to Hicoria, Florida, during the 1920s. There Bob cleared pines from sandy land and tried again, with poor results. So by the road at the edge of his property he built a small general store from rough lumber. At the end of the 1930s he still had little business, but his large family benefited from food and durables he could buy at wholesale because he was a storekeeper. Franklin also performed day labor for neighboring farmers.[7] Many more southern mi-

5. Mary A. Hicks, "A Waitress," life history of Eva Truelove, January, 1939 (Typescript, *ibid.*); Bill Boyd, interview with Johnny Washington, May 15, 1974 (Audio tape in Delta and Pine Land Company Oral History, Mississippi State University Library); Ruth Clark, "Finis Evitis," November 10, 1938 (Typescript in FWP life histories files, SHC).

6. Quoted in J. Wayne Flynt, *Dixie's Forgotten People: The South's Poor Whites* (Bloomington, Ind., 1979), 70.

7. Barbara Berry Darsey, "Jack Dillin," life history of Bill Griffin, January 27, 1939 (Typescript in FWP of Florida files, University of Florida Library); Darsey, "Albert and

grants to Florida lacked the Griffins' and Franklins' modest capital, and they simply drifted. A tobacco sharecropper left southern Georgia for a share of a three-acre northern Florida berry farm. A too-short growing season and small crops could not support his family of seven, so the migrant worked irregularly at jobs supplied by the WPA and finally, late in 1938, found regular work as an elevator operator at a Jacksonville paper mill. He was delighted with his position and his pay, 35 cents per hour; but his wife still dreamed of "a little farm of our own."[8] Many other former tenants and croppers squatted in tar-paper shacks between Orlando and the Everglades, hunting, fishing, and working seasonally for fruit and vegetable farmers. Others hoed grass in orange groves, pruned trees in winter, and took New Deal and local workfare or welfare in the fall. Their diets improved—few had ever encountered fruits and vegetables in such abundance—but most of those who spoke to interviewers felt abandoned and betrayed by the great bonanza state and refuge of the South.[9]

Elsewhere life was at least as cruel to the landless, and the weather was not so kind, perhaps, as Florida's. Tenants and sharecroppers had moved from the country directly to city jobs during World War I and again during the boll weevil onslaughts of the 1920s. When farm price collapses in 1929–1930 were accompanied by an industrial depression as well, however, *at least* one million southerners were caught in a terrible economic vise. Most of them did not enjoy the privilege of squatting in Florida. In the cotton and wheat plains of Oklahoma and Texas, where large farmers already used tractors, grain combines, and cotton-picking "strippers," tenants were evicted as early as 1926, as landowners reduced costs. Between 1926 (when the combine became common on the plains) and 1933, an estimated 150,000 wheat harvest hands were eliminated between Texas and the Dakotas. Most of these were single men, but mechanization of cotton in the Southwest affected families, and waves of the dispossessed began to appear as refugees three years before the New Deal produced the same effects farther east. Oklahoma City experienced an invasion of the landless beginning dur-

---

Anne Denkman," n.d. (1938 or 1939) (Typescript in FWP life histories files, SHC). Darsey revealed the couple's actual names in the typescript.

8. Lillian Steadman, "Robert Smith," December 22, 1938 (Typescript in FWP life histories files, SHC).

9. See Barbara Berry Darsey, "Lollie Bleu, Florida Squatter," November 29, 1938, "We Is Victims," February 8, 1939, "Mary Windsor," n.d. (1938 or 1939), and "Marie Gonzales," December 7, 1938 (Typescripts all *ibid.*).

ing the winter of 1930–1931. Failing to find employment in the city, the former tenants gathered in camps of jerry-built shacks on the banks of the North Canadian River on the outskirts of the city. In January 1931 there were about 350 white families living in one camp, which became known as Elk Grove. A smaller number of black families lived in a separate camp known as Sand Town. Oklahoma City police subsequently herded other destitute newcomers into the camps, which became prototypes for similar "okie" ghettoes in California after 1932. Elk Grove and Sand Town were starting places for the journey to the Far West over Route 66 for those with cars and trucks. For others—a population of between fifteen hundred and two thousand through 1940—they were a dead end. Many more displaced Oklahoma tenants—about fifty thousand of them in 1940—fell into a migratory pattern: in winter and early spring they picked vegetables in southern Texas, then moved northward, back as far as Oklahoma, chopping, then picking cotton.[10]

After 1933 other former tenants and sharecroppers flocked into Jackson, Mississippi, into Memphis, Little Rock, and scores of other cities. Local governments and New Deal agencies sustained them in crowded rooming houses and new shantytowns during the winter, but welfare and workfare were usually cut off in spring and fall when planters and farmers in the surrounding countryside needed labor. Then trucks rolled into urban ghettos and loaded inhabitants for work chopping or picking. Local police often assisted in recruitment. Laborers were returned to city homes each evening if they worked close by, but more often they were housed in former tenant cabins, in barns, or in new barracks. Often landlords and their riding bosses locked such laborers in at night, and the Southern Tenant Farmers' Union (headquartered in Memphis) received complaints of peonage—laborers held against their will long after contracted work terms.[11]

Throughout the 1930s, the second half of the 1940s, and the 1950s,

10. See Louise V. Kennedy, *The Negro Peasant Turns Cityward: Effects of Recent Migrations to Northern Centers* (New York, 1930); Robert Higgs, "The Boll Weevil, the Cotton Economy, and Black Migration, 1910–1930," *Agricultural History,* L (April, 1976), 335–50. On Oklahoma and Texas, see Carey McWilliams, *Ill Fares the Land: Migrants and Migratory Labor in the United States* (Boston, 1942), 102–103, 194–96, 205–207.

11. On former tobacco tenants in Wilson County, N.C., see Stanley Combs, "One of Them Might Be President," May 20, 1939 (Typescript in FWP life histories files, SHC). On tenant displacement and day labor in Texas, see McWilliams, *Ill Fares the Land,* 222. On eastern Arkansas and Memphis, see letters and depositions on microfilm rolls 2 and 10, STFU Papers, SHC (*e.g.,* typescript depositions of Henry Rover and Mary E. Hicks, both dated June 23, 1938, roll 2, concerning peonage).

neoplantations were created; the numbers of southern farms, tenants, and croppers plummeted; and the numbers of hired farm workers soared. Day labor was the fate—temporary for most—of the displaced. No one counted farm laborers systematically until the Bureau of the Census finally undertook the task as part of the 1935 agricultural enumeration. This count revealed 751,339 hired laborers in fourteen southern states; but since the count was made in January, it was without doubt grossly low. The 1940 census took place in March, before the heaviest spring chopping time, but still totalled 853,829 hired workers. The wartime 1945 enumeration occurred in January again and yielded only 243,919. In 1950 the census was moved to April, a heavy work time, and produced 724,228 workers. At last, in 1954, the bureau counted hired laborers during fall harvest, and reported the highest figure ever—1,342,745. By 1959, when the bureau again conducted its enumeration in the fall, combines and cotton harvesters were becoming common; yet the census still reported 843,998 hired workers in the region, about the same number as in 1940. Census after census, hired workers were distributed among the states rather evenly. Florida's numbers, for example, were not remarkable, totaling less than Georgia's in most reports. Alabama, Mississippi, and Arkansas also reported comparable numbers most years, although Alabama fell behind the other two states after World War II. Rugged West Virginia never had many. Texas stood out at the other extreme, averaging two to three times the typical average among southern states of about fifty thousand hired farm workers each census.[12] Many Texan workers were probably Mexicans who had never been tenants or sharecroppers, however.

Of these hundreds of thousands of part-time workers, many were not shunted off to urban ghettos right away but remained in the country in tenant cabins or squatted in tents and new shacks or lived in automobiles or trucks. The demographic flux of World War II vastly reduced their numbers, hastened further labor-saving mechanization, and induced many farmers to raze old tenant housing that stood in the way of enlarged, machine-driven operations.[13] By the middle and late 1950s, ap-

12. Regional totals aggregated from state tables in *Census of Agriculture, 1959*, Pts. 24–37, p. 8 each part. (This census report provides data from the 1935 census through 1959.) On methods and times of ennumerations, see *Census of Agriculture, 1954*, Vol. 1: *Counties and State Economic Areas*, Pt. 26—Texas, xvi.

13. See USDA, AAA, "Farm Wage Worker Schedule" series, 1939, (Typescript in University of Arkansas Department of Agricultural Economics and Rural Sociology records, University of Arkansas Library, Fayetteville); letters from displaced tenants, rolls 2 and 10, STFU Papers. On mechanization and housing, see Charles Shelton Aiken,

parently nearly all seasonal farm workers were recruited from among the poor in nearby towns and cities, or they belonged to corps of well-organized migrants who had begun to specialize in harvesting.

Southern-based migratory farm work dates at least to World War I, when southern blacks (mainly Virginians and Marylanders) replaced Italian and Polish immigrants from the Baltimore and Philadelphia areas who had traveled through the Middle Atlantic states harvesting vegetables. During the 1920s, as Florida vegetable and citrus growers ditched their fields and organized markets—and as the boll weevil drove ruined lower South tenants and sharecroppers into the state—the so-called Atlantic Coast Stream of agricultural migrants began to take shape. By 1928 the stream was operative. The flow began (and continues still) in southern Florida. Having wintered in rented shacks near Miami, the migrants started their year in February with early vegetable harvests from Dade County to Lake Okeechobee. Then northward to the next vegetable crops around Hastings, Florida, in early May, and on to Meggett, South Carolina, and Bayboro, North Carolina. By early June they reached the Eastern Shore of Virginia in time to dig potatoes around Exmore, then up to Pocomoke for the Maryland potato crop. Mid-July found the migrants picking green vegetables again, around Freehold, New Jersey; they moved on to Long Island in August. In September many of them continued up to Maine. All returned to southern Florida some time in the fall to rest until the flow began anew before the winter was gone.[14]

The stream's main course and cataracts having been established, internal organization of migrant laborers took shape early, too. In 1933 Congress passed the Wagner-Peyser Act, forming a national employment service for agriculture under supervision of the Department of Labor. Amid massive tenant-sharecropper evictions and crop adjustments across the South, the new agency soon became a means of channeling the dislocated into areas with wage labor needs. The Wagner-Peyser Act also legitimized the functions of crew leaders (also known as freewheelers), who recruited, transported, and managed the migrants. Crew leaders contracted laborers to farmers along the route of the stream, then trucked them to crops at appointed times. Crew leaders

"Transitional Plantation Occupance in Tate County, Mississippi" (M.A. thesis, University of Georgia, 1962), 67–70.

14. Donald Hughes Grubbs, "A History of the Atlantic Coast Stream of Agricultural Migrants" (M.A. thesis, University of Florida, 1959), 4–18; McWilliams, *Ill Fares the Land*, 175–77; Earl Loman Koos, *They Follow the Sun* (Jacksonville, 1957), 1–35.

also usually collected and distributed laborers' pay, deducting charges for transportation, food, and various supplies (often including liquor and drugs). The system's potential for abuse was manifest early. Crew leaders operated like country lien merchants and landlords, commonly overcharging laborers and leaving them with little cash at the end of the working season. They also connived with farmers to hold and work migrants against their will—in effect extending peonage into a new field, just as the gradual death of sharecropping was eliminating the traditional opportunity for enslavement of agricultural labor.[15]

Even with supposed federal supervision, estimates of the numbers of Atlantic Coast Stream migrants through the decades remain at best informed guesses. Carey McWilliams, the Los Angeles–based attorney, writer, and migrant advocate, estimated that during the 1930s and early 1940s there were usually about eight thousand people in the truck "battalions" but that occasionally the stream included as many as fifteen thousand. Many of these people disappeared into military service and war industries during World War II, and contractors shifted to "offshore" sources of labor—especially Jamaicans, Bahamians, and Puerto Ricans. By 1952 the migrant force was dominated by Americans once more. The Department of Labor estimated their numbers at 24,000, mainly native Afro-Americans. Later, an official Florida estimate for the year 1954 reached the figure of 60,000: about 41,000 American blacks, 2,700 American whites, and 16,000 West Indians. Conceivably, the migrant force actually more than doubled during the early 1950s: both new farm machinery and herbicides came into wide use during those years, bringing about enormous labor savings in most agricultural work, except harvesting, and displacing many tenants and stationary workers; and great strides in the marketing and distribution of produce also took place. Several demographic facts about the eastern migrants seem clear, however. Most were southern blacks traveling and working as families. Few were either lifelong migrants or natives of Florida. The Department of Labor study showed that 86 percent of heads of migrant households were former tenants or sharecroppers. Georgia was the most frequently named place of origin; South Carolina was second. Migrants were poorly educated and in ill health, and both conditions became hereditary, for their children were seldom able to complete elementary

15. L. A. Winokur and Chip Hughes, "Workers and the Harvest," *Southern Exposure,* XI (November/December, 1983), 55–61. Labor contractors for lower Mississippi Valley planters early in the century were also deeply involved in peonage. See Pete Daniel, *The Shadow of Slavery: Peonage in the South, 1901–1969* (New York, 1972), 82–109.

school and spent their young lives in grubby housing and beneath pesticide sprays.[16]

Another migrant stream, made up primarily of whites, took shape along the Gulf Coast and up the western side of the Mississippi River. This system began to form about 1922, as "quick chilling" of strawberries and other fruits, and truck and railroad transportation networks to faraway urban markets, came into being. By the early 1930s this stream was fully programmed. The migrant pickers—once more, mainly former tenants and croppers from the lower South—began their journey in northwestern Florida, then followed the shore to Louisiana. Local black pickers dominated the great strawberry operations above New Orleans in Tangipahoa Parish and environs, so the white families traveled on northward to Arkansas, especially to Judsonia in White County, the center for north-central Arkansas strawberry production, and to Benton and Washington counties in northwestern Arkansas, which produced peaches and other fruits as well. From there, migrants moved into Missouri, then eastward into Kentucky, Illinois, Indiana, Ohio, and finally to the Benton Harbor area of Michigan, for the last strawberry harvest. The annual migrant trek covered nearly two thousand miles.[17]

Carey McWilliams estimated that Mississippi Valley strawberry crops alone required approximately 150,000 pickers about 1932. Most of these people doubtless were locals who did not travel with the stream, and many (like the Louisiana pickers) were probably blacks. The Farm Security Administration, which surveyed migrants during 1937–1938, found that those who did follow the stream were mainly young (in their twenties) whites with dependents. Unlike black families in the Atlantic Stream, they traveled in their own battered autos and trucks, apparently without exploitative crew leaders. Their living conditions at work were probably at least as poor as those of East Coast agricultural laborers, however. In Arkansas they were housed in old frame buildings without screens, water, or electricity. Enclosed pits served as privies. Some

16. McWilliams, *Ill Fares the Land,* 175. See Koos, *They Follow the Sun,* 31–47, for the Department of Labor data; Grubbs, "Atlantic Coast Stream," 17–18; Winokur and Hughes, "Workers and the Harvest," on offshore laborers; Florida Legislative Council and Legislative Reference Bureau, *Migrant Farm Labor in Florida* (Tallahassee, 1963), 5, for the Florida data for 1954. McWilliams, *Ill Fares the Land,* 172–73, also reported extremely high rates of syphilis infection among migrant workers in Florida, 1938–41: about half the black vegetable pickers and packers of Belle Glade, above Miami; and in 1941 Public Health Service officials treated 2,000 cases per week among them in Palm Beach County.

17. McWilliams, *Ill Fares the Land,* 148–56. See also USDA, AAA, "Farm Wage Worker" series, for Hempstead, Benton, and Washington counties, Arkansas.

lived in barns. One large family was lodged in a Washington County chicken house. Others lived in their cars, in tents, or slept under the stars. By 1939, according to Agricultural Adjustment Administration studies, migrants hailed not only from the lower South but from Tennessee, Arkansas, eastern Oklahoma, Texas, Missouri, Kansas, Illinois, and even Arizona.[18]

The near abandonment of tenancy and sharecropping on the plantations on the lower Mississippi Valley both augmented and changed this central migratory stream. The fate of the thousands of evicted southeastern Missouri sharecroppers—nearly all of them black—who staged the famous "roadside demonstration" is illustrative. The Farm Security Administration settled many of the demonstrators in a camp nearby. Others drifted into St. Louis and other cities. By the early 1940s, however, a study of migratory cherry pickers in Michigan revealed that 60 percent hailed from southeastern Missouri. And while former cotton croppers left to pick berries, peaches, and cherries, folks from as far away as Texas and Mexico and as near as Mississippi and Tennessee began to arrive in Arkansas and southeastern Missouri to pick cotton. They included displaced white and black southern farmers and Mexican laborers who, beginning in 1937, were extending their established migratory trek northward. The mechanization of the cotton harvest (or the abandonment of cotton) would erase part of this complex stream after World War II. White families would almost disappear, too, along with much of the lower Mississippi Valley strawberry crop (which succumbed during the 1950s to California competition). By the 1960s, what remained of the central stream would be, like the West Coast Stream, largely Hispanic.[19]

The most important intra-South migrations were the ones directed toward towns and cities. Larger southern cities gained astoundingly in both population and area between 1900 and 1930. Atlanta, for example, grew from 179,420 to 440,906; Birmingham from 140,420 to 431,493. Knoxville and Nashville passed 200,000; Memphis topped 300,000. Memphis doubled in area, Atlanta tripled, and Birmingham increased

18. McWilliams, *Ill Fares the Land,* 152–56; USDA, AAA "Farm Wage Worker" series.
19. See Louis Cantor, *Prologue to the Protest Movement: The Missouri Sharecropper Roadside Demonstrations of 1939* (Durham, N.C., 1969); Missouri demonstrations materials, roll 10, STFU Papers. The Michigan study is cited in McWilliams, *Ill Fares the Land,* 283. On Mexicans in Missouri and the effects of mechanization, see T. H. McConnell to H. L. Mitchell, n.d. (*ca.* August 28, 1937), roll 5, STFU Papers; Winokur and Hughes, "Workers and the Harvest."

about ten times. Small industrial places, from coal camps in Appalachia to mill villages in the piedmonts, appeared and grew, too. A few foreigners and a larger number of Yankees helped swell southern towns and cities, but the greatest part of the increase derived from the southern countryside. In the larger cities, proportionately more newcomers were white, too, for in 1930 most populations were somewhat whiter than they had been in 1900. Although many rural blacks came to southern cities before continuing north, before World War II industrial jobs (especially in textiles) were closed to them; so the urban South fed particularly upon young white migrants from farms.[20]

Blacks had three significant southern opportunities for nonfarm work before 1930. Two possibilities were the coal mines of Alabama and southern West Virginia and the tobacco warehouses and factories of Virginia and North Carolina. Between about 1900 and 1915 West Virginia coal company recruiters lured black men from as near as Virginia and as far away as the lower South cotton areas. Men from the Deep South were sometimes transported in sealed train cars to prevent other employers from enticing them elsewhere and perhaps to discourage migrants from changing their minds. The cars disgorged them upon company-owned towns, where travel expenses were deducted from their wages. Once settled in West Virginia, however, blacks discovered their employers (mostly nonsoutherners) cared less about color than efficiency and production. So black men did well, often receiving promotions, higher pay, and relative security for their families. As the coal industry became troubled, however (especially during the 1920s), all miners became more mobile than ever; and there is some evidence that blacks moved more often than whites, reversing the rule of mobility among cotton tenants farther south.[21] Black migration to the tobacco towns appears to have been short-range: piedmont families moved at most a hundred miles, usually much less, to Richmond, Petersburg, Durham, Raleigh, Wilson, and so on. The tobacco companies did not

20. Blaine A. Brownell, *The Urban Ethos in the South, 1920–1930* (Baton Rouge, 1975), 12–16 and *passim;* Daniel M. Johnson and Rex R. Campbell, *Black Migration in America: A Social Demographic History* (Durham, N.C., 1981), 71–89; Pope, *Millhands and Preachers,* x, 12–13; USDA, BAE, "Rural-Urban Migration in North Carolina, 1920 to 1930," by C. Horace Hamilton (Typescript, 60 pages, with tables, October, 1933, RG 83, NA). See also Allen Tullos, interview with Jessie Lee Carter, May 5, 1980, Mary Fredrickson and Brent Glass, interview with Flossie Moore Durham, September 2, 1976 (Both typescripts in the Southern Oral History Program, SHC [SOHP]), on racial exclusion at the Bynum, N.C., mill, where blacks did not hold "inside" jobs until 1971.

21. David Alan Corbin, *Life, Work, and Rebellion in the Coal Fields: The Southern West Virginia Miners, 1880–1922* (Urbana, 1981), 40–41, 61–67.

provide housing. Theirs was an old enterprise, always located in easily expandable cities. So migrants settled into crowded, established black neighborhoods, where there was little or no room for gardens, livestock, or the other requisites of living at home. The warehouses and factories employed men and women of both races and rigorously discriminated against blacks. They might load boxes or baskets of tobacco, sweep floors, sort tobacco, or work as "stemmers," performing the dirty, tedious task of stripping leaves from stems at the beginning of the manufacturing process. White men and women were stemmers, too, but they usually worked in separate areas of factories, and their efforts could win them cleaner jobs and promotions.[22]

The third opportunity available to blacks was a perverse one. Poor whites who left tenant and sharecrop farms made sufficient weekly cash in mills to hire black women to do their washing and, sometimes, to provide day care for children while both parents worked. In Bynum, North Carolina, during the 1910s, according to a white woman, "you could get a nigger to work for you a month for five dollars." By the 1930s "cleaning help" cost about five dollars per week, loads of washing 25 cents each.[23] Another North Carolina mill worker paid a black woman only four dollars per week for child care in 1939. And in Greenville, South Carolina, though white mill women usually cooked for their own families, black women "always" did the washing. Whites who reported such domestic services seem never to have inquired about their servants' origins and situations. They were merely available—to the working mother, to the expectant mother in need of a midwife, to the widower in need of a surrogate mother for his children.[24] Many of these black women may well have been migrants themselves, and considering

22. See the "Durham" collection of interviews, SOHP. The typescript interview with Mary Bailey, January 26, 1979, provides an excellent view of black life and work in Durham and at the Liggett and Myers factory, *ca.* 1912–40. Stemmers of both races earned lower wages than textiles mill workers, too. Durham and Winston-Salem tobacco workers averaged only $14.50 (for men) and $9.00 (for women) per week about 1929. North Carolina textiles workers averaged $17.19 (men) and $14.06 (women) about the same time. See typescript notes for interview with Hallie Caesar, May 21, 1979 (SOHP), on tobacco; Rupert B. Vance, *Human Geography of the South: A Study in Regional Resources and Human Adequacy* (Chapel Hill, 1932), 293, on textiles.

23. Frederickson and Glass, interview with Durham.

24. Ethel Deal, life history of Rosa Kanipe, June 29, 1939 (Typescript in FWP life histories files, SHC); Allen Tullos, interview with Myrtle Spencer Cleveland, October 22, 1979 (Typescript in SOHP). See also I. L. M. [Ida L. Moore], "May Is a Lonesome Time," March 25, 1939 (Typescript in FWP life histories files, SHC). Valerie Quinney, interview with Mrs. Wade Bland,'April 17, 1974 (Typescript in SOHP), relates cases of women as midwives and a day-care provider for a white widower's children.

the high incidence of reported single-adult households among rural blacks, they may well have been the sole providers for their own families.

Whether they were recruited to distant mines or factories or appeared in towns on their own initiative, blacks and whites alike often migrated in the "stem-family" pattern first described in Europe and among trans-atlantic migrants. One or two members of a family would pioneer settlement in a mine or mill town and establish employment and housing, forming a branch capable of supporting additional newcomers. The way prepared, other branches from the "stem" followed, often along with new branches from other families in the base community. Ultimately, entire families—stems and all—resettled, and the old community was much diminished or abandoned.[25] The peopling of piedmont mill towns and cities provides many examples and variations of the stem-family pattern of resettlement and renewal as well as the pathos of family and community disintegration.

Piedmont migrants seldom traveled far for industrial employment. Most seem to have been natives of the piedmont itself—small farm owners, share tenants, and sharecroppers who had grown corn, tobacco, and cotton. They usually moved within their native states, but the great mills of Greensboro and Burlington attracted a great many piedmont Virginians from Halifax, Henry, Carroll, Floyd, and Pittsylvania counties; and South Carolinians flocked to Charlotte and other North Carolina cities, too. Appalachian highlanders were the second most common migrants to the mills and factories. Southern West Virginians, western North Carolinians, and eastern Tennesseans usually, they commonly settled in towns such as Martinsville and Danville, Virginia; Burlington, Winston-Salem, Hendersonville, and Gastonia, North Carolina; and Spartanburg, Greenville, and Anderson, South Carolina—all in the western piedmont and relatively close to their origins. Before World War I highland migrants appear to have been farming families. Later they seem just as often to have had other industrial experiences, such as mining coal.[26]

25. The mode is described in Harry K. Schwarzweller, James S. Brown, and J. J. Mangalam, *Mountain Families in Transition: A Case Study of Appalachian Migration* (University Park, Penn., 1971), 96–97 and *passim*.

26. The sources of piedmont industrial labor are surmised from approximately 250 typescript interviews and indexes/summaries of audio tape interviews in the "Piedmont Social History Project" (1976–80), SOHP; and about two dozen FWP life histories (1938–39), SHC. The procedure is admittedly impressionistic, but in that most interviewees described migrations, and many also described family and neighbors' moves as well, the sample is a respectable one, considering that the federal censuses do not enumerate intrastate or rural-to-urban migrants. David L. Carlton, in *Mill and Town in*

For many southerners, going to work in a town merely meant daily commuting. In 1928 a Raleigh man, an official of the North Carolina Cotton Growers Co-operative Association, wrote: "Through the Piedmont section I find that a large percent of those living on the farm are working in the cotton mill, some growing a few bales of cotton on the side and depending on their wages from the cotton mill for their main support." [27] A decade later, seven miles west of Durham, there lived a family of eleven who successfully cash-rented a three-hundred-acre farm because of the proximity of a mill. The father and a teenaged son cleaned looms by day while the mother and older daughters kept small children and maintained a large garden. Evenings and weekends they worked a five-acre tobacco field for more cash, and raised corn and small grains to feed their two mules and two milk cows. Other families remained on farms and sent willing children to nearby mills during the day. A Chatham County brother and sister began to commute to the cotton mill at Bynum (near Pittsboro) during the 1910s. Their parents stayed home to garden and grow cotton, as did other young workers' elders. Later the girl moved permanently (as a single woman) to the Bynum mill village. Her family did not follow, but many former rural neighbors did, finally regrouping extended branches and stems. A Catawba County, North Carolina, boy began work in a glove factory during summers, beginning about 1930. One of a family of eight children on a dairy farm, he helped his family and avoided hot, disagreeable outside work when not in school. Later, however, when his father was obliged to sell the farm, he became a full-time hand—a mechanic, a supervisor, and finally owner of small mills in Conover. Yet for all the disruption of a move from farm to town, the boy was prepared gradually, and the man spent his entire life in one county. [28]

Children and adults, in fact, often found towns and mills alluring. A Catawba woman recalled her bitterness when (during the 1920s) her father, who disliked work in a Hickory mill, moved the family back to the

---

South Carolina, 1880–1920 (Baton Rouge, 1982), 146–49, confirms that migrants to S.C. mills came from the rural piedmont and the mountains, but his research is based only upon piedmont townspeople's impressions. Pope, in *Millhands and Preachers*, 9–10, confirms from a 1914 survey that the first Gaston County, N.C., millhands "came from counties immediately bordering Gaston," then primarily from the mountains to the west.

27. S. P. Jones to Howard W. Odum, April 23, 1928, Howard W. Odum Papers, SHC.

28. W. O. Saunders, "Sycamore Hill," n.d. (1938 or 1939) (Typescript in FWP life histories files, *ibid.*); Kennette Nowell, interview with Mary Council, November 1, 1978 (Typescript of tape index), Jacqueline Hall, interview with Fred Fox, December 15, 1979, (Typescript), both in SOHP.

country. "Us young'uns didn't like being in the country." She particularly hated the rural school; she complained about it and finally quit altogether. So the father gave in and the family returned to Hickory.[29] Although factory hours were long and most work tedious, the mills and mill villages offered sociability as well as cash wages. "I enjoyed the mill work more than anything I have ever done," said a Huntersville, North Carolina, woman during the 1930s. "I enjoyed being with other people and it was so much better than having to work out in the hot sun in the fields."[30] Mill hands may have been disparaged as "lint heads" by the middle and upper classes, but to poor and ambitious farm folk, including young children, the mills meant advancement, often without loss of home and family. Another Catawba woman, for example, reflected on her girlhood: "I wanted to get a job at public works where I'd have a little future and make a little more money." So her grandfather spoke to a supervisor at the Ridgeview Hosiery Mill, and she began work. Because Ridgeview was near her farm home, she lived with her family until she married, then began her own family in town.[31] Thus for some migrants, extended families included both mill hands and farmers, all fortunate enough to remain physically close. For them there was not so much a stem-pattern migration as a mere enlargement of family and community into nearby industrial centers.

Yet another western North Carolina farm-owning family followed the stem pattern, gradually, to a Newton (Catawba County) mill. About 1915 two daughters left for Newton. Too far from home to commute, they boarded with a lady in town. Later the remaining family sold the farm and followed, buying land in Newton and building their own house with proceeds from the sale. A cow, hogs, and chickens came along to help feed them. In 1939 the mother declared they were satisfied: "we prospered in the mill. . . . we own this home, about sixteen acres of ground, and several lots scattered around." The children were still in Newton, the parents having helped them acquire their own homes.[32] Many sharecroppers and tenants (though they seldom moved in such security) also managed to move short distances gradually, in the stem-family mode. The Glenn family, sharecroppers of Alamance County, North Carolina, for example, ran afoul of plummeting tobacco prices

29. Jacqueline Hall and Patty Dilley, interviews with Mareda Sigmon Cobb and Carrie Sigmon Yelton, June 16, 18, 1979, SOHP.

30. Mary Wilson, "Married to a Sorry Man," life history of Catherine Jones, June 19, 1939 (Typescript in FWP life histories files, SHC).

31. Jacqueline Hall, interview with Eunice Austin, July 2, 1980 (Typescript in SOHP).

32. Deal, life history of Kanipe.

and crop reductions during the early 1930s. So one or two members of the family went off to nearby Burlington for part-time mill work while the rest made little crops. After a few years the entire family moved to company housing in Burlington. It was "common," recalled the wife-mother, for croppers "to go gradually." A Wilkes County (Appalachian) family of share tenants represents the classic stem-family mode. A neighbor had taken work in Charlotte. Returning home for a visit, he reported the availability of more jobs at his mill. Young men, including J. M. Robinette, followed him back to Charlotte. Then gradually much of the rest of the Robinette family sold their farming equipment and moved, along with other Wilkes County neighbors.[33]

Earlier in the century, mountain neighborhoods moved longer distances in response to traveling recruiters for piedmont mills. About 1905 an agent from the Brandon Mill of Greenville, South Carolina, scoured the country around Newport, Tennessee. Entire families pulled up stakes, loaded their belongings in wagons, and walked with their cows and hogs to Greenville. Once such piedmont connections were made, other highland families followed, ultimately recreating parts, at least, of old farming communities in the mill towns.[34]

Piedmont migration also presents some complex odysseys. Harry Adams, for instance, was born on a Halifax County, Virginia, tobacco farm in 1908. As a boy he left to work in a South Boston machine shop, making buggies, then to weaving in a cotton mill. When his father died he returned to the family farm, but after tobacco prices fell in 1929 he returned to weaving. When he was laid off, Adams farmed again, only briefly, until he found another weaving job in Danville. There he was fired for his union activities. Finally Adams made his way down to Burlington, a magnet for piedmont farmers and mill hands alike, even in 1933, for its mills specialized in the seamed "full-fashioned" hosiery that sold well despite the Depression. In Burlington, Adams became the pioneer branch for his Halifax family, most of whom ultimately joined him. Part of a Pittsylvania County, Virginia, family made their way to Burlington by another route. During the late 1920s the eldest of a farm family of seven girls bravely struck out on her own to find work in the

33. Cliff Kuhn, interview with Mrs. Howard K. Glenn, July 27, 1977 (Typescript in SOHP). See Kuhn, interview with J. M. Robinette, July, 1977 (typescript, *ibid.*), on the Wilkes-Charlotte migration.

34. Tullos, interview with Carter. See also Allen Tullos, interview with Paul Cline, November 8, 1979 (Typescript in SOHP), on a Newport-Spartanburg (Arcadia Mills) connection.

north-central Carolina textiles belt. She succeeded, then married a Reidsville man and moved to Burlington. Within a few years two of her sisters met mill workers while visiting, married them, and also settled in Burlington. Almost half a century later the three sisters still lived in the same neighborhood.[35]

Perhaps just as often (one cannot be certain), migration to piedmont towns was occasioned by tragedy. Families and old neighborhoods were not recreated elsewhere but simply shattered, or individuals and families never settled comfortably. Widowhood could produce such pathos. During the mid-1910s a Tennessee woman struggled for two years with farming after her husband's death. She took in others' washing for twenty-five to thirty cents per day, and as her son recalled, "she'd have to hoe corn two or three days for somebody, to get them to plow for her one [day]." Exhausted, she quit Tennessee for the Woodside Mills of Greenville, South Carolina. There she worked all day while her son, then eight years old, watched the younger children.[36] The young, fatherless family apparently came to Greenville alone. A complete family from western North Carolina came to Greenville in 1915 because, as a daughter remembered, some unspecified farming disaster had befallen them. "That's why we came," she said. Her parents "would have preferred to stay on the farm, but you've heard of famines in the Bible. It was kind of like that."[37] Other families moved so often and to so many places that it seems impossible for them to have maintained contact with other relatives or old neighbors. Icy Norman's family, for example, were mining coal near Welch, West Virginia, just before American entry into World War I. By about 1918 they were textiles hands in the Danville, Virginia, area; and by the early 1930s they were in Burlington. In the meantime there were no fewer than three attempts at farming in Virginia and West Virginia. The J. W. Prosser family of northeastern South Carolina were also hard-luck itinerants who must have lost contact with their relatives and original community. Married before World War I, Prosser was a blacksmith. When his shop burned he turned to sharecropping tobacco. The second year was a wet one; his tobacco scaled and he made

35. Allen Tullos, tape index and notes for interview with Harry and Janie Adams, May 11, 1979, Mary Murphy, interview with Edward and Mary Harrington, February 28, 1979 (Typescripts both in SOHP). On Burlington's relative prosperity in 1933, see Murphy, interview with Carroll Lupton, M.D., May 18, 1979 (Typescript, *ibid.*).

36. Allen Tullos, interview with Grover Hardin, March 25, 1980 (Typescript, *ibid.*).

37. Allen Tullos, interview with Paul and Pauline Griffith, March 30, 1980 (Typescript, *ibid.*).

no money. There were by that time four young children, so the Prossers moved to a cotton mill in Darlington where Prosser worked for ten cents an hour. Between 1922 and 1926, he recalled, "We'd sharecrop for a while, and then we'd rent. I'd work at a sawmill, and then blacksmith again." At last they "settled down and come to Columbia" and mill work once more, which after a decade of moving represented stability.[38] Most mills, however, were in such economic and labor turmoil during much of the 1920s and 1930s that many families were unable to settle— or to remain together. Frances Medlin and her siblings, for example, were raised by her mother's parents in Carrboro, North Carolina, while her mother and father moved all over North Carolina, working in one mill after another. "A whole lot of Daddy's people I never knew," she remembered. "I don't even recall ever meeting some of my cousins. . . . It's the same way with the rest of the family. We don't know them. We just got away . . . and it was so far to travel."[39]

Yet other itinerants regarded farming as the ultimate refuge, and worked in mills only as a means of returning to the country. About 1939 a Greensboro woman in her sixties, who had worked in the mills all her life, declared: "When they get through with me down yonder [at the mill] I've got a home to go to. One hundred and sixty-eight acres of land bought and paid for, and I've got the lumber already sawed to build me a house with." It was her parents' "old home place down in Randolph County" below Greensboro. Whether she would actually leave her grandchildren in Greensboro and return to the country at her age is unknown. But her pathetic discontent with city life and labor and her yearning for rural community and old roots were not uncommon.[40]

Writing about industrialization in *The Mind of the South,* W. J. Cash declared that "the *plantation* remained the single great basic social and economic pattern of the South. . . . For when we sound the matter, that is exactly what the Southern factory almost invariably was: a plantation, essentially indistinguishable in organization from the familiar

38. Mary Murphy, tape index, notes, and life history form for interviews with Icy Norman, April 6, 30, 1979 (Typescript, *ibid.*); Mattie T. Jones, "Ain't It So, Corrie?" life history of John William Prosser, February 6, 1939 (Typescript in FWP life histories files, SHC).

39. Valerie Quinney, interview with Frances Medlin Albright, August 24, 1975 (Typescript in SOHP).

40. Quotation from Ida L. Moore, "Almeda Brady," n.d. (1938 or 1939) (Typescript in FWP life histories files, SHC). Other variations of discontented urban workers are represented in Ida L. Moore, "When a Man Believes," life history of James Evans, February, 1939 (Typescript, *ibid.*); Cliff Kuhn, interview with Alice Copeland, June 29, 1977, Rosemarie Hester, interview with T. J. Cotton, June 17, 1977 (Typescripts both in SOHP).

plantation of the cotton fields."[41] What Cash referred to in particular was the physical and political organization of cotton mill villages and other industrial plants and towns. Beginning with William Gregg's pre–Civil War model mill at Graniteville, South Carolina, southern industrialists had built their mills in unincorporated rural areas; surrounded them with company-owned housing, churches, schools, and other social facilities; and invited lower-class rural whites to come and work and live under the entrepreneurs' terms. Sharecropper and tenant families who had farmed as families, arrived at the mills as working families. In the nineteenth and early twentieth centuries children as young as six went into the mills. The most paternalistic of the mill men, however, from Gregg himself to B. B. Comer of Alabama during the early twentieth century, saw to workers' welfare. Children received time off for elementary schooling, all were encouraged to attend church services conducted by ministers paid by the mill men, housing was kept clean and in good repair, and sometimes medical and recreational programs were instituted as well. Operatives worked sixty-hour weeks on the average. Many received their pay in company script, redeemable in goods at the company store. When workers got out of line—or sought to organize unions—they were dealt with by company police, who always had the cooperation of county sheriffs. Mill owners and managers were thus as much lords of this industrial creation as planter-landlords were in their black belt and delta domains.[42]

As we have already seen, too, many Appalachian coal towns were organized similarly. One of the most self-consciously paternalistic of coal operators was Major William P. Tams. Born in Staunton, Virginia, in 1883 and trained as an engineer, Tams began to mine the great Beckley, West Virginia, coal seam in 1908. Southwest of the town of Beckley he built the village of Tams—about two hundred houses, a church and school. Workers were native whites and blacks and immigrants, almost a microcosm of the southern West Virginia coal boom mining population. Like entrepreneurs everywhere else, Tams abominated unions and even reduced his workday to nine hours and increased pay somewhat above union scale to avoid having to share his power with the United Mine Workers. (He finally accepted the UMW during the 1930s.) As a

41. W. J. Cash, *The Mind of the South* (New York, 1941), 205. A similar argument in a neo-Marxist framework is elaborated in Dwight B. Billings, Jr., *Planters and the Making of a "New South": Class, Politics, and Development in North Carolina, 1865–1900* (Chapel Hill, 1979).

42. Pope, *Millhands and Preachers*, 16–20 and *passim*.

very old man Major Tams declared that he had become a coal operator to perform public service, to help and care for people. Yankee operators were not so involved in miners' personal lives and welfare, Tams reflected, as he and his fellow southern businessmen had been.[43]

That many southern industrialists self-consciously patterned their enterprises after plantations is obvious. B. B. Comer of Alabama was and remained a planter-landlord while founding Avondale, Cowikee, and other mills. And Major Tams, a privileged native of the Valley of Virginia, was a sort of missionary for Old South idealism. Yet too much can be made of the plantation analogy. A better term is welfare capitalism. This sort of paternalism began soon after the industrialization of Britain got underway. Samuel Slater, "Father of American Manufactures," established a school and Sunday school for boy workers at his Pawtucket, Rhode Island, mill in the 1790s, following the English industrial rather than the southern plantation model. New England and other northern manufacturers persisted in some form of welfarism, too. By 1900 welfare capitalism had become a national movement, reaching a peak during the 1920s. Everywhere, twentieth-century welfare capitalism had more to do with discouraging unionization than keeping alive some romantic notion of the Old South.[44]

In actuality, too, southern workers' communities, pay, and relationships with authority varied much more than Cash allowed, both from industry to industry and within industries. Many coal miners and textiles mill hands (as we have seen) never lived in company towns or received pay in scrip but commuted to work from farm homes beyond the bosses' reach and took cash wages with them to spend on themselves and their own property. Urban tobacco warehouses and factories, too, lacked company housing and the guiding hand of the paternalist. By the 1930s (and probably before, as well), tobacco factories did not employ entire families, including children, either. A former eastern North Carolina sharecropper complained bitterly of his lot as a stemmer in Wilson, where only his eldest boy (apparently a teenager) had found work, and that in a poolroom rather than a factory. In lumber work (the South's most important industrial employer after textiles), most laborers were poor rural folk who farmed on shares part of the year and did public work at sawmills during the winter. Other lumber workers, however,

43. Ron Eller, interview with Major William P. Tams, Jr., March 8, 1975 (Typescript in SOHP).

44. See Stuart D. Brandes, *American Welfare Capitalism, 1880–1940* (Chicago, 1976), 10–11 and *passim*.

dwelled in corporate towns such as Kirbyville in eastern Texas, were paid in scrip, and traded at company stores where prices were marked up comparably to those in plantation commissaries. Company stores were more common in lumber company towns than in textiles mill villages. Company-owned towns, stores, and elaborate private welfare systems declined rapidly after about 1925, however. Textiles managers, in particular, came to regard them as too expensive, and workers said they preferred the equivalent of social services in wages.[45]

Some industrial "plantations" survived well into the 1930s. The Comer family continued to preside as before over several mills. And in Birmingham, the U.S. Steel corporation operated perhaps the most unusual workers' settlement of all, Docena. Docena had been created by southern managers when the Tennessee Coal, Iron, and Railroad Company owned the steel mills. Following the U.S. Steel takeover in 1907, social welfare professionals administered in detail most aspects of village life—housing, schools, churches, medical care, and well-organized athletic and recreational programs. Yankee managers thus modernized southern paternalism. U.S. Steel was not so modern as to pay workers in cash, however. They received instead copper coins called "clacker" (or "clackers") stamped with the company emblem in various denominations. The equivalent of eastern Arkansas plantation "bronzene," clacker was redeemable at the Docena store or could be exchanged (about 1920) for United States currency at eighty cents on the dollar.[46] Whether or not they lived under surveillance on company-owned property, many farm-to-mill and farm-to-mine migrants found comfort and

45. See Combs, "One of Them Might Be President"; George B. Tindall, *The Emergence of the New South, 1913–1945* (Baton Rouge, 1967), 326, 329–30; Baynard Kendrick, "Florida's Perpetual Forests" (Typescript, 1967, in University of Florida Library); Wayne Greenhaw, "Echoes of Change in the South's Backwoods: Woodcutters Organize," *Southern Changes,* III (December, 1980), 16–19, 22; Lawrence F. Evans, "Sam, the Turpentine Chopper," September 21, 1938, R. V. Waldrep, "The Andrew Jackson of Southern Labor," 1939 (Typescripts both in FWP life histories files, SHC); oral history of Emmett R. Conerly, August 30, 1977 (Audio tape), oral history of Lawrence Thompson Wade, December 30, 1977 (typescript), both in Mississippi Department of Archives and History, Jackson—all on corporate lumbering; Theodore Rosengarten, *All God's Dangers: The Life of Nate Shaw* (New York, 1975), 182, 184, and *passim,* on freelance, part-time lumbering by a farmer; Harriet L. Herring, *The Passing of the Mill Village: Revolution in a Southern Institution* (Chapel Hill, 1929); Tindall, *Emergence of the New South,* 327.

46. See the thirteen Docena Project typescript interviews in the Samford University Oral History Program, Birmingham; N. S. MacDonald, "If I Had My Life to Live Over Again," life history of Sam Brakefield, n.d. (1938 or 1939) (Typescript in Alabama Writers' Project files, Alabama Department of Archives and History, Montgomery), which relates the "clacker" exchange rate.

much that was familiar when they settled in towns. First (as observed already) was the presence of family and former rural neighbors. Those who had been tenants and sharecroppers were accustomed to living in rented quarters, too, even though few country folk had ever dwelled in the close proximity of mill and mine housing. The mill work itself was least familiar—always inside in hot, humid rooms, and it went on all week, all year, changing weather notwithstanding, without cycle or variety. Mining coal from slopes was not unfamiliar to mountaineers. Nor was lumber work to any rural southerner. Yet the sociability of village and city work and life seems to have been more than adequate compensation for many if not most migrants, no matter how unfamiliar, boring, or difficult their work. Most also enjoyed an important transitional buffer as they settled into village or town life: they brought animals with them, planted gardens, and lived at home.

In southern West Virginia during the difficult 1920s, for example, probably at least two-thirds of coal-mining families—most of whom lived in company housing and many of whom were paid in scrip—kept cows, hogs, chickens, and substantial gardens. Living at home reduced families' dependence on company stores and tided them over frequent work stoppages, when there was no pay. Many gardens measured an acre and more. Some were in steep backyards, others in meadows away from the coal camps. Women and girls preserved vegetables for winter by drying or canning, crucial work in huge mountain families with unreliable cash incomes. Keeping animals and gardens also preserved familiar contacts and part, at least, of the sustaining rural culture.[47]

Piedmont textiles mill villages, usually built in rural areas, typically had space for gardens and animals, and company owners and managers usually encouraged tenants in company housing to live at home. Migrants able to rent or buy their own property near mills invariably brought milk cows, hogs, and chickens, too, and planted their large gardens in the spring. At "Company Hill" in Burlington, at the Durham Hosiery Mill, in Carrboro, Bynum, and elsewhere in North Carolina, and at the Woodside, Brandon, Poe, and Judson mill villages around Greenville, South Carolina, workers milked, slaughtered, and harvested most of their food on company property. Some had brought animals with them from their farms, from early in the century into the 1950s.

47. Corbin, *Life, Work, and Rebellion*, 33–34; oral history of Frank Brooks, n.d. (*ca.* 1974), Anna Laura Kovich, oral history of Joseph Anderson Kovich, n.d. (*ca.* 1975), Patty Clark, oral history of William T. Arnold, n.d. (*ca.* 1974) (Microfilmed typescripts in Marshall University Oral History of Appalachia Collection [MUOHA]).

Others, often former sharecroppers, earned cash in the mills and acquired the wherewithal to live at home for the first time in their lives. In some mill villages each family had sufficient room on rental property for gardens and cow, hog, and chicken lots. In others there were centralized pastures, somewhat like early New England or English commons, where all animals were maintained. "So, in a way," as a surprised young interviewer remarked to a former Carrboro mill hand, "you didn't leave the farm entirely." The same conditions prevailed at the southwestern end of the textiles crescent, in Alabama. The Comer family encouraged living at home among workers at Avondale Mills. And at Comer's Cowikee Mill village in Eufala, the company provided a free pasture, and virtually all mill families—whether they lived in the village or not—kept gardens and chickens.[48]

When migrants found space close to work too narrow for their truck gardening, they settled in semirural working-class suburbs. The Dan River Mills area of Danville, Virginia, was too crowded for some former farmers, who decided to live and raise extensive gardens in Schoolfield instead. By the 1940s, when possession of automobiles made commuting convenient, this phenomenon seems to have become common throughout the South. Former tobacco farmers from northeastern North Carolina and a great many Virginia and West Virginia mountaineers flooded into Portsmouth, Virginia, and environs during the 1940s and 1950s. They sought work in the Norfolk Naval Shipyard or at the Seaboard Air Line Railroad's northern terminal yard. Black migrants crowded into the established ghetto, but many white newcomers settled beyond the western and southern fringes of the city in Norfolk County. There they planted fields of corn, sweet potatoes, and other vegetables, and kept cows, hogs, chickens, and large numbers of dogs for winter racoon hunting in the Dismal Swamp nearby. During the 1950s Ports-

48. Quotation from Valerie Quinney, interview with Mrs. Wade Bland. See also Douglas DeNatale, interview with Mary Gattis, August 13, 1979 (Typescript tape index and notes), Allen Tullos, interviews with Ethel M. Faucette, November 16, 1978, January 4, 1979; Mary Murphy, interview with Fannie Marcom, July 17, 1979 (tape index and notes), Lanier Rand, interview with Luther Riley, July, 1977, Allen Tullos, interview with Geddes Elam Dodson, May 26, 1980, Tullos, interview with Paul and Pauline Griffith, all in SOHP. See Ida L. Moore, "John Pierce," September, 1938, (Typescript in FWP life histories files, SHC), which describes the Royal Cotton Mill's "hogpen lane" at Wake Forest. On Alabama, see Gertha Couric, "The Jim Bittingers—Cotton Mill Workers," in James Seay Brown (ed.), *Up Before Daylight: Life Histories from the Alabama Writers' Project, 1938–1939* (University, Ala., 1982), 155–57 (on Avondale); and Couric, life histories of the Alsocrock, Anderson, and Hughes families (of Eufala), n.d. (1938 or 1939) (Typescripts in FWP life histories files, SHC).

mouth's boundaries expanded, Norfolk County disappeared, property values and taxes increased, and urban zoning laws forbade farm animals. In the meantime, however, rural folk had eased their way into city life with familiar ways and creatures.[49]

Another compensation to migrants was the impetus mill villages and factory towns gave to recreation and sports. Scholars have only recently begun to address this subject in systematic fashion, and much remains to be learned. Of the contrast between the activities of poor rural folk and townspeople, however, a pattern seems rather clear. Scattered farmers went to town on Saturdays, played cards and checkers on courthouse squares and in country stores, hunted and fished, bred and fought gamecocks, and in many (but not all) places supported and played baseball. Radio broadcasts of games came to augment newspapers in promoting enthusiasm for major league and regional teams. But until high schools became common—not until the late 1920s and 1930s in many parts of the South—organization of baseball and other team sports was sporadic and rather weak. Cockfighting may well have generated more interest and participation than did baseball. For most ordinary southerners, recreation was merely visiting. Women gathered to share such work as quilting. Men loafed on rainy days at their "poor farmers' clubs"—stores and filling stations. The propinquity of mill villages and towns, however, naturally promoted organization of group activities and team sports. And for better or worse, southerners' now legendary athletic enthusiasms seem to have been unleashed by urbanization.[50]

When the Columbia University anthropologist Frank Tannenbaum studied the South's "darker phases" early in the 1920s, he found an appalling lack of recreational activities among farmers in the tobacco and cotton belts. In one unspecified North Carolina locality Tannenbaum discovered that more than 70 percent of the inhabitants had not attended a single party or public meeting in an entire year; more than 80 percent had neither attended nor participated in an athletic event, and more than 90 percent had not been to a dance.[51] Tannenbaum apparently did not

49. See Mary Murphy, interview with Stella Foust Carden, April 25, 1979 (Typescript in SOHP). Having been born in Portsmouth in 1938 and raised on what was the western fringe of the city, I participated in what is described. It might also be noted that a few migrants living in the midst of large cities also managed partly to live at home. During the 1930s an Atlanta autoworker had a deep lot near the Chevrolet plant, where he pastured a cow and calf and kept chickens. See Jacques Upshaw, "The Family of an Auto Worker," n.d. (1938 or 1939) (Typescript in FWP life histories files, SHC).

50. Generalizations are based upon reading of the FWP life histories files and sources cited below.

51. Frank Tannenbaum, *Darker Phases of the South* (New York, 1924), 139–140.

inquire about hunting, fishing, unorganized visiting, or cockfighting. Yet his doleful portrait may have been largely true. Late in the 1930s a white North Carolina tobacco-cotton-corn farmer recalled the privations along his family's road upward from sharecropping: "During those years of struggle we had very little recreation. Church and Sunday school and reading, that's practically all. Of course, we did visit occasionally." Their only treats were local fairs. Later, when they had acquired their own farm, the family attended the state fair. The farmer's wife had taken their daughters to movies in town a few times, but he had never seen one.[52] As North Carolina schools were consolidated and as many large landholders withdrew to towns, leisure and recreation for those remaining suffered with the rest of organized existence. At the end of the 1930s a fifty-three-year-old white farmer in Seaboard (Northampton County) bemoaned the loss of community amenities: "Folks has got to leave the neighborhood these days to look for a good time." He regretted especially the decline of congenial visiting, "ice cream suppers and singin's and basket picnics every Fourth of July."[53]

The two white Carolinians told individual and local truths, without doubt; yet they were not sustained everywhere. Children, especially, amused themselves singly and in groups. They had pets, played games, and roamed. Mountain children and adults skated and played on frozen ponds and creeks in winter. West Virginians were fond of hunting rabbits with ferrets. In the country towns and rural areas of black-belt Georgia (in 1927 and 1934), Arthur Raper observed adults playing marbles behind courthouses. Everyone played checkers—occasionally blacks and whites together—and poker and bridge. The towns had swimming pools for whites and frequent dances. Country folk of both colors had swimming holes but few formal affairs. Traveling carnivals attracted crowds of black and white rural people, but movies were still difficult to get to during the mid-1930s.[54]

By that time the great contrast between town and country was becoming starkly apparent, to the latter's disadvantage. Georgia towns had not only swimming pools and society but baseball teams. Some towns had more than one, and intertown rivalry was fierce. High schools had

52. Mary A. Hicks, "Crazed by Fear," life history of Ernest Foster, n.d. (1938 or 1939) (Typescript in FWP life histories files, SHC).

53. Bernice Kelly Harris, "Sharecropping's the Best," n.d. (1938 or 1939), *ibid.*

54. See the oral history of Wilsie L. Pierson, April 4, 1974, and Larry K. Lane, oral history of Edward C. Jackson, March 23, 1974 (Both microfilmed typescripts in MUOHA); Arthur F. Raper, *Preface to Peasantry: A Tale of Two Black Belt Counties* (Chapel Hill, 1936), 387–92.

appeared in the towns, too, and with them organized adolescent sports—football and basketball as well as baseball—magnifying town spirit and recreational participation. Much the same sports craze seized the coal-mining towns and county seats of eastern Kentucky during the 1930s, when baseball teams, especially, preoccupied everyone, it seemed, during spring and summer. In piedmont mill villages, meanwhile, company management had sponsored baseball teams at least since 1920. A 1926 survey of 322 North Carolina mill villages revealed that, though companies had begun to abandon much of their welfare program for workers, they still supported 127 baseball teams. During the late 1920s and 1930s mill village schools were virtually all merged with local public schools, including high schools. So, as in the Georgia black belt, mill hands became avid fans of their sons' teams. Then, as athletic boosterism extended beyond mill to town and as mill children became sports heroes, mill hands gradually came to take proud places in the towns. A weaver at the Cowikee Mills in Eufala, Alabama, mother of the captain of the Eufala High School football team in 1938, announced the transformation: "It used to be we were just factory folk or 'lint heads.' Now we are 'mill operatives' and we hold our heads high. All work is honorable, you know, and we are proud of ours." Her son was bound for Auburn, no doubt to participate in that great southern passion play, college football, which late in the 1930s approached baseball as an abject folk devotion.[55]

During the 1930s and 1940s town high schools also supported varsity sports for girls. Basketball was most popular. Textiles mill sports enthusiasts watched for good players and recruited them to work at the mills and play basketball on the industrial teams. (Late in the 1940s, when jobs for women were difficult to find, high school athletes were particularly eager to be recruited.) The industrial teams and leagues came to dominate regional and national (American Athletic Union) play. Coach Virgil Yow's Hanes Hosiery team from Winston-Salem was the great power between 1949 and 1954, when Eunies Futch (six feet, two and a half inches tall) and Evelyn Jordan (only five feet, two and a half) starred. They toured the United States, the Soviet Union, Brazil, and

55. Raper, *Preface to Peasantry,* 387–92; "Our Lives" project files, WPA in Kentucky, Kentucky State Archives, Frankfort; Tindall, *Emergence of the New South,* 327; Gertha Couric, life history of Mrs. Lee Snipes, October 13, 1938 (Typescript in FWP life histories files, SHC). See Larry Goodwyn, "Wonder and Glory in Another Country," *Southern Exposure,* VII (Fall, 1979), 42–47, on the college football craze in Texas during the late 1930s and early 1940s.

other countries. In 1953 the North Carolina legislature in effect out-
lawed high school girls' tournaments; the notorious 1950s antifeminist
wave of restrictions on women's sports was underway. And in 1954 the
Hanes executive who had sponsored the team retired. So the Hanes Hosiery team and soon North Carolina women's basketball withered and
died. Their place was taken by the team from the Nashville Business
College. NBC coach John Head used secretarial students as players;
then college President Hermon O. Balls would hire star graduates for
low-wage jobs so they could continue to play. Like Hanes Hosiery, NBC
played the few women's college teams in existence during the 1950s and
1960s, as well as other industrial groups, and won the AAU championship no fewer than eleven times between 1950 and 1969. Sue
Gunter, a native of Mississippi and star of 1960s teams, became coach
of the United States women's basketball team for the 1980 Olympics.[56]

The story of cockfighting in the South is quite different, as one might
well expect. Cockfighting is a blood sport, primarily for men, which
seems to have been changed only in a superficial organizational sense
by the urbanization of the rural population. An ancient sport, cockfighting was popular over much of the world. Both the Spanish and the English brought gamecocks to the Americas. In the United States cockfighting has been pursued in all regions, but in the twentieth century
most devotees have lived in a great arc stretching from Virginia to New
Mexico. The sport is illegal in most states, so keeping gamefowl has
been necessarily a rural and small town custom of farmers and the
working class, hobbyists with perhaps thirty or forty fowl each. A few
wealthy men, such as E. R. Alexander of Tuskegee, Alabama, kept
large numbers of fowl, employed full-time specialists to care for them,
and gambled considerable sums on the outcomes of contests. During the
late 1920s and 1930s certain changes occurred in the sport, which parallel urbanization and the decline of farms. Upper-class cockfighters
achieved a high level of organization, especially in Florida, where the
sport was legal. Each year members of the Deer Island Game Club held
a "main" on their grounds outside Orlando. Mains were never publicly
advertised, but owners of the best gamecocks in the United States, Canada, Mexico, Cuba, and Central and South America were invited to enter. Entry fees were $2,000 during the 1920s, $500 during the 1930s;
and spectators paid $15 to $25 during the more prosperous decade, $5

56. Elva Bishop and Katherine Fulton, "Shooting Stars: The Heyday of Industrial
Women's Basketball," *Southern Exposure*, VII (Fall, 1979), 50–56.

during the Depression. The top prize in 1936 was $4,000. Middling and ordinary folks called their regularly scheduled contests (which began about 1929) derbies, hacks, and meetings. These took place in towns and on farms all over the South and brought together poor and middle-class amateurs and a few professionals. The amateurs made up the bulk of the gamecocking breed, who from the 1930s until the present day were supporters of the magazines *Grit and Steel, Gamecock, Feathered Warrior,* and *Knights of the Pit.* By the 1970s an estimated half million Americans, most of them southerners, had contact with the sport.[57]

World War II was devastating to men's team sports, to living at home, and to the stem-family pattern of migration. Not that mill villages or semirural working-class suburbanites were displaced; rather, the war magnified the exodus from farms so dramatically, sent off the young singly to the services and to war plants, and so impacted many cities that housing, let alone gardens and cow pastures, was impossible to find. Between 1940 and 1943 the South's civilian population declined almost one and a half million, as southerners fled or were ordered out of the region. And during 1940–1945 the farm population shrank by one-fifth, or 3,347,000 souls. Those not in the service or working at plants in the North or West, flocked to southern cities, particularly seaports. Pascagoula, Mississippi (site of the Ingalls shipyard), grew from 4,000 to 30,000; Panama City, Florida from 20,000 to 60,000. Norfolk's population grew 57 percent, Mobile's 61 percent. The newcomers came from near and far. According to observers they were country people—frightened, suspicious, and cut off from kin and community. Crammed into old tenements or cheaply built new housing, they worked in around-the-clock shifts, and their children attended impossibly overcrowded schools, also in shifts, and formed troublesome street gangs. A Washington *Post* writer who toured this seething South in 1943 entitled her report *Journey Through Chaos.*[58]

The seaport cities may have seemed most chaotic to single migrants.

57. Harold Herzog and Pauline B. Cheek, "Grit and Steel: The Anatomy of Cockfighting," *ibid.,* 36–40; Roland Phillips, "Cock Fighting" (Typescript, 9 pages, n.d., in the "American Guide" series of the FWP of Florida, University of Florida Library). See also the gamecock correspondence (most for 1936) and the collection of spurs in the E. R. Alexander section of the Varner-Alexander Papers, Alabama Department of Archives and History. Harry Crews has written about cockfighting in *Florida Frenzy* (Gainesville, 1982), 35–41.

58. Tindall, *Emergence of the New South,* 700–703; Agnes E. Meyer, *Journey Through Chaos* (New York, 1944).

Roy Ham, for example, left his mountain family in Ashe County, North Carolina, for work in the Norfolk Naval Shipyard about 1942, when he was sixteen or seventeen. He lived in the Portsmouth YMCA, near the shipyard on the Elizabeth River waterfront. Lonely and scared, he soon found the company of other mountain boys. They kept together for comfort in a noisy, crowded environment they thought decidedly unfriendly, playing guitars, singing songs, and telling tall stories from home. Ultimately Ham returned to western North Carolina, his attachments to hill folk and ways strengthened.[59]

Such demographic flux had lasting effects, too. Many migrants found permanent homes in cities of the South and elsewhere and never returned to old farm communities. Temporary as wartime production was, the South's industrial capacity increased about 40 percent during the early 1940s, and continued strong following peacetime conversion. Between 1939 and the end of 1943 the region's production work force leaped from 1,422,143 to 2,835,000. In 1947 there were 2,133,326 production workers in the South; so places for about half the wartime peak were retained. Surging chemical, petroleum, construction, and metal works, and garment, furniture, automotive, and other kinds of manufacturing more than provided for the other half and many thousands of new farm-to-city migrants after 1947.[60] Indeed, as Figure 12 demonstrates, it was during the 1950s that production work at last overtook farming in the region.

Quickened postwar migration seems to have returned to prewar patterns: the stem-family mode to familiar urban destinations, usually not far away. For example, Portsmouth, Virginia (as well as its neighbors, South Norfolk, Norfolk, Newport News, and Hampton), drew thousands of farm migrants from the tobacco counties of nearby northeastern North Carolina—especially Gates, Hertford, Bertie, and Northampton—and from such hamlets as Ahoskie, Aulander, Jackson, and Weldon. They went into Norfolk Naval Shipyard as helpers and laborers, for few of the Tar Heels possessed trades; or just as commonly, they went to work as carmen in the vast Seaboard Railroad shops and yard. Carmen worked with hammers, sledgehammers, and wrecking bars, repairing and dismantling box cars. Occasionally, went the local

59. Patty Dilley, interview with Roy Ham, July, 1977 (Typescript in SOHP).

60. Tindall, *Emergence of the New South*, 700–701. Figures aggregated from state tables in Dodd and Dodd (comps.), *Historical Statistics of the South*, 66–73. Charles P. Roland, *Improbable Era: The South Since World War II* (Lexington, Ky., 1976), 12–15.

FIGURE 12

Farms, 1920–1959, and Production Workers, 1919–1958,
in the South
(in thousands)

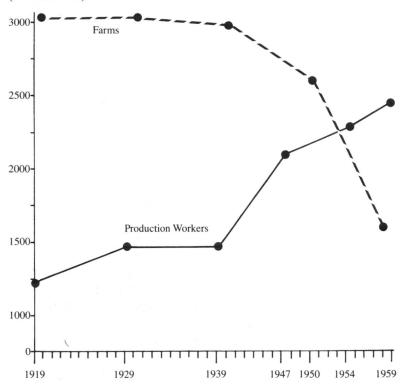

SOURCE: Donald B. Dodd and Wynelle S. Dodd (comps.), *Historical Statistics of the South, 1790–1970* (University, Ala., 1973).

NOTE: The South is the former Confederacy, plus West Virginia, Kentucky, and Oklahoma.

saying, carmen were privileged to use large screwdrivers or wrenches. The white migrants came in families with their farm animals, made homes and large gardens, and gradually assimilated with native whites and other newcomers, many making their way into the middle class before 1960. Black migrants faced housing and employment difficulties. Crowded into old ghettos, they found trades and other well-paid work more difficult to acquire than did whites. Old, established black communities comforted them, however, and the Norfolk *Journal and Guide,* edited by P. B. Young, himself a former Carolina migrant, fought for opportunity.[61]

Portsmouth and Norfolk had always served as market towns for northeastern North Carolina. By the 1940s the servant and supplier to the countryside had become the great magnet. So, too, did the relationship between Jacksonville and rural southeastern Georgia reverse. The poor farm people of Wayne, Bacon, Pierce, Ware, Brantley, Camden, Charlton, Clinch, and Echols counties, according to Harry Crews (a native of Bacon born in 1935), always went to Jacksonville. Bacon countians moved specifically to the Springfield section, near the King Edward cigar factory. The "Springfield Section of Jacksonville was where all of us from Bacon County went," wrote Crews of his boyhood. "Jacksonville came up in conversations like the weather. Farmers' laconic voices always spoke of Jacksonville in the same helpless and fatalistic way." The Florida city loomed like a death warrant over the old life in everyone's consciousness. "*Everybody* had to" go, wrote Crews. "Sooner or later everybody ended up in the Springfield Section." Jacksonville was synonymous with dread in Crews's Georgia neighborhood because so many migrants had already brought back news of Springfield and the King Edward factory. The city stank with "the odor of combustion," and Crews's divorced mother hated the grueling, tedious work of making cigars on machines. Springfield housing was little better than Georgia tenant cabins, with thinner walls. Noisy crowds jammed the apartment buildings, and there was no room for gardens or animals. Crews's mother hardly had time for gardening, anyway; and her young sons ran the streets. Harry learned to steal and sell hubcaps and scrap metal.[62]

After the Crewses' brief sojourn there early in the 1940s, however, Jacksonville sprawled. Military installations and shipyards planted during the war were maintained and grew apace during the late 1940s and after. Manufacturing and other businesses boomed, too, especially the Seaboard Railroad's southern terminal yards. Such sprawl accommodated migrants who wanted more room than the Crewses had enjoyed.

61. Portsmouth information based upon author's recollections. Daniel Johnson and Rex Campbell, *Black Migration in America,* 94–98, 105–107; and see Wilmoth Arnette Carter, "The Negro Main Street of a Contemporary Urban Community" (Ph.D. dissertation, University of Chicago, 1959), 217, 290–92, and *passim* (on Raleigh's black migrants and their accommodation in the existing black neighborhoods). On P. B. Young, see H. L. Suggs, "P. B. Young and the Norfolk *Journal and Guide*" (Ph.D. dissertation, University of Virginia, 1976).

62. Harry Crews, *A Childhood: The Biography of a Place* (New York, 1978), 128–42.

Then during the 1960s the railroad's managers closed the northern terminal yards in Portsmouth, Virginia, and many Tar Heel migrants (or
their Virginia-born sons) left for Jacksonville to work in the expanding
Florida yards. By this time most intra-South migration had become
interurban, like the Portsmouth-Jacksonville connection. The great age
of farm-to-city movement was over.[63]

63. The Seaboard Railroad and Portsmouth-Jacksonville migration is based upon the
author's recollection of his Portsmouth neighborhood and a family of boyhood friends,
who made the trek south with other Seaboard employees. On the change from farm-to-city
to interurban migration, see Karl E. Taeuber and Alma F. Taeuber, *Negroes in Cities: Residential Segregation and Neighborhood Change* (Chicago, 1965), 129.

Those were draining years on the cotton farms—the 1920s. . . . Popcorn [a black boy] left for New York, Harve [a white boy] for the steel mills of Ohio. Mr. Tom's oldest boy went to work with Westinghouse Electric Company in Pittsburgh. Winnie Mae and Dazarene and Lulu left on the day coach for Harlem, and my Aunt Bettie began to regard her kitchen as a training school for servants for Park Avenue; she said that as soon as she taught a colored girl the difference between a tablecloth and a sheet the girl left her for Philadelphia and New York.

—BEN ROBERTSON

Going north was one of the worse difficulties you can imagine. Pulling yourself away from the family, you know, church on Sundays, Sunday dinner at one of the houses, and visit two or three times a week.

—A KENTUCKY WHITE MAN, ON MOVING TO DETROIT
IN 1942

Those poor Kentuckians! They're in worse shape than the Negro. It's their accent, you know. You can tell them anywhere.

—A HAMILTON, OHIO, NATIVE WHITE
WOMAN, ca. 1960

Chapter 9
Southerners Abroad

ALL THE WHILE SOUTHERN COUNTRY REFU-gees were urbanizing their own region they were flooding into the cities of the Northeast, Middle West, and West. From early times the South contributed more migrants to other regions than it received in return. The southern deficit was relatively small, however, until the floodgates opened after the census of 1910. Then, in less than half a century, nine million left. Cumulatively, the migrants were equal to 34 percent of the entire 1910 population. Massive as it was the migration did not bring an end to southern history; it was hardly the equal of the diasporas of West Africans through the slave trade or of the ancient Jews.[1] Yet nothing ap-

1. *South* here includes thirteen states—the old Confederacy plus West Virginia, Kentucky, and Oklahoma, but *minus* Florida, which is exceptional for reasons given below. *Migration* here refers to a negative net figure; that is, nine million more southerners left than nonsoutherners entered the region. The out-migration total is 9,067,000, aggregated from net migration figures by states in Bureau of the Census, *Historical Statistics of the United States, from Colonial Times to 1957* (Washington, D.C., 1961), 45–47, *Historical*

proaching this population movement has occurred elsewhere in recent American history, and the migrants left effects upon the South they departed and the regions they joined that may be impossible to calculate.

Measurement of the migration itself is not easy. The primary source on the phenomenon is, of course, the federal censuses. The Bureau of the Census has long counted migrants and published net aggregates by race. Some censuses also divide migrants by sex, age, and educational level. There are no census data on gross (as opposed to net) migration flows for the 1910s, 1920s, or 1940s, however; and the bureau has never counted individuals or used counties as a base for enumeration. (Resident populations and agricultural activities are registered by counties.) Rather, migrants are counted by states and, beginning in the 1940s, by metropolitan areas as well. Scholars, therefore, cannot directly study the movements of the rural population that are central to the southern exodus. Following the 1940 census there was hope, for the Bureau began an ambitious project to measure migration between 1935 and 1940 by rural areas as well as metropolitan ones, employing an elaborate map broken down into small, useful, homogeneous blocks. The project was halted by World War II, however, and when demographers reconstructed pieces of it during the 1950s the results were of little use to historians. So one cannot follow specific persons or families from place to place, or even faceless migrants from one agricultural crop area to another. One cannot study migration in a single year either. Finally there is the problem of the censuses' credibility. Some scholars estimate that the black population, particularly, has been undercounted by as much as 20 percent.[2]

Statistics of the United States . . . Continuation to 1962 and Revisions (Washington, D.C., 1965), 9–10. The thirteen states' population nevertheless grew, from 26,807,974 to 45,710,616 between 1910 and 1960, an increase of 70.5 percent and testimony to southerners' vaunted procreativity. Aggregates made from Donald B. Dodd and Wynelle S. Dodd (comps.), *Historical Statistics of the South, 1790–1970* (University, Ala., 1973), 2–63.

2. See the censuses of population, 1910–60; Flora Gill, *Economics and the Black Exodus: An Analysis of Negro Emigration from the Southern United States, 1910–1970* (New York, 1979), 10, 48, 117, and *passim;* and on the Bureau of the Census project and its aftermath, Donald Bogue, Henry S. Shryock, Jr., and Siegfried A. Hoermann, *Streams of Migration Between Subregions: A Pilot Study of Migration Flows Between Environments* (Oxford, Ohio, 1957), esp. 28, Vol. I of Bogue et al. (eds.), *Subregional Migration in the United States, 1935–1940,* 2 vols. There is, however, a complex statistical technique for extrapolating net migration from county population data. See Neil Fligstein, *Going North: Migration of Blacks and Whites from the South, 1900–1950* (New York, 1981), Appendix C (202–209). On the issue of undercounting the black popu-

Scholars and journalists have been interested in the great southern exodus since it began, before American entry into World War I. Historians have contributed little to measurement or analysis of the subject, but sociologists, economists, and geographers have produced a huge bibliography. A few of the social scientists have worked as historians— that is, they have carefully reconstructed events in chronological context. Most, however, have been preoccupied with testing abstract "laws" of migration or with data collection and analysis for future policy formulation.[3] Those who would discover human and regional fates must be prepared, then, for some methodological and bibliographical discrimination.

First is an appropriate definition of *South*.[4] Most social scientists and historians employ the Bureau of the Census model—the old Confederacy plus Oklahoma, Kentucky, West Virginia, Maryland, Delaware, and the District of Columbia—although hardly anyone seems satisfied with such a vast and diverse area. In that Maryland's and Delaware's populations were classified as urban as early as 1920, it would seem obvious that they, along with the nation's capital, might readily be excluded from the region. Whatever scheme united southerners (there is no consensus on this either), everyone might agree they were statistically a rural and poor people until recently. Migration data that includes these urban and

---

lation, see Marcus E. Jones, *Black Migration in the United States, with Emphasis on Selected Central Cities* (Saratoga, Calif., 1980), 10–11.

3. The most historical of social scientific works are Louise V. Kennedy, *The Negro Peasant Turns Cityward: Effects of Recent Migrations to Northern Centers* (New York, 1930); Robert Higgs, "The Boll Weevil, the Cotton Economy, and Black Migration, 1910–1930," *Agricultural History,* L (April, 1976), 335–50; Daniel M. Johnson and Rex R. Campbell, *Black Migration in America: A Social Demographic History* (Durham, N.C., 1981); Gill, *Economics and the Black Exodus.* Most historical of all is sociologist Fligstein's *Going North,* which virtually alone among social scientific or historical works treats whites as well as blacks in the context of agricultural conditions and other aspects of the southern socioeconomic structure that provided "pushes." Fligstein's study is restricted to nine cotton-producing states, however, excluding not only Florida but nearly all the upper South. Social scientific works concerned with "law" testing include Richard J. Cebula, *The Determinants of Human Migration* (Lexington, Mass., 1979), which treats migration as an "investment"; and Donald J. Bogue and Warren S. Thompson, "Migration and Distance," *American Sociological Review,* XIV (April, 1949), 236–44, which debates Ravenstein's 1885 "distance law" as applied to the U.S. experience.

4. David F. Sly, "Migration," in Dudley L. Poston, Jr., and Robert H. Weller (eds.), *The Population of the South: Structure and Change in Social Demographic Context* (Austin, 1981), 109–36 (esp. 110–11), refers to "thirty-odd definitions" of the region. Sly's own "redefined South" comprises only seven states: Kentucky, Tennessee, the Carolinas, Georgia, Alabama, and Mississippi.

TABLE 1

Net Migration, 1910–1960

(in thousands)

	Census South	Thirteen-State South*
1910s	−430.2	−1042.2
1920s	−1419.1	−1589.1
1930s	−1391.4	−1147.5
1940s	−1908.4	−2472.3
1950s	−2022.7	−2815.9

SOURCES: *Eighteenth Census, 1960,* Subject Reports, *State of Birth* (Washington, D.C., 1963), 1; Bureau of the Census, *Historical Statistics of the United States from Colonial Times to 1957* (Washington, D.C., 1961), 45–47; *Historical Statistics of the United States . . . Continuation to 1962 and Revisions* (Washington, D.C., 1965), 9–10.

*Figures exclude small numbers of the white foreign-born.

relatively prosperous states atop the "real" South skew the southern experience, especially in overrepresenting white in-migrants.

Florida, a state of the census South as well as the old Confederacy, also presents a problem. Since the early 1920s Florida has enjoyed rapid and rather steady population growth, most of it urban, along with a flourishing tourist, vegetable, and citrus economy. Florida's allure, in fact, attracted enough white migrants to skew the statistical portrait of the entire census region. Elimination of Florida, as well as Maryland, Delaware, and Washington, D.C., from the census South actually increases the totals of out-migrants in four of five decennial census periods, as seen in Table 1. The impact of Florida alone on census South aggregates is apparent in Figure 13. During a half century when blacks fled nearly every other southern state every decade, Florida gained nonwhite population through migration. Numbers of white in-migrants skew census South net migration totals even more significantly.

Twentieth-century Florida, then, is not a southern state, at least in terms of migration; so it should be excluded from regional generalizations. None of the remaining thirteen states is a perfect representative of the preferred model. Two in particular—Virginia and Texas—present very irregular migration profiles. Like the rest of the region they were rural and poor until well after World War II, but both gained white population during most of the half century under study because of metro-

FIGURE 13
Net Migration by Race: Florida, 1910–1960
(in thousands)

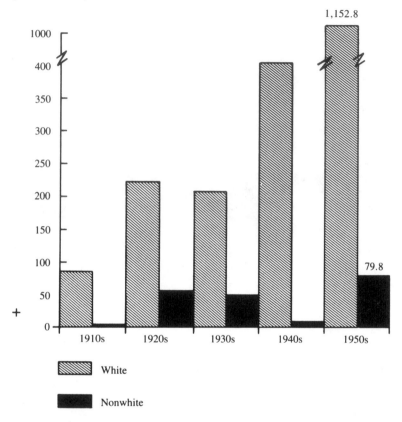

SOURCES: Bureau of the Census, *Historical Statistics to 1957,* and *Historical Statistics to 1962.*

politan growth, agricultural renewal, or the opening of new farm land.[5] A "typical" southern state's migration experience would be shown entirely on the negative (lower) side of a graph, but as figures 14 and 15 demonstrate, both Virginia and Texas left checkered records.

Aside from the atypical infusions of white migrants in Virginia and Texas, there are few important exceptions to the thirteen-state South's

5. Generalization, which is based upon county tables, censuses of agriculture, 1920–59, is developed at length in Jack Temple Kirby, "Agricultural Souths, 1920–1960" (Paper read November 13, 1981, Southern Historical Association, Louisville).

FIGURE 14

Net Migration by Race: Virginia, 1910–1960
(in thousands)

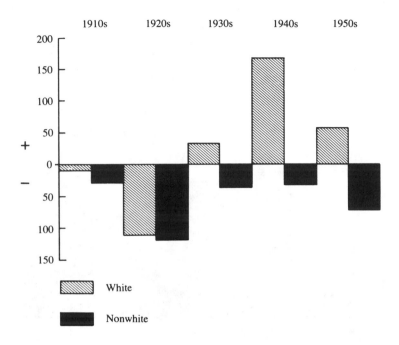

SOURCES: Bureau of the Census, *Historical Statistics to 1957,* and *Historical Statistics to 1962.*

half-century record of negative migration. Oklahoma gained whites during the 1910s, as did Louisiana in the 1920s and 1950s. Oklahoma and West Virginia gained a few blacks during the 1910s, Oklahoma again in the 1920s, and Tennessee actually gained black migrants, too, during the 1930s (probably rural Mississippians and Arkansans into Memphis).[6] Such exceptions notwithstanding, these states and Virginia and Texas (by virtue of Confederate tradition, poverty, and rural populations) can be considered part of a credible and workable South.

Once *South* is defined, the more important divisional criterion for migration studies is not states but race. Proportionately more nonwhite southerners left the region than whites, and massive black flight, beginning about 1915, has always been perceived as more significant. This is

6. Bureau of the Census, *Historical Statistics to 1957,* 45–47, *Historical Statistics to 1962,* 9–10.

FIGURE 15

Net Migration by Race: Texas, 1910–1960
(in thousands)

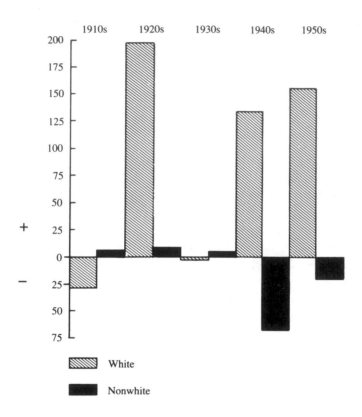

SOURCES: Bureau of the Census, *Historical Statistics to 1957,* and *Historical
Statistics to 1962.*

overwhelmingly obvious in the attention scholars have lavished upon
black migration. Owing to this attention, dating back to World War I, a
rather good portrait of the southern black exodus exists.

Sociologist Louise Venable Kennedy first collated and interpreted
data during the late 1920s. She and other scholars drew their data for the
1910s from local and state chamber of commerce and other estimates,
published in the *Literary Digest* for 1916 and 1917. Kennedy connected
the migration of southern blacks to the dramatic decline in European
immigration to the United States after the outbreak of World War I. By
1915–1916 there was a vacuum in the northern industrial labor market,

creating for the first time since the Civil War a substantial "pull" to southern blacks. Long-standing racial oppression, including low wages and the sharecropping system, as well as the encroaching boll weevil, were more than adequate "push."[7] Economic opportunity at last gave southern blacks a means of making essentially *political* statements, too, with their feet and tongues. A newcomer in Philadelphia explained this eloquently during World War I. "If I had the money," he said, "I would go back south and dig up my father's and mother's bones and bring them up to this country. I am forty-five years old, and these six weeks I have spent here are the first weeks of my life of peace and comfort. And if I can't get along here I mean to keep on goin', but no matter what happens, I'll never go back."[8]

The flow of blacks abated only momentarily when northern industries adjusted to peacetime production in 1919. Between 1919 and 1924 the boll weevil advanced to the limits of cotton culture in North Carolina and southern Virginia, while New Era consumer production got underway; so "the Great Migration," as it is termed, resumed. During the mid-1920s the weevil was relatively quiescent, and migration ebbed once more, but between 1927 and 1929 the weevil surged again, and so did southern blacks to the North.[9]

The Great Depression reduced industrial employment and the flow of black migrants. Even so, 458,000 more blacks left the South than moved in. Many were probably sharecroppers and other tenants displaced by New Deal crop-reduction programs. That migration continued in times of economic depression, however, is remarkable and may be explained at least in part by the interregional network of families and friends established during the 1910s and 1920s. Many southern blacks, in other words, migrated via the stem-family pattern. Pioneer emigres had set up contacts and shelters that tended to perpetuate the flow even in the worst of times. Federal censuses tell nothing of such networks, only that there were rather distinct directional streams from subregions of the

7. Kennedy, *Negro Peasant Turns Cityward*, 43–44.

8. Quoted in Arna Bontemps and Jack Conroy, *Anyplace but Here* (New York, 1966), 309.

9. See Daniel Johnson and Rex Campbell, *Black Migration in America*, 72–76; Higgs, "Boll Weevil, the Cotton Economy, and Black Migration." See also Kennedy, *Negro Peasant Turns Cityward*, 71–80, 88–92, which reports growing northern industrial employment for blacks, especially for women who had been domestic workers. Arthur F. Raper, *Preface to Peasantry: A Tale of Two Black Belt Counties* (Chapel Hill, 1936), 209–10, discusses the varying experiences of black-belt folk with the weevil and migration.

South. South Atlantic folk tended to move to the Northeast (especially New York and Pennsylvania); Mid-South people (from Kentucky to the Gulf east of the Mississippi River) decamped for the Middle West; trans-Mississippi southerners usually went west, especially to California. Minor variations were provided by West Virginians and Georgians, who divided between the Northeast and the Middle West, and Arkansans and Louisianians, who divided between the Middle West and West. [10] Of individuals and families we know little, except where diligent scholars have tracked down migrants as such, beginning with either the destination or the community of origin.

During the 1960s a sociologist studied the North Lawndale section of Chicago, for instance. North Lawndale is a black working-class neighborhood that had been a magnet for migrants from the lower Mississippi Valley since before World War II. Of nearly one hundred subjects interviewed, almost two-thirds had come from Mississippi. Most had followed known earlier migrants in some variant of the stem-family pattern. Most were also married and somewhat better educated than blacks back home, and though most had difficulty adjusting to urban life and labor, most liked Chicago better than their southern homes. Interviews with elderly Newark women late in the 1970s confirm many generalizations in the Chicago sample. The women had come to New Jersey from the South Atlantic states between 1920 and the 1950s. Most came from strong families who had migrated together, and in old age few had regrets. There were demurrers, however. Some marriages went bad in the North, and city streets were corrupting and occasionally deadly to children. [11] Women who had been domestic workers in the South were sometimes shocked by the different terms northern white women offered, too. Maids in New Jersey were better paid than in the South and were usually treated with formal courtesy, but the work was more difficult. "The thing about Carolina work and this work is, it wasn't as long as this

10. Bureau of the Census, *Historical Statistics to 1957*, 46–47; Howard Kester, *Revolt Among the Sharecroppers* (New York, 1936), *passim;* Daniel Johnson and Rex Campbell, *Black Migration in America*, 74–77.

11. Frank T. Cherry, "Southern In-migrant Negroes in North Lawndale, Chicago, 1949–1959: A Study of Internal Migration and Adjustment" (Ph.D. dissertation, University of Chicago, 1965), 25–30, 82–83. Many other scholars confirm Cherry's finding that black migrants were generally better educated than nonmigrants. See, *e.g.*, Marcus Jones, *Black Migration in the U.S.*, 86–89; C. Horace Hamilton, "The Negro Leaves the South," *Demography*, I (1964), 273–95. On Newark, see Audrey Olsen Faulkner *et al.* (eds.), *When I Was Comin' Up: An Oral History of Aged Blacks* (Hamden, Conn., 1982), 112–13 and *passim.*

work," complained one woman. "And it wasn't as hard as jobs in the North, not as hard as here." [12] Newark migrants soon learned the Yankee version of white racism, too, and though none harbored illusions about white southerners, their disillusionment with northerners was bitter. "You don't know where you stand with them," said one respondent. "It's Mrs. this and Mrs. that, or Mr. this or Mr. that—as long as you spend your money with them." Yet if one attempted to rise above one's poorly defined place, "to get up there with them," then "they'll let you know where you at. Up here they're two-faced, they're hypocritic and nasty." [13]

Revealing glimpses of migration, focusing on place of origin, are to be found in the history of the tiny all-black community of Promised Land, South Carolina. The community, which survives to this day, has contributed many of its sons and daughters to the North. Promised Land's historian, Elizabeth Rauh Bethel (a sociologist by profession), found some of the migrants and in retelling the stories of their travels, recreates and humanizes early migration networks that persisted until recent times. One young man, for example, moved first to Atlanta, where he worked as a railroad porter, then after some years settled into New York City and a job in the garment industry. His home served as shelter for several Promised Land relatives when they migrated. Another example provides another route. Before World War I a married couple without land set out for Mississippi, where the wife's family offered promises of opportunity. The sharecropping venture failed, but a few years later the couple and their children were drawn to Chicago by a labor recruiter. There the family pooled resources, acquired property, and finally moved to a black suburb. All the while they acted as migration contact for relatives and friends in both South Carolina and Mississippi. [14] Such pioneers prepared the way for those who left the South in the less propitious times of the 1930s, as well as for the floods of the 1940s and 1950s.

By 1940 more than half (58 percent) of all urban blacks had migrated from other urban areas, often cities within the South. By the 1960s nearly all black migration was interurban. Demographers are fairly certain, then, that though many southern blacks were long-distance migrants from the beginning, most (especially after World War I) probably

12. Quoted in Faulkner *et al.* (eds.), *When I Was Comin' Up,* 58.

13. Quoted *ibid.,* 101.

14. Elizabeth Rauh Bethel, *Promiseland: A Century of Life in a Negro Community* (Philadelphia, 1981), 177–81, 241–54. On the eastern stream of black migrants during the 1960s, see Dwayne E. Walls, *The Chickenbone Special* (New York, 1970).

TABLE 2

Out-migration by Race, 1910–1960

	Whites from Kentucky and West Virginia	Blacks from Alabama and Mississippi
1910s	5.7	10.4
1920s	7.1	8.1
1930s	3.7	6.2
1940s	11.1	20.6
1950s	15.0	23.2

SOURCES: Calculated from Donald B. Dodd and Wynell S. Dodd (comps.), *Historical Statistics of the South, 1790–1970* (University, Ala., 1973); Bureau of the Census, *Historical Statistics to 1957,* and *Historical Statistics to 1962.*

NOTE: Figures represent migrants as percentage of racial population at the beginning of each decade.

moved to northern cities in stages, beginning with southern cities. Southern metropolitan areas such as New Orleans, Atlanta, Memphis, and Norfolk-Portsmouth, Virginia, as we have seen, burgeoned with rural blacks throughout the era of interregional migration.

Great numbers of southerners, black and white, continued to leave the region, but toward the end of the 1950s net migration for both the census and thirteen-state Souths began a great change. The rate of out-migration began to falter, but more important, nonsoutherners' rate of migration into the region became significant. In the 1960s, as two demographers put it, "the counterstream . . . [became] the dominant migration stream." Thereafter, blacks on the move in urban America were not usually southerners at all, but probably second-, even third-generation "Americans." [15]

The published literature on the odyssey of white southern migrants is very limited. Scholars have neglected white migrants, perhaps because they are less visible, often disappearing into white host societies in less than a generation. (By contrast southern black migrants, segregated and

15. Daniel Johnson and Rex Campbell, *Black Migration in America,* 94–98, 105–107, 141, 169; Karl E. Taeuber and Alma F. Taeuber, *Negroes in Cities: Residential Segregation and Neighborhood Change* (Chicago, 1965), 129; Marcus Jones, *Black Migration in the U.S.,* 101–103, 106; Larry H. Long and Kristin A. Hansen, "Trends in Return Migration to the South," *Demography,* XII (November, 1975), 601–14. For brilliant impressionistic portraits of black and white migrants (most interurban) during the 1960s see Robert Coles, *The South Goes North* (Boston, 1971), Vol. III of Coles, *The Children of Crisis,* 7 vols. to date.

TABLE 3
Net Migration, 1910–1960
(in thousands)

	Whites	Blacks
1910s	−559.9	−482.3
1920s	−764.4	−824.7
1930s	−689.5	−458.0
1940s	−1126.9	−1345.4
1950s	−1453.0	−1362.9

SOURCES: Bureau of the Census, *Historical Statistics to 1957,* and *Historical Statistics to 1962.*

most noticeable, provoked alarm, curiosity, and research in northern universities.) A smaller proportion of the southern white population migrated, too, and this may constitute another reason for their neglect. Racial proportions may be well expressed by comparisons of black and white migrants as percentages of racial populations from two Appalachian states (white majority) and two lower South states (black majority). As elsewhere throughout the South, a smaller proportion of whites migrated each decade. Yet net migration aggregates for the thirteen-state South reveal that white migrants were more numerous than blacks in three of five decades. The grand totals for the half century are whites, 4,593,700, and blacks, 4,473,300—or 120,400 more white migrants, enough to populate a sizable city.

No historical synthesis that traces these migrants and explains their journeys by decades and by "pushes" and "pulls" yet exists. Instead, one must read of the mechanization of agriculture and coal mining to find only a broad context. The 1910s and 1920s are particularly mysterious. Whites were not driven from their homeland by the racial oppression that pushed blacks. One must assume that economic pushes and pulls comparable to those affecting blacks also drove out whites—1,324,300 of them—even before the Great Depression. The boll weevil, continued failures of white (as well as black) farmers, and the spectacular overproduction of children everywhere in the South must have pushed whites as much, or nearly as much, as blacks.[16]

16. A very general summary of white migration is Lewis M. Killian, *White Southerners* (New York, 1970), 91–119. See also J. Wayne Flynt and Dorothy S. Flynt (comps.), *Southern Poor Whites: A Selected Annotated Bibliography of Published Sources* (New

The only well-known southern white migrants are the "okies," not because of scholarly attention (given only recently) but because of John Steinbeck's *The Grapes of Wrath* (1939); Carey McWilliams' exposé of California agriculture, *Factories in the Field,* published almost simultaneously; and an excellent and popular film version of Steinbeck's book. Unlike Steinbeck's Joad family, most migrants from Oklahoma, Texas, Arkansas, and Missouri (collectively, okies) were not hard-up former farm owners but tenants of varying classes shut out of homes and work by the process of mechanization that began in the 1920s and by New Deal crop reductions. Few migrants came from those parts of the southern plains affected by the infamous dust storms either. Rather, landless rural folk were first attracted to the cotton fields of Pinal County, Arizona, and Kern County, California, by labor recruiters. Once Route 66 was discovered and the interpersonal and family networks established, a great migration stream began to flow. During the 1930s about 100,000 Oklahomans became Californians. The best estimate of migrants to the West from all four okie states is 350,000, nearly all white. [17]

Like other migrants, many okies followed the stem-family pattern and, once arrived, remained clannish. In 1934 three young men from Carroll County, northwestern Arkansas, drove to Greenfield, California, in the Salinas Valley. By 1940 Greenfield had a shantytown community of two hundred, virtually all of them from Carroll County, Arkansas. Across Oklahoma some families and neighborhoods skipped the gradual process of sending out branches, then stems. Pentecostal preachers led entire congregations en masse to California. Communities formed motor convoys on Route 66, settled together, then rebuilt their churches. In Modesto a drainage canal divided one such group from a settlement of Arkansans who had apparently migrated in the same fashion. [18]

In California the okies encountered an agricultural factory system fraught with dangerous strife. Between mid-1933 and mid-1939 there were about 180 farm labor strikes affecting thirty-four of California's

---

York, 1981), Chap. 6. Fligstein (*Going North,* 93–114) is convinced that whites migrated during 1910–30 for the same economic reasons blacks left, but his evidence is inferential.

17. Walter J. Stein, *California and the Dust Bowl Migration* (Westport, Conn., 1973), 6, 10, 15, 20, 201–10; Carey McWilliams, *Ill Fares the Land: Migrants and Migratory Labor in the United States* (Boston, 1942), 13–15, 25–26, 32, 72–75, 194–96, 247–56.

18. McWilliams, *Ill Fares the Land,* 35; Walter J. Stein, "The 'Okie' As Farm Laborer," in James H. Shideler (ed.), *Agriculture in the Development of the Far West* (Washington, D.C., 1975), 202–15.

fifty-eight counties. Mexican workers were already union-minded before 1930, when they were swept up by the militant, Communist-led Cannery and Agricultural Workers' Industrial Union. The CAWIU spread rapidly from processing plants into the huge ranches of the Imperial and San Joaquin Valleys. Growers formed the Associated Farmers of California to organize their counterattack, in league with railroads, banks, power companies, and local police. So just as the okies began to arrive in force, bloody confrontations between the CAWIU and the growers and their allies were underway. A leader of the ill-fated 1933 cotton pickers strike in the Woodville area was "Big Bill" Hammett, a man in his mid-fifties, father of five sons, and recently arrived from Oklahoma. The Woodville strikers were a grand mixture of Mexicans, Filipinos, blacks, and okies, and Hammett's lieutenants represented every ethnic group, forming a precursor to the racial balancing act attempted by the Southern Tenant Farmers' Union beginning the following year. Most okie migrants were not members of the CAWIU, however. Indeed, they were a factor in the union's defeat during 1933–1934. Arriving as tired, scared families, many of them took jobs left by strikers and accepted the protection of the police and the growers' hired gunmen while they picked cotton and peas.[19]

The next three years, 1934–1937, were relatively quiet, as the okie migrants poured into the West. Weak unions reluctantly sponsored by the American Federation of Labor made little headway or stir. Then in 1937 another militant farm labor group emerged—the United Cannery, Agricultural, Packing, and Allied Workers of America, a branch of the AFL Committee on Industrial Organization (soon to be the separate Congress of Industrial Organizations). UCAPAWA aimed not only to reassemble CAWIU's Mexicans but to organize the okies, too. For the most part they failed. Families of poor newcomers once more scabbed on Mexican and other strikers, who were usually single men or men whose families did not accompany them. The Hotchkiss Ranch near Los Banos—a model San Joaquin agricultural factory with about ten thousand acres in cotton, plus other production—fought UCAPAWA with yet another group of migrants. In 1937 Hotchkiss imported around 250

19. McWilliams, *Ill Fares the Land,* 15, 25–26, 32; McWilliams, *Factories in the Field: The Story of Migratory Farm Labor in California* (Boston, 1939), 219–24; Stein, *California and the Dust Bowl Migration,* 220–60; Cletus E. Daniel, *Bitter Harvest: A History of California Farmworkers, 1870–1941* (Ithaca, 1981), 185–86, 195–96. Despite the CAWIU's defeat and demise, San Joaquin cotton pickers' wages per hundredweight of lint rose from 40 cents in 1932 to 75 cents in 1933. (Daniel, *Bitter Harvest,* 179.)

OKIE SHANTYTOWN NEAR THE RAILROAD TRACKS, SAN JOAQUIN VAL-
LEY, CALIFORNIA, *ca.* 1938
USDA No. 83-G-41449, National Archives

black workers from Louisiana to pick cotton. These migrants were kept
in company housing and fed from a high-priced company store, conditions perhaps familiar to southerners. The United States Senate investigated western farm labor conditions in 1937, but Congress sealed
UCAPAWA's fate in 1938 with a second Agricultural Adjustment Act,
which reduced California cotton acreage from 618,000 to 400,000. The
new AAA produced a huge surplus of cotton workers who, as early as
May, 1938, crowded out of the San Joaquin into the Sacramento Valley
to compete with pea harvesters for jobs. There was a cotton strike in
Kern County in 1939, and a citrus worker's strike farther south in 1941.
Both were broken, the latter in particular with okie scabs from the San
Joaquin's saturated labor market. At last American rearmament and entry into World War II "solved" the West's labor problem. The okies hap-
pily withdrew from the fields to the urban factories and the armed
services.[20]

Before the okies left farm work for city jobs during World War II they
were as visible and oppressed as a white minority might be. *Okie* (like
arkie and *texie*) was a slur word. The migrants lived in cars, in tents,
and in tin shacks next to irrigation ditch banks on company property for

20. Stein, *California and the Dust Bowl Migration,* 76–77, 260–78; McWilliams,
Factories in the Field, 195; McWilliams, *Ill Fares the Land,* 40.

six months to a year, then went on to garages and barns and jerry-built shacks, which were gradually improved into suburbs of sorts—"Little Oklahomas" and "Little Arkansas" on the outskirts of Bakersfield, Delano, Shafter, and so on. Their children, like those of black migrants elsewhere, fell behind in school and became habitual truants and fighters. Natives thought okies innately inferior, a transplanted "poor white trash" prone to violence, alcoholism, and incest. Legislatures both in Arizona and California discriminated against migrants in welfare residence requirements, and in 1939 a sign was placed in a San Joaquin Valley theater, "Negroes and Okies Upstairs." [21]

Sad to say, native Californians (and, as we shall see, middle westerners) held no monopoly on bigotry, even toward whites. Urban southern whites mocked and shunned rural newcomers during the same years of movement and troubles. In Virginia's tidewater cities natives laughed at migrant North Carolinians (renewing a custom dating from at least the time of William Byrd II), creating a variation of ethnic jokes at their expense. Late in the 1930s a young white man in Knoxville, a recent high school graduate obliged to work in a factory after his father's death, related his own cultural shock over mountaineer newcomers to a Federal Writers' Project interviewer: "I'll tell you I never before knew that such people existed. Most of them had come in off of the mountains somewhere and they had such a funny way of talking that plenty of times I wouldn't know what they were saying." The migrants seemed a separate breed in physical appearance, too. "The girls were usually either sloppy fat or thin and dried up. Their hair all hung in strings and a good many of them dipped snuff and spit all the time. They wore the doggonedest clothes I ever saw" and "told each other the slimiest jokes. . . . I've seen them have fights, pulling hair and scratching and biting." The men, he averred, "were funny people . . . most of them awfully measly. . . . Not a beefy man among them. But they were tough. Always getting in knife fights on Saturday night." [22] The perspective, of course, was a matter not only of subregional culture but of class. It prevailed everywhere.

The white masses who moved to the Northeast and Middle West have no historian, although several social scientists have done fine studies of migrants in a few northern communities. Research on these migrations is confounded by many problems: the large numbers of migrants, the

21. Stein, *California and the Dust Bowl Migration,* 51–63, 126–27 (quotation 63).

22. Author's recollection (on Virginia). Quotation from W. T. Couch (ed.), *These Are Our Lives* (Chapel Hill, 1939), 248–49.

five decades of their travels, the Census Bureau's method of identifying migrants by state of birth rather than by county, and the persistent Yankee practice of referring to all working-class white southern new-comers as "hillbillies," a term inappropriate for most and as stigmatizing as okie in the West. A scholar who studied "hillbilly" migrants in Chicago during the late 1940s estimated that no more than 20 percent of Kentucky newcomers to Illinois were Appalachian highlanders. Another investigator found that Detroit's white southerners included no more than 30 percent highlanders.[23]

Even Appalachia is an unworkable basis for study and synthesis. Much as scholars (and politicians) would like to treat the southern highlands as a coherent and homogeneous subregion, they are not—either culturally or as a source of migrants. Appalachia is huge and complex, and as demographers have demonstrated, its migratory streams took several directions, not all of them northward. The remainder of the South is no less culturally diverse, and considering the inadequacies of the censuses for migration research, perhaps it is no wonder that so little work on the sources and streams of the migrants has been accomplished. One is left with a number of social profiles of white migrants in their new middle western communities, along with a few valuable testaments of migrants themselves.[24]

Detroit and its environs were major destinations for migrants from the mid-South, black and white, highlanders and flatlanders alike. During the early 1940s pioneers found jobs and neighborhoods, and their relatives and friends came in droves. Many Kentucky and Tennessee

23. Killian, *White Southerners,* 102–103. The references to his chapter on migration include valuable journalistic studies of hillbillies in Great Lakes cities. See also Killian, "The Adjustment of Southern White Workers to Northern Urban Norms," *Social Forces,* XXXII (October, 1953), 66–69; James S. Brown and George A. Hillery, Jr., "The Great Migration, 1940–1960," in Thomas R. Ford (ed.), *The Southern Appalachian Region: A Survey* (Lexington, Ky., 1967), 76–78.

24. George A. Hillery, Jr., James S. Brown, and Gordon F. De Jong, "Migration Systems of the Southern Appalachians: Some Demographic Observations," *Rural Sociology,* XXX (March, 1965), 33–48; Lewis M. Killian, "Southern White Laborers in Chicago's West Side" (Ph.D. dissertation, University of Chicago, 1950); Todd Gitlin and Nanci Hollander, *Uptown: Poor Whites in Chicago* (New York, 1970); Alan Clive, *State of War: Michigan in World War II* (Ann Arbor, 1979), 170–84; Gene B. Petersen, Laure M. Sharp, and Thomas F. Drury, *Southern Newcomers to Northern Cities: Work and Social Adjustment in Cleveland* (New York, 1977); William W. Philliber and Clyde B. McCoy (eds.), *The Invisible Minority: Urban Appalachians* (Lexington, Ky., 1981); "Urban Appalachians" issue of *Mountain Life and Work,* LII (August, 1976); John D. Photiadis, *West Virginians in Their Own State and in Cleveland, Ohio* (Morgantown, W.Va., 1970); Dan M. McKee and Phillip J. Obermiller, *From Mountain to Metropolis: Urban Appalachians in Ohio* (Cincinnati; 1978).

whites arrived to work in the great bomber plant at Willow Run. Settling into production work and crowded city life, they encountered a host of troubles and predictable disdain from natives. Their clothes were too thin for Michigan winters. They had difficulty being understood in conversation. A Tennessee boy, unfamiliar with urban directions, counted trees along the bus route between home and work in order to determine where he should get off. Mothers-to-be from Kentucky searched for midwives. Nashville's Grand Ole Opry broadcasts suddenly became popular, and the migrants patronized a new institution, the "hillbilly bar," where they were understood and where they could indulge shared perspectives and solace.[25]

In July, 1942, Jim Hammitte and his wife arrived in Detroit from eastern Kentucky. The trials of wartime apartment hunting were compounded both by their rural concepts of adequate space and by problems of speech. The Hammittes wished to have their two children join them, but many landlords would not accept youngsters. The place they finally found was cheap and cramped. Adjusting to such quarters was, Hammitte recalled, "one of the hardest things" they endured; they felt "all cooped up." Then landlords, too, were "local people and this created a problem 'cause the language we talked and the language they spoke was entirely different." Detroit teemed with newcomers, but the Hammittes were apparently migrant pioneers; so they enjoyed few of the benefits of peacetime stem-family newcomers. "Detroit . . . was really mixed up," Hammitte remembered. "There was a lot of people there came from the South, but it was hard to get acquainted with them. . . . You pass people on the street they don't talk to you, you don't talk to them." Personability begat suspicion: "If you tried to smile and talk to somebody, why they thought you's up to something, gonna rob them." The Hammitte children adjusted more quickly than their parents, however. After the war the family moved to a suburb and the children assimilated with ease.[26]

Ohio, located alongside and directly above the upper part of the southern Appalachians, was the most important destination of genuine hillbilly migrants. Scholars have presented a valuable if incomplete portrait of the protracted movement of highlanders into its midst. By World War I much of the highland timber had been cut and shipped and many coal mines were already worked out. The poor, rocky soil would support little more than subsistence agriculture, but highlanders' human re-

25. Clive, *State of War*, 173–76.
26. Mary Thompson, oral history of Jim Hammitte, November 23, 1974 (Typescript in Samford University Oral History Program, Birmingham).

production rate continued to be the highest in the nation. In 1940, when 1000 statistical American women of child-bearing age bore 73.7 children, 1000 women of Wolfe County, Kentucky, birthed 174.3. Ohio received the huge surpluses. As early as 1930, 54,043 Tennesseans, 206,353 Kentuckians, and 130,363 West Virginians were living in Ohio. The 1940 census figures are much smaller because the Depression slowed migration and because the bureau counted only people who had lived in another state in 1935 (instead of 1930). But the 1950 and 1960 censuses reported the enormous continued flow to Ohio from all three mountain states: Tennessee—77,280 (1950) and 119,388 (1960); Kentucky—301,500 (1950) and 409,059 (1960); and West Virginia—190,000 (1950) and 311,134 (1960).[27] So by 1960 there lived in the Buckeye State 839,581 people born in the nearby South, the overwhelming majority of them highlanders.

They appeared and mingled in all parts of the state. During the 1920s and 1930s, for example, an agricultural corporation specializing in onion production in northwestern Ohio recruited West Virginians and especially Kentuckians, most from Magoffin County, as laborers. Many of them remained in Hardin County, Ohio. Most West Virginians apparently migrated to the nearby steel and rubber industrial cities of northeastern Ohio. Kentucky and Tennessee mountaineers met in Columbus, Cleveland, Lorain, and Toledo. But the industrial towns of southern Ohio—Ironton, Portsmouth, Chillicothe, Dayton, Middletown, Hamilton, Cincinnati—were favorites with eastern Kentuckians because of these cities' proximity to the homeland.[28]

The migration to Ohio apparently began, like the black exodus, with recruitment. One witness in Hamilton reported that Kentuckians were brought up to help clear debris following the 1913 Miami River flood. Then from 1915 to 1917, when new European immigrant laborers were no longer available, the Champion Paper Company of Hamilton sent re-

27. John L. Thompson, "Industrialization in the Miami Valley: A Case Study of Inter-regional Labor Migration" (Ph.D. dissertation, University of Wisconsin, 1956), 126; *Fifteenth Census, 1930,* Vol. II, *General Report—Statistics by Subjects,* Table 21, "Native Population of Each Division and State, by Division and State of Birth, 1930," pp. 155–56; *Seventeenth Census, 1950,* Special Report No. 4A, *State of Birth,* Table 13, "Native Population of Each Division and State, by Division and State of Birth: 1950," p. 4A–22; *Eighteenth Census, 1960,* Subject Report No. 2A, *State of Birth,* Table 18, "Native Population of Each Region, Division, and State, by Region, Division, and State of Birth, 1960," pp. 22–23.

28. McWilliams, *Ill Fares the Land,* 130–37; Harry K. Schwarzweller, James S. Brown, and J. J. Mangalam, *Mountain Families in Transition: A Case Study of Appalachian Migration* (University Park, Penn., 1971), 73–118 and *passim.*

cruiters to the mountains, then special trains to transport workers to the plant. The Lorillard Tobacco Company of Middletown (just north of Hamilton) probably also recruited. Armco Steel of Middletown and Champion Paper actively encouraged the stem-family pattern of migration, too. During the 1950s a geographer confirmed that Champion recruited in five Kentucky counties and Armco primarily in another five. Inside Armco's plant people who had been neighbors in Kentucky worked in the same departments. A sign over a doorway between departments read, "Leave Morgan County and Enter Wolfe County." On weekends these Ohio branches returned to family stems in Morgan, Wolfe, Clay, or Laurel and reported on job prospects at the plants in Middletown and Hamilton. The companies gave preference to members of employees' families in hiring new workers. Thus migration did not so much destroy neighborhoods and families as transport them.[29]

Family and friends sustained hillbillies in the Ohio environment, where, as in California, Chicago, and Detroit, working-class white southern migrants were scorned. In southern Ohio natives favored "briar" (or "briarhopper") over "hillbilly." During the Depression, they said, briars took scarce jobs from "decent" people, shunned underwear and shoes, knifed one another like blacks, and lived in filth and ignorance. Briar jokes became fashionable: "The hot-air registers were recommended . . . as built-in spitoons, the bathtub . . . as a convenience for storing ashes, and the commode . . . as a fine spring on the second floor." In truth, as a sociology student discovered early in the 1940s, migrant children in Hamilton *were* often truants, their families were disproportionately represented on welfare rolls, and migrant married couples split more often than natives.[30] Another sociologist, who stud-

29. John Thompson, "Industrialization in the Miami Valley," 132–39; William D. Worley, "Social Characteristics and Participation Patterns of Rural Migrants in an Industrial Community" (M.A. thesis, Miami University, 1961), 49; Schwarzweller, Brown, and Mangalam, *Mountain Families in Transition,* 96–97. The stem-family mode also describes the migration of singer Loretta Lynn's family to Wabash, Indiana. See Loretta Lynn with George Vecsey, *Loretta Lynn: Coal Miner's Daughter* (New York, 1976), 94–95. See also Richard A. Ball, "The Southern Appalachian Folk Subculture as a Tension-Reducing Way of Life," in John D. Photiadis and Harry K. Schwarzweller (eds.), *Change in Rural Appalachia: Implications for Action Programs* (Philadelphia, 1970), 69–84.

30. Raymond P. Hutchens, "Kentuckians in Hamilton: A Study of South-Born Migrants in an Industrial City" (M.A. thesis, Miami University, 1942), 4–5, 9–11, 111–14. Hutchens estimated that the Kentucky-born were 22 percent of Hamilton's population in 1940; yet 39 percent of the city's WPA employees were Kentucky-born; and of direct relief clients, 43 percent were Kentuckians, 41 percent Ohio-born (pp. 90–91).

ied mountain-born Cincinnatians during the mid-1970s, concluded that Appalachian migrants and their children were maladjusted and "little more assimilated . . . now than they were when first coming to the area." [31] If this judgment is correct (I think it harsh and dubious), it would not appear an adequate basis for a generalization. For most Kentuckians in Hamilton and other Ohio towns, like the okies of Bakersfield, rapidly improved their status, dispersing from slums to good working-class and middle-class neighborhoods.

In Hamilton the newly arrived usually lived in housing provided by Champion or in Peck's Addition, arguably the worst slum in town. Peck's Addition was bounded by the Miami River, the small black ghetto, and a smoldering dump. Housing consisted of converted chicken coops and shacks built from scrap lumber and metal. Only about half had city water and electricity, even though Peck's Addition was a short distance from downtown. Inhabitants of this miserable enclave (and of company housing) were most self-conscious about their origins and most noticeable—and disliked—by natives. But many of the Kentuckians moved on in a short time to detached housing in Kentucky-dominated working-class neighborhoods such as Gobbler's Knob and Happy Top and in semirural Fairfield Township south of Hamilton. Their children graduated from high school and moved on to Armondale, a neighborhood of well-kept bungalows at the northwestern edge of the city. Armondale was a lower-middle- to middle-class area with many Ohio-born residents. By the 1950s, in fact, only the least successful (or the poorest among latecomers from the mountains) remained in identifiable Kentucky enclaves. Peck's Addition succumbed to urban renewal. [32]

In the meantime, mountain migrants suffered from a peculiar ethnic-class prejudice at the hands of natives. Italian- and German-Americans in Hamilton had long maintained strong, self-perpetuating organizations that put on well-publicized parades and all-day picnics at the fair-

31. William W. Philliber, *Appalachian Migrants in Urban America: Cultural Conflict or Ethnic Group Formation?* (New York, 1981), 36, 56, 86, 99, 111–20. Petersen, Sharp, and Drury, in *Southern Newcomers to Northern Cities*, did not study Cleveland migrants in the same manner Philliber surveyed Cincinnati, but insofar as their work may be compared with Philliber's, their Cleveland findings do not confirm Philliber's grim generalizations on the Appalachians' adjustments to Ohio cities. See also Hutchens, "Kentuckians in Hamilton," 111–14; Worley, "Social Characteristics and Participation Patterns," 56, 59–60, 89–92, 102–109; John Thompson, "Industrialization in the Miami Valley," 139–45.

32. Hutchens, "Kentuckians in Hamilton," 57–62; Worley, "Social Characteristics and Participation Patterns," 89–92.

grounds. Working-class Kentuckians, however, were recognized only for their strange ways and accent. Nevertheless, Ohioans were well prepared to discriminate among southern whites. If someone said "you all" but dressed well, he or she was a southerner. If someone said "you all" but also "tote" (for carry), "reckon," and "yonder," then the southerner became a briar to be mocked and shunned. "Local merchants," as an eyewitness put it in 1942, never considered advertising "a Briar-day or a Kentucky-day sale." But as most of the mountaineers moved into the respectable working class, to the middle class and beyond, and as they dispersed to a variety of neighborhoods, the shunning subsided. During the 1960s middle-class arrivistes finally established their own social and public-service organization based on "ethnic" pride—the O'Tucks, Ohioans from Kentucky.[33]

Class, both in the mountains and in the North, was the most important determinant of migrants' well-being and acculturation in new communities, as a team of scholars who conducted a twenty-year study of a Kentucky hamlet and its Ohio branches between the early 1940s and the 1960s confirmed. "Upper class" remote mountaineers (actually modest landowners with high school educations and a little capital) shared middle-class values—pride in property ownership and appearance, ambition, respect for schooling—with the majority of their bosses and new neighbors. They rose quickly and disappeared as briars (or perhaps helped found the O'Tucks). Such migrants were from the beginning less dependent upon Kentucky stems and had more contact with native Ohioans than brother and sister Kentuckians. They regarded trips to the hamlet of origin less as escapes than as vacations. "Lower class" migrants (usually former tenants or owners of the poorest ridge land, with elementary school educations or less) felt alienated in Ohio and depended upon Kentucky stems and other migrants for refuge and support. Such folk as these were the last to leave company housing or identifiably Kentucky slums in Ohio cities.[34]

What remained of stems and communities of origin, especially in Appalachia, fared poorly in the most obvious material senses. The Kentucky hamlet in the longitudinal study remained poor by Ohio standards in 1961. By that date virtually all Ohio branches (of all classes) pos-

33. Hutchens, "Kentuckians in Hamilton," 8, 133–34; Worley, "Social Characteristics and Participation Patterns," 90–92. Ercel Eaton (a Kentucky-born feature writer for the Hamilton *Journal-News*) has anthologized her experiences (including information on the O'Tucks) in *Appalachian Yesterdays* (Hamilton, Ohio, 1982).

34. Schwarzweller, Brown, and Mangalam, *Mountain Families in Transition*, 166–95.

sessed automobiles, television sets, electric refrigerators and washing machines, piped-in water, and flush toilets. Of the Kentucky stems almost all had refrigerators and washers, but hardly 59 percent owned cars, not quite 40 percent had piped-in water, only a little more than 20 percent had televisions, and but 15.6 percent enjoyed the luxury of bathtubs or showers. The departure of the young, able, and better educated, meanwhile, devastated southern county tax bases and further impoverished the elderly and disabled who remained behind. The population of Logan County, West Virginia, for example was reduced from 86,000 to 46,000 in only eight years, between 1956 and 1964. Working-age men and women deserted in droves for Ohio, Michigan, and Indiana, often leaving behind school-age children in the care of nonworking or underemployed grandparents, whose tax payments were hardly sufficient to support schools.[35]

Ultimately most children rejoined their parents in the North, went to new schools their parents supported with their taxes, and soon assimilated. Some of the younger migrants have lost their southern accents and in effect ceased being hillbillies. But many who were raised in the Middle West and most of their migrant parents, still maintain strong ties to the homeland. This attachment is most apparent at bluegrass music festivals in the Middle West. Kentucky, Tennessee, and other southern migrants may be depended upon to object vociferously to "progressive" styles of play and to electronic amplification of instruments. They applaud with tears in their eyes the "purists"—Bill Monroe, the aged founder of bluegrass, and Larry Sparks, who is, significantly, an Ohio-born son of Kentucky parents.[36]

Southerners in other irredenta have not championed purism so much as they have geographically enormously extended the popularity and production of "country and western" music. In 1970 there were 650 AM radio all country stations in the United States and Canada. In California alone, 24 claimed the largest block audience. By 1975 the number of AM and FM stations devoted entirely to this music approached a phenomenal 1,150. Market researchers attributed much of the 1970s

35. *Ibid.,* 144; William E. Cole, "Social Problems and Welfare Services," in Thomas Ford (ed.), *Southern Appalachian Region,* 245–56. On Logan County, West Virginia, see Ann M. Berry, oral history of Roscoe Spence, December 3, 1973 (Microfilmed typescript in Marshall University Oral History of Appalachia Collection).

36. Bill C. Malone, *Southern Music/American Music* (Lexington, Ky., 1979), 143–45. The author has witnessed the phenomenon at Monroe's festivals in Bean Blossom, Indiana. See also Lynn with Vecsey, *Loretta Lynn,* 230–31, on Lynn's preference for accompanists with northern factory experience.

switchover of radio stations to a belated acceptance of country by middle-class nonsoutherners, but the core of the supporters who perpetuated this music outside the South were doubtlessly southern migrants and their children. Cincinnati, Detroit, and Chicago, for instance, had "barn dance" type radio programs before World War II. After the war Bakersfield, California, an okie city in the lower San Joaquin Valley, emerged as a major outpost of musical production with its own styles. Texas-born and Arizona-bred Alvis Edgar "Buck" Owens was the first Bakersfield-based star to win national recognition. Appearing first on a Mesa, Arizona, radio show, Owens moved to the Compton, California, *Town Hall Party* program, then to Bakersfield, whence he has made both recordings and television broadcasts. Merle Haggard is the best known singer of the West Coast version of "honky-tonk blues." Haggard was born in Bakersfield of working-class Oklahoma parents and, having grown up surrounded by okies, sounds very much like a native of Muskogee County.[37]

The existence of such irredenta as Bakersfield and the mass or stem-family patterns of migration that provided their musical stimuli might settle an old debate concerning the consequences of urbanization and migration. At the end of the nineteenth century European (and then American) social scientists and philosophers raised a foreboding thesis regarding the demise of rural communities and country towns. These small circles of closely related people had provided security and individual identity within a web of traditional obligations, thought scholars. All would be lost in the alienation of large cities. Ferdinand Tönnies introduced the concepts of *Gemeinschaft* and *Gesellschaft* to illustrate the Manichean contrast. The former, describing the small settlement, implied close interpersonal relationships and supporting clannishness—community in the best premodern sense. The latter concept represented modernity in the worst sense, loss of old institutional ties in favor of membership in "artificial," impersonal corporate structures. Thus migration and urban settlement amounted to a dreadful sequential step from *Gemeinschaften* to *Gesellschaften,* community to alienation.[38]

Of course, the scholars of doomsday were wrong. Urban life has been hell for some migrants. (So was rural life for some.) Most appear to have formed new *Gemeinschaften* in cities of the North and West as

37. Patrick Anderson, "The Real Nashville," *New York Times Sunday Magazine,* August 31, 1975, p. 42; Malone, *Southern Music/American Music,* 88–90; Malone, *Country Music, USA: A Fifty-Year History* (Austin, 1968), 290–94.

38. Thomas Bender, *Community and Social Change in America* (New Brunswick, N.J., 1978).

well as in the South. Settling with family and old neighbors, southern rural folks retained much that was familiar and supportive, from personal relationships, gardens, and farm animals to manners of speech and tastes in music. Like immigrants from overseas before them, they adapted in neighborhoods of their own until, if they wished and were financially able, they moved on again, into other *Gemeinschaften* that were not southern. Migrants of all social classes belonged to enlarged communities, as well—*Gesellschaften* such as the paper, steel, or aircraft industries where they worked; the armed services; and later professions such as teaching, law, and medicine. All this proceeded as the variety of communities we call southern were extended throughout the nation, were changed by the experience, and changed those not-so-foreign places, too.

Mules was gettin scarce then. . . . Tractors was in style, you know, and a mule just can't cover the ground a tractor can. . . . So the ones that stayed in farmin . . . they commenced to buyin tractors so they could work more land and make a bigger crop to meet their expenses.
—NED COBB ON THE LATE 1940s

It is ready on Monday or Saturday. It don't get drunk. It don't have to be bailed out of jail. It don't borrow money all year to gripe when the work is to be done. . . . You can sleep at night because you can get the tobacco.
—A NORTH CAROLINA TOBACCO GROWER ON HIS NEW HARVESTING MACHINE, *ca.* 1973

More is known about the nutrition of chickens than of any other animal, including man.
—*FEEDSTUFFS*, SEPTEMBER, 1969

Epilogue
Giants, Commuters, and Chicken Feed

LIGHT, MULTIPURPOSE, GASOLINE-POWERED tractors were the perfect tool for commercial agriculture. They seemed so "democratic," too. With them ordinary farmers could cultivate more land, raise more cash crops, reduce labor costs, and earn more money, which might be invested in the further rationalization of operations. Farming has ever been both a business and a way of life. The earliest animal-drawn planting and grain-harvesting machines pushed farming toward an emphasis upon capitalism and scale economies and away from community labor and traditional rural society. Tractors were another step, and a large one. Their manufacturers understood this. So did the Department of Agriculture Extension Service. Both promoted tractorization as a means of producing cheap food for the nation's growing population and power and dignity for individual farmers during an age when their importance was waning.[1] Whether anyone understood the

1. John L. Shover, *First Majority—Last Minority: The Transforming of Rural Life in America* (DeKalb, Ill., 1976), 230 and *passim*. See also Texas Agricultural Extension Service, "Annual Report, 1920–21" (Typescript in Texas A & M University Archives, College Station), 6, which celebrates the conversion of a rice farmer from horses to a tractor and successes in educating cotton farmers in labor saving and equipment acquisition.

PROGRESSIVE ALABAMA FARMER PULLS 1930S DISC RIG WITH 1920S
FARMALL
ACES Photo Collection, Auburn University Archives

great paradox—that mechanization would ultimately doom most ordinary farmers—is impossible to say.

By the 1920s single-row Fordsons and newer, lighter Farmalls had become ubiquitous in the northern and western countryside, and manufacturers introduced new, much larger machines designed to magnify efficiencies. International Harvester, for example, marketed the McCormick-Deering "10-20" and "15-30" tractors, with two and three plows respectively. The "15-30" was capable of turning twelve acres per day, the maker claimed, in comparison with only three acres a three-horse team might plow—an efficiency factor of four. International Harvester also promoted sales of disc harrows four to ten feet wide—"sizes for everyone"—to replace farmers' primitive little tooth harrows. Cotton harvesters, too, were improving. The first recorded stripper, a homemade affair consisting of wooden fence pickets tied with wire, was drawn through a northwestern Texas field in the fall of 1914. During the 1920s manufacturers mounted metal stripping teeth on wooden boxes with skids, then wheels. Horses pulled these devices, then (before the end of the 1920s) tractors. Western Texas, Oklahoma, and New Mexico growers waited until frost caused the leaves on their cotton plants to

drop, lessening the trash to be gathered with lint, then drove their contraptions over the fields. As early as 1926–1927 manufacturers and agricultural experiment station scientists (especially John Deere and the
station at Texas A&M College) began experimentation with chemical
defoliants that would permit earlier use of strippers.[2]

Such progress was little felt in the Southeast, however. Relatively
prosperous middle-sized farmers in the upper South bought some tractors, as did a few black-belt planters who were affected by heavy labor
migration. Southern grain farmers with sufficient level land used tractors and either owned or rented powered threshers at harvest. But until
the 1940s mechanization made little headway in the region. The Depression nearly ruined John Deere's cotton stripper business. With picking labor so abundant and cheap, the machines could not be sold, even
at low prices; so in 1941 Deere disposed of its remaining stock, at a
loss, for fifteen dollars each. In the humid cotton country to the east,
where there was no practical harvesting machine, planters bought tractors *and* mules as they converted tenants and sharecroppers to wage
hands. But they also expanded acreage so much that by 1937, work-
stock per thousand acres remained about the same as in 1934. Many
thousands of hungry people still vied for farm work, and farmers, lacking chemicals to kill weeds and defoliate cotton, did not rush to buy
existing machinery. In tobacco and peanuts, also, there was virtually no
labor-saving machinery before the 1940s, save a thresher that separated
peanuts from vines and leaves. So, where tractors could only break the
land and cultivate until crops were a foot or so high and where huge
labor requirements remained for all other operations, there were neither
incentives nor means to become thoroughly "modern."[3]

2. See International Harvester advertisements in *Farmer and Stockman* (Jacksonville,
Fla.), XXVI (October 1, 1924), 159, and XXVII (January 1, 1925), 37; Harland Padfield
and William E. Martin, *Farmers, Workers, and Machines: Technological and Social
Change in Farm Industries in Arizona* (Tucson, 1965), 78–79; Gilbert C. Fite, "Mechanization of Cotton Production Since World War II," *Agricultural History*, LIV (January,
1980), 193.

3. In addition to Chapter 2 herein, see (on early black-belt migration and tractors)
Debra Ann Burks, oral history of Allen Buster, November 29, 1974 (Typescript in Sam-
ford University Oral History Program, Birmingham); (on grain threshers) Gail Hatton,
oral history of Dr. Donald Hatton, July 22, 1973, and D. L., oral history of Mr. and Mrs.
Clarence S. Rule, n.d. (*ca.* 1974) (Both microfilmed typescripts in Marshall University
Oral History of Appalachia Collection); (on John Deere) Padfield and Martin, *Farmers,
Workers, and Machines*, 79–80; (on eastern cotton) Work Projects Administration, Divi-
sion of Research, *The Plantation South, 1934–1937*, by William C. Holley, Ellen
Winston, and T. J. Woofter, Jr. (Washington, D.C., 1940), xvi; (on peanuts) USDA, Farm
Economics Division, Economic Research Service, Agricultural Economics Report No. 7,

Yet great breakthroughs lay only shortly ahead. Most important was the final development of a spindle-type cotton harvester suitable for the humid Southeast. John and Mack Rust, Memphis inventors and Socialists, had produced a working prototype during the Depression. But the Rust brothers refused to release patents or to manufacture their machine for wide distribution, fearing their invention would compound hardship among the South's poor. The Rusts hoped that a "co-operative commonwealth" would "supplant our decaying capitalist society" so that workers themselves might control the machines.[4] But corporate inventors were also busy. International Harvester, whose engineers and mechanics had tinkered with spindles since the mid-1920s, introduced a one-row picker in 1941. This rig was designed to be mounted on the rear of a Farmall-type tractor, which was then driven in reverse through cotton. During World War II, IH sold about a hundred of these on a "job" basis, then after the war built a large plant near Memphis and began mass production. Other corporations—Allis-Chalmers, Deere, and Pearson—joined the competition. Respectable sales in the lower Mississippi delta country and in California hastened confrontation of the next great problems: weed control and defoliation. For a while some cotton growers attached racks of butane-fueled flamethrowers to tractors and burned out weeds in cotton and corn. But the Southeast was often so wet that this weird by-product of combat in two world wars was unsatisfactory. Too, spindle picking machines (like strippers) accumulated so much leaf trash with lint that the value of a bale of machine-gathered cotton was always reduced. In the humid subregions, complete defoliation through chemistry was absolutely necessary if hand labor was to be eliminated.[5]

So immediately after the war, the federal government, the land-grant colleges, and agri-industry joined to attack weeds and cotton leaves systematically. In 1946 Congress increased appropriations to the colleges and experiment stations through the Research and Marketing Act. The

---

Peanut-Cotton Farms: Organization, Costs, and Returns, Southern Plains, 1944–1960, by W. Herbert Brown (Washington, D.C., 1962), 13; (on tobacco) Charles Kellogg Mann, *Tobacco: The Ants and the Elephants* (Salt Lake City, 1975), 120–25.

4. John Rust and Mack Rust, "The Cotton Picker and Unemployment" (Typescript, [probably 1937], microfilm roll 6, STFU Papers, Southern Historical Collection, University of North Carolina), 1.

5. Fite, "Mechanization of Cotton Production," 193–95; Padfield and Martin, *Farmers, Workers, and Machines,* 88; John Turner, *White Gold Comes to California* (Bakersfield, 1981), 89–100; James H. Street, *The New Revolution in the Cotton Economy: Mechanization and Its Consequences* (Chapel Hill, 1957).

next year the Cotton Council of America, a trade group representing growers, ginners, and textiles manufacturers, conducted its first "Belt-wide Cotton Mechanization Conference" at the Stoneville, Mississippi, experiment station. There and at subsequent conferences in the South and West, cotton men, USDA observers, and government and corporate researchers coordinated the focus of money and effort. Their successes were remarkable. By the early 1950s preemergent herbicides were available. Applied to fields (usually in dried, granulated form), they obviated the hoeing (or chopping) that had occupied so many hundreds of thousands of southerners every spring for so many generations. Chemical defoliants, meanwhile, were improved to the extent that by the 1960s, when spindle pickers and gins had also been refined, machine-harvested cotton was nearly as clean as the hand-picked. The researchers also developed commercial insecticides and fungicides to cope with virtually every pest and plant disease and anhydrous ammonia fertilizers that magnified yields. Together they created the much-heralded "Green Revolution." [6]

These ultimate leaps to rationalized farming were so expensive that they benefited few southerners. In 1960, for example, when the machine-picked part of the American cotton crop attained the 50 percent mark, it was westerners who accounted for most of the "progress." Early one-row harvesters cost five thousand dollars, plus transportation. Two-row pickers, developed and available during the 1960s, cost more. Growers who wanted to do without most hired labor faced huge and escalating bills for chemicals—fertilizers, herbicides, pesticides, and defoliants—and ever more finely tuned hybrid seeds, which they could not supply themselves. Debt, always a fact of farm life, became astronomical. Middling and small farmers were last in line at federal credit offices and at banks, and most southerners, like the aging Ned Cobb, watched the technological blitz from behind their mules or from the North. [7]

Even the largest of Mississippi delta plantations moved cautiously into the new era. During the early 1940s the Delta and Pine Land Company continued its custom of buying about 150 mules each year. Oscar Johnston, corporate president, liked to maintain a huge stable of mules averaging five to six years old; so in 1941 D&PL purchased a group of

6. Fite, "Mechanization of Cotton Production," 200–207; Turner, *White Gold,* 101–107.

7. Gilbert C. Fite, "Recent Progress in the Mechanization of Cotton Production in the United States," *Agricultural History,* XXIV (January, 1950), 19–28; Fite, "Mechanization of Cotton Production," 203–204; Shover, *First Majority—Last Minority,* xiv, 152, 156–58, and *passim.*

TWO-ROW, ENCLOSED-CAB COTTON HARVESTER, *ca.* 1960
ACES Photo Collection, Auburn University Archives

fourteen-month-olds and an equal number of seven-month-olds. Plans were to phase them into work in 1942 and 1943, respectively, as the company retired comparable numbers of its oldest mules. As late as 1949 D&PL owned but a few tractors and was only considering a full commitment to machine picking. Its resident force of sharecroppers was smaller than prewar averages of three thousand but still very substantial. Company croppers continued to chop and pick as mules slowly gave way to machines. During the late 1940s hands picked the first bolls, which opened late in August and early September. In October company planes finally sprayed calcium cyanide to defoliate, and only then did D&PL's first few mechanical pickers begin to roll. Hands went through fields once more at the end of the fall to gather cotton left by the un-discriminating machines. For a while D&PL experimented with flame throwers to control weeds in cotton but during the 1950s abandoned that operation in favor of cross-plowing (an old method of cultivating both between and across rows, first employed by the company in 1932).

Johnston embraced pesticides early, however. In 1956 his corporation sprayed 1.2 million pounds of poison dust on its fields. D&PL was fully in the arms of mechanization and agricultural chemistry only in the 1960s. Corporate accounts reveal the extent. Total expenses for 1966 crops of cotton, wheat, corn, rice, and soybeans amounted to $1,385,756. Weed control alone (including flames in corn) cost $257,048; pesticides were $173,410; defoliants and the cost of spraying reached $21,544. D&PL, like most southeastern growers, reduced cotton acreage in favor of rice and soybeans, the bonanza crops of the postwar era, but yields in all staple enterprises soared. The company made somewhat better than two 500-pound bales of cotton per acre in 1965.[8] Only such production as this might compete with that of the San Joaquin cotton ranchers.

Farther to the east, the better part of wisdom was abandonment of cotton in favor of pasturage and cattle production. As early as 1947 the Extension Service agent for Colbert County, Alabama, reported the idling of fields in the rugged southern part of Colbert and great increases in the planting of perennial clovers for soil-building and pasturage in the north (through which the Tennessee River flowed). Tractor purchases were up more than 50 percent over 1946 sales; the number of grain combines had increased threefold since 1944, and farmers showed more interest in hay binders, corn pickers—machines of every kind—than the agent had ever seen. To the south, in the black belt, sharecropper-raised cotton was still common, but by 1947–1948 the pattern of transformation was becoming clear. Small farmers without access to generous credit were struggling, many giving up their land to lumber companies, which were busy consolidating huge tracts, cutting out mature stands and planting pine seedlings that would mature in only fifteen years. The largest plantation in one black-belt county was by 1948 about half de-

8. See the following documents in the Delta and Pine Land Company Records in the Mississippi State University Library: "Statement and President's Report for the Year Ended March 31, 1941" (Typescript), Oscar Johnston, "Will the Machine Ruin the South?" (Typescript, 1947, for *Saturday Evening Post* article), "Around the Clock on the South's Largest Cotton Plantation" (Offprint of 1956 *Cotton Trade Journal* article), "Accountant's Report" (Typescript, March 31, 1968), "Planting Division—Statistical Information Comparison for Fiscal Years Ended March 31" (Typescript, 1966, including cotton yields for 1961–65). In addition see Billy Burkett, oral history of J. O. Dockery, n.d. (*ca.* 1978) (Audio tape in Arkansas County Agricultural Museum, Stuttgart), which reports pesticide spraying for D&PL. A 1960s D&PL plantation manager also reported corporate caution in mechanization and releasing labor. Bill Boyd, interview with Ed Hester, May 16, 1974 (Audio tape in Delta and Pine Land Company Oral History, Mississippi State University Library).

PEANUT THRESHING IN SOUTHERN OKLAHOMA WITH 1920S EQUIP-
MENT, *ca.* 1940

E. E. Dale Collection, Western History Collections, University of Oklahoma Library

voted to cattle production. Tenant-raised cotton (without mechanization except tractors) made up an important part of production, too; but the landlord was already hiring labor for his new creosoting plant, where he prepared pine posts cut from the property for fencing enlarged pastures. Some of the creosote workers were also cotton tenants; so they were in effect taking wages for labor that led to the demise of their rented farms. Another plantation had already completed the transformation. A new owner had arrived during the 1930s. His chalk land was so poor he was not tempted to persist with cotton. Instead, the planter consulted his county agent and sowed scientifically selected pasture grasses and acquired purebred Hereford cattle. By the end of the 1940s he had a fully developed cattle-grain neoplantation. Salaried skilled employees—all white—lived in neat bungalows near his machinery shed on the main plantation road. Wage hands—all black—cleaned barns and herded Herefords. There were no tenants or croppers at all.[9]

9. "Annual Narrative Report of D. G. Sommerville, County Agent, Colbert County, Alabama, November 30, 1947" (Typescript in Alabama Extension Service Records, Auburn University Archives); Morton Rubin, *Plantation County* (Chapel Hill, 1951), 24–25, 45–49, 52–53.

Over in hilly Coosa County in northeastern Alabama farm implement dealers feared they would be unable to satisfy demand for combines, tractors, and corn pickers during the winter of 1947–1948.
Coosa's relatively few substantial farmers and river valley planters made
huge profits on 1947 crops. The great majority of Coosa's farmers were
small hillside owners and tenants, however. Their crops had been too
small either for big profits or for big credit. So, as the county agent reported, they were "indifferent toward farming" and drifted off for industrial work.[10] Such would be the fate of most southern farmers, now
that machines, chemicals, and the economies of scale had combined in
irresistible array against them.

Peanut culture underwent a similar dynamic during these years. Before World War II making crops was largely a mule and hand-work business. At harvest many hands carried shocks of dried vines to a stationary
thresher that separated trash from peanuts. During the 1930s threshers
were often powered by a long belt connected to a rear truck wheel,
jacked off the ground for the occasion. Peanut farmers turned to tractors
for cultivating crops almost wholesale during the late 1940s and 1950s.
Meanwhile the first harvesters appeared. These tractor-drawn machines
moved through fields, digging vines and delivering them from the side
to a hopper leading to a thresher. In addition to the driver, another
worker atop the harvester sacked peanuts and dropped the closed bags
on the ground behind the machine. Other workers followed, retrieving
the sacks. Finally, during the 1950s, peanut combines appeared. These
self-propelled contraptions dug, shook, separated vines from nuts, and
discharged peanuts (without sacks) directly into trucks. Small-time
operators in the old peanut belt of southeastern Virginia and northeastern North Carolina had difficulty capitalizing these rapid and costly
successive "generations" of equipment and were largely surpassed by
new, extensive growers in southwestern Georgia and southeastern Alabama, who were converting from cotton.[11]

Sugar and rice culture had always been well capitalized, but after
1940 important labor-saving refinements were added to the mechanization of both commodities. Sugar growers introduced mechanical cane
cutters and loaders to hasten and cheapen the movement of their crop
from field to refinery. Rice planters universally came to employ self-

10. "Annual Narrative Report of A. D. Jackson, County Agent, Coosa County, Alabama, November 30, 1947" (Typescript in Alabama Extension Service Records).
11. USDA, *Peanut-Cotton Farms*, 13–14; Dru Flowers, oral history of Carl and Ted
Forrester, January 18, 1975 (Typescript in Samford University Oral History Program).

Second-Generation Peanut-Harvesting Rig, Alabama, *ca.* 1950
ACES Photo Collection, Auburn University Archives

propelled combines at harvest and later bought "hedge-hogs" to maintain their levees. These tiny tractors with large wheels, which looked
rather like recreational vehicles, replaced the horses with turning plows
that had performed the task of shoring up the serpentine mounds that
separated fields and held water during the growing season.[12]

Tobacco resisted thoroughgoing mechanization. Despite some labor-
saving technology in the eastern flue-cured belts, this crop remained the
great province of the small farmer until the 1960s and 1970s. Even tobacco could not resist high-cost technology, however. During the 1940s
tobacco growers, like many other southern farmers, acquired tractors
for breaking land and cultivating young crops. Tractors also pulled
new four-row transplanting rigs. Seedlings from covered winter beds
were loaded on the transplanters, which were then drawn over prepared
fields. Still, in addition to the tractor driver, motorized transplanting
required two workers for each row to handle the planting. All rode, and
the work progressed relatively quickly, but tobacco remained labor in-

12. On sugar, see J. Carlyle Sitterson, *Sugar Country: The Sugar Cane Industry in the
South, 1753–1950* (Lexington, Ky., 1953), 361–70. On rice, see the exhibits (pictures
and machinery) at the Arkansas County Agricultural Museum.

tensive. Automatic tobacco "stringers," portable "sewing machine" devices first developed in Canada, were another example of intermediate technology—this appearing in the 1950s. With stringers, farmers might sew (instead of hand tie) small bundles ("hands") of pulled tobacco leaves onto long sticks, which were then hung in curing barns as of old. This work also proceeded more quickly, but stringers made little impact on the total labor requirements to produce tobacco. So-called "taxi rigs," which first appeared in 1954, probably represented the limit of innovation within the traditional mode of flue-cured tobacco culture. Like stringers, they affected harvest. Taxi rigs were tractor-drawn platforms on which "primers" (leaf pickers) sat, selecting ripe leaves as the rig moved slowly between rows. Primers placed tobacco on conveyors to the center of the platform, where other workers employed automatic stringers to attach hands to curing sticks. Such harvest rigs commonly bore four primers and two stringers, in addition to the driver. Work was faster and much easier on backs and legs, and women and children were expected to accomplish more during long hours at the task. Yet since taxi rigs, like walking, stooping humans, were still obliged to make successive passes through the fields as leaves ripened gradually, this was no breakthrough. Moreover, before the later 1950s, agricultural chemistry had little impact on tobacco, either in labor savings or yields. So it is little wonder that tobacco farms remained small and cropping on halves remained common into the 1960s.[13]

A fundamental reason for the technological "backwardness" of tobacco culture was the federal acreage allotment policy left over from the New Deal. Farm owners with an established record in tobacco had received in effect perpetual franchises, with subsidies, to grow tobacco on strictly limited acreages. (Between 1933 and 1965 the government switched from acreage to poundage and back again.) The first Agricultural Adjustment Act franchisees were virtually all small; their allotments typically measured from half an acre up to five. Excess production was not subsidized, and allotments could not be combined. So the dynamic of aggrandizement that had rampaged through the cotton country did not obtain, but gradually pressures began to build for belated technological and legal breakthroughs. During the 1950s and early 1960s larger operators who invested in nitrogen fertilizers and newly developed tobacco pesticides began to distance themselves in per-acre

13. Mann, *Tobacco*, 4, 127; John Fraser Hart and Ennis L. Chestang, "Rural Revolution in East Carolina," *Geographical Review*, LXVIII (October, 1978), 435–58.

yield from small farmers. Leaf quality deteriorated, too, and tobacco manufacturers complained. The USDA responded in 1965 with a subsidy limitation based upon poundage (as opposed to acreage). With this imposed limit on the benefits of chemistry and intermediate-technology mechanization, larger operators and their allies looked to labor savings as their best hope. The R. J. Reynolds Tobacco Company, in league with researchers at North Carolina State and Clemson universities, had already begun the task of developing a "once-over" tobacco harvester, along with new seed adapted to the machine to be, in 1961. In 1962 federal regulations were altered to permit allotment holders to rent or sell within a county, and in 1967 the USDA permitted unlimited leasing within a county. The next year Reynolds introduced a prototype of the harvesting machine. So at last all the elements for an upheaval in flue-cured tobacco began to merge.[14]

Early consolidations are evident in comparisons of the 1964 and 1969 censuses of tenants in the flue-cured tobacco belts. In the first enumeration traditional share renting and sharecropping were still the common systems for raising the crop, and 44 percent of all eastern tobacco-growing nonowners were black. By 1969, 80 percent of the black tenants and croppers were gone, along with substantial numbers of white nonowners as well. Following the appearance of a production tobacco harvester in 1971 the consolidation movement quickened, and tobacco tenancy was finally redefined. During the 1970s the "one-third/two-thirds" system evolved. Renters paid one-third of their net proceeds to owners for the use of allotments, while supplying most capital and equipment (as well as management) themselves. The tenancy rate remained high in the flue-cured belts—from about 20 percent in Georgia to a high of about 45 percent in eastern North Carolina—but most tenants more closely resembled middle-class middle western tenants than southern renters before World War II. Many tenants, indeed, were large operators, busy taking advantage of relaxed federal regulations, combining scattered allotments into efficient and lucrative agribusinesses.[15]

In a short time, the labor-intensive culture of flue-cured tobacco was almost utterly transformed. Shortly before the introduction of the harvester, the old Virginia–North Carolina practices of grading, then tying

14. Anthony J. Badger, *Prosperity Road: The New Deal, Tobacco, and North Carolina* (Chapel Hill, 1981), 92, 200–207, and *passim;* Mann, *Tobacco,* 58–59, 69–70, 83–84.

15. Mann, *Tobacco,* 33, 42, 158; Pete Daniel, *Breaking the Land: The Transformation of Cotton, Tobacco, and Rice Cultures Since 1880* (Urbana, 1985), 256–70. Figures represent tenancy rates in 1972.

PRIMING TOBACCO THE NEW WAY, FLOODS CHAPEL, NORTH CAROLINA, 1983
Photo by Pete Daniel, courtesy Smithsonian Institution

tobacco into hands before delivery to warehouses were at last abandoned. Buyers in particular objected that the requirement of hand tying unduly delayed the opening of markets. Growers eagerly complied, for the savings in labor were theirs. Now cured leaf could be delivered to warehouses in lots weighing about two hundred pounds, bundled and wrapped in sheets. This innovation and others hastened abandonment of thousands of old unpainted curing barns, those ubiquitous structures tourists often mistook for shabby houses. In their place growers adopted so-called "bulk curers"—rectangular sheet-metal buildings resembling small motor homes but without the usual doors and windows. (Nonetheless some tourists thought these were improved housing for the poor who formerly dwelled in curing barns.) Into these shiny things farmers jammed racks of harvested leaves, then turned on heaters (sometimes electric, usually butane or a similar gas) and watched gauges. There being no flues on bulk curers, the expression *flue-cured* began to pass from the language before the end of the 1970s. Bulk curing suited the new harvesters well. The machines are high, self-propelled affairs with rollers that twist off leaves and convey them to a hopper. New hybrid seed led to tobacco which matured in a less protracted period than before. Still, operators set their harvesters so that immature leaves would be taken along with prime ones. They calculated that loss of profit through grade degradation would be more than offset by labor savings. Machine priming and bulk curing reduced the labor requirement for tobacco by a factor of four: five workers could accomplish what twenty did before.[16]

To nonsavants all tobacco may be the same, but burley culture is elementally different from that of the eastern bright leaf cured by heat. Burley growers with tiny allotments are scattered throughout much of Appalachia and over into the plateaus of Kentucky and Tennessee. Unlike flue-cured tobacco, which had to be stripped, tied, barned, cured, graded, retied, and marketed in a rather short time, burley's harvest and preparation was and remains almost leisurely. Burley is cut by the stalk (rather than by the leaf), stacked, and dried in the late-summer sun in the fields. Later it is taken to barns and hung on sticks for final curing. Labor is thus spread over several months, between work on other crops. Families could almost always manage without outside help. For this reason burley growers seldom joined the flue-cured tobacco farmers' campaigns for eased regulations on allotment sizes or conspired with manufacturers and experiment stations for the development of machinery. Chemicals to fertilize, treat fungi, and kill nematodes have been sufficient, along with the use of tractors and trucks. Burley has remained an important cash crop, even in postage-stamp-sized fields, and these growers' involvement in high-cost mechanization has been directed toward other crops on their land, such as corn and small grains, if indeed they have participated in the so-called Green Revolution at all.[17]

Indeed small farmers—particularly those on rugged land not suited to heavy machinery—seemed doomed to follow sharecroppers and old-style renters off the land. In 1959 there were 508,061 small farms in the South, which accounted for 14.9 percent of all regional farm sales. (A small farm during the 1960s was defined as one with annual sales under five thousand dollars.) By 1969 their numbers had shrunk by 39 percent to 307,697, and small farmers sold only 5.8 percent of the South's agricultural goods. Medium-sized farms (with sales between five thousand and twenty thousand dollars) declined relatively slightly—from 290,227 to 243,900—but their share of sales shrank from 31.8 percent to 19.1. The most remarkable statistics for the 1960s concern large

16. Hart and Chestang, "Rural Revolution in East Carolina"; Mann, *Tobacco*, 61–62.
17. Mann, *Tobacco*, 66, 83–84, 144.

farms with annual sales above twenty thousand dollars. There were only 81,009 in 1959, but 133,777 in 1969. Most dramatic of all, large farmers increased their share of sales from 47.2 to 72.1 percent.[18]

The dynamics of capitalization, aggrandizement, and scale have already been observed. Planters and larger farmers collected federal subsidies, reduced their labor costs, mechanized, and expanded their acreage while creating neoplantations specializing in cattle, grains, soybeans, corn, rice, cotton, and even timber. Economies of scale had their limit, however, as two agricultural economists demonstrated before the end of the 1950s. The scholars studied production costs and returns in four categories of farms in the Mississippi delta during 1957–1958: farms with less than 60 acres of cropland, with 60 to 399, with 400 to 999, and with more than 1000 acres. Their conclusion was that farms in the third category—400 to 999 acres—achieved the greatest returns per acre. "It is probable," they added, "that internal economies are largely exhausted as a farm . . . expands in size to 1000 acres of cropland." [19] Yet southern and other American farmers continued to expand both acreage and share of sales through the following decade and after, always at the relative expense of small farmers.

Resolution of this apparent defiance of economics and logic is to be discovered in part in federal farm policy. Despite many legislative peregrinations after the New Deal, Congress has consistently rewarded large operators disproportionately, rendering further capitalization and expansion irresistible. An excellent means of understanding the federal factor in the triumph of the farming giants after World War II is to measure the percentage distribution of government payments to the top 20 percent of producers of the major southern commodities. During the early 1960s, 20 percent of southeastern cotton growers received 61 percent of all payments; 20 percent of rice producers took 64 percent of subsidies; 20 percent of Louisiana sugarcane growers got 72 percent. Among peanut farmers the top 20 percent in the old belt of Virginia and North Carolina received 58 percent; 20 percent of the top growers in the new belt of Georgia and Alabama gained 62 percent. Tobacco culture remained a small farmer's crop during these years; so subsidies for the

18. Ray Marshall and Allen Thompson, *Status and Prospects of Small Farmers in the South* (Atlanta, 1976), 27. Marshall and Thompson's South includes thirteen states—all those termed southern in this book except West Virginia.

19. USDA, Farm Economics Division, Economic Research Service, Agricultural Economics Report No. 21, *Crop Production Practices and Costs by Size of Farm: Delta Area of Mississippi, 1957–58,* by Irving R. Starbird and James Vermeer (Washington, D.C., 1962), iv.

sotweed were the most "democratically" distributed: the top 20 percent of producers received a mere 53 percent.[20]

No wonder, then, that not only individuals and families but corporations eagerly undertook or expanded farming operations. By 1970 corporate farms were more prevalent in the South than in any other region of the United States except the three contiguous western states of California, Nevada, and Arizona. About 20 percent of all Florida's farmland, for example, was owned by corporations. Ten corporations owned 119,000 of the state's 636,000 acres of citrus. Coca Cola's Minute Maid Division alone held 30,000 acres. Food processors, grain and soybean dealers, and even oil and gas companies acquired enormous acreage for crops elsewhere in the region. During 1966–1970 soybean acreage in the deltas of Mississippi, Louisiana, and Arkansas trebled the 1946–1950 average. Much of the expansion replaced cotton, but in Louisiana more than a million new acres of land were leveed and drained during the 1960s, 90 percent of it for soybeans. Corporate farms that were subsidiaries of energy companies accounted for most of the expansion.[21]

Profits, fueled by inflation as well as federal subsidies, soared so that federal statisticians were obliged to redefine categories of American farms during the 1970s. The "expanding sector" of the agricultural scene included large farms averaging 1,299 acres and sales of $100,000–$199,999 each, and a new category, "largest" farms, which averaged 2,826 acres and annual sales in excess of $200,000. Medium-sized farms (with an average of 761 acres and sales between $40,000 and $99,999) remained relatively stable. A troubled "declining sector" included two other old categories—small, and part-time and subsistence farms. Combined they amounted to more than 1.8 million units but accounted for only 21.6 percent of national sales in 1974. There were only 101,153 large and 51,446 largest farms, but they sold 53.8 percent of all agricultural goods.[22]

Not only corporations but many families operated these giant farms. Some were owners who expanded as smaller neighbors quit farming.

20. Arthur M. Ford, *Political Economics of Rural Poverty in the South* (Cambridge, Mass., 1973), 52–53; Ingolf Vogeler, *The Myth of the Family Farm: Agribusiness Dominance of U.S. Agriculture* (Boulder, Colo., 1981), 95 and *passim.*

21. Robert Bildner, "Southern Farms: A Vanishing Breed," *Southern Exposure,* II (Fall, 1974), 75; Bill Rushton, "The South Coast Conspiracy," *ibid.,* 15; Shover, *First Majority—Last Minority,* 164–65; Bill Finger, Cary Fowler, and Chip Hughes, "Special Report on Food, Fuel, and Fiber—State-by-State Profiles: Florida," *Southern Exposure,* II (Fall, 1974), 186.

22. U.S. Congress, General Accounting Office, *Changing Character and Structure of American Agriculture: An Overview* (Washington, D.C., September 26, 1978), 77.

Others were tenants of a sort never dreamed of in the old domain of the mule-coaxing sharecropper. In 1976 H. L. Mitchell wandered around eastern Arkansas, surveying scenes of his struggles on behalf of tenants four decades before. Near Pine Bluff he encountered the Chadwick brothers, who rented three thousand acres of cotton, rice, and soybean land from a list of retired farm owners who had moved to towns. The two brothers owned a quarter of a million dollars' worth of farming equipment, including tractors and combines with air-conditioned cabs— one with a stereophonic sound system as well. With three other men the Chadwicks cultivated land where at least a hundred families had once lived and labored. Such new-style tenants were respectable and influential men, too. Buddy Chadwick was president of the Jefferson County Farm Bureau Federation.[23]

At the beginning of the 1970s there were still many medium-sized family farmers in the South, although they were aging and declining in numbers. According to the criteria of the 1960s, they numbered 243,900, or 21.8 percent of the region's farmers. Among them, however, were farmers sufficiently capitalized, diversified, and vigorous to survive. Such people worked to maintain the sort of motorized, enlarged rural communities that existed a generation after World War II. Aubrey and Juanita Ward and their three young sons exemplified this small corps. Celebrated as a model rural family by the Florida Agricultural Extension Service and Farm Bureau, the Wards raised tobacco (their chief cash crop), cattle, hogs, small grains (for feed and cash), and gladiolus bulbs on their place in Suwannee County in the northern part of the state. Their farming equipment was adequate and flexible enough to serve both large and small operations that involved the entire family. Winters and other slack times were devoted to a staggering number of organizations concerned with farming and the broader rural community. The Wards were pillars of their Baptist church and the Suwannee County Farm Bureau. Their boys were members of 4-H and the Future Farmers of America. Aubrey Ward was principal founder of the county Grain Association, which dried and stored corn and small grains, and he was also a member of the Cattlemen's Association, the Swine Producers' Association, Tobacco Services, and the Rural Areas Development Council—not to mention the Masons and Elks.[24]

23. H. L. Mitchell, *Mean Things Happening in This Land: The Life and Times of H. L. Mitchell* (Montclair, N.J., 1979), 344–45.
24. Figure from Ray Marshall and Allen Thompson, *Status and Prospects of Small*

Models are hardly ever representative, however. The great majority of southern farmers belonged in the two categories below the Wards, small and marginal. (Marginal corresponds to the 1970s designation of part-time and subsistence.) Of the region's 1,116,838 farms, 736,161— or 66.2 percent—were such undersized and undercapitalized businesses, rapidly losing their already small share of sales. By 1969 they accounted for only 8.8 percent of the South's marketed agricultural goods. Small and marginal farmers were statistically the oldest, least educated, and poorest of rural folks. Few earned the major part of their incomes from their farms. They hired out to larger farmers nearby or held full-time jobs in town and farmed their little places evenings and on weekends. Some of them produced commodities economically suited to small parcels of land—tobacco, broilers, or small fruits—but most did not, accounting for their shrinking share of farm sales. Established scales necessary to grow grains, soybeans, and cotton were far beyond them. Extension Service agents (with few exceptions) did not advise these farmers. Nor did they benefit much from land-grant college or other federally funded research or from federal tax and subsidy policies. During the 1960s and 1970s a new small-farmer cooperative movement spread through the region, attempting to negate some of the disadvantages of smallness. The Southern Cooperative Development Fund (SCDF), in particular, sought to assist these farmers in such essential matters as bulk purchases of fertilizers and other chemicals, marketing, and especially credit. The SCDF and other groups tried in effect to replace the New Deal's defunct Farm Security Administration, but they struggled in an apparent losing battle.[25]

Some of the region's 432,464 marginal farmers (in 1969) were not part of the rural working class or the poor. They were "hobbyists," professional people such as veterinarians and business managers who enjoyed both country living and generous federal investment and depreciation tax advantages. Others were upper-middle-class or wealthy retirees from cities who realized similar advantages in the country. The methods the Bureau of the Census used to count farmers during the 1960s and 1970s do not provide the number of such well-off "marginal farmers,"

Farmers, 27 (my percentage calculation). Florida Agricultural Extension Service, *The Story of Suwannee County* (N.p., [1963]), 10–11.

25. Ray Marshall and Allen Thompson, *Status and Prospects of Small Farmers,* 12–15, 26–27, 36, 53–68.

but data on rural income and a variety of impressionistic evidence indicate that hobbyists and affluent retirees were relatively few.[26]

In 1960, according to the President's National Advisory Commission on Rural Poverty, there were 829,000 rural farm families in the South with annual incomes below the official poverty level of three thousand dollars. (Nearly two-thirds of the families were white.) Another 1,646,000 southern rural nonfarm families also met this doleful criterion. Together the rural poor—farm and nonfarm—outnumbered the southern urban poor by nearly half a million families. The poor were distributed throughout the region. In eastern Arkansas, H. L. Mitchell found them in the shabby, shrunken remains of formerly populous country towns and neighborhoods, too old or infirm and financially unable to retire to cities. This predicament doubtless prevailed everywhere neoplantations had evolved. To the west, in the Ozarks (here broadly conceived, to include northwestern Arkansas, most of southern Missouri, and eastern Oklahoma), the rural poor consisted of the leftovers of a massive demographic transformation. During the 1950s almost half a million people had migrated from the rugged subregion. Ozark migrants (like most) were primarily the young, able, and better educated. Those who remained in the 1960s were mainly the elderly, the widowed, the infirm, and many households headed by single women. At the end of the 1960s, in a sample of Ozark counties studied by the USDA Economics Research Service, a quarter of all families lived well below the government's poverty line, and another quarter lived on the borderline. So the USDA classified half of all Ozark families as poor. Elsewhere in commodity-producing subregions, a few old-fashioned sharecroppers were still to be found in the 1960s and 1970s. In Franklin County, North Carolina, for example, several elderly blacks cropped tobacco and earned $1,600–$2,400 per year as late as 1975.[27]

A significant portion of the rural nonfarm working poor of the South

26. *Ibid.*, 19. On the difficulty of counting and classifying farms, see also Vogeler, *Myth of the Family Farm*, 27–30.

27. John F. Kain and Joseph J. Persky, "The North's Stake in Southern Rural Poverty," in President's National Advisory Commission on Rural Poverty, *Rural Poverty in the United States* (Washington, D.C., 1968), 306; Mitchell, *Mean Things Happening*, 296–97; USDA, Economic Research Service, Agricultural Economics Report No. 182, *Human Resources in the Ozarks Region . . . With Emphasis on the Poor*, by Herbert Hoover and Bernard L. Green (Washington, D.C., 1970); Steven Petrow, "The Last of the Tenant Farmers in the Old New South: A Case Study of Tenancy in Franklin County, North Carolina," in Robert L. Hall and Carol B. Stack (eds.), *Holding on to the Land and the Lord: Kinship, Ritual, Land Tenure, and Social Policy in the Rural South* (Athens, Ga., 1982), 131–45.

were woodcutters. These people either lived in their country homes and worked part-time, as in Ned Cobb's day, or they were full-time "independents" who, with their own chainsaws and old trucks, performed contract work for giant lumber and pulp-paper corporations. A handful of these manufacturers—International Paper, Weyerhaeuser, Georgia-Pacific, St. Regis, Scott, Union Camp, and U.S. Plywood-Champion—owned or controlled more than thirty million acres in ten southern states in 1970. The federal Forest Service permitted cutting on additional land in the national forests and parks and discriminated in favor of corporations in its leasing policies and practices, compounding the dependency of small-time timber workers. By 1980, according to one estimate, there were more than 150,000 families in the pine barrens of western Florida and southern Georgia, Alabama, and Mississippi alone, who gleaned small incomes from harvesting and hauling pulp wood for the corporations.[28]

Much of the rural South (indeed, of rural America) after 1960 consisted not of struggling middling family farmers, the elderly and destitute, or piney backwoods folks but of working-class country commuters. Many of these people owned marginal or small farms, where they raised a few animals and feed grains and kept gardens. Five days and forty hours per week they worked in nearby mines or industrial plants. More, probably, were not farmers at all but residents of along-the-highway housing developments. They, too, were full-time industrial workers. These patterns of part-time farming with full-time industrial work and rural nonfarm blue collar communities, both dependent upon the automobile, had begun to appear as early as 1930 and had become common by the end of the 1950s. The phenomenon of rural industries made continued rural occupance possible for many folks not eager to live in cities. That southern and western country people were disinclined to join unions, in turn, made parts of the rural South and West inviting to industrialists. During the 1970s, as coal mining revived and as northeastern and middle western manufacturers sought cheaper energy and labor, many rural counties grew in population more rapidly than metropolitan areas. This growth was most noticeable in southern West Virginia and in the strip-mining sections of Montana and Idaho. Descendants of 1930s okie migrants moved from California to rural

28. Bill Finger, Cary Fowler, and Chip Hughes, "Tree Killers on the Rampage," *Southern Exposure,* II (Fall, 1974), 175; Si Kahn, "The Government's Private Forests," *ibid.,* 141; Wayne Greenhaw, "Big Profits and Little Pay in South's Backwoods—Woodcutters Organize, II," *Southern Changes,* III (February/March, 1981), 14–17.

Oklahoma, bought land, and retired or sought work in small industries. Back roads radiating from remote Mountain Home, Arkansas, filled with the new houses and mobile homes of workers in electrical components factories. And as hundreds of light industries built plants in and around Rocky Mount, North Carolina, the rural population of Nash County outstripped those of Rocky Mount and other towns in the county.[29]

The mechanization of flue-cured tobacco production in eastern North Carolina hastened development of a rural-industrial commuter culture in at least a dozen counties. Eviction of tenants, delayed so long by tobacco's labor intensiveness, began in earnest before the end of the 1950s and accelerated toward the end of the 1960s, as the heralded mechanical harvester approached production. Some tenants decamped for the North, but for the most part the belated tobacco revolution did not cause massive out-migration. Instead, textiles and other light industries relocated or opened new mills and plants in eastern Carolina. County industry hunters sold industries particularly on the availability of nonunion labor. White former farmers often moved to towns, but most displaced black tobacco tenants remained in the country. By the mid-1970s many had built little brick houses along main highways, from which men and some women commuted as much as twenty and forty miles each day to the factories. Along-the-highway living also permitted many women and children and a few men to work as occasional tobacco wage hands. Thus was "community" reformed in much of North Carolina and the rest of the South by the 1970s. Both tenant shacks and small owners' homes had been razed. Small factory towns burgeoned. And the automobile—the "energy crisis" of that decade notwithstanding—was as necessary to existence as it had become in southern California.[30]

Another mode of rural community transformation and the development of commuting is exemplified by the experience of Mount Pleasant, South Carolina, on the north bank of the Cooper River above Charleston. After the Civil War many former slaves acquired little farms of ten to

29. Glenn V. Fuguitt, "Part-time Farming and the Push-Pull Hypothesis," *American Journal of Sociology,* LXIV (January, 1959), 375–79; John Herbers, "Americans Migrating . . . Countryside," New York *Times,* March 23, 1980, pp. 1, 50, and March 25, 1980, Sec. D, 9.

30. Hart and Chestang, "Rural Revolution in East Carolina"; Joseph Giovannini, "Farms and Industry Mix in North Carolina Area," New York *Times,* June 3, 1984, p. 29. See also (on tenant evictions) Phaye Poliakoff, "Thought We Were Just Some Poor Old Country People," an interview with Alice Balance, *Southern Exposure,* XI (November/December, 1983), 30–32.

forty acres around Mount Pleasant. They fed themselves from their gardens and nearby waters, harvested nearby planters' crops for wages, and avoided dependency on lien merchants. During the early twentieth century they sold surplus produce and seafood on the streets of Charleston. Then during the 1920s and 1930s local planters gradually abandoned cotton in favor of vegetable production. They and developers of self-service groceries systematized produce marketing and by the end of World War II had virtually driven the Mount Pleasant truckers and street salespeople from the scene. Some of Mount Pleasant's blacks fled to New York. Others turned to construction work in Charleston's expanding suburbs. Women became domestics, unskilled hospital workers, or home weavers and roadside sellers of baskets. Most families clung to their land, even as greater Charleston encroached. By the 1970s, descendants of the former rural community were all commuting city workers, even as they remained on their ancestral ground.[31]

Far more commuters, as well as many stationary small and marginal farmers, were participants in perhaps the most remarkable agribusiness of post–World War II America—the production of broiler chickens. For many generations before the war virtually every family farm in the nation included a chicken house and yard, some surplus eggs, and at least a few spring cockerels for consumers' frying pans. The Middle West was the great egg basket of the country, and nearby feed mills nurtured that region's primacy in poultry. The chicken meat industry as such, however, was decentralized. So broilers were relatively scarce and expensive. This situation began to change during the early 1920s. In the upper piedmont and mountains of northern Georgia and a few other badly weevil-infested areas of the cotton South, feed dealers easily persuaded farmers to raise chicks for shipment to Atlanta or other urban butchers within easy reach. Two successive apple crop failures in northwestern Arkansas produced similar results among farmers around Fayetteville and Springboro. The great explosion in chicken production took place on the Delmarva Peninsula, however. In 1923 a woman reportedly took a chance with a few thousand birds, sold them all in Baltimore for a good profit, and reinvested in many thousands more with great success. Managers of a feed-milling company took notice, set up local operations, and financed many more eager chicken farmers. By 1926 the Peninsula was producing more than a million birds a

---

31. Kay Young Day, "Kinship in a Changing Society: A View from the Sea Islands," in Robert Hall and Carol Stack (eds.), *Holding on to the Land and the Lord*, 11–24.

year, live or plucked, for the great Baltimore, Philadelphia, and New York markets.[32]

The Delmarva ascendancy lasted through the 1930s and produced at least two developments crucial to the industry's future expansion. First, the early decades of growth in chicken farming paralleled and materially assisted the elaboration of a new marketing institution, the self-service grocery, later known as the supermarket. Dressed chickens were easily chilled and displayed for customers in such stores, freeing butchers for other work. Mass-produced broilers were cheaper, too, encouraging more demand and prompting chain grocerymen to prod poultry producers for more and better chickens. Expanded demand led to the second development, the creation in 1935 of the National Poultry Improvement Plan, a federal-state governmental and private enterprise collaboration dedicated to better fowl nutrition and the eradication of poultry diseases, especially pullorum. Over the following two decades researchers at land-grant colleges, feed mill laboratories, and drug companies wrought several miracles. They not only wiped out pullorum but improved "feed conversion"—that is, the amount of feed required to produce a pound of chicken meat—beyond the dreams of chicken producers, from nearly four pounds to two and even less. Another problem for science was breeding a chicken perfect for the supermarket—large breasted, tender, and pinkish white, without dark feather marks. To this end the Great Atlantic and Pacific Tea Company, operators of A & P supermarkets, announced in 1946 a national "Chicken of Tomorrow" contest, with a prize of five thousand dollars to the breeder of a superbird. Finals of the first contest were held on the Delmarva Peninsula in 1947, with the prize going to a California breeder. A second contest was held in Arkansas in 1951.[33]

Meanwhile Delmarva's ascendancy ended rather abruptly during World War II. Peninsula growers' success was their undoing, for the War Food Administration closed the subregion's market and made the government prime buyer of its poultry, for the armed services. Southern poultrymen made their move. Among them the most daringly innovative was Jesse Dixon Jewell, a small fertilizer and feed dealer of Gainesville, Georgia. Jewell and banker friends had been promoting broilers among depressed local farmers for some time when, in 1936, Jewell conceived a plan to integrate the production of chicken meat vertically. By 1940 he

32. Gordon Sawyer, *The Agribusiness Poultry Industry: A History of Its Development* (Jericho, N.Y., 1971), 36–51.

33. *Ibid.*, 54–61, 115–22; Shover, *First Majority—Last Minority,* 143–44.

owned a large hatchery, distributed chicks to farmers in several north-ern Georgia counties, along with feed and medicines, then collected the broilers after eight weeks. Jewell also processed the broilers—that is, killed, plucked, eviscerated, cut, and packaged them—before trucking his product to Atlanta distributors. In 1951 Jewell decided to market all his chicken frozen, giving him added flexibility and security in distri-bution. Thus, except for the farms and chicken houses in which his chicks were grown, Jewell owned and controlled his product from eggs almost to consumers' tables. Farmers were grateful for a cash business to replace cotton and eager to accept Jewell-arranged credit to build chicken houses and buy feed and drugs. Jewell was no doubt grateful they were willing to relieve him of the need to capitalize chicken houses and pay for full-time labor to raise chicks and that they were willing to share to an extent in the risk of the business. It was a new sort of sharecropping.[34]

Delmarva production had never been integrated. Feed millers had provided impetus for enlargement, especially through provision of credit for feed, but they dealt with independent farmers through middle-men dealers, who marketed the poultry with minimal processing. Del-marva farmers, indeed, resisted direct contracts with feed mill men who wished to integrate vertically, referring to such contracts as sharecrop-ping, a condition they feared. Farther south desperate farmers did not resist. The first known contract between a feed and chick supplier and a farmer was signed in the Valley of Virginia in 1933. The farmer had been unable to pay his bills, so the feed dealer persuaded him to share profits fifty-fifty while the supplier in effect assumed more responsibility for the farmer's debts if he lost an entire flock. Farmers feared losing their farms as a result of failure in what during the 1940s amounted to a mere sideline enterprise. After the war it was they, apparently, who ne-gotiated new contracts in which their liabilities *and* profits were reduced to only 10 percent. Later, yet another type of contract evolved all over the South, in which farmers received a flat rate of a few cents per broiler plus bonuses for added weight, which demonstrated good care and feed-conversion ratios. So the contract system moved past something resem-bling sharecropping to something resembling wage labor. A constant, however, was rather close supervision, a feature of both cropping and wage labor in the old plantation system. Even though chicken farmers owned their places, chicken houses and all, the "integrators" (as Jewell

34. Sawyer, *Agribusiness Poultry Industry*, 85–96.

and his many imitators were known) had such a stake in chicks, feed, and drugs that they insisted upon the right to inspect farmers' operations at every turn. In the early days Jewell himself traveled about the country to inspect his broilers-in-progress. But as his company grew into a corporation, he sent out representatives called "service men" to perform the supervision. Service men gradually became bosses. Farmers enlarged their own investments (and debts) until chickens were not a sideline but their primary business. Thus dependent on their contracts with the corporations, farmers could not resist when service men ordered them to adopt a new feed mixture, invest in new, automated watering devices, ventilating fans, heating systems—whatever. Loss of the contract through noncompliance with corporate orders would mean loss of a considerable investment. By 1980 a fully automated chicken house cost about sixty to eighty thousand dollars. Broiler operations became so specialized that a farmer might not convert his investment to turkey production or any other remunerative purpose either. He became in effect a hostage. As a North Carolina farmer complained about 1980, the corporate service "man has total control over me. He has no investment in my operation, but he's got complete say-so over the future of my farm." [35]

Meanwhile other integrators were at work in the South during the 1940s and 1950s. In northwestern Arkansas John Tyson and his son created Tyson Foods, and Harold Snyder built Arkansas Valley Feed and nearly half a dozen other coordinated poultry companies. In Wilkes County, North Carolina, a group of men founded Holly Farms. Later they expanded into eastern Texas and extended Jewell's model further, into the retailing of prepared chicken to consumers. They contracted with a supermarket chain to provide parking lot takeout service. Similar industry growth occurred in northern Alabama and eastern Mississippi. According to a USDA study, southern poultry production increased 365 percent between 1947 and 1960, while man-hours of labor grew but 5 percent. Rapid automation developed by the integrators, mill companies, and college researchers made these remarkable statistics possible. Farmers built ever larger chicken houses with mechanical feeding and watering devices requiring minimal human attention. Feed bags and their handling disappeared, too, as special tanker-type trucks delivered precise mixtures from mill to farm hoppers, which in turn conveyed the feed automatically to the chicks. Processing of broilers was also

35. *Ibid.,* 129, 145–47; Hope Shand, "Billions of Chickens: The Business of the South," *Southern Exposure,* XI (November/December, 1983), 76–82.

MONUMENT TO POULTRY, GAINESVILLE, GEORGIA
Photo by Lyra M. Cobb

dramatically refined and speeded. Plants quickly passed any resemblance to butcher shops as they adopted moving "dis-assembly lines,"
where workers killed birds, used defeathering machines, eviscerators,
and so on.[36]

The southern integrators' striking success spelled doom for most of
them as independent regional businesses. During the early 1960s a wave
of horizontal integration swept over the region. Huge national and international corporations, most of them grain millers, bought out southern
poultry producers. Having already established feed mills in the region
during the 1950s (Pillsbury had leased Jewell's Gainesville mill then),
Ralston-Purina, Central Soya, Pillsbury, and Perdue now acquired
southern operations outright, along with their contracts with many
thousands of southern chicken farmers. This first major shake-out of the
industry rendered marketplace competition keener and in turn applied a
greater squeeze on the farmers. By 1969 more than 98 percent of all
American poultry was raised under contract. Broilers became the most
important farm product in Arkansas, Georgia, and Alabama, and was
second only to tobacco in North Carolina. These four southern states,
ranked in this order, led the nation in poultry production by 1980. Mis-

36. Sawyer, *Agribusiness Poultry Industry,* 139–43, 162–66, 211–13; Shover, *First
Majority—Last Minority,* 145–46.

sissippi was fifth, Texas seventh, and Virginia tenth. Yet this ranking was of doubtful value to contract farmers. A 1967 examination of Georgia chicken farmers' operations found that the contractors earned only fifty-three cents per hour for their work. A 1969 USDA study of northern Alabama growers revealed that they received an average of *minus* thirty-six cents an hour of labor. The latter year set a record for poultry profits, but the average chicken farmer netted only about two thousand dollars. Such labor was, of course, exempt from the federal minimum-wage law. In 1970 there was an abortive strike by contract growers in northern Alabama.[37]

More horizontal integration left only 137 producers nationally in 1981, and some of those were for sale. (There had been 286 broiler companies in 1960.) Merciless corporate cost accounting, lower prices, and ever more costly automation and credit made chicken farmers' lives yet more difficult. Successive corporate takeovers, combined with over-production relative to poultry prices, meant loss of contracts and ruin for many small farmers. The federal Farmers' Home Administration, principal lender to these operators, grew wary and called in loans. Early in the 1980s a former chicken farmer bitterly summarized his fate: "You're just like a dog. You follow the crumbs along, and you get poorer every day." Such men had no unemployment compensation or corporate insurance, merely property and labor to lose.[38]

Those southerners who remained in the country after the great exodus and the triumph of agribusiness found little security, then. A steadily shrinking quarter million middle-sized family farmers struggled on against the economies of scale and subsidy. They alone maintained a semblance of independence. The great majority were dependent to various degrees upon corporate giants, whether as commuters to industrial jobs, as woodcutters, or as chicken farmers, those new-style rural hostages whose very existence was manipulated by forces beyond their reach and region. Thus had the modern South completed a circle of sorts, or perhaps a spiral, from undercapitalized colonial dependency to complex, well-capitalized colonial dependency, complete with motors of every sort and faceless coercion. A new New South had appeared, but whether it was better than the old one was a question not easily and fairly answered.

37. Sawyer, *Agribusiness Poultry Industry*, 201–206; Shover, *First Majority—Last Minority*, 147; Shand, "Billions of Chickens"; Ray Marshall and Allen Thompson, *Status and Prospects of Small Farmers*, 55.
38. Shand, "Billions of Chickens," 82.

Essay on Sources

Structural Change

STRUCTURE HERE MEANS FUNDAMENTAL elements of agriculture and rural life: numbers of farms and farmers, tenure systems, types of farm power, crops. The most valuable and elemental sources on structure are the federal censuses of agriculture, 1920 through 1959. Beginning in 1920 the Bureau of the Census and the Department of Agriculture began to take and publish farm censuses every five years. This innovation was particularly fortuitous, for it permits the tracking of structural variables at briefer intervals than the previous decennial censuses, during the decades of particularly intense change in farming. Basic data from both state and (especially) county tables of all nine censuses were used in the preparation of this book.

There are approximately twelve hundred counties in what is here termed the South—the former Confederacy, minus western Texas, plus Kentucky and parts of West Virginia, Oklahoma, and Missouri. To aid me in subdividing this enormous region and grouping by crop types and topography I was fortunate to discover Charles S. Johnson and his associates' compilation, *Statistical Atlas of Southern Counties: Listing and Analysis of Socio-economic Indices of 1104 Southern Counties* (Chapel Hill, 1941). Based in large part upon the county tables of the 1930 agricultural census, the *Statistical Atlas* was most valuable in providing a classification system for each county in what Johnson *et al.* called the South—the former Confederacy, minus central and western Texas, plus Kentucky and Maryland. Johnson's system designated each county as Cotton, Crop Specialty, Self-Sufficient, Grain-Dairy-Livestock, Vegetable-Fruit, or Unclassifiable (urban, wilderness, or rural-industrial without significant agriculture). In classifying counties in Oklahoma, Missouri, and West Virginia—not included in *Statistical Atlas*—I consulted the county tables of the 1930 agricultural census and classified them myself. (As noted in Chapter 3, a number of Appalachian counties designated as General Farming in the census had so few farms and so little farm income that I might have designated them Unclassifiable instead of Self-sufficing. Johnson had the advantage of a large corps of assistants who made personal observations and often consulted with county Extension Service agents and other local authorities. The actual difference between Unclassifiable and Self-sufficing may have been negligible in any case.) Making my own county maps based on this classification system and comparing them with topographical maps, I selected eight or ten counties to represent each of the five crop groups Johnson used, adding one more—Cotton and Other Crops. This modification of Johnson's system discriminates between counties where more than 50 percent of acreage harvested was cotton and those where between 25 and 50 percent was cotton. The latter usually turned out to be counties described in Chapter 4 as developing, that is, relatively prosperous areas where farmers were able to diversify rather early and find market outlets for commodities other than the old staple. The sample counties, meanwhile, became a base for tracing the various crop Souths over the nine census periods. The crop maps for 1959 in Chapters 2 and 3 were made from the tables for all twelve hundred–odd counties in the 1959 census.

New Deal farm programs accelerated southern agricultural changes and pushed farming into the specific directions of labor-saving mechanization and depopulation. On this complex subject there is an abundance of able scholarship in print. An excellent compendium of the broader subject is Theodore Saloutos, *The American Farmer and the New Deal* (Ames, Iowa, 1982). Also of benefit is Richard S. Kirkendall, *Social Scientists and Farm Politics in the Age of Roosevelt* (Columbia, Mo., 1966), which links what I have called the middle-class rural education movement to the middle western–dominated Department of Agriculture during the New Deal. On the South, one must consult Paul E. Mertz, *New Deal Policy and Southern Rural Poverty* (Baton Rouge,

1978); David Eugene Conrad, *The Forgotten Farmers: The Story of Sharecroppers in the New Deal* (Urbana, 1965); and Donald H. Grubbs, *Cry from the Cotton: The Southern Tenant Farmers' Union and the New Deal* (Chapel Hill, 1971). On specific programs, other than the Agricultural Adjustment Acts, that affected southerners, see Sidney Baldwin, *Poverty and Politics: The Rise and Decline of the Farm Security Administration* (Chapel Hill, 1968); and Donald Holley, *Uncle Sam's Farmers: The New Deal Communities in the Lower Mississippi Valley* (Urbana, 1975). For the perspective of the southern agricultural establishment, one should consult Roy V. Scott and J. G. Shoalmire, *The Public Career of Cully A. Cobb: A Study in Agricultural Leadership* (Jackson, Miss., 1973); and Lawrence J. Nelson, "Oscar Johnston, the New Deal, and the Cotton Subsidy Payments Controversy, 1936–1937," *Journal of Southern History,* XL (August, 1974), 399–416. Two additional secondary sources also influenced my approach to the New Deal, the Farm Bureau Federation, and the triumph of what is now termed agribusiness: Grant McConnell, *The Decline of Agrarian Democracy* (Berkeley, 1953); and Arthur M. Ford, *Political Economics of Rural Poverty in the South* (Cambridge, Mass., 1973).

The mechanics of mechanization have invited study by able scholars since the end of the 1940s. Gilbert C. Fite, for instance, published two excellent articles on cotton, thirty years apart: "Recent Progress in the Mechanization of Cotton Production in the United States," *Agricultural History,* XXIV (January, 1950), 19–28; and "Mechanization of Cotton Production Since World War II," *ibid.,* LIV (January, 1980), 190–207. Dated but still useful is James S. Street's *The New Revolution in the Cotton Economy: Mechanization and Its Consequences* (Chapel Hill, 1957). Fite's latest work, *Cotton Fields No More: Southern Agriculture, 1865–1980* (Lexington, Ky., 1984), summarizes technical advances in all major southern crops. Pete Daniel's *Breaking the Land: The Transformation of Cotton, Tobacco, and Rice Cultures Since 1880* (Urbana, 1985) is much more detailed on three commodities. On tobacco, see also Anthony J. Badger, *Prosperity Road: The New Deal, Tobacco, and North Carolina* (Chapel Hill, 1981). Charles Kellogg Mann's *Tobacco: The Ants and the Elephants* (Salt Lake City, 1975) is a useful overview of federal policy since 1933, which also emphasizes differences between burley and flue-cured cultures. I am aware of no overview of peanut culture, but U.S. Department of Agriculture, Farm Economics Division, Economic Research Service, Agricultural Economics Report No. 7, *Peanut-Cotton Farms: Organization, Costs, and Returns, Southern*

Plains, 1944–1960 by W. Herbert Brown (Washington, D.C., 1962), is useful. Advertisements for peanut shellers and harvesting machinery are to be found in farmers' and planters' records, including some of those cited below, and Dru Flowers, oral history of Carl and Ted Forrester, January 18, 1975 (Typescript in the Samford University Oral History Collection, Birmingham), is an interesting chronicle of the rise of a peanut farmer in southeastern Alabama. J. Carlyle Sitterson's *Sugar Country: The Sugar Cane Industry in the South, 1753–1950* (Lexington, Ky., 1953) might profitably be brought up to date, but the volume remains basic and most useful on the considerable mechanization sugar culture underwent before 1950. On post–World War II crop changes (which imply certain forms of mechanization and use of chemicals), see Harry D. Fornari, "The Big Change: Cotton to Soybeans," *Agricultural History,* LIII (January, 1979), 245–53; Clifton Paisley, *From Cotton to Quail: An Agricultural Chronicle of Leon County, Florida, 1860–1967* (Gainesville, 1968); Sam B. Hilliard, "Birdsong: Biography of a Landholding" (Paper read September 23, 1983, History of Rural Life in America Symposium, Florida A & M University); and Merle C. Prunty, Jr., "The Woodland Plantation as a Contemporary Occupance Type in the South," *Geographical Review,* LIII (January, 1963), 1–21.

The University of Georgia geographer Merle C. Prunty, Jr., and his many students produced a great many important articles, theses, and dissertations on crop transformations, even while their principal concern was patterns of changing plantation occupance—that is, concentrations and spreads of human domiciles on plantations. The typology of "neoplantations" employed in this book is derived from Prunty, whose seminal work on the subject is "Renaissance of the Southern Plantation," *Geographical Review,* XLV (October, 1955), 459–91. Significant works of Prunty's graduate students are cited in the notes to Chapter 2.

On old tenant-sharecropper plantations (which Prunty called fragmented), there are many able published studies. I think that Roger L. Ransom and Richard Sutch, *One Kind of Freedom: The Economic Consequences of Emancipation* (Cambridge, Eng., 1977), is the ablest and most comprehensive on the origins and evolution of post–Civil War tenancy and the fragmented plantation. Older social scientific works still of considerable value are USDA, *Agriculture Yearbook, 1923* (Washington, D.C., 1924), especially 507–600, on tenancy; Charles S. Johnson, *Shadow of the Plantation* (Chicago, 1934); and especially Rupert B.

Vance's *Human Factors of Cotton Culture: A Study in the Social Geography of the American South* (Chapel Hill, 1929). There are also two invaluable federal studies that were conducted during the New Deal by gifted social scientists: Works Progress Administration, Division of Social Research, *Landlord and Tenant on the Cotton Plantation,* by T. J. Woofter, Jr. (Washington, D.C., 1936); and Work Projects Administration, Division of Research, *The Plantation South, 1934–1937,* by William C. Holly, Ellen Winston, and T. J. Woofter, Jr. (Washington, D.C., 1940).

Available records of twentieth-century plantations and farms are infinitesimal compared with the bounties scholars of the antebellum South find in Chapel Hill, Baton Rouge, and elsewhere. The following records and papers do, however, represent plantations small and large, from western South Carolina to northwestern Louisiana and central Arkansas: the Sam Bowen Farm Records, 1921–1930, Clemson University Archives (a small planter of Anderson County with one share tenant and four sharecroppers); the Dugger Family Papers, Auburn University Archives (a middle-sized cotton and livestock plantation operated by an agronomist); the Edward A. O'Neal Papers and the Walter Leon Randolph Papers at the Alabama Department of Archives and History, Montgomery (with incomplete farm records but much on the Alabama and national Farm Bureau Federation); the Varner-Alexander Papers at the same depository (containing the E. R. Alexander Papers and some plantation materials); the J. E. Little Plantation Records, Arkansas History Commission, Little Rock (a huge Arkansas River estate with about three hundred sharecroppers); the John P. Murphy Store and Plantation Ledgers, University of Arkansas Library, Little Rock (a large through-and-through plantation); the Thomas Hottel Gist Plantation and Business Records, University of Arkansas Library, Fayetteville (excellent records on two eastern Arkansas plantations); the Frierson Company Records, and the J. E. Cupples and Son Ledgers in the William V. Robson Plantation Records, both in the Louisiana State University–Shreveport Archives (corporate plantations).

Appropriately, the largest extant set of plantation records belonged to the largest southern plantation, The Delta and Pine Land Company, headquartered at Scott, Mississippi. The D&PL Records are stored in the Mitchell Library at Mississippi State University. In addition to the records, one might consult several able articles by Lawrence J. Nelson, who for more than a decade has been publishing pieces of his University of Missouri dissertation and newer research. Most descriptive and comprehensive on D&PL is "Welfare Capitalism on a Mississippi Plantation During the Great Depression," *Journal of Southern History,* L (May, 1984), 225–50.

In addition to the best published work on 1930s plantations, the WPA's *The Plantation South,* one finds excellent materials on the subject in many other studies: for example, Vance's *Human Factors of Cotton Culture* and Arthur F. Raper, *Preface to Peasantry: A Tale of Two Black Belt Counties* (Chapel Hill, 1936). William Alexander Percy provided elaborate information on his Trail Lake estate in his famous memoir, *Lanterns on the Levee: Recollections of a Planter's Son* (1941; rpr. Baton Rouge, 1973). Among unpublished sources there are excellent interviews with planters among the Federal Writers' Project life histories in the Southern Historical Collection at the University of North Carolina (SHC) and at the Alabama Department of Archives and History. The interviews conducted by Bernice Kelly Harris during 1938 and 1939 (at the SHC) are best on this and any other subject. Students at the University of Arkansas, Little Rock, conducted interviews during the 1970s, too; and among the better planter subjects is Rebecca Yarbrough's oral history of Mr. and Mrs. Robert H. Alexander, October 5, 1973 (Typescript in the university library). County agents of the Extension Service had close contact with planters and sometimes referred to them specifically in their annual narrative reports. These typescripts (some microfilmed) collectively amount to an enormous (if largely dull) resource. I sampled them for the various crop-type Souths over the period covered in the book in the following repositories: the Auburn University Archives; the Texas A & M University Archives; and the Mississippi State University Library (which houses microfilmed annual reports for Georgia, Tennessee, and other states as well as for Mississippi).

Structural change in the southern highlands is a rather discrete subject, although one will find valuable description in such broader works as Rupert Vance's *Human Geography of the South: A Study in Regional Resources and Human Adequacy* (Chapel Hill, 1932) and Howard W. Odum's *Southern Regions of the United States* (Chapel Hill, 1936). An excellent (and more recent) overview by social scientists is Thomas R. Ford (ed.), *The Southern Appalachian Region: A Survey* (Lexington, Ky., 1967); and Ronald D Eller, a historian, has written a fine synthesis of highland modernization, *Miners, Millhands, and Mountaineers: Industrialization of the Appalachian South, 1880–1930* (Knoxville, 1982). Two descriptive and polemical works, published at either end of this book's chronology, should also be consulted: John C. Campbell (an outland missionary), *The Southern Highlander and His Homeland* (New York, 1921); and Jack E. Weller, *Yesterday's People: Life in Contemporary Appalachia* (Lexington, Ky., 1965), a bitter account of ruined arcadias. David E. Whisnant's brilliant *All That Is Native and Fine: The Politics of Culture in an American Region* (Chapel Hill, 1983) not only examines outsiders' "politics of culture" but offers important details on highlanders' adaptation to what is called modernization. There are also two invaluable published federal studies: USDA, Bureau of Agricultural Economics and Forest Service, *Economic and Social Problems and Conditions of the Southern Appalachians,* by L. C. Gray and C. F. Clayton (Washington, D.C., 1935); and USDA, Economic Research Service, Agricultural Economics Report No. 69, *An Economic Survey of the Appalachian Region* (Washington, D.C., 1965). Modernization in subregions of the highlands is very effectively presented in several recent monographs, as well: David Alan Corbin, *Life, Work, and Rebellion in the Coal Fields: The Southern West Virginia Miners, 1880–1922* (Urbana, 1981); John W. Hevener, *Which Side Are You On? The Harlan County Coal Miners, 1931–39* (Urbana, 1978); and William Lynwood Montell, *The Saga of Coe Ridge: A Study in Oral History* (Knoxville, 1970). Michael J. McDonald and John Muldowny's *TVA and the Dispossessed: The Resettlement of the Population in the Norris Dam Area* (Knoxville, 1982) is a fine case study of the role of the New Deal in the transformation of one area. The first section of the book is based upon local inventories housed in Record Group 142 of the National Archives, Atlanta Branch. Since McDonald and Muldowny had arrived before me and done a thorough job of research, I sampled the records for only two counties, Anderson and Campbell.

Ozarkia has not been so well served by scholars as Appalachia. The notes for Chapter 3 include a number of semischolarly travelogue-folkloric sources. My work (including the maps) is based primarily upon the county tables of the censuses of agriculture and Johnson *et al.* (comps.), *Statistical Atlas of Southern Counties.* Also of great value are some of the New Deal Federal Emergency Relief Administration "Rural Problem Area Survey Reports" for the "Appalachian-Ozark Area," to be found in Record Group 83 at the National Archives in Washington. These typescripts were prepared by on-the-scene agents who consulted with county Extension Service agents, observed local conditions for themselves, and compiled statistics.

Discussion of southern structural change in the first part of this book is guided by the perspective afforded by development in other American regions and by the role of the South in the agricultural education movement. Here, I am most indebted to previous scholars, of whom the following are most important: Clarence H. Danhof, *Change in Agriculture: The Northern United States, 1820–1870* (Cambridge, Mass., 1969); Douglas F. Dowd, "A Comparative Analysis of Economic Development in the American West and South," *Journal of Economic History,* XVI (December, 1956), 558–74; Donald L. Winters, *Farmers Without Farms: Agricultural Tenancy in Nineteenth Century Iowa* (Westport, Conn., 1978); Gilbert C. Fite, *The Farmers' Frontier, 1865–1900* (New York, 1966); James H. Shideler (ed.), *Agriculture in the Development of the Far West* (Washington, D.C., 1975); Thomas R. Wessell (ed.), *Agriculture in the Great Plains, 1876–1936* (Washington, D.C., 1971); Reynold M. Wik, *Steam Power on the American Farm* (Philadelphia, 1953); Carey McWilliams, *Factories in the Field: The Story of Migratory Farm Labor in California* (Boston, 1939); Donald Worster, "Hydraulic Society in California: An Ecological Interpretation," *Agricultural History,* LVI (July, 1982), 503–15; Moses S. Musoke and Alan L. Olmstead, "The Rise of the Cotton Industry in California: A Comparative Perspective," *Journal of Economic History,* XLII (June, 1982), 385–412. John Turner's *White Gold Comes to California* (Bakersfield, 1981) is not a scholarly book in the conventional sense, and Turner makes no attempt to conceal his association with seed distributors and ranchers, but it is an excellent source for the origins and development of western cotton. Frank C. Diener, who began planting cotton in Fresno County in 1930, spoke with me at length aboard the *Mississippi Queen* in July, 1982, about California farming and sent me a copy of Turner's book (which, unsurprisingly, has not had wide distribution).

In this book modernization (including structural change) is regarded as the work primarily of government and a corps of middle-class educator-activists who began their labors during the mid-nineteenth century. A narrower version of this interpretation is to be found in David B. Danbon, *The Resisted Revolution: Urban America and the Industrialization of Agriculture, 1900–1930* (Ames, Iowa, 1979). On the rise of "progressive farming" in the early twentieth-century South, see Jack Temple Kirby, *Darkness at the Dawning: Race and Reform in the Progressive South* (Philadelphia, 1972), 131–76. One should also see Alfred Charles True's compendious *A History of Agricultural Education in the United States, 1785–1925* (Washington, D.C., 1929); and especially Joseph Cannon Bailey's *Seaman A. Knapp, Schoolmaster of*

American Agriculture (New York, 1945). My argument that the South lagged far behind other regions in accepting "modern" farming is largely based upon data in Roy V. Scott, *The Reluctant Farmer: The Rise of Agricultural Extension to 1914* (Urbana, 1970).

Continued structural change since about 1950 and the emergence of agribusiness in the South are discussed and documented in the epilogue. Generalizations are based mainly upon the federal censuses of agriculture, Gilbert Fite's articles on the mechanization of cotton, his and Pete Daniel's 1984 and 1985 books, Charles Mann's *Tobacco,* and Arthur Ford's *Political Economics of Rural Poverty in the South.* Ford, and Ray Marshall and Allen Thompson, *Status and Prospects of Small Farmers in the South* (Atlanta, 1976), are especially useful in measuring the impact of federal subsidies among classes of farmers. U.S. Congress, General Accounting Office, *Changing Character and Structure of American Agriculture: An Overview* (Washington, D.C., September 26, 1978), does not provide adequate regional statistics but updates and redefines classes of farmers by acreage and income for the 1970s, and relates the classes to amounts and percentage of federal subsidies. USDA, Economic Research Service, Agricultural Economics Report No. 21, *Crop Production Practices and Costs by Size of Farm: Delta Area of Mississippi, 1957–58,* by Irving R. Starbird and James Vermeer (Washington, D.C., 1962), demonstrates the logical limits of growth without the factor of subsidies.

On poultry I relied upon Gordon Sawyer, *The Agribusiness Poultry Industry: A History of Its Development* (Jericho, N.Y., 1971), an uncritical industry document, which nonetheless is well organized and informative; John Shover's *First Majority—Last Minority: The Transforming of Rural Life in America* (DeKalb, Ill., 1976); and Hope Shand, "Billions of Chickens: The Business of the South," *Southern Exposure,* XI (November/December, 1983), 76–82, a very critical example of exposé journalism. Marshall and Thompson, *Status and Prospects of Small Farmers* also presents important information about the structure of the poultry industry.

Rural Life

Local economies and "life-styles" underwent modernization at different times and at a variety of paces. *Modernization* here means the arrival of paved roads, the automobile, electricity, and commercial farming to the virtual exclusion of live-at-home semisubsistence farming. It also means the end of isolation, animal power, self-sufficiency (or something close to it, including reliance upon family and community labor). Most of these matters may be measured in the county tables of the censuses of agriculture (using, once more, Johnson *et al.* (comps.), *Statistical Atlas of Southern Counties* as a base). *First Majority—Last Minority,* an impressionist work by John L. Shover, is an engrossing overview of national changes since World War II. Pete Daniel's *Breaking the Land* and Gilbert Fite's *Cotton Fields No More* concern changes in rural life as well as mechanization and other structural changes in the South. J. Wayne Flynt's *Dixie's Forgotten People: The South's Poor Whites* (Bloomington, Ind., 1979) does not discriminate clearly among southern whites of the various subregions, ·but it evokes well the semiprimitive old rural existence and some aspects of the transformation to commercial farming. Thomas D. Clark's delightful *Pills, Petticoats and Plows: The Southern Country Store* (Indianapolis, 1944) describes and dates the demise of traditional stores (*ca.* 1920), an important institution of the premodern South. Herman Clarence Nixon's *Possum Trot: Rural Community, South* (Norman, Okla., 1941) charts the virtual disappearance of his family's rural community in Alabama. Several other books by scholar-participants of Nixon's generation, notably Raper's *Preface to Peasantry* and Vance's *Human Factors of Cotton Culture,* are also invaluable descriptions of rural life and the beginnings of transformation.

Much of the description in Chapters 4 through 7 is based upon the testimony of ordinary southerners—interviews, life histories, oral histories, and autobiographies. Some of this material has been published. First was a selection of Federal Writers' Project life histories collected by the FWP's director in Chapel Hill, W. T. Couch, *These Are Our Lives* (Chapel Hill, 1939). Recently, additional collections from the FWP files have appeared: Tom E. Terrill and Jerrold Hirsch (eds.), *Such as Us: Southern Voices from the Thirties* (Chapel Hill, 1978); John L. Robinson (ed.), *Living Hard: Southern Americans in the Great Depression* (Washington, D.C., 1981); and James Seay Brown (ed.), *Up Before Daylight: Life Histories from the Alabama Writers' Project, 1938–1939* (University, Ala., 1982). Audrey Olsen Faulkner *et al.* (eds.), *When I Was Comin' Up: An Oral History of Aged Blacks* (Hamden, Conn., 1982), presents memories of southern migrants to Newark, most of which focus on the rural South Atlantic states between 1915 and the 1950s. Among autobiographies the most indispensable to me was Theodore Rosengarten, *All God's Dangers: The Life of Nate Shaw* (New

York, 1975). Shaw, whose real name, Ned Cobb, is used throughout this book, dictated his life story to Rosengarten, who transcribed tapes, edited the story, and dubbed himself author. Also valuable are H. L. Mitchell, *Mean Things Happening in This Land: The Life and Times of H. L. Mitchell* (Montclair, N.J., 1979); Loretta Lynn with George Vecsey, *Loretta Lynn: Coal Miner's Daughter* (New York, 1976); and Harry Crews, *A Childhood: The Biography of a Place* (New York, 1978). Flynt's *Dixie's Forgotten People* and Elizabeth Rauh Bethel's *Promiseland: A Century of Life in a Negro Community* (Philadelphia, 1981) also include good interview materials.

Most of the testimony of common folks remains unpublished, however, and there is a great deal of it. The Southern Historical Collection contains about 900 FWP life histories. The Kentucky State Archives in Frankfort holds about 450 more; and the P. K. Yonge Library at the University of Florida, the Alabama Department of Archives and History, and the Arkansas History Commission each hold a few more. During the 1970s, especially, a great many oral histories of elderly southerners were taped and transcribed. Among the best-executed projects is the Samford University Oral History Program in Birmingham, which includes typescripts of interviews with miners, steel mill hands, former tenants and sharecroppers, and housewives. Among the several highland oral history programs undertaken in recent years, I had best access to the Marshall University Oral History of Appalachia Collection (which is available on microfilm and microform). I also traveled to West Point, Mississippi, to see the "Sharecropper Project" in the library of Mary Holmes College. The students who conducted these interviews were not well prepared; and though the typescripts as a whole convey convincing messages about blacks at the bottom of the tenure ladder in Mississippi, much tape, paper, and effort were wasted, and opportunities were lost, because interviewers were ignorant of farming.

Use of such testimony in writing history has its risks—as does, indeed, use of most other kinds of documentation. Leonard Rapport, a veteran of the North Carolina FWP, indicted the 1938–1939 life histories in "How Valid Are the Federal Writers' Project Life Stories: An Iconoclast Among the True Believers," *Oral History Review,* III (1979), 6–17. Rapport reminded his readers that most interviewers lacked tape recorders, were biased toward "fiction" in setting the scene and casting their interviewees, and injected themselves into the imaginations of their subjects. I have little doubt that most of Rapport's charges are fair, and I cannot be absolutely certain that my selection of life histories avoided every flawed one. In using the interviews, however, I never tried to reconstruct an important historical event entirely from these sources, and I believe I was successful in discerning instances where interviewers' own imaginations assumed center stage. Life stories and oral histories are most useful in documenting certain conditions of life—housing, family size, child rearing, husband-wife relationships, and the nature of work. My generalizations on such matters are based upon multiple citations of interviews, and often other evidence as well. Reading through dozens, then hundreds, of these typescripts, one grows to respect certain individual interviewers, too, and to trust their observations. This was the case especially with the many North Carolina life histories gathered and composed by Bernice Kelly Harris, one of the minority of professional writers who served the project.

Excellent correlation of interview materials is to be found in the many unpublished social studies of the Department of Agriculture Bureau of Agricultural Economics and of various New Deal agencies, especially the Tennessee Valley Authority, the Resettlement Administration, and the FERA. (Most of these are filed in Record Group 83 at the National Archives in Washington.) The Land Tenure Section project files of the USDA (also in Record Group 83) are useful not only on conditions of farm tenure but on income and other basic matters. The Land Tenure Section, along with various state Extension Services, also conducted studies of tenure (including family relationships between landlords and tenants) in the states and certain counties during the 1930s. (Copies of these, as well as the FERA's "Area Studies," are also housed in the National Archives.)

Another important resource on the lives of the so-called inarticulate is the Southern Tenant Farmers' Union Papers, in the SHC. I used the collection for the years 1934–1940 (which fill thirteen rolls of microfilm). Included in the STFU Papers are printed and typescript materials—copies of the union's short-lived newspaper, the *Sharecropper's Voice;* the *Ritual;* the Rust brothers' declaration on their cotton-picking machine; and a great deal of the correspondence of the Memphis headquarters. Many of the documents in this collection are letters from poor people—tenants, sharecroppers, hired laborers, the drifting unemployed—usually written in pencil on cheap, lined paper. Most of this correspondence came from eastern Arkansas and southeastern Missouri, but there are also letters from Mississippi, Texas, Oklahoma, western Arkansas, and Tennessee. Acute distress often occasioned such letter writing; so perhaps one might at least partially discount the weight of this correspondence. Yet on the other hand, we know from the well-established context of farming conditions and federal policies that such distress was not exceptional in the cotton belt; and there are so many pained letters, year after year. It is no wonder that the principal historians of the New Deal and the cotton tenants, David Eugene Conrad, Donald H. Grubbs, and Paul E. Mertz—all of whom used the STFU Papers—excoriate the Agricultural Adjustment Acts and write sympathetically of the rural poor.

In addition to the primary materials, I was guided in writing about various social and economic subjects by a number of valuable published works. On the expansion of communities during the process of modernization, David J. Russo, *Families and Communities: A New View of American History* (Nashville, 1974); Wayne E. Fuller, *RFD: The Changing Face of Rural America* (Bloomington, Ind., 1964); and Eugen Weber, *Peasants into Frenchmen: The Modernization of Rural France, 1870–1914* (Stanford, 1976) were valuable. On the advantages of mixed farming near urban markets (as opposed to monoculture and semisubsistence farming), I was guided by Anthony M. Tang, *Economic Development in the Southern Piedmont, 1860–1950: Its Impact on Agriculture* (Chapel Hill, 1958). On sexuality and birth control, James Reed, *From Private Vice to Public Virtue: The Birth Control Movement and American Society Since 1930* (New York, 1978) was useful. On the social impact of the automobile, I consulted Michael L. Berger, *The Devil Wagon in God's Country: The Automobile and Social Change in Rural America, 1893–1929* (Hamden, Conn., 1979); and Raper, *Preface to Peasantry.* On white southern Baptists *ca.* 1920–1970, see J. Wayne Flynt, "Southern Baptists: Rural to Urban Transition," *Baptist History and Heritage,* XVI (January, 1981), 24–34, which includes data from a Southern Baptist Convention study of churches. On diseases, see Thomas D. Clark, *The Emerging South* (New York, 1961), 24–39; Daphne A. Roe, *A Plague of Corn: The Social History of Pellagra* (Ithaca, 1973); Elizabeth W. Etheridge, *The Butterfly Caste: A Social History of Pellagra in the South* (Westport, Conn., 1972). On chain gangs and other penal institutions, see Jesse F. Steiner and Roy M. Brown, *The North Carolina Chain Gang: A Study of County Convict Road Work* (Chapel Hill, 1927); Ray A. March, *Alabama Bound: Forty-five Years Inside a Prison System* (University, Ala., 1978). On geophagy, see Robert W. Twyman, "The Clay Eater: A New Look at an Old Southern Enigma," *Journal of Southern History,* XXXVII (August, 1971), 439–48. On burial practices, see Charles R. Wilson, "The

Southern Funeral Director: Managing Death in the New South," *Georgia Historical Quarterly,* LXVII (Spring, 1983), 49–69.

On mules, the basic source is Robert Byron Lamb, *The Mule in Southern Agriculture* (Berkeley and Los Angeles, 1963); but there are many other less comprehensive sources of special value. Not the least among them is Harry Crews's delightful autobiography, *A Childhood.* On the prohibition of alcoholic beverages, one might consult Andrew Sinclair, *Prohibition: The Era of Excess* (Boston, 1962); and Dewey W. Grantham, *Southern Progressivism: The Reconciliation of Progress and Tradition* (Knoxville, 1983), 160–77 and *passim.* In addition to unpublished life histories, my discussion of moonshining and bootlegging is largely based upon the federal Internal Revenue Service *Annual Reports,* 1920–1959, which are cited in their various formats with page numbers in the notes to Chapter 6. On music and its broader cultural implications, I am indebted to Bill C. Malone, author of *Country Music, USA: A Fifty-Year History* (Austin, 1968) and *Southern Music/ American Music* (Lexington, Ky., 1979); to William Ferris, *Blues from the Delta* (Garden City, N.Y., 1979); and especially to David Whisnant, *All That Is Native and Fine.*

Relations between white and black southerners are an enormous subject much written about. Among many works that influenced the writing of Chapter 7 are W. J. Cash, *The Mind of the South* (New York, 1941); V. O. Key, *Southern Politics, in State and Nation* (New York, 1949); Pierre L. van den Berghe, *Race and Racism: A Comparative Perspective* (New York, 1967); George B. Tindall, *The Emergence of the New South, 1913–1945* (Baton Rouge, 1967); C. Vann Woodward, *The Strange Career of Jim Crow* (1955; 3rd rev. ed; New York, 1973); and Joel Williamson, *New People: Miscegenation and Mulattoes in the United States* (New York, 1980). Readers may have already noted the many citations in the chapter of Raper's *Preface to Peasantry* and Rosengarten's *All God's Dangers,* as well. Unfortunately, most writing about racial relations has been trapped within the segregation-integration dichotomy that so colored perception during the 1950s and 1960s. I think the dichotomy oversimplified and overly concerned with urban environments. Most southerners, white and black, lived in the country until recently, and there, especially in plantation subregions, economic arrangements did not permit segregation as customarily perceived. I wrote about this some years ago in "Clarence Poe's Vision of a Segregated 'Great Rural Civilization,'" *South Atlantic Quarterly,* LXVIII (Winter, 1969), 27–38. Chapter 7 of this book is probably only a small step beyond, toward an understanding of the varieties and ambiguities as well as the fixities of black-white relations.

Most of the chapter is based upon primary materials already discussed—the FWP life histories and the STFU Papers—along with a serendipitous selection of published memoirs, including H. L. Mitchell's *Mean Things Happening in This Land,* and J. E. McTeer's *Adventure in the Woods and Waters of the Low Country* (Beaufort, S.C., 1972), the autobiography of a white sheriff. Because FWP interviewers were white, I was cautious about using their quotations of blacks about class and racial relations. White and black STFU members were generally confident in stating their views to union officials, however; so I have felt confident about using their letters.

Migration

Probably everyone knows that in addition to swelling cities in the North and West, migrants from southern farms flooded into southern towns and cities and became operatives in southern industry. Yet there is neither a synthesis nor a body of monographs on intra-South rural-to-urban migration. Much of this book is organized around what I think is a rational subdivision of the region by crops and topography. I had hoped to pursue refugees from these rather specific subregions into new urban homes. Existing literature and the population censuses do not permit such a procedure, however, except by strong inference in a few cases that will be mentioned below. Broadly speaking, one may begin by simply charting the rise of urban populations and decline of rural ones, in the censuses. The censuses, however, provide only statewide and metropolitan area (after 1940) data, not county or subregional figures. One cannot trace migrants within states, except by inference when county populations decline and city ones rise. One can count numbers of farms and numbers of industrial production workers, and this critical comparison is charted in Chapter 8 from the tables in Donald B. Dodd and Wynelle S. Dodd (comps.), *Historical Statistics of the South, 1790–1970* (University, Ala., 1973), a most useful and convenient aid to researchers. Blaine A. Brownell, *The Urban Ethos in the South, 1920–1930* (Baton Rouge, 1975) is also helpful with statistics.

Rural-to-urban migration began with the disruption of traditional farms and plantations and increased rural mobility. This pattern is evident in a number of reliable secondary sources, such as the *Agriculture Yearbook, 1923,* Conrad's *The Forgotten Farmers,* and the FERA "Area

Studies," which were discussed earlier. One of several results of the disruption was creation of two South-based migrant labor streams, the Atlantic Coast Stream (which survives to this day) and a central, Mississippi Valley one, which was dominated by young white southerners before World War II. The basic source on early migratory farm labor is Carey McWilliams, *Ill Fares the Land: Migrants and Migratory Labor in the United States* (Boston, 1942). The Atlantic Coast Stream has received considerable attention since McWilliams' time—*e.g.,* Earl Loman Koos, *They Follow the Sun* (Jacksonville, 1957); Florida Legislative Council and Legislative Reference Bureau, *Migrant Farm Labor in Florida* (Tallahassee, 1963); Donald Hughes Grubbs, "A History of the Atlantic Coast Stream of Agricultural Migrants" (M.A. thesis, University of Florida, 1959); and L. A. Winokur and Chip Hughes, "Workers and the Harvest," *Southern Exposure,* XI (November/December, 1983), 55–61. Migrant labor has been intimately connected with peonage, too, as Pete Daniel demonstrates in *The Shadow of Slavery: Peonage in the South, 1901–1969* (New York, 1972), especially 82–109.

Many intra-South migrants moved to rural or small-town mill villages and mining camps whose increased populations are not represented as urban in the federal censuses. The economist Mitchell brothers, Broadus and George Sinclair, understood this phenomenon when they wrote *The Industrial Revolution in the South* (Baltimore, 1930). The rural-industrial phenomenon was best demonstrated, however, in the early chapters of Liston Pope's classic, *Millhands and Preachers: A Study of Gastonia* (New Haven, 1942). Pope also took care to trace the origins of mill hands in Gastonia: early migrants came from the surrounding piedmont, later ones from the eastern slopes of the Appalachian South. David Alan Corbin also describes the origins of migrant miners in West Virginia in his *Life, Work, and Rebellion in the Coal Fields.* David L. Carlton, in *Mill and Town in South Carolina, 1880–1920* (Baton Rouge, 1982), uses impressionistic evidence to confirm Pope's generalization about the origins of textiles operatives. On more recent short-range migration and the creation of along-the-highway commuter neighborhoods, see John Fraser Hart and Ennis L. Chestang, "Rural Revolution in East Carolina," *Geographical Review,* LXVIII (October, 1978), 435–58; Joseph Giovannini, "Farms and Industry Mix in North Carolina Area," New York *Times,* June 3, 1984, p. 29; and John Herbers, "Americans Migrating . . . Countryside," New York *Times,* March 23, 1980, pp. 1, 50, and March 25, 1980, Section D, 9.

The best source on migration to piedmont textiles villages, towns, and cities is a newly available primary one, the "Piedmont Project" of the Southern Oral History Program (SOHP) at the SHC. Directed by Professor Jacqueline Hall of the University of North Carolina, the project includes about 250 interviews of elderly inhabitants of North and South Carolina, who relate experiences not only of work but of migration from farms as early as the first decade of the twentieth century. This is altogether the most professionally executed collection of oral histories I have encountered and one of the most valuable not only on industrial work and migration but on moonshining, bootlegging, sexuality and birth control, health, and other subjects social and economic. (The story of quilling, for example—the use of snuff and a sipping straw to induce childbirth—derives from this project.) Regarding migration, it seems clear from the body of this collection that most newcomers did not travel far; that central and eastern piedmont towns drew people from the piedmont; and that western piedmont towns attracted migrants from the piedmont and nearby mountains. Pope's surmises about Gastonia thus seem to have been generally true.

Methods of migration were many, as I submit in Chapter 8, but the stem-family mode was common in both intra- and extra-regional migration. Described in Europe and among transatlantic migrants long ago, the stem-family pattern is well documented in the twentieth-century South by sociologists Harry K. Swarzweller, James S. Brown, and J. J. Mangalam, *Mountain Families in Transition: A Case Study of Appalachian Migration* (University Park, Penn., 1971). The FWP life histories and SOHP interviews offer many examples, as do some of the oral histories in the "Docena Project" within the Samford University Oral History Program in Birmingham.

The basic sources of the out-migration of southerners are the decennial federal censuses of population, 1910–1960. I used the state tables for thirteen states—the fourteen termed southern throughout this book, minus Florida, owing to its exceptional record of in-migration (which is discussed early in Chapter 9).There are also three volumes of statistics handy for state aggregates: Bureau of the Census, *Historical Statistics of the United States, from Colonial Times to 1957* (Washington, D.C., 1961), and *Historical Statistics of the United States . . . Continuation to 1962 and Revisions* (Washington, D.C., 1965); and Dodd and Dodd (comps.), *Historical Statistics of the South*.

Literature on the black out-migration is quite large, but writings on whites' travels remain rather small, and some of the best remain unpublished. No other scholar of regional migration uses the definition of the

South employed in this book either; yet some restricted generalizations and many details from these works are quite valuable. On black migration I made good use of Louise V. Kennedy, *The Negro Peasant Turns Cityward: Effects of Recent Migrations to Northern Centers* (New York, 1930); Robert Higgs, "The Boll Weevil, the Cotton Economy, and Black Migration, 1910–1930," *Agricultural History,* L (April, 1976), 335–50; and Flora Gill, *Economics and the Black Exodus: An Analysis of Negro Emigration from the Southern United States, 1910–1970* (New York, 1979). Daniel M. Johnson and Rex R. Campbell, *Black Migration in America: A Social Demographic History* (Durham, N.C., 1981), is a serviceable survey; and David F. Sly, "Migration," in Dudley L. Poston, Jr., and Robert H. Weller (eds.), *The Population of the South: Structure and Change in Social Demographic Context* (Austin, 1981), 109–36, summarizes the problem of defining the region and includes valuable bibliography on both black and white migrations. Neil Fligstein, *Going North: Migration of Blacks and Whites from the South, 1900–1950* (New York, 1981), an important work, not only assays the travels of both races but attempts a complex quantitative speculation on out-migration from counties. Fligstein's South is considerably smaller than the region considered in this book, but unusually for a social scientist, he wrote in the context of economic and political history. On black migrants in new northern settings, see Frank T. Cherry, "Southern In-migrant Negroes in North Lawndale, Chicago, 1949–1959: A Study of Internal Migration and Adjustment" (Ph.D. dissertation, University of Chicago, 1965); Kennedy, *Negro Peasant Turns Cityward;* Marcus E. Jones, *Black Migration in the United States, with Emphasis on Selected Central Cities* (Saratoga, Calif., 1980); Karl E. Taeuber and Alma F. Taeuber, *Negroes in Cities: Residential Segregation and Neighborhood Change* (Chicago, 1965); and Robert Coles, *The South Goes North* (Boston, 1971), Vol. III of Coles, *Children of Crisis,* 7 vols. to date. Elizabeth Bethel's *Promiseland,* and Arna Bontemps and Jack Conroy's *Anyplace but Here* (New York, 1966) include interview materials and quotations of black migrants in the North.

A brief summary of southern white out-migration is to be found in Lewis M. Killian, *White Southerners* (New York, 1970), 91–119; and for bibliography, one should consult J. Wayne Flynt and Dorothy S. Flynt (comps.), *Southern Poor Whites: A Selected Annotated Bibliography of Published Sources* (New York, 1981), Chapter 6, "Migration/Urbanization." So-called okies are the most written-about of southern white migrants. See Carey McWilliams, *Factories in the Field,* and *Ill*

Fares the Land; Walter J. Stein, *California and the Dust Bowl Migration* (Westport, Conn., 1973); Cletus E. Daniel, *Bitter Harvest: A History of California Farmworkers, 1870–1941* (Ithaca, 1981); and Stein's "The 'Okie' As Farm Laborer," in Shideler (ed.), *Agriculture in the Development of the Far West,* 202–15. Southern whites in the Northeast have received virtually no attention, except in passing and impressionistically in such works as Coles's *The South Goes North.* Migrants to the Middle West, many of them highlanders, have received a great deal of scholarly attention, however. See James S. Brown and George A. Hillery, Jr., "The Great Migration, 1940–1960," in Ford (ed.), *Southern Appalachian Region,* 54–78; George A. Hillery, Jr., James S. Brown, and Gordon F. De Jong, "Migration Systems of the Southern Appalachians: Some Demographic Observations," *Rural Sociology,* XXX (March, 1965), 33–48; Lewis Killian, "Southern White Laborers in Chicago's West Side" (Ph.D. dissertation, University of Chicago, 1950); Killian, "The Adjustment of Southern White Workers to Northern Urban Norms," *Social Forces,* XXXII (October, 1953), 66–69; Alan Clive, *State of War: Michigan in World War II* (Ann Arbor, 1979), 170–184; William Philliber and Clyde B. McCoy (eds.), *The Invisible Minority: Urban Appalachians* (Lexington, Ky., 1981); John D. Photiadis, *West Virginians in Their Own State and in Cleveland, Ohio* (Morgantown, W.Va., 1970); and the "Urban Appalachians" issue of *Mountain Life and Work,* LII (August, 1976). Schwarzweller, Brown, and Mangalam, *Mountain Families in Transition,* is the only study that traces migrants from their home community through adjustment in northern ones. The connection between mountain Kentucky and the industrial cities of the Miami Valley in southwestern Ohio, and the adjustment of migrants especially in Hamilton and Middletown, Ohio, however, are well established in several unpublished works: John L. Thompson, "Industrialization in the Miami Valley: A Case Study of Interregional Labor Migration" (Ph.D. dissertation, University of Wisconsin, 1956); Raymond P. Hutchens, "Kentuckians in Hamilton: A Study of South-Born Migrants in an Industrial City" (M.A. thesis, Miami University, 1942); and William D. Worley, "Social Characteristics and Participation Patterns of Rural Migrants in an Industrial Community" (M.A. thesis, Miami University, 1961).

As for testimony from migrants, themselves, there are quotations, vignettes, and a few life stories in many of the sources mentioned in the previous two paragraphs. Todd Gitlin and Nanci Hollander, *Uptown: Poor Whites in Chicago* (New York, 1970), is largely composed around the oral history format and includes lengthy segments on a one-armed wino from West Virginia. Among oral history collections, sad to say, there are few out-migrant testaments. This small handful—from the FWP files, the Samford University Oral History Program, and the Marshall University Oral History of Appalachia Collection—are cited in the notes to Chapter 9.

Index